MERGERS AND THE CLAYTON ACT

MERGERS AND THE CLAYTON ACT

By DAVID DALE MARTIN

UNIVERSITY OF CALIFORNIA PRESS

Berkeley and Los Angeles · 1959

UNIVERSITY OF CALIFORNIA PRESS
BERKELEY AND LOS ANGELES, CALIFORNIA
CAMBRIDGE UNIVERSITY PRESS, LONDON, ENGLAND

LIBRARY OF CONGRESS CATALOG CARD NUMBER: 59-13085

DESIGNED BY HARRY MARKS

Acknowledgments

Much of the research and writing included in this volume originated in the preparation of the author's doctoral dissertation submitted to the Department of Economics of the University of California, Los Angeles. The study was first suggested by Professor Dudley F. Pegrum, who directed the dissertation with a degree of efficiency and understanding greater than any graduate student is entitled to expect, and who also read and criticized the manuscript of this book at several stages. Professor Paul F. Homan's criticism, advice, and encouragement at all stages were also invaluable. It is impossible adequately to acknowledge the debt owed these two inspiring and stimulating teachers.

The author also wishes to thank Professors Warren C. Scoville, J. Fred Weston, Marvel M. Stockwell, George H. Hildebrand, and Wytze Gorter, all of the University of California, Los Angeles, for their help at various points in the preparation of this work. Several members of the staffs of the Federal Trade Commission and the Department of Justice greatly facilitated the research on which this book is based by providing information and criticism. Dr. Irston R. Barnes and Dr. Frank J. Kottke of the Federal Trade Commission, Dr. John M. Blair, formerly with that agency, and

Mr. John T. Duffner, of the antitrust division, are due special thanks. They are, of course, in no way responsible for the views herein expressed.

The Graduate School of Arts and Sciences and the Social Science Research Institute of Washington University, Saint Louis, helped the author complete this study by providing several grants for stenographic services. A research grant from the Graduate School enabled the author to devote the summer of 1956 exclusively to this project.

Most of the real cost has been borne by the author's wife and children. For most of their lives the latter have not known what it would be like to have a father not engaged in the writing of a book.

D. D. M.

Bloomington, Indiana
December, 1958

Contents

Abbreviations

C.C.A., 3d Cir.	United States Circuit Court of Appeals, Third Circuit
CCH	Commerce Clearing House
Cong.	United States Congress
(D.C., D. of Col.)	Federal District Court, District of Columbia
(D.C., D. Conn.)	Federal District Court, District of Connecticut
(D.C., D. Del.)	Federal District Court, District of Delaware
(D.C., D. Mass.)	Federal District Court, District of Massachusetts
(D.C., E.D. Mo.)	Federal District Court, Eastern District of Missouri
(D.C., M.D. Tenn.)	Federal District Court, Middle District of Tennessee
(D.C., N.D. Ill.)	Federal District Court, Northern District of Illinois
(D.C., N.D. Ohio, E.D.)	Federal District Court, Northern District of Ohio, Eastern Division
(D.C., S.D. N.Y.)	Federal District Court, Southern District of New York
Fed. Rept.	Federal Reporter
Fed. Rept., 2d Ser.	Federal Reporter, Second Series
Fed. Supp.	Federal Supplement
F.T.C.	Federal Trade Commission Decisions
F.T.C. Act	Federal Trade Commission Act

F.T.C. Annual Report	Federal Trade Commission Annual Report
F.T.C. Docket No.	Federal Trade Commission Docket Number
F.T.C. Exhibit No. 168	"Digest of Formal Complaints Issued by the Federal Trade Commission under Sections 7 and 8 of the Clayton Act," F.T.C. Exhibit No. 168 (typewritten, n.d.), admitted to the record during hearings held March 1, 1939, by the Temporary National Economic Committee and included within *T.N.E.C. Exhibit No. 305,* National Archives, Washington, D.C.
F.T.C. Exhibit No. 192	"Digest of Informal Investigations Made by the Federal Trade Commission under Section 7 of the Clayton Act," F.T.C. Exhibit No. 192 (typewritten, n.d.), admitted to the record during hearings held March 1, 1939, by the Temporary National Economic Committee and included within *T.N.E.C. Exhibit No. 305,* National Archives, Washington, D.C.
Ga.	*Georgia Reports*
H.R.	House of Representatives Bill
H. Doc.	House Document
H. Rept.	House Report
I.C.C.	Interstate Commerce Commission Reports
Ill.	Illinois Reports
Mich.	Michigan Reports
N.E.	North Eastern Reporter
N.J. Eq.	New Jersey Equity Reports
Ohio St.	Ohio State Reports
Par.	Paragraph
Public Res. No.	Public Resolution
S.	Senate Bill
Sess.	Session
S. Doc.	Senate Document
S. Rept.	Senate Report
T.N.E.C.	Temporary National Economic Committee
T.N.E.C. Hearings, part 5-A	*Hearings Pursuant to Public Resolution Number 113,* U.S. Temporary National Economic Committee, 76th Congress, 1st sess. (Washington: 1939), part 5-A.
U.S.	*United States Supreme Court Reports*
U.S. Stat. at L.	*United States Statutes at Large*

Introduction

The Clayton Act was enacted in 1914 as a supplement to the Sherman Act—the basic statute embodying the antitrust law policy of the United States. Section 7 of the Clayton Act, as originally enacted, prohibited the acquisition by one corporation of the *stock* of another corporation where the effect may be substantially to lessen competition or to restrain trade between the corporations, or tend to create a monopoly. In 1950, after a long campaign "to plug the loophole" in Section 7, the section was amended to include the prohibition of asset as well as stock acquisitions. The purpose of this study is to examine the reasons for the passage by Congress of the original and the amended Section 7, and to analyze the administration of the section and the implications of its amendment. Some observations are offered on the basic economic issues in the corporate merger policy of the United States.

It will be shown that the amendment of Section 7 in 1950 was a major change in the substantive provisions of the antitrust laws of the United States and not the mere plugging of a loophole; that merger by means of asset acquisition was not a new stratagem devised to avoid the prohibitions of Section 7 after 1914;

that the original Section 7 was part of a legislative program designed to limit the freedom of large corporations to engage in aggressive business practices rather than a change in the Sherman Act policy with respect to corporate mergers.

In addition, the Federal Trade Commission, in administering the section, failed to develop a workable policy with which to apply the general criterion of illegality of the statute to specific cases of stock acquisition, and, therefore, the responsibility for the emasculation of the section rests as much with the commission as with the courts.

Aside from the substantive change implied in the inclusion of asset acquisition in the prohibitions of Section 7, the amendment of 1950 changed the standard of illegality in such a way that it is necessary for the Justice Department and the commission, in the process of administration of the section with the review of the courts, to develop anew a workable policy with which to apply the general criterion of illegality to specific cases. It appears that the commission, in administering the amended Section 7, is doing a much better job of implementing and giving specific content to the statute than it did with the original Section 7.

The study begins with a brief investigation and analysis of the development of the corporate combination movement, its effect on public opinion, and the development of the law of mergers before the enactment of the Clayton Act in 1914. The legislative history of Section 7 is reviewed for the purpose of defining the reasons for its enactment. On the basis of the published records, as well as material from the files of the Federal Trade Commission filed with the Temporary National Economic Committee and deposited in the National Archives, the policies of the commission are analyzed along with the construction of the statute by the courts. The legislative history and the implications of the 1950 amendment are examined. An attempt is made in the concluding chapters to bring into focus some of the theoretical economic questions implicit in the administration of the law.

1. The Institutional Setting of the Clayton Act

The many changes in American institutions and thought during the period of rapid growth of the economy around the turn of the century resulted in the enactment of the Clayton Act twenty-four years after Congress passed the Sherman Act in 1890. The Clayton Act supplemented, but did not replace, the Sherman Act as the basic Congressional statement of federal antitrust policy. The Sherman Act was couched in the general language of the old common law prohibitions against restraint of trade and monopolization, but the 1914 antitrust statute provided for prohibitions of four specific business practices: price discrimination, tying contracts, interlocking directorates, and intercorporate stockholding. This chapter will provide general background to the action taken by Congress in 1914 to supplement the Sherman Act policy on corporate combinations and to its decision to prohibit intercorporate stockholding as one means to that end.

Public Reaction to the Changing Industrial Structure

Popular belief in the American antitrust policy has long been based on hostility toward great combinations of capital. The hostility reflected the fear of aggressive suppression of competition and monopoly control of markets. This attitude was deeply rooted in the English common law. The Sherman Act embodied these traditional ideas in federal statute law, but the great merger movement after 1890 created a feeling that the statute was inadequate.

The Merger Movement—The first industrial combination of large size was created in 1879 with the formation of the original Standard Oil trust in Ohio. Several other combinations were formed in the succeeding decade, using the trustee form of organization.[1] At that time, however, close combinations were far less important than various kinds of loose agreements between firms on price and output policy.[2] This early wave of mergers continued until the panic of 1893. With the passage of the Sherman Act in 1890, the Ohio court decision in the Standard Oil case dissolving that trust in 1892,[3] and the liberalization of the New Jersey incorporation law in 1889,[4] the form of combination switched from trust to holding company or a single large corporation. The period from 1897 to 1904 witnessed the all-time high rate of formation of important combinations of previously independent firms into large corporations or holding companies.[5]

[1] See Jesse W. Markham, "Survey of the Evidence and Findings on Mergers," *Business Concentration and Price Policy,* a Conference of the Universities-National Bureau Committee for Economic Research (Princeton: Princeton University Press, 1955), p. 157.

[2] See Dudley F. Pegrum, *Regulation of Industry* (Chicago: Richard D. Irwin, 1949), p. 143.

[3] See p. 10.

[4] See p. 11.

[5] Markham's study shows 257 combinations involving 4,227 plants during this period. *Op. cit.,* p. 157.

During this period the general pattern of the twentieth-century industrial market structure was created.[6] The great importance of this merger movement lies in the fact that many combinations were of large numbers of firms including the largest firms existing prior to the fusion. As a result, the business units created were much bigger than any firm previously existing in the affected industries.[7]

In commenting on this period of combination activity, Arthur S. Dewing said:

> During 1900 and 1901, the movement continued, but the new promotions were fewer in number, owing to the fact that most opportunities for the formation of "trusts" had already been fully exploited by the bankers and promoters. Accordingly, the ground was combed over again. The trusts themselves were consolidated. A pyramid was built of pyramids. The United States Steel Corporation, capitalized at over 1300 millions of dollars, was built up out of half a dozen smaller "trusts," themselves, in several cases, the combinations of smaller combinations.[8]

From 1904 to 1914, relatively few combinations were formed. Professor Markham found that too few were formed to attract attention.[9] There were, however, a few mergers of merchandising and automotive manufacturing firms in 1908 and 1909, including, for example, the General Motors Corporation.[10]

One fact is clear from the information available on the extent of mergers before 1914. The degree of combination activity varied considerably through the years with the peak rate occurring during the period 1896 to 1904. Before this merger movement was half over, the changes taking place in the structure of ownership

---

[6] See Paul T. Homan, "Trusts," *Encyclopedia of the Social Sciences*, vol. 15 (Macmillan, 1931), p. 114.

[7] John Keith Butters, John Lintner, and William L. Cary, *Effects of Taxation: Corporate Mergers* (Boston: Division of Research, Grad. School of Bus. Ad., Harvard University, 1951), p. 289.

[8] *Financial Policy of Corporations*, 4th ed. (New York: Ronald Press, 1941), pp. 924–925.

[9] *Op. cit.*, p. 146.

[10] W. Z. Ripley, ed., *Trusts, Pools and Corporations*, rev. ed. (Boston: Ginn, 1916), p. xxi.

of American industry had become a major issue of public policy.[11]

Public Opinion on Antitrust Policy—As early as 1899, the Civic Federation of Chicago called a conference of persons representing all shades of opinion to discuss the "trust" problem. More than seven hundred delegates attended, including governors of several states, representatives of many business, industrial, and labor organizations, journalists, and university economists. More than ninety persons addressed the conference.[12] Few ideas on the monopoly problem have been presented in the past half-century that cannot be found in the record of the discussions in Chicago. Some of the participants took an uncompromising antitrust position, some favored giving full rein to the growth of large firms, and many others advocated the acceptance of the "trusts" but control of their abuses. The arguments presented and the issues raised were not limited to economic questions. The discussions centered in the basic question of public policy, which Allyn A. Young later defined: "In short, it is a question less of the relative 'economy' of monopoly or competition than of the kind of economic organization best calculated to give us the kind of society we want." [13]

Some participants in this conference expressed the fear of the agricultural regions that the merger movement was creating firms with power to raise the prices of manufactured goods while lowering the prices paid for raw materials.[14] Others warned of the political and social consequences of the threatened disappearance

[11] For an excellent, detailed analysis of developments in antitrust opinion, enforcement, and legislation from 1890 to 1903, see: Hans B. Thorelli, *The Federal Antitrust Policy, Origination of an American Tradition* (Baltimore: Johns Hopkins Press, 1955), part II.

[12] The proceedings were recorded in detail and provide a very good source of information on the reactions of the leaders of public opinion to the merger movement at its peak. See: *Chicago Conference on Trusts: Speeches, Debates, Resolutions, Lists of Delegates, Committees, etc.* (Held Sept. 13–16, 1899) (Chicago: Civic Federation of Chicago, 1900).

[13] "The Sherman Act and the New Antitrust Legislation: 1," *The Journal of Political Economy,* vol. 23 (March 1915), p. 214.

[14] See Dudley G. Wooten, "Principles and Sources of the Trust Evil as Texas Sees Them," *Chicago Conference on Trusts,* p. 45.

of the middle class of small independent businessmen and artisans.[15] A spokesman of the Knights of Labor decried the "trusts" as not only controlling production and prices, but also depriving individuals of their inherent right to labor.[16] Other labor leaders, however, accepted industrial combinations as a part of the American economic system that eliminated many evils of competitive business and made possible higher wages.[17] Samuel Gompers feared that any new legislation would be used "to deprive labor of the benefit of organized effort." [18]

John Bates Clark presented to the conference a proposal for legislation very much like the Clayton Act that was adopted fifteen years later. He said:

> The present effort of the people is to stop centralization in order to preclude monopoly, while their effort will ultimately be to crush the element of monopoly out of massed capital and let massing continue. The line of cleavage between what is good and will abide, and what is harmful and must go, is not between capital and concentration, but between centralization and monopoly.[19]

In subsequent years Clark reaffirmed his view that the advantages of centralization of capital should be retained while the abuses to which it gives rise are prohibited.[20]

Similar diverse opinions on the problem of industrial combinations were expressed thirteen years later in the papers read before the annual meeting of the American Academy of Political and

---

[15] See Hazen S. Pingree, "The Effect of Trusts on Our National Life and Citizenship," *Chicago Conference on Trusts*, pp. 266–267.

[16] John W. Hayes, "The Social Enemy," *Chicago Conference on Trusts*, pp. 331–332.

[17] See Henry White, "A Period of Doubt and Darkness in a New Industrial Era," *Chicago Conference on Trusts*, p. 323.

[18] "The Control of Trusts," *Chicago Conference on Trusts*, p. 330.

[19] "The Necessity of Suppressing Monopolies While Retaining Trusts," *Chicago Conference on Trusts*, p. 405.

[20] See John Bates Clark, *The Control of Trusts, An Argument in Favor of Curbing the Power of Monopoly by a Natural Method* (New York: Macmillan, 1901), p. 81, and *The Problem of Monopoly: A Study of a Grave Danger and of the Natural Mode of Averting It* (New York: Columbia University Press, 1904), pp. 120–122.

Social Science.[21] Like the Chicago conference in 1899, this meeting was addressed by a number of representatives of labor and business organizations, as well as journalists, political leaders, lawyers, and university professors.

The Sherman Act had been enacted to incorporate the common law into the federal statutes. The state incorporation laws had been liberalized sufficiently to allow the merger movement to transform the structure of ownership of industry between 1896 and 1904. Many persons desired an uncompromising antitrust policy designed to reëstablish and preserve a pattern of many small firms. Some argued strongly for a policy of noninterference with the growth of large firms under state incorporation laws. Most writers on the subject, or perhaps the most influential writers, advocated the type of policy that was in fact adopted in 1914 with the enactment of the Federal Trade Commission Act and the Clayton Act—the establishment of a commission and the explicit prohibition of a few predatory practices. Such a policy was designed to preserve the economic advantages of centralization of capital while promoting competition.

An examination of the evolution of the law in relation to mergers helps to explain why Congress chose to include in the Clayton Act a provision dealing with intercorporate stockholding.

The Development of Antitrust Law Prior to 1914

The legal environment in which the early combination movement developed in the United States consisted of three parts—common law, state statutory law, and federal statutory law—all closely interrelated. Since the common law, as interpreted by the courts, set up barriers to the process, the combination of small firms into larger aggregations eventually developed along with the state incorporation laws. The courts, however, interpreted these statutes in the light of the earlier common law doctrines.

[21] The entire meeting in July, 1912, was devoted to this question. See American Academy of Political and Social Science, *Industrial Competition and Combination, The Annals,* vol. XLII (July, 1912).

Because of the federal form of the government of the United States, which explicitly gives the national government jurisdiction over interstate commerce, the statutes of the federal government—or their absence—form an important part of the legal environment.

The Common Law—The two primary points of common law bearing on industrial combinations during the period in which the basis was laid for our present corporate structure were (1) the rule against agreements in restraint of trade and (2) the *ultra vires* principle.

The *ultra vires* principle was important in many of the early cases dealing with combinations, some involving the acquisition of stock and some involving the acquisition of property of one corporation by another. In some cases of this sort, the combination was declared illegal at common law on the basis of the *ultra vires* principle without the court's having to invoke the principle against agreements in restraint of trade. The law of corporations forbade "a corporation from exercising any power or authority not expressly conferred upon it or necessarily incident thereto."[22] Under this principle, in several early cases it was considered *ultra vires*—that is, contrary to the purposes of the corporation as set forth in its charter—for a corporation either to surrender control of its own affairs to another corporation, or to acquire control of another corporation, in the absence of expressly conferred legislative authority.[23]

In 1879 the United States Supreme Court declared to be void as an *ultra vires* act, against public policy, a lease by one railroad of the rolling stock, road, and buildings of another railroad without charter authority.[24] In an Illinois case in which one corporation gained control over another by purchasing a majority of its stock, the court held that the minority stockholders could void the purchase.[25] Another early case of stock acquisition involved the principle against contracts in restraint of trade as well as the

[22] *Trust Laws and Unfair Competition* (Washington: Bureau of Corporations, Department of Commerce, 1916), p. 58.

[23] *Ibid.*

[24] *Thomas* v. *Railroad Co.* (1879), 101 U.S. 71.

[25] *Dunbar* v. *American Telephone and Telegraph Co.* (1906), 224 Ill. 9.

ultra vires principle. In *Central Railroad Company* v. *Collins,* the court held that the purchase of capital stock by one railroad in another railroad with intent to hold it and to use it to obtain control of the management came within both of these common law principles.[26]

In discussing the legality under the common law of combinations effected by the acquisition by one corporation of another's plants, W. W. Thornton said:

> If a corporation be organized to take over the plants and monopolize the business of other corporations, its purpose and business will be illegal, even though the public may not suffer from the raise of the prices of its manufactured product. Thus a corporation was organized under the law of Connecticut for the purpose of securing the ownership of all of the match factories in the United States. Thirty-one concerns went into this combination, and out of these all except thirteen were closed and ceased to manufacture matches. This was not a case of combination of stock interests, but by the purchase of the principal match factories in the country. Many of the factories were paid for by the issuance of stock. The agreements for the acquisition of certain properties were held void.[27]

In the case referred to by Thornton, the judge said that the Diamond Match Company was engaged in an unlawful enterprise and that the contract in question was designed to further that enterprise and was, therefore, against public policy.[28]

Before 1890, in the United States the right of contract had been restricted more extensively than in England, especially through limitations imposed by public policy. Both loose agreements to fix prices and combinations of various forms were generally held illegal at common law. The trust form of organization was an attempt to get around these legal restrictions. But this, also, was held to be contrary to law and against public policy. For example, the Ohio court held the oil trust to be void, in a suit begun about 1890, on grounds that it was *ultra vires* and contrary to public policy.[29]

---

[26] 40 Ga. 582 (1896).

[27] W. W. Thornton, *A Treatise on Combinations in Restraint of Trade* (Cincinnati: W. H. Anderson Company, 1928), 112.

[28] *Richardson* v. *Buhl* (1889), 77 Mich. 632.

[29] *State* v. *Standard Oil Company* (1892), 49 Ohio St. 137.

After the Ohio oil trust case and the passage of the Sherman Act in 1890, combination of firms through stock or asset acquisition or through both became of increasing importance. Changes in state incorporation laws counteracted the effect of the actions of the courts in declaring such acquisitions unlawful at common law.

State Incorporation and Antitrust Statutes—New York adopted a general incorporation law in 1811, but other states followed slowly, so by the middle of the nineteenth century only a minority of the states had such laws.[30] Even with state statutes permitting incorporation without a special act of the state legislature, the strict interpretation of corporate charters by the courts in the light of the common law limited the usefulness of the corporate form in making possible large firms. The authority of two or more corporations to consolidate was not granted in New York, for example, until 1867. This authority was limited to corporations engaged in the same branch of industry and was extended in 1892.[31]

The development of state statutes allowing intercorporate stockholding was similar to that allowing consolidation. Until the latter half of the nineteenth century, almost universally a corporation was forbidden to hold the stock of another for purposes of control. One of the first relaxations of this restriction was the New York statute of 1853, which permitted the purchase of mining stock by a manufacturing corporation under certain conditions. Not until 1892 did New York allow an industrial corporation to purchase the stock of a competitor. The New Jersey statutes were changed frequently, the first limited authority being granted in 1883.[32] As to this development of state incorporation laws, Whitney said:

> The present statutes, which permit any company to purchase stock of a rival for control, are more recent even than the Sherman Anti-trust Law. They were in all probability adopted, although the legislatures did not

[30] *Trust Laws and Unfair Competition*, p. 8.

[31] *Ibid.*

[32] Edward B. Whitney, "Governmental Interference with Industrial Combinations," *Publications of the American Economic Association*, 3d ser., VI, 2 (1905), 4.

know it, for the very purpose of circumventing that law. They date in New York from 1892. In New Jersey their development was from 1888 to 1893. Before that the holding company, now so familiar, was a rarity.[33]

After the growth of a few very large trusts in the 1880's, there was a public demand for antitrust legislation. At about the same time that Congress passed the Sherman Act, several state legislatures passed state antitrust laws. These appear to have had very little effect on the combination movement. Writing in 1929, Seager and Gulick, in commenting on the interpretation of the Sherman Act in 1895, said:

There remained some uncertainty as to what might result from the antitrust legislation of the states. But as time went on and the futility of the spasmodic efforts that were made by a few of the states to enforce their antitrust acts became apparent, this danger, too, ceased to have any terrors for the would-be trust organizer.[34]

From the point of view of social control, the legal problem of limiting the size of business firms organized under the corporate form has become a problem of counteracting to some extent the broad grants of authority that have come to be given to corporations by the state incorporation laws, which superseded the common law doctrines. The legal efforts to impose such limitations on business firms organized under charters of incorporation granted by the various states have been made primarily by the federal government, under the constitutional power to regulate commerce among the states and with foreign countries.

On the power of Congress to impose conditions on business corporations, Edward B. Whitney, writing during the period of the greatest public interest, said:

Congress has the power of regulation here—a power which knows no limits except those which are put upon it by the Federal Constitution. Congress itself may grant a charter of incorporation to persons engaging in such commerce. A state cannot exclude therefrom any corporation which Congress permits to engage in it. Congress has always given tacit permission to corporations of the various states to engage in such commerce, but

[33] *Ibid.*

[34] H. R. Seager and C. A. Gulick, Jr., *Trust and Corporation Problems* (New York: Harper & Bros., 1929), p. 59.

I think that if it shall change this policy and impose conditions upon the participation of a foreign corporation in their own internal commerce, the courts will sustain it.[35]

The federal government played an important part in the evolution of the legal environment of the early combination movement, although it never adopted a federal incorporation law.

The Sherman Act—The first positive action taken by the federal government with respect to the manner of organization of industrial business enterprise in the United States was the enactment of the Sherman Antitrust Act in 1890.[36] In spite (or perhaps because) of the general language of the prohibitions of that statute against combinations in restraint of trade in the form of trusts or otherwise, it was not clear in the years immediately following its enactment just how far the courts would go in interpreting the act as prohibiting the union of two or more firms under common control by means of the corporate device.

As a result of the passage of the Sherman Act and several state cases[37] against the trust form of organization at about the same time, it became evident during the last decade of the century that the trust would not be permitted. This fact, along with the changes in the incorporation laws of New Jersey, encouraged the holding company form of organization for large combinations. Several trusts were transformed into New Jersey holding companies under the new statutes by the simple procedure of chartering a corporation to take over the assets held by the trustees. The owners then held common stock instead of trust certificates. The protection that a New Jersey holding company charter would give against the new federal antitrust act, however, was not definitely established in the early years.[38]

The uncertainty about the applicability of the Sherman Act to combinations organized under the New Jersey incorporation statutes was greatly lessened in 1895 by the United States Su-

[35] Whitney, *op. cit.*, p. 7.

[36] 26 *U.S. Stat. at L.* (1890), 209. For an excellent account of the forces leading up to the enactment of the Sherman Act, see Thorelli, *op. cit.*, pp. 9–232.

[37] For example, the Standard Oil Company of Ohio case, 49 Ohio St. 137, and the North River Refining Company case (1890), 24 N.E. 834.

[38] See Seager and Gulick, *op. cit.*, p. 55.

preme Court decision in the E. C. Knight Company case.[39] The Court ruled that manufacturing is not commerce and that the combination of manufacturing plants in different states was legal under the Sherman Act, as the effect of restraint on commerce was not direct and did not "necessarily determine the object of the contract." [40] Seager and Gulick stated:

> This narrow interpretation was given official confirmation and support in statements to Congress by both President Cleveland and Attorney General Olney that the federal law was ineffective and that the remedy must be sought in state action.[41]

As pointed out, this decision was followed by what is generally considered to be the most significant period of combination activity at any time in the long development of our present corporate structure. The end of this first great combination movement coincided with the second important Sherman Act case dealing with the applicability of the antitrust statute to combinations formed by the device of a holding corporation.

The Northern Securities Company decision in 1904 [42] showed conclusively that a combination formed by means of a New Jersey holding corporation charter was not sufficient to remove it from the jurisdiction of the federal government's action under the Sherman Act. It was not made certain, however, that the act would be applied to such combinations of manufacturing companies, since the Northern Securities case involved railroad companies, which were considered to be natural monopolies and were under federal regulation by positive act of Congress.

The Northern Securities decision was one of many causes for the decrease in the number of combinations created after 1904. The decision appears to have been also an important factor in determining the form of some important existing and some subsequently formed combinations. For example, the American Tobacco Company, which had originally been organized primarily

[39] *United States* v. *E. C. Knight Company* (1895), 156 U.S. 1.
[40] *Ibid.*
[41] Seager and Gulick, *op. cit.*, p. 59.
[42] *Northern Securities Company* v. *United States* (1904), 193 U.S. 197.

as a holding company, was reorganized shortly after the decision to merge the properties of the principal companies in the combination. While the Northern Securities case was in progress, the International Harvester Company was organized by uniting under the ownership of one corporation the properties of several previously independent corporations.[43]

Regarding the form of industrial combinations subsequent to the Northern Securities case, Bruce Wyman, professor of law and lecturer in economics in Harvard University, writing in 1911, said:

> All this time it had been recognized that there was a safer way, if one chose to take it. The approved form among lawyers during the last few years for making a consolidation of interests is by the formation of a single gigantic corporation intended to take over, by purchase, all the different concerns that are to be brought together.[44]

The legality of this form of combination was not, however, definitely established in 1911, although the creation of a combination by acquisition of physical properties had been frequently used at the turn of the century. It was not even definitely established that combinations of this sort were legal in cases not involving interstate commerce and the Sherman Act. In one case, a state court in New Jersey declared such a combination to be legal because the authority granted by the state to the acquiring corporation in its charter was sufficient to counteract the common law prohibition against a combination in restraint of trade.[45] In an Illinois case, however, the court had ruled that, as the whiskey trust had been illegal because it was against public policy, the corporation taking its place by acquisition of the assets of the constituent corporations was also illegal under the common law.[46] The legal status of such combinations under the Sherman Act was no more clear. Before the passage of the Clayton Act in 1914, there had

[43] *Trust Laws and Unfair Competition,* p. 15.

[44] Bruce Wyman, *Control of the Market; a Legal Solution of the Trust Problem* (New York: Moffat, Yard and Company, 1911), p. 160.

[45] *Trenton Potteries Company* v. *Oliphant* (1899), 58 N.J. Eq. 507.

[46] *Distilling and Cattle Feeding Company* v. *People* (1895), 156 Ill. 448.

been no antitrust case in which a single corporation owned all the properties combined under common control. Several cases under the Sherman Act, however, involved combinations brought about in part by the merger of properties under a single corporation as well as by the acquisition of capital stock in other companies. In none of these cases did the courts consider the legality of an asset acquisition or of a stock acquisition as an isolated feature.[47]

In *Cincinnati Packet Company* v. *Bay* (1906),[48] the United States Supreme Court held that the Sherman Act did not prevent the purchase of the business of one corporation by another since any effect on commerce was merely incidental to the sale of property. In a case decided just the year before Congress enacted the Clayton Act, the Supreme Court dismissed a Sherman Act criminal indictment against the man who engineered the combination resulting in the United Shoe Machinery Company on the grounds that the purpose of the combination was greater efficiency rather than the elimination of competition.[49] On the other hand, in *United States* v. *E. I. du Pont de Nemours & Company* (1911),[50] a lower court ruled that the combination created an illegal monopoly. The du Pont Company had acquired from 1903 through 1908 either the assets or the stock of most of the powder and explosive firms in the United States. The firms involved had previously been members of an association. The circuit court ruled that the combination was the continuation of the illegal association in a new form and was therefore illegal.

The 1911 oil and tobacco cases[51] were the most important pre-1914 cases, concerning the legality of combinations brought about by either stock or asset acquisitions, and they were important in creating the demand for the passage of the Clayton Act. The American Tobacco Company was primarily the result of a

---

[47] *Trust Laws and Unfair Competition*, p. 98.

[48] 200 U.S. 179.

[49] *United States* v. *Winslow* (1913), 227 U.S. 202.

[50] 188 Fed. 127.

[51] *Standard Oil Company* v. *United States* (1911), 221 U.S. 1, and *United States* v. *American Tobacco Company* (1911), 221 U.S. 106.

series of asset acquisitions, although it involved as well the acquisition of the stock of competitors. The Standard Oil Company of New Jersey was primarily a combination brought about as a holding company by the acquisition of stock. In neither case was the court concerned with the legality of a particular asset or stock acquisition, but rather with the combination as a whole and the purposes and results of its organization.

The government won both cases and thus demonstrated that under the Sherman Act a combination of manufacturing concerns could be dissolved whether organized under the corporate form as a holding company or as a single corporation. In both cases, however, the actions of the defendants were so obviously designed to achieve domination of their respective markets that the same decision would have resulted under almost any interpretation of the Sherman Act. The most important aspect was that the defendants were found to have violated the Sherman Act not because of a restraint of trade, but because of an *unreasonable* restraint of trade. The cases offered little more than the Northern Securities decision as a criterion by which to judge the legality of a *particular* acquisition by a corporation of the capital stock or assets of a competitor. Applying the rule of reason, the court found in these cases that the whole pattern of behavior of each of these consolidated firms constituted an unreasonable restraint of trade and an attempt to monopolize because their actions were injurious to the public.

Thus, by 1914 the law on corporate mergers and acquisitions had evolved through several stages: first, the period before 1890, during which the common law did not permit corporations to acquire the stock or assets of another corporation or to merge with another corporation unless specifically authorized to do so by charter authority; second, the period around the turn of the century, during which state incorporation statutes were so general and liberal as to allow any corporation to acquire the property of others, to merge with another, or to hold stock in another corporation, and during which the state and federal antitrust statutes were not a deterrent to such combinations; and third, the period after the Northern Securities decision, during which the Sherman Act served as a deterrent to combinations, but had no definite criterion of illegality for a particular acquisition. During the second period, the great combination movement had occurred.

Conclusions

After Congress had, with the Sherman Act, enunciated the basic policy of maintaining competition in industrial markets, the market structure underwent a major change as small firms were combined into giant corporations during the great merger movement. The Sherman Act had been ineffective in counteracting the power granted by liberal state laws to newly created corporations. The merger movement made antitrust policy a major political issue from 1899 to 1914, when the Federal Trade Commission was established and the Clayton Act was enacted. During this period, public opinion on the "trust" problem was divided, but the newly created industrial combinations gradually were accepted as an evolutionary development in the form of industrial organization. The problem of public policy shifted to the question of the manner in which the activities of large firms should be circumscribed in the interest of the public.

The general incorporation laws of the states had been liberalized to allow a corporation to consolidate with other corporations, acquire the physical assets of other corporations, and acquire the capital stock of other corporations. In the two decades of discussion of antitrust policy before 1914, public writings and Congressional proposals gave very little consideration to the desirability of prohibiting intercorporate stockholding. The change in the structure of ownership of industrial plants, however, led most students of the problem to advocate some new form of federal legislation to supplement the Sherman Act. By 1914 the climate of opinion forced new legislation to prohibit some specified business practices that might otherwise enable large firms to avoid competition and gain monopoly power. The final result was a commission with power to prohibit "unfair methods of competition" and a specific prohibition against four business practices. The institutional framework underlying the 1914 legislation was much more conducive to legislation designed to regulate the practices of industrial combinations than to legislation designed to alter the corporate structure any more than the Sherman Act made possible. As will be shown in the following chapter, the prohibition against intercorporate stockholding was a part of a policy concerned with corporate practices rather than basic corporate structure.

2. The Legislative History of Section 7 of the Clayton Act

In enacting the Clayton Act in 1914, Congress intended to supplement the Sherman Act in several ways. This chapter examines the question of Congress' intent to change the antitrust law with respect to mergers generally. An analysis of the political environment surrounding the Clayton Act and of the development of Section 7 in Congress leads to the conclusion that Congress intended merely to prevent the particular evils thought to be associated in some instances with the practice of intercorporate stockholding.

The Political Environment in Which the Clayton Act Was Enacted

During the decade and a half preceding the enactment of the 1914 legislation, the important political leaders of the nation had expressed opinions on the "trust problem," official proposals had been made for changing the antitrust law policy, and the question was a major issue in the presidential campaign of 1912.

The Recommendations of the Bureau of Corporations—The creation of the Bureau of Corporations constituted a new conception of the "trust problem," since it was a recognition of the inevitability of industrial combinations, in spite of the prohibitions of the Sherman Act. Congress expected the bureau to provide indirect regulation of combinations. Public opinion, exerted in response to information made available by a permanent administrative agency, was expected to prevent the abuse of corporate power. The work of the bureau during its twelve years of existence was narrow in scope, but its investigations of the oil, tobacco, and harvester industries led to the antitrust cases in those fields.[1]

Until the change of personnel in 1913, occurring with the advent of the Wilson Administration, the Commissioner of Corporations held the opinion that most problems of social control of business could be solved by adequate publicity of corporate practices. In this period the commissioner made no recommendations to change the law to prohibit mergers in any form. Requests were made, however, for new legislation to create an agency with sufficient powers to extend the investigative and publication activities of the bureau to all interstate corporations. For example, in 1907 Herbert Knox Smith, the Commissioner of Corporations, said:

> As has been stated in previous reports, the primary object of the Bureau is to set before the President, Congress, and the public reliable information as to the operation of the great interstate corporations in such clear and concise form as to show the important permanent conditions of such corporate operations. With such information as a basis, it is believed that the great corrective force of public opinion can be intelligently and efficiently directed at those industrial evils that constitute the most important of our present problems. . . .
>
> Corporate combination, as such, appears to be not only an economic necessity, but largely an accomplished fact. The mere prohibition of commercial power, simply because such power is the result of corporate combination, by no means meets the real evils. It is not the existence of industrial power, but rather its misuse, that is the real problem. . . .
>
> Thus, the experience of the Bureau seems to point logically to the need

[1] W. Stull Holt, *The Federal Trade Commission, Its History, Activities and Organization,* Institute for Government Research, Service Monographs of the U.S. Government, no. 7 (New York: D. Appleton & Co., 1922), pp. 4–5.

for an extension of such results by the creation of a general administrative system of supervision of interstate corporations which shall give, in substantially the same form as is furnished now for a few corporations, the essential facts relating to all the great interstate corporations. . . . Whether the system take the form of a Federal licence plan or a simple requirement that interstate corporations shall make reports and submit their books to a Federal bureau is of little consequence so long as the information necessary for publicity is obtained.[2]

The following year Oscar S. Straus, Secretary of Commerce and Labor, reiterated this same general approach to the problem of social control of industrial corporations:

It is becoming more and more obvious that the work of the Government in regulating corporations should not be directed at the mere existence of combination itself, as such, but should deal rather with the way in which the combination powers are used, so as to prevent as far as possible the misuse of these great industrial forces. . . . It is useless to ignore the operations of the economic law that has brought about the present concentration in business. It is useless to ignore the fact, further, that this concentration is already largely accomplished.[3]

The first reports on antitrust law policy of the Secretary of Commerce and the Commissioner of Corporations in the administration of President Wilson show a marked change of attitude from the reports of the secretary and commissioner in earlier administrations. In his 1913 report, Secretary of Commerce William C. Redfield renewed the requests of his predecessors that information from corporations engaged in interstate commerce should be submitted to some government agency, but his report spelled out in detail what information he thought should be required and included, among other things,

. . . the names of other corporations in which it holds stock, and names of other corporations which hold its stock, and the respective amounts held; other companies in which its officers or directors are either officers or directors, and their stockholdings in such other companies; . . .[4]

[2] *Reports of the Department of Commerce and Labor, 1907* (Washington: 1909), p. 33.

[3] *Ibid., 1908*, p. 33.

[4] *Ibid., 1913*, p. 70.

As contrasted with previous recommendations, the purpose of such information would be to obtain a basis for legislation rather than relying on public opinion. Secretary Redfield, however, went beyond this and proposed some immediate changes in the anti-trust laws:

That there are immediate and well-known conditions that should and can be remedied by law is apparent. Some of these remedies are, for instance . . . that corporations shall not hold stock in other competing companies, and that neither a person nor a corporation shall at the same time own a controlling interest in two or more competing corporations, or that the officers of corporations shall not be affiliated directly or indirectly by holding office in other corporations.[5]

Joseph E. Davies, Commissioner of Corporations, expressed essentially the same views in his report.[6]

Other Proposals for Restricting Combinations—In the years immediately preceding the enactment of the Clayton Act, several proposals dealt specifically with the question of prohibiting combinations in one form or another. Consideration of some of these proposals may place in better perspective the proposals that were in fact adopted.

In a message to Congress in 1911, President William Howard Taft renewed a previous request for legislation providing for voluntary incorporation under federal charter of corporations engaged in interstate and foreign commerce. He recommended that the law prohibit corporations organized under the act from either acquiring or holding stock in any other corporations (whether competing or not) except upon approval of a federal agency for special reasons. There was no suggestion of the prohibition of mergers or asset acquisitions since he thought the Sherman Act was sufficient to prevent monopoly.[7]

In the previous session of Congress, Senator Robert W. La Follette had introduced a bill to amend the Sherman Act by adding several sections to it. This bill proposed that in Sherman Act cases

[5] *Ibid.*, p. 71.

[6] *Report of the Commissioner of Corporations* (Washington: 1914).

[7] *Congressional Record*, 62d Cong., 2d sess., 48:1 (1911), 25–26.

several actions on the part of the defendants would be considered conclusive evidence of unreasonable restraint of trade. Among these actions, the bill included doing business under any name other than a corporation's own corporate name, and concealing or misrepresenting the ownership or control of a business or the identity of a manufacturer. This was apparently aimed at what was considered to be evils of the holding company.[8]

In 1912, Senator John Sharp Williams introduced a bill that would have specified certain charter provisions as prerequisites to the privilege of doing business in interstate commerce. Senator Williams included prohibitions against owning stock in any other corporation or having its stock owned by any other corporation. He made no attempt in this bill to prohibit mergers or asset acquisitions.[9]

In the same session of Congress, Senator Albert B. Cummins introduced a bill that would have prohibited a corporation from engaging in interstate commerce if its officers and directors included men who were officers or directors or under the control of officers or directors in another corporation engaged in business "of the same general character." This bill would have prohibited intercorporate stockholding irrespective of the similarity of the businesses. It would have attempted to prevent a community of interest between competitive corporations by prohibiting a person from owning more than 10 per cent of the stock of each of two competing interstate companies. Section 3 of the bill would have restricted mergers and asset acquisitions as well as internal growth of firms. It would have prohibited a corporation from engaging in interstate commerce if it employed capital to the extent that it would "destroy or prevent substantially competitive conditions" in the industry.[10]

One proposal made during the second session of the Sixty-second Congress specifically dealt with the question of the acquisition by one corporation of the property of another. Judge

---

[8] U.S. 62d Cong., 1st sess., S. 3276. Reprinted in William S. Stevens, *Industrial Combinations and Trusts* (New York: Macmillan Co., 1913), pp. 530–537.

[9] U.S. 62d Cong., 2d sess., S. 4747. Reprinted in Stevens, *op. cit.*, pp. 537–540.

[10] U.S. 62d Cong., 2d sess., S. 5451. Reprinted in Stevens, *op. cit.*, pp. 540–547.

Elbert H. Gary was requested by the Senate Committee on Interstate Commerce to submit a draft of a bill.[11] The proposal of Judge Gary would have set up a corporation commission to license interstate corporations as a prerequisite to engaging in interstate commerce. No corporation so licensed and whose business constituted more than 50 per cent of the business "of the same character" in the national market would have been allowed to acquire the property or business of another corporation whose business was similar without the approval of the corporation commission. The commission would give its approval only if it concluded that the acquisition would not result in a monopoly or restraint of trade in violation of the Sherman Act. This proposal would have made no change in the criterion of illegality under the Sherman Act, but would have required a judgment prior to the achievement of a degree of market control sufficient to constitute a Sherman Act violation.[12]

All the proposals discussed above were reactions to the enunciation of the rule of reason by the Supreme Court in 1911.[13] With the exception of Judge Gary's suggestions, all were designed to be an enunciation by Congress of a policy toward combinations more stringent than the Sherman Act, as it was interpreted at the time. They aimed, however, at specific practices that apparently accompanied the development of the combinations that had been given wide publicity by the major antitrust cases. The holding company was considered an obvious evil with which the Sherman Act was not capable of dealing effectively. The holding company was an easily understood, well-defined device, used by the "trusts" and unpopular with the voters. Only Judge Gary dealt with the more difficult question of establishing a criterion by which to judge the degree of integration consistent with public policy, and he proposed the retention of the Sherman Act test of illegality, that is, whether the combination unreasonably restrains trade to the injury of the public.

---

[11] See *Hearings on the Control of Corporations, Persons, and Firms Engaged in Interstate Commerce,* U.S. 62d Cong., 2d sess., pp. 2407–2412.

[12] Stevens, *op. cit.,* p. 552.

[13] See pp. 16–17.

The Election Campaign of 1912—In the presidential election campaign of 1912, all three parties recognized the necessity of advocating strengthening the antitrust laws. There was general agreement that some new agency should be set up to regulate industrial corporations engaged in interstate commerce. The differences in approach to the problem, indicated by the recommendations of the commissioners of Corporations and the secretaries of Commerce in the Republican and Democratic administrations, were also manifested in the campaign pronouncements of those two parties. Some pronouncements of the group of Republicans who broke away to form the Progressive party were stronger than those of either of the other two parties. All these groups, however, pledged to give the voters some type of positive legislation to supplement the Sherman Act.

The platform of the Republican party included the following statement:

> The Republican Party favors the enactment of legislation supplementary to the existing anti-trust act which will define as criminal offences those specific acts that uniformly mark attempts to restrain and to monopolize trade. . . .[14]

The platform did not state the acts to be prohibited. On the question of the creation of a new administrative agency, the platform was also couched in very general terms:

> In the enforcement and administration of Federal Laws governing interstate commerce and enterprises impressed with a public use engaged therein, there is much that may be committed to a Federal trade commission, thus placing in the hands of an administrative board many of the functions now necessarily exercised by the courts.[15]

In his speech in acceptance of renomination, President Taft discussed antitrust policy at length. He renewed his suggestion for a federal incorporation law, but made no specific reference to the question of changing the law to prohibit combinations effected by either stock or asset acquisitions. He expressed his general satisfaction with the Sherman Act and opposed any "drastic amendments," saying:

[14] *Official Report of the Proceedings of the Fifteenth Republican National Convention* (New York: Tenny Press, 1912), p. 345.

[15] *Ibid.*

The measure has been on the statute book since 1890, and many times under construction by the courts, but not until the litigation against the Standard Oil Company and against the American Tobacco Company reached the Supreme Court did the statute receive an authoritative construction which is workable and intelligible.[16]

Taft called for new legislation to prohibit specific unfair trade practices, but he gave no indication of which practices should be prohibited. He went on to call for a competent agency to supervise business transactions and thus preclude violation of the antitrust laws:

[T]here is great need for . . . constructive legislation of a helpful kind. Combination of capital in great enterprises should be encouraged, if within the law, for everyone must recognize that progress in modern business is by effective combination of the means of production to the point of greatest economy.[17]

Some Republicans differed on the degree to which the antitrust laws should be strengthened. A minority report of the platform committee at the Republican convention strongly denounced the Standard Oil and American Tobacco decisions and declared that the "present law is impotent to destroy monopoly." It called for supplementary legislation placing the burden of proof on the defendants in restraint of trade cases, prohibiting community of interest between corporations set up by dissolution decrees, and giving the proposed commission authority to administer all the antitrust laws. The report made no proposal, however, on specific prohibition of stock or asset acquisitions.[18]

The Progressive party, formed in 1912 by dissident Republicans under the leadership of Theodore Roosevelt, also advocated strengthening the antitrust laws, but its proposals would have changed the basic policy embodied in the Sherman Act to allow large combinations under government regulation. The Progressive party platform stated:

To that end we urge the establishment of a strong Federal administrative commission of high standing, which shall maintain permanent active super-

[16] *Ibid.*, p. 429.
[17] *Ibid.*, pp. 429–430.
[18] *Ibid.*, pp. 354–356.

vision over industrial corporations engaged in interstate commerce, or such of them as are of public importance, doing for them what the Government now does for the national banks, and what is now done for the railroads by the Interstate Commerce Commission.[19]

In the campaign of 1912, the Democratic party also offered general promises with respect to strengthening the antitrust policy, but it made specific statements concerning holding companies. The platform said:

We favor the declaration by law of the conditions upon which corporations shall be permitted to engage in interstate trade, including, among others, the prevention of holding companies, of interlocking directorates, of stock watering, of discrimination in price, and the control by any one corporation of so large a proportion of any industry as to make it a menace to competitive conditions.[20]

The record of the 1912 campaign thus reveals that the political leaders of the nation believed that the public was interested in new legislation to supplement the Sherman Act as interpreted by the Supreme Court. Most discussions of the problem were couched in highly general terms. Everyone recognized the need for some new form of administrative agency to deal with industrial corporations, but the nature and duties of such a body were in dispute. The public discussions definitely placed on the defensive those who were satisfied with the substance of the Sherman Act as interpreted. With the Democratic party winning the election and Taft running third, it was evident that positive action had to be taken by the new administration, but the campaign had not crystallized public opinion on the basic question. The discussions resulted in no substitute for the rule of reason as the basis of deciding the extent to which the government should allow control of markets for industrial products to be concentrated in the hands of single firms. Nor did the legislative process answer this question. The new provisions of law accomplished primarily

[19] Quoted in: *Interstate Trade Commission, To Accompany H.R. 15613,* U.S. House Interstate and Foreign Commerce Committee, 63d Cong., 2 sess., H. Rept. 533 (1914), part 3, p. 2.

[20] *Ibid.,* p. 3.

the aim of appearing to have satisfied the promises made during the campaign.

The Antitrust Legislative Program of the Wilson Administration—On January 20, 1914, President Wilson to a joint session of Congress delivered an address officially requesting legislation to fulfill the campaign promises on antitrust policy. He discussed at length the evils of interlocking directorates, which he proposed should be prohibited.[21]

> We are all agreed that "private monopoly is indefensible and intolerable," and our programme is founded upon that conviction. It will be comprehensive but not a radical or unacceptable programme and these are its items, the changes which opinion deliberately sanctions and for which business waits:
>
> It waits with acquiescence, in the first place, for laws which will effectually prohibit and prevent such interlockings of the *personnel* of the directorates of great corporations . . . as in effect result in making . . . those who affect to compete in fact partners and masters of some whole field of business.[22]

President Wilson was asking for the same things that he and his party had promised during the campaign, and he felt the public wanted. He went on to say:

> The business of the country awaits also . . . further and more explicit legislative definition of the policy and meaning of the existing antitrust law. . . . Surely we are sufficiently familiar with the actual processes and methods of monopoly and of the many hurtful restraints of trade to make definition possible, at any rate up to the limits of what experience has disclosed.[23]

In discussing the practices that should be prohibited, President Wilson made no mention of mergers or asset acquisitions. He called for some prohibition of common control of more than one corporation through a community of interest, but his message

---

[21] This proposal was the outgrowth of the investigations by the Pujo Committee, which was concerned with combinations among financial institutions. See *Report of the Committee Appointed Pursuant to House Resolutions 429 and 504 to Investigate the Concentration of Control of Money and Credit,* U.S. 62d Cong., 2d sess. (1913).

[22] *Trusts and Monopolies,* U.S. 63d Cong., 2d sess., H. Doc. 625 (1914), p. 5.

[23] *Ibid.,* p. 5.

gave little attention to his request for prohibitions against stock acquisitions, since he took it for granted that holding companies should be prohibited:

Enterprises, in these modern days of great individual fortunes, are oftentimes interlocked, not by being under the control of the same directors, but by the fact that the greater part of their corporate stock is owned by a single person or group of persons who are in some way intimately related in interest. We are agreed, I take it, that holding *companies* should be prohibited, but what of the controlling private ownership of individuals or actually cooperative groups of individuals? [24]

In this message Wilson called for a trade commission, but did not specify what powers it should have, except to say that businessmen "desire the advice, the definite guidance and information which can be supplied by an administrative body." [25]

Wilson's recommendations were embodied in five bills, but, after several weeks of hearings, the portions of these bills relating to antitrust policy were placed in two bills—the Trade Commission Bill and the Clayton Bill. Although Clayton introduced the Trade Commission Bill under the rules of the House it was referred to the Committee on Interstate and Foreign Commerce. The Judiciary Committee, of which Clayton was chairman, considered only the bill containing substantive changes in the antitrust laws.[26] A third bill relating to railroad securities was to have been part of the program, but was postponed to a later session of Congress.[27]

The Development of Section 7 in Congress

The House Judiciary Committee reported the Clayton Bill on May 6, 1914.[28] In addition to several sections concerning the application of the antitrust laws to labor unions and the pro-

[24] *Ibid.*, p. 7.
[25] *Ibid.*, p. 5.
[26] H. Rept. 533, part 1, p. 9.
[27] Seager and Gulick, *op. cit.*, p. 424.
[28] *Antitrust Legislation*, U.S. 63d Cong., 2d sess., H. Rept. 627 (1914).

cedures to be used by the judiciary in issuing injunctions, four sections of the bill proposed substantive changes in the antitrust laws by way of supplementing the Sherman Act and several sections dealt with the administration of these sections. These four sections proposed to declare illegal under certain circumstances (1) price discrimination, (2) exclusive dealing and tying contracts, (3) holding companies, and (4) interlocking directorates. The language of the holding company section—eventually to become Section 7 of the Clayton Act—changed frequently during the legislative process. In order to ascertain the intent of Congress, it is necessary to examine the step-by-step changes made in the section and the reasons given for each change.

Section 7 as Presented to the House—Under the bill reported by the House committee, the Attorney General, acting through the district courts, would have enforced these provisions in the same manner as the Sherman Act. The bill provided criminal penalties for violations. At the time that the Judiciary Committee reported the Clayton Bill, the Interstate and Foreign Commerce Committee had already reported the Trade Commission Bill and it was pending before the House. The trade commission proposed in that bill would have been primarily an instrument of information and publicity, as the provision relating to unfair methods of competition had not yet been added.[29]

The holding company section (Section 8, later renumbered Section 7) of the Clayton Bill was explained by the majority report of the committee as follows:

> Section 8 deals with what is commonly known as the "holding company," which is a common and favorite method of promoting monopoly. "Holding company" is a term, generally understood to mean a company that holds the stock of another company or companies, but as we understand the term a "holding company" is a company whose *primary* purpose is to hold stocks of other companies. It has usually issued its own shares in exchange for these stocks, and is a means of holding under one control the competing companies whose stocks it has thus acquired. As thus defined a "holding company" is an abomination and in our judgment is a mere incorporated form of the oldfashioned trust. . . .
>
> At common law a corporation had no right to own stock in another

[29] H. Rept. 533.

corporation, but from time to time the various States have, by special statutes, permitted it, until now certainly more than a majority of all the States permit corporate stockholding either generally or of certain kinds and under certain conditions. This legislation in its early operation may have served a useful, economic purpose. Trade and commerce could do as well without steam and electricity as without the idea of the commercial unit which is embodied in the word "corporation." Hence there are certain corporations which may properly be interested with individuals other than its own stockholders, but experience has taught us that the "holding company" as above described no longer serves any purpose that is helpful to either business or the community at large when it is operated purely as a "holding company." Section 8 is intended to eliminate this evil so far as it is possible to do so, making such exceptions from the law as seem to be wise, which exceptions have been necessary by business experience and conditions, and the exceptions herein made are those which are not deemed monopolistic and do not tend to restrain trade.[30]

This statement shows that the original framers of Section 7 were unwilling to force corporations engaged in interstate commerce to return to the common law rule against intercorporate stockholding. Nor were they concerned with prohibiting mergers or consolidations apart from those taking the form of "monopolistic" holding companies.[31]

The holding company section of H.R. 15657, as reported by the House committee, was worded as follows:

Sec. 8. That no corporation engaged in commerce shall acquire, directly or indirectly, the whole or any part of the stock or other share capital of another corporation engaged also in commerce where the effect of such acquisition *is* to *eliminate or* substantially lessen competition between the corporation whose stock is so acquired and the corporation making the acquisition, or *to create a monopoly of any line of trade in any section or community.*

No corporation shall acquire, directly or indirectly, the whole or any part of the stock or other share capital of two or more corporations engaged in commerce where the effect of such acquisition, or the use of such stock by the voting or granting of proxies or otherwise, *is to eliminate or sub-*

---

[30] H. Rept. 627, p. 17. This statement was reprinted and sanctioned by the Senate Judiciary Committee in *Unlawful Restraints and Monopolies, Report to Accompany H.R. 15657,* U.S. 63d Cong., 2d sess., S. Rept. 698 (1914), p. 13.

[31] The intent of Congress in enacting Section 7 of the Clayton Act is analyzed in detail in a later section of this chapter.

stantially lessen competition between such corporations, or any of them, whose stock or other share capital is so acquired, *or to create a monopoly of any line of trade in any section or community.*

This section shall not apply to corporations purchasing such stock solely for investment and not using the same by voting or otherwise to bring about, or in attempting to bring about, the substantial lessening of competition. Nor shall anything contained in this section prevent a corporation engaged in commerce from causing the formation of subsidiary corporations for the actual carrying on of their immediate lawful business, or the natural and legitimate branches or extensions thereof, or from owning and holding all or a part of the stock of such subsidiary corporations, when the effect of such formation is not to eliminate or substantially lessen competition.

Nothing contained in this section shall be held to affect or impair any right heretofore legally acquired: *Provided,* that nothing in this paragraph shall make stockholding relations between corporations legal when such relations constitute violations of the antitrust laws.

Nor shall anything herein contained be construed . . . to prevent any railroad company from extending any of its lines through the medium of the acquisition of stock or otherwise of any other railroad company where there is no substantial competition between the company extending its lines and the company whose stock, property, or an interest therein is so acquired.

A violation of any of the provisions of this section shall be deemed a misdemeanor, and shall be punishable by a fine not exceeding $5,000, or by imprisonment not exceeding one year, or both, in the discretion of the court.[32]

The Minority Reports on the Proposal—The Judiciary Committee's report to the House on the Clayton Bill contained three separate statements of minority views. Congressmen George S. Graham, Henry G. Danforth, and L. C. Dyer opposed the bill on the grounds that it was too strong. Graham said:

The antitrust laws on the statute book at this time have been carefully considered by the Supreme Court and judicially interpreted through a period of 24 years, and if properly enforced are believed by us to strip corporations and trust of any power to injure or oppress. . . .

The proposed legislation contains many new phrases and sets up new standards, all of which would require a period of years of interpretation by the courts before their meaning can be definitely known by the business world.

[32] H. Rept. 627, p. 3. Italics indicate phrases in the wording of the section, which were later to become points of contention in the discussions of the bill.

It is very undesirable to bring about such a period of uncertainty and doubt to worry and harass the business of the country.[33]

Graham said about the holding company section:

This provision goes further than the Sherman Act of 1890 with relation to holding companies. Under that act the doing of any of these things with intent to create or actually creating a monopoly or restraint of trade is forbidden; and the law in this respect is fully ample and competent to take care of all such offenses and the offenders. This act, however, goes beyond and leads us into a most dangerous realm, for it makes "elimination or lessening of competition" the test of illegality; while the Sherman Act makes "monopoly" or "restraint of trade" the test of illegality.

The only excuse and justification for legislation against holding companies lies in the fact that the holding company intended to be reached by the law creates a monopoly, or attempts to do so, or restrains trade.[34]

The views of this minority of the committee disclose that they were explicitly opposed to any attempt to change the basis of antitrust policy from the concept of *a monopoly* to the concept of maintaining competition.

A second minority report was written by John M. Nelson and concurred in by A. J. Volstead. These gentlemen opposed the bill because they felt that its provisions were not strong enough. They voiced a criticism that the record indicates was soundly based:

After months of hearings before the Judiciary Committee upon certain tentative bills prepared by a partisan subcommittee, in consultation with the President, the outcome has been this compromise measure, which is clearly intended as an assurance to big business and a sop to public opinion. . . . The spirit of compromise which runs through every section of this bill is something quite apart from the spirit of the brave declaration that "A private monopoly is indefensible and intolerable," but rather in it we detect the "atmosphere of accommodation and mutual understanding" between the Government and big business which the President advocated in his trust message.[35]

Nelson's report offered several specific objections to the wording of the holding company section of the bill. He pointed out that the prohibitions against holding companies and interlocking di-

[33] *Ibid.*, part 2, p. 1.
[34] *Ibid.*, p. 6.
[35] *Ibid.*, part 3, pp. 1–2.

rectorates were aimed at mere manifestations of the real evil, "common stock ownership and other forms of interlocking control." He criticized the section for exempting holding companies already organized.[36] He levied his major criticism of the section, however, against the criterion of illegality, saying:

It prohibits one corporation from holding the stock of another corporation where the "effect" of such acquisition is to eliminate or substantially lessen competition. In the Northern Securities case the criterion when the holding by one corporation of the stock of another is unlawful under the Sherman antitrust law was laid down as being, not that the holding of the stock of such other corporation must be shown to have had the effect of lessening competition, whether that power has been exercised or not. Had this section of the bill been the law, the Northern Securities case would have been decided against the government. . . . If this section were genuinely intended to strengthen the Sherman Act in dealing with the evil of the holding company, why did it not simply declare that no corporation shall acquire any of the stock of another corporation where the acquisition of the whole of the stock of such other corporation would constitute a violation of the Sherman Antitrust Act? Instead of thus strengthening the Sherman law by preventing one competing corporation from edging toward the control of another, it provides that the potential power to lessen competition shall no longer be the criterion.[37]

Dick T. Morgan presented the third minority view of the bill. He felt that the Sherman Act was adequate, if it could be properly administered. He deplored the assignment of the Trade Commission Bill and the Clayton Bill to separate committees.

In my judgment it is unfortunate that one committee should not have had exclusive jurisdiction over the proposed legislation to create a Federal trade commission and all antitrust legislation. The creation of a Federal commission with certain jurisdiction over industrial corporations engaged in interstate trade will mark an epoch in our national policy in Federal control of private business. Manifestly all legislation for the supervision, regulation, and control of private business engaged in interstate commerce will and should center in and around the national commission, whether its jurisdiction and power be great or small. So it seems to me, if the Sherman law is to be amended, the new statutory provisions should be drawn with the

[36] *Ibid.*, pp. 7–8.

[37] *Ibid.* This criticism of the original wording of the section was later met in the Senate by substituting "may be" for "is" in the phrase "where the effect is to eliminate."

trade commission and its power in view. Because we are entering upon a new field of Federal activity in the control of private business; all our enactments should be suited to our new enforcing agency—the proposed Federal commission. But over this proposed legislation the Judiciary Committee has no jurisdiction, and it is not proper for me to discuss any of the provisions relative thereto.[38]

The Debates in the House—The House of Representatives began debate on the Clayton Bill on May 22, 1914.[39] The discussions on the floor of the House reiterated the points of criticism against the holding company section expressed in the minority reports. Kelly of Pennsylvania, a member of the Progressive party, opposed including any specific prohibitions in the bill. Instead, he would have given the trade commission the power to root out "every trade practice which leads to monopoly."[40]

The Republican members of the Judiciary Committee who had opposed the bill for being too ineffectual stressed the view that the criterion used was weaker than the Sherman Act criterion laid down in the Northern Securities case. In answer to this argument, Carlin, a Democratic member of the subcommittee that wrote the bill, maintained that the Supreme Court in the Northern Securities case had held that the holding company had eliminated competition and thus restrained trade. He said:

Under this bill there has to be only a lessening of competition. Competition may be lessened without restraint of trade. Competition may be lessened without attempt to monopolize.[41]

Volstead moved to strike out all of Section 8 (later to be numbered Section 7) and to substitute a new section. The proposed section would have removed the standard of illegality proposed in the bill and would have used, instead, the Sherman Act standard. It also would have prohibited absolutely the practice of acquiring stock by exchange of stock.[42] This amendment was rejected.[43]

---

[38] H. Rept. 627, part 4, p. 5.
[39] *Congressional Record,* 63d Cong., 2d sess., 51:9 (May 22, 1914).
[40] *Ibid.,* p. 9086.
[41] *Ibid.,* p. 9271.
[42] *Ibid.,* p. 9591.
[43] *Ibid.,* p. 9597.

On June 5, 1914, the House of Representatives passed the Clayton Bill by a vote of 277 to 54, with three present but not voting and ninety-nine absent.[44]

Senate Judiciary Committee Changes—On July 22, 1914, the Senate Committee on the Judiciary reported the Clayton Bill with the recommendation that it be amended and that it be passed.[45] The committee recommended several amendments in the holding company section. The bill, as passed by the House, had specified that a stock acquisition would be prohibited where its effect is "to create a monopoly of any line of trade in any section or community." The committee substituted "commerce" for "trade," since commerce was defined in the bill and trade was not.[46] The words "in any section or community" were stricken out here as well as in the price discrimination section because the committee thought that

> . . . they are either surplusage, when applied to "commerce" as defined in the bill; or if they are used in a more restricted sense, in a sense which would apply them to local transactions merely, they would attempt to regulate intrastate commerce and be void.[47]

The only other major change recommended by the Senate Committee was the striking out of the last paragraph of the House version, which would have declared violations of the section misdemeanors and imposed criminal penalties. The committee added a new section providing for the administration by the Federal Trade Commission of the four sections of the Clayton Bill dealing with prohibitions of corporate practices.[48] No minority views were expressed in the report.

The Debates in the Senate—The Senate began its deliberations on the Clayton Bill on August 17, 1914.[49] Sitting as a committee of the whole, the bill was discussed section by section with amendments being offered. Some senators objected to the re-

[44] *Ibid.*, p. 9911.
[45] S. Rept. 698.
[46] *Ibid.*, p. 46.
[47] *Ibid.*, p. 43.
[48] *Ibid.*, p. 48.
[49] *Congressional Record*, 51:14 (Aug. 17, 1914).

moval of the criminal penalties on the ground that some of the subjects being dealt with were so closely related to the provisions of the Sherman Act that the same penalties should apply in order to avoid the effect of repealing the criminal penalties provided in that act.[50] Nevertheless, the Senate voted 29 to 22 to strike out the penalty provisions of the House bill.[51] The new section inserted by the Judiciary Committee, providing for administration by the Interstate Commerce Commission for common carriers and by the Federal Trade Commission for corporations within its jurisdiction, was amended [52] to make the procedure conform to that provided in the Federal Trade Commission Act for the administration of Section 5 of the latter act.[53]

The statement of the criterion of illegality, in each of the first two paragraphs of the stock acquisition section, was discussed at length on the floor of the Senate. The House version would have prohibited acquisitions "where the effect of such acquisition is to eliminate or substantially lessen competition between such corporations . . . or to create a monopoly of any line of trade in any section or community." The Senate accepted an amendment by Senator Walsh of Montana to strike out, in the first and second

[50] *Ibid.*, pp. 14314 and 14317.

[51] *Ibid.*, p. 14319.

[52] *Ibid.*, p. 14322. See the appendix for the text of Section 11 of the Clayton Act as enacted in 1914, which sets forth the procedures for administration of Sections 2, 3, 7, and 8 of the Clayton Act by the commissions.

[53] 38 *U.S. Stat. at L.* (1914), 717–724. Section 5 of the Federal Trade Commission Act provided that "unfair methods of competition in commerce are hereby declared unlawful." this provision empowered the commision to serve a complaint against any person using unfair methods of competition, if it thought a proceeding would be in the public interest. The act did not define "unfair methods of competition in commerce." The commission was empowered to issue a cease and desist order after a hearing, if in its judgment such a method had been used. Section 5 provided for appeal by the accused person to a Circuit Court of Appeals. Also the section provided for appeal by the commission to a Circuit Court for an order of enforcement if its own order were ignored. The Wheeler-Lea Act, 52 *U.S. Stat. at L.* (1938), amended Section 5 of the Federal Trade Commission Act to give force to the orders of the commission in cases arising under Section 5, but the amendment did not apply to cases arising under the Clayton Act. For additional comments on Section 5 of the Federal Trade Commission Act, see pp. 54–55, 93–97, 112–118.

paragraphs, the words "eliminate or" on the grounds that competition is lessened if it is eliminated.[54]

Walsh also moved to strike out altogether the phrase "or to create a monopoly of any line of trade in any section or community," which the committee had recommended should be changed to "or to create a monopoly of any line of commerce." The Senate did not accept this amendment.[55]

As a substitute for the first paragraph of the section, Senator Reed offered the following amendment:

> That no corporation engaged in commerce shall acquire, directly or indirectly, the whole or any part of the stock or other share capital of another corporation engaged also in commerce in the same line or lines of business.[56]

In support of this amendment, Senator Reed said:

> . . . It saves all the equivocation and all the trouble that will arise from the construction of the section as written.
>
> It is easy to ascertain whether a corporation is engaged in the same line or lines of business in which another corporation is engaged, but it is very difficult to tell whether the ownership of stock has substantially lessened competition, and yet there may be a very grave lessening of competition. You avoid the difficulty of proving that most difficult question of fact.[57]

Senator Culberson, the author of the Committee Report and the Democratic leader responsible for steering the bill through the Senate, was asked whether the committee would accept the amendment. He said that he was not authorized to answer in its name, since only a few of the members of the committee were present and they were divided on the question.[58]

---

[54] *Congressional Record,* 51:14, p. 14419. This seemingly innocuous attempt to perfect the language of the bill proved to have unanticipated results, since the Supreme Court later interpreted the words "to substantially lessen competition" to mean a lessening of substantial competition. See chap. 4.

Senator Walsh's amendment also resulted in the use of a split infinitive in the Clayton Act—an error which was not corrected until the passage of the 1950 Amendment to Section 7!

[55] *Ibid.,* p. 14462.

[56] *Ibid.,* p. 14419.

[57] *Ibid.*

[58] *Ibid.*

In the discussions of this amendment, some senators expressed a desire to go even further and absolutely prohibit intercorporate stockholding. Senator Thomas, for example, advocated the latter. He pointed out that the Federal Trade Commission would be so busy with unfair competition cases arising under Section 5 of the Federal Trade Commission Act that it would not have time to investigate and prove a substantial lessening of competition.[59] The fears of Senator Thomas and Senator Reed concerning the difficulty of administration were borne out in the succeeding twenty years. Senator Reed did not, however, foresee the difficulty to be encountered by limiting the prohibition to the acquisition of stock rather than including asset acquisitions. When an opponent of the bill asked whether the acquisition of the property of another corporation in the same line of business would not result in the same evil, Senator Reed replied that such an acquisition would be aboveboard and known to the world. Senator Thomas agreed. Thus the proponents of the strongest test of legality of a stock acquisition were not concerned with the prohibition of asset acquisitions.[60]

By a vote of 22 to 27, the Senate rejected Senator Reed's amendment.[61] A similar but stronger amendment by Senator Walsh to substitute for paragraph two a paragraph prohibiting the acquisition of any part of the stock of two or more corporations engaged in commerce was also rejected.[62]

The Senate defeated two other attempts to strengthen the test of illegality. An amendment by Senator Poindexter of Washington would have forbidden stockholding between corporations with no other standard than that they "compete." [63] An amendment by Senator Cummins would have stricken out all the section as reported and substituted in its stead a section using the phrase "corporations engaged in commerce and carrying on business of the same kind or competitive in character." His proposal would

[59] *Ibid.*, p. 14454.
[60] *Ibid.*, p. 14457.
[61] *Ibid.*, p. 14459.
[62] *Ibid.*, p. 14462.
[63] *Ibid.*, p. 14467.

have excepted acquisition for investment only and acquisitions involving banks and common carriers.[64]

At this point the Senate made one very significant change in the standard of illegality—a change incorporated in the final version of the bill as enacted. Instead of forbidding an acquisition where the effect "*is* to substantially lessen competition," the Senate substituted the words "*may be* to substantially lessen competition." The chairman of the Judiciary Committee offered no objection to this change. The grounds for making the change were that, under the Sherman Act as interpreted by the Supreme Court in the Northern Securities case, it was necessary to prove merely that the power to restrain trade had been created. Thus the Senate met the objections raised in the House that the criterion was weaker than that of the Sherman Act.[65]

Without debate the Senate accepted an amendment to strike out the word "substantially" in the phrase "to substantially lessen competition." [66]

On September 2, 1914, the bill as amended was passed by the Senate.[67] The Senate moved to insist on its amendments[68] and agreed to the conference requested by the House.[69]

The first two paragraphs of the stock acquisition section, as amended by the Senate, were as follows:

> That no corporation engaged in commerce shall acquire, directly or indirectly, the whole or any part of the stock or other share capital of another corporation engaged also in commerce, where the effect of such acquisition may be to lessen competition between the corporation whose stock is so acquired and the corporation making the acquisition, or to create a monopoly of any line of commerce.
>
> No corporation shall acquire, directly or indirectly, the whole or any part of the stock or other share capital of two or more corporations engaged in commerce where the effect of such acquisition, or the use of such stock by the voting or granting of proxies or otherwise, may be to lessen

[64] *Ibid.*, p. 14476.
[65] *Ibid.*, p. 14464.
[66] *Ibid.*
[67] *Ibid.*, p. 14610.
[68] *Ibid.*, p. 14737.
[69] *Ibid.*, p. 14718.

competition between such corporations, or any of them, whose stock or other share capital is so acquired, or to create a monopoly of any line of commerce.[70]

The Compromises Reached by the Conference Committee—The conference committee made several changes in the wording of the bill as it passed the Senate. It reinstated the word "substantially" in the phrase "may be to substantially lessen competition" and also in two other places in the section. The House conferees accepted the Senate amendment which struck out the words "in any section or community" in the phrase "or to create a monopoly of any line of trade in any section or community," but the phrase was made to read "or *tend* to create a monopoly." To satisfy the desire of the House conferees for some limitation on the geographical extent of the market in which the evil effect must take place, the committee inserted a new phrase prohibiting a stock acquisition where the "effect . . . may be to . . . restrain such commerce in any section or community."[71] The first two paragraphs of Section 7 as finally agreed upon were:

That no corporation engaged in commerce shall acquire, directly or indirectly, the whole or any part of the stock or other share capital of another corporation engaged also in commerce where the effect of such acquisition may be to substantially lessen competition between the corporation whose stock is so acquired and the corporation making the acquisition, or to restrain such commerce in any section or community, or tend to create a monopoly of any line of commerce.

No corporation shall acquire, directly or indirectly, the whole or any part of the stock or other share capital of two or more corporations engaged in commerce where the effect of such acquisition, or the use of such stock by the voting or granting of proxies or otherwise, may be to substantially lessen competition between such corporations, or any of them, whose stock or other share capital is so acquired, or to restrain such commerce in any section or community, or tend to create a monopoly of any line of commerce.[72]

After considerable discussion in both houses of Congress, the bill as agreed to by the conference committee was passed by the

[70] *Federal Antitrust Bill, Comparative Print,* U.S. 63d Cong., 2d sess., S. Doc. 584 (1914), p. 8.

[71] *Ibid.*

[72] *Ibid.*

Senate on October 5,[73] and by the House on October 8.[74] President Wilson signed the bill on October 15, 1914.[75]

The Purposes and Meaning of Section 7

On the basis of the preceding historical review, it is possible to infer the following reasons underlying the enactment of the original Section 7 of the Clayton Act in 1914.

The Economic Philosophy Underlying the Bill—The legislative history of this section of the Clayton Act clearly indicates that the discussions of the need for legislation to supplement the Sherman Act, during the election campaign of 1912 and during the legislative process, were an attempt to define more clearly the basic policy of the United States with respect to the organization and control of industry. The conceptual tools used by the political leaders were inadequate for the development of a clear, unambiguous statement of policy to be implemented by the newly created administrative agency. The framers of the Clayton Act were thinking primarily in terms of the quasi-legal, quasi-economic concept of "a monopoly." Everyone agreed that the law should prohibit the existence of "the trusts," which were definitely known to be considered undesirable by the people of the nation. The problem was to frame a statute, the interpretation and administration of which would succeed in preventing the evil more satisfactorily than had been done under the Sherman Act alone. More was needed than the prohibition of what the Supreme Court might consider to be an unreasonable restraint of trade or a monopoly. The long, detailed debates over the wording of the standard of illegality to be incorporated into Section 7 prove, however, a struggle to develop a concept of "workable competition."

The legislators, on the whole, were attempting to create a legal framework in which private enterprise could operate with market

---

[73] *Congressional Record,* 51:16, p. 16171.

[74] *Ibid.*, p. 16344.

[75] Public Law No. 212, 38 *U.S. Stat. at L.* (1914), 730–740.

conditions not necessarily perfectly competitive, but more competitive than the conditions that had come to be described as a monopoly in a particular market. They were searching for a middle ground along the lines suggested by John Bates Clark in the preceding decade and a half. The discussions in Congress clearly exemplify an attempt to do more than merely condemn a "monopoly" after it has reached that legal state. For example, in his synopsis of the entire bill, which opened the discussions on the floor of the House, Congressman Webb said:

We condemn the individual acts which lead to a restraint of interstate trade, whereas at present you must show a sufficient number of such acts of restraint to make such a restraint as the Supreme Court will declare illegal under the trust laws.[76]

In its report, the Senate Judiciary Committee indicated the purpose of the bill to be as follows:

Broadly stated, the bill in its treatment of unlawful restraints and monopolies, seeks to prohibit and make unlawful certain trade practices which, as a rule, singly and in themselves, are not covered by the act of July 2, 1890, or other existing antitrust acts, and thus, by making these practices illegal, to arrest the creation of trusts, conspiracies, and monopolies in their incipiency and before consummation.[77]

In explaining the purposes of the bill on the floor of the Senate, the chairman of the Judiciary Committee said:

It is proposed, without amending the Sherman Act . . . to supplement that act by denouncing and making unlawful certain trade practices which, while not covered by that act because not amounting to restraint of commerce or monopoly in themselves, yet constitute elements tending ultimately to violations of that act.[78]

This same basic idea was very clearly expressed also on the floor of the Senate by Senator Walsh, a member of the committee:

I do not understand that any one of these sections applied to trusts and monopolies. I understand that the bill was not intended to reach the practices of trusts and monopolies. The members of the Judiciary Committee,

[76] *Congressional Record,* 51:9, p. 9070.

[77] S. Rept. 698, p. 1.

[78] *Congressional Record,* 51:14, p. 13848.

at least, did not intend that it should. It was the common belief that the practices of actual trusts and monopolies are already amply taken care of by the law. It was intended to reach the practices that were not the practices of things which have developed into trusts and monopolies, but were practices of trade which, if persevered in and continued and developed, would eventually result in the creation of a monopoly or a trust.[79]

The ideas expressed in the foregoing excerpts from the debates all show a desire to implement the policy of the Sherman Act by prohibiting some trade practices because they lead to the development of monopoly, rather than because they lessen competition and increase monopoly power. Some members of Congress, however, were unwilling thus to strengthen the antitrust laws. For example, one of the minority reports of the House Judiciary Committee said:

The only possible excuse and justification for legislation against holding companies lies in the fact that the holding company intended to be reached by the law creates a monopoly, or attempts to do so, or restrains trade.[80]

The mere possibility of a situation of monopoly power contrary to the public interest and yet not sufficiently widespread to cover the whole country was not admitted by Senator Chilton, a member of the conference committee, who, in answer to why the conference committee struck out the words "in any section or community," said:

They were stricken out simply because a monopoly is a monopoly anywhere and everywhere. There is no such thing as monopoly in interstate commerce in a county, or monopoly in interstate commerce in a section or community. It is a monopoly in interstate commerce, that is what we have power to deal with, and to put in the words "in any section or community" would simply becloud the definition and make it, possibly, inconsistent with itself and with everything else. A monopoly in interstate commerce is a monopoly in interstate commerce; you cannot qualify it; you cannot limit it; you cannot extend it. If it is not a monopoly, it is not one; and if it is, it is; and it was the deliberate judgment of the Judiciary Committee of the Senate and of the Senate itself that the words "in any section or community" were either meaningless or else a restriction that might destroy

[79] *Ibid.*, part 16, p. 15820.
[80] H. Rept. 627, part 2, p. 6.

the law, and therefore should be stricken out; and your conferees carried out the judgment and the direction of the Senate in leaving them out.[81]

The discussions of the criterion of illegality to be used in Section 7 of the Clayton Act showed, however, a desire to define a situation intermediate between the two extremes of competition and monopoly—a desire to shift from the essentially negative policy of preventing the extreme of monopoly to a positive policy of maintaining reasonably competitive conditions in the markets of industrial products. For example, in one of the few places in the record in which the concept of price was mentioned, Webb pointed out that "in holding corporations the company controls the policy and price of commodities of constituent or subsidiary corporations." [82] Senator Cummins said:

The only protection we can secure is the willingness of one seller to dispose of his product at a fair price, knowing that he has a competitor who will if he does not. If we lose that protection, we shall be compelled to resort to the power of Government itself in fixing prices, and when we are compelled to employ the force of the Government in fixing the prices of all the commodities that we sell and use we will have entered the field of State socialism. For that reason those of us who do not want to resort to that power of the Government in protecting the people against the rapacity and the avarice of monopoly are so insistent upon preserving independence and competition.[83]

This shift in policy toward emphasis on maintaining competition rather than merely preventing a monopoly or an unreasonable restraint of trade is best indicated by the fact that Congress expressed the criterion of illegality in terms of the lessening of competition and the *tendency* toward monopoly.

The Criterion of Illegality—In the legislative history of the section, one finds no unanimity of opinion among the members of Congress either on what was desired from, or what would result from, the legislation. There was nothing that could clearly be called "the intent of Congress." As previously related, practically every phrase in the statement of the test to be applied in deter-

[81] *Congressional Record,* 51:16, pp. 16047–16048.
[82] *Ibid.,* part 9, p. 9073.
[83] *Ibid.,* part 14, p. 14256.

mining the legality of a stock acquisition was debated at length and frequently changed during the legislative process. It is possible, however, to ascertain from the record the intent of Congress within broad limits. Clearly, Congress did not wish to prohibit all stock acquisitions or all holding companies. The question then becomes which stock acquisitions were to be made illegal. Congress was laying down a general policy to be implemented by administrative commissions and the courts. The policy was stated in phrases and words that had no generally accepted meaning either in economics or law.

The use of the term "to substantially lessen competition" raises the question of the legal meaning of competition. It was generally assumed that this meant something different from restraint of trade. But the use of the phrase in conjunction with "between the corporation whose stock is so acquired and the corporation making the acquisition" indicates that the authors of the bill were thinking of competition in terms of rivalry *between* firms rather than in terms of control of the market.

The over-all discussions of the section indicate that its proponents may have wished to forbid the union by stock acquisition of any two corporations engaged in the sale of similar commodities in the same market regardless of the relative proportions of the market controlled by the two firms. If this interpretation is correct, then the use of "substantially lessen" rather than "eliminate" can be explained by the desire of Congress to deal with the problem of acquisition of *part* of the stock of a competitor. Such a partial acquisition might not result in complete control of the competitor, and the degree of control would not necessarily be related in the same way in each instance to the proportion of stock acquired. Therefore, the words "substantially lessen" were included with the word "eliminate." Then "eliminate" was removed as surplusage, since presumably the courts would hold that the elimination of competition between two corporations by acquisition of *all* the stock would constitute a substantial lessening of competition between the two corporations.

Nowhere in the record is there any definite indication that the members of Congress who were supporting the bill thought of the part of the criterion dealing with a lessening of competition between the corporations as a test of the degree to which competition in the market might be lessened by the acquisition. In the debates in the Senate on the adoption of the conference version of the bill, Senator Walsh said about the removal of "substantially":

> It went out [on the floor of the Senate] without argument, because there is not enough in the word to provoke argument. If it were out, the language would receive the same construction, because no court would find that competition was lessened unless it was "substantially" lessened. . . . How much reason there is to dread disastrous results from such a construction is exhibited by the decision in the Union Pacific–Southern Pacific case, in which the traffic affected by the combination amounted only to eighty-eight one-hundredths of one per cent of the total tonnage of the Southern Pacific. Yet the court held that the restraint of trade was substantial enough to bring the combination under the condemnation of the law.[84]

The effect of an acquisition on the control of the market was taken care of in the second part of the criterion as written by the House—"or to create a monopoly in any line of commerce in any section or community." This phrase included the words "in any section or community" in order to make the criterion stronger than that of the Sherman Act. When they were omitted by the Senate, the House conferees insisted on inserting the word "tend" and another phrase about restraint of trade in a section or community.[85] The substitution of "may be" for "is" was designed to strengthen the law and to avoid proving that the required effect had actually taken place, although no clear definition was given of "may be." The net result was a compromise wording of the standard of illegality, its exact meaning unknown to the members of Congress, about which many fears were expressed during the process of adoption of the bill.

This lack of a consensus in Congress on the question of the prevention of the evils that might be associated with the union of two previously independent firms is not difficult to understand

[84] *Ibid.*, part 16, p. 16149.

[85] As will be seen later in this study, the Court interpreted the lessening of competition phrase in the light of the others and reverted to the Sherman Act criterion —the requirement that injury to the public must be proved.

upon consideration of the inherent difficulties involved in the analysis of the effect of such an action on the public welfare, the state of development of the tools for such an analysis at that time, and the political conditions under which the bill was passed. In reference to the latter, writing soon after the passage of the bill, Allyn A. Young said:

> The Clayton Act was thus the outcome of about eight months of deliberation, but in less degree than is true of most important federal statutes, and in a markedly less degree than is true of the establishment of a trade commission, did it represent a real focus of the opinion of a majority of the members of Congress. Despite the large majority recorded in its favor the general attitude of Congress was that of unwillingly doing a set task. For many members of Congress the casting of a favorable vote was a matter of political exigency. Administrative pressure, party discipline, the political power of organized labor, and the undoubted fact that a majority of the voters at home would interpret a Congressman's vote against an "anti-trust" statute as a vote for monopoly were the dominant factors in the situation. And so many things were lumped together in the bill that it was impossible to segregate the good from the bad.[86]

What Young has said of the bill as a whole is probably even more applicable to Section 7, which was not given much discussion until the later stages of the legislative process. Congress framed this section, along with the price discrimination section and the tying and exclusive contract section, without the benefit of detailed recommendations of an administrative agency experienced in advising on the language needed. The criterion of illegality was formulated primarily on the floor of the Senate and in the conference committee during the rush of the last days before the adjournment of Congress just before the midterm elections.

In spite of the fact that one of the reasons for supplementing the antitrust laws was the feeling that the Supreme Court had preëmpted the power to determine policy by its enunciation of the rule of reason in the 1911 cases, the criterion adopted in the Clayton Act was so ambiguously formulated that the result was to give the court an almost free hand in interpreting the new law.

The Intent of Congress Regarding Asset Acquisitions—In view

[86] "The Sherman Act and the New Anti-trust Legislation, Part II," *Journal of Political Economy*, 23 (April, 1915), 326.

of the problems that arose in the administration of Section 7 and its later amendment, it is important to ascertain whether Congress inadvertently or deliberately failed to include asset acquisitions among the prohibitions of the Clayton Act. The consolidation of previously independent firms by means of the purchase of the physical properties of one firm by another was a common occurrence around the turn of the century. Why did Congress not prohibit asset acquisitions? Was Section 7 designed to prohibit stock acquisitions among competitors as a means of prohibiting mergers, or was it designed merely to prevent the evils of the holding company itself? [87]

In the election campaign, denunciation had been made of "the holding company." Throughout the legislative record of the bill, the section is referred to as the "holding company section." In the record frequent reference was made to the need for prohibiting holding companies. Most of the debate on Section 7 centered on the question of which holding companies should be prohibited and which permitted, rather than which forms of combination should be prohibited. "Holding company" had taken on overtones similar to those of "trust." For example, the analysis of the bill by the House Committee contained the statement, quoted previously, that a " 'holding company' is an abomination and in our judgment is a mere incorporated form of the oldfashioned trust." [88] In the debate on the floor of the Senate over the question of criminal penalties, Senator Reed said:

> . . . It was meant to strike the favorite device of the monopolist. At common law it was illegal for one corporation to hold the stock of another corporation. And why? Because it was contrary to good morals, because it was contrary to good government for a corporation that was organized under the law, and given specific powers and required to have certain officers to manage its affairs, the stockholders of which were also given certain privileges and responsibilities, to have its affairs governed not by individuals, but by some other corporation. Hence it was regarded as bad policy to permit one corporation to acquire the control of another.

[87] On the answer to this question hinges the answer to whether the enactment of the 1950 Amendment to Section 7 was merely the "plugging of a loophole" or a major substantive change in the nation's antitrust law policy.

[88] H. Rept. 627, p. 17.

But what happened? That rule was relaxed; and so we find in this country a corporation organizing a brood of corporations, every day whelping a new litter, and operating them secretly and using them to deceive the public. . . . [T]he device has been commonly employed by the monopolies of the country. You, my brethren, have denounced these monopolistic devices upon the stump until you were hoarse and until your audience rose and applauded you to the echo.[89]

The fact that the same purpose might be achieved, and had in the past been achieved, by outright consolidation of the property of two firms was recognized and discussed at several places in the debates. In his analysis of the bill on the floor of the House, Webb said:

After the holding company came the complete merger, where the stock of the constituent companies is actually bought in and cancelled, the only stock being that of the master company. This act does not prohibit all holding companies, but only those which substantially lessen competition.[90]

The Democratic leader in the House here implies that the holding company device was used before the device of acquiring property of a competitor was originated and that the acquisition of stock is a first step in the acquisition of property. Nothing was said about the effect of the bill in prohibiting this last step of asset acquisition. Progressive party leader Murdock, however, explicitly stated the possibility of changing the form of combination:

The Clayton bill also attacks the form of monopoly, not its substance, in its attempt to eliminate "holding companies." When in time the courts reach with banning decrees this provision the offenders will change the form of monopoly and escape with the substance of monopoly as before.[91]

The question of the possibility and the desirability of combination by acquisition of property rather than stock was recognized and discussed in the debates in the Senate. While arguing against the wording of the section which prohibited one small corporation from acquiring the stock of another, Senator Chilton said:

---

[89] *Congressional Record,* 51:14, p. 14226.
[90] *Ibid.,* 51:9, pp. 9073–9074.
[91] *Ibid.,* p. 8974.

Now, take a small company. It will go to one section. It will find there a certain condition as to another small company. It may want to take that over as a line of opposition to the great octopus. Now, it may be so that it cannot buy the physical property. It may be that it will have to buy part of the stock.[92]

Senator Cummins replied:

Of course, if we are not going to try to do anything with the big corporations that are holding stocks that they ought not to hold . . . then there is a good deal of force in the suggestion of the Senator from West Virginia; but I want to destroy that, and so far as all corporations are concerned, other than common carriers, there is no reason in the law why the corporation shall not own all the property with which it carries on its business. There is no reason which has ever come to my notice which requires that a single business shall be divided into a series of corporations. . . . It is a sound, wise policy for any country to adopt and maintain. That is the policy, I think, intended to be announced in the section.[93]

The difference between a consolidation by means of outright purchase of property and by means of purchase of stock was discussed. The chief evil incident to the latter was felt to be the possible secrecy of control. Regarding two relatively small firms in a combination not constituting a violation of the Sherman Act, Senator Cummins said:

It would lessen competition as between the two, but of course, if one had a right under the law to buy the other it could not be any offence against the law, as it is now, for one to acquire the control of the other. It is just that case that we want, as I think, to prohibit, so that if a consolidation can lawfully occur under the antitrust law it shall be an open, public consolidation, so that everybody can know what is transpiring. . . . whenever the law permits the sale of the business then it ought to be open and public, and a corporation ought not to acquire control of a business simply through the purchase of the stock of a company which continues under its own name and, so far as the public knows, is independent in its management. That is what I think this section is inteded [*sic*] in the main to prevent.[94]

These discussions indicate a deliberate intent, at least on the part of some of the strongest proponents of the bill, to provide a more stringent criterion of illegality for acquisitions of stock than

[92] *Ibid.*, 51:14, p. 14255.
[93] *Ibid.*
[94] *Ibid.*, p. 14314.

already provided for acquisitions of assets by the restraint of trade provisions of the Sherman Act. That this would result in different criteria for the two types of combinations was explicitly pointed out by Senator Colt, who was against the bill and satisfied with the Sherman Act as interpreted.

> This proposed amendment forbids corporation A from acquiring stock in corporation B. Now, I should like to ask the Senator from Missouri if the same effect, so far as the elimination of competition is concerned, would not be accomplished if corporation B was wound up and corporation A bought the property and paid for it in stock of the company? I cannot quite understand the reason upon which this provision is founded if its purpose is to prevent the suppression of competition. . . .
>
> I agree entirely with the Senator that monopoly should be prohibited; but again I ask if such a transaction [the acquisition of the stock of an unsuccessful firm by a well-managed corporation] . . . is wrong—and I cannot see why it is—is there any difference between that transaction and consolidating the two corporations by the actual purchase of the property of one of them? If the wrong consists in the elimination of competition, then we are forced to this conclusion: The elimination of competition is permitted until we reach the corporate unit, but here it must stop.
>
> In other words, you allow individuals to crush each other by competition. You allow the combination of individuals in the form of a partnership which results in the elimination of competition. You allow the combination of partnerships in the form of a corporation, the effect of which is to stifle competition, and then you say at this point: We will stop the elimination of competition, but in effect you do not do this, because you still permit the corporate unit to crush competition by consolidation; that is to say, you forbid the union of A and B corporations by the purchase of stock by A, but you do not forbid the consolidation of the property of these corporations in the hands of A.[95]

Better than anyone else, Senator Colt pointed out the dichotomy between the standards being applied to the two types of acquisitions. As an opponent of the bill, however, he did not advocate that asset acquisitions be included among the prohibitions of the Clayton Act; instead, he argued that the prohibition against stock acquisitions was undesirable. No attempt was made at any point in the legislative process to apply the criterion of a "substantial lessening of competition" to asset acquisitions or mergers. The

[95] *Ibid.*, pp. 14456–14457.

intent of the proponents of the bill was made quite plain by Senator Reed's reply to Senator Colt:

> It is no answer, either, to say that the corporation might sell all of its assets to another corporation, or that a corporation might go out of business and its properties might be acquired by another corporation. When that is done, it means an increase of capital stock. It means that there is given to the world knowledge of the fact that the property and the business are thus controlled; whereas, under the method of stock ownership, there has been exercised in this country for years a secret control, and frequently monopoly is almost completely worked out through it.[96]

Senator Thomas then cited the case of the New York, New Haven & Hartford Railroad Company: 326 subsidiary corporations "were utilized for the purpose of wrecking that great concern." [97]

It thus appears that the failure of Congress to include asset acquisitions among the prohibitions of the Clayton Act was deliberate. It can be attributed neither to the device of asset acquisition being as yet nonexistent, nor to an unawareness of the device by the members of Congress. The omission of asset acquisitions from the prohibitions of the original Section 7 was based on, instead, the deliberate intention to prohibit "monopolistic holding companies" and the evils incident thereto.

The Provisions for Administration of the Section—The Clayton Bill originated in the House of Representatives as part of the Wilson administration's program to supplement the antitrust laws. The bill to establish a trade commission was another part of this same program. There was, however, little coördination between the two bills because of their assignment to different committees in both Houses of Congress. The framers of the trade commission legislation were not concerned with the substantive changes to be made in the antitrust laws. The trade commission bill that passed the House of Representatives would have created a merely investigative agency.[98]

The Senate Committee on Interstate Commerce reported its own bill as a substitute for the trade commission bill passed by

---

[96] *Ibid.*, p. 14457.
[97] *Ibid.*
[98] H. Rept. 533.

the House. The Senate bill was designed to create a trade commission with administrative powers and it included a section declaring unlawful "unfair competition." The committee report on that bill read:

> It is believed that the term "unfair competition" has a legal significance which can be enforced by the commission and the courts, and that it is no more difficult to determine what is unfair competition than it is to determine what is a reasonable rate or what is an unjust discrimination. The committee was of the opinion that it would be better to put in a general provision condemning unfair competition than to attempt to define the numerous unfair practices, such as local price cutting, interlocking directorates, and holding companies intended to restrain substantial competition.[99]

This report was submitted after the Clayton Bill had already passed the House with the provision for enforcement by the same methods as provided for the Sherman Act. The Clayton Bill did not go to the same Senate committee for consideration. If it had done so, it is quite possible that the Interstate Commerce Committee would have recommended the removal of Section 7 from the bill. The Senate Judiciary Committee did take cognizance of the fact that the Federal Trade Commission Bill was proceeding through the Senate with the possibility of being enacted with provisions for the creation of an agency suited to the administration of the substantive antitrust sections of the Clayton Bill. They recommended that the criminal penalties be stricken out and administration of those sections given to the trade commission about to be established.[100]

The final version of the Clayton Bill as agreed to by the conference committee provided several means by which appropriate agencies might implement the policy laid down by Congress. Section 4 provides that any person who shall be injured by any-

---

[99] *Federal Trade Commission, Report to Accompany H.R. 15613,* by Mr. Newlands, U.S. Committee on Interstate Commerce, 63d Cong., 2d sess., S. Rept. 597.

[100] S. Rept. 698, p. 47. On the floor of the Senate, however, Senator Culberson, as the spokesman of the committee, moved to strike out the price discrimination and tying contract sections on the grounds that they were covered under Section 5 of the Federal Trade Commission Bill. See *Congressional Record,* 51:14, p. 14227.

thing forbidden in any of the antitrust laws can sue for treble damages. Section 16 provides that any person can sue for injunctive relief against threatened loss resulting from a violation of the antitrust laws, including Sections 2, 3, 7, and 8 of the Clayton Act. Section 15 gives jurisdiction of violations of the Clayton Act to the United States district courts and says that it is the duty of the various United States district attorneys, under the direction of the Attorney General, to institute suits in equity to prevent and restrain violations. Section 11 of the Clayton Act gave the Federal Trade Commission, the Federal Reserve Board, and the Interstate Commerce Commission the authority to enforce Sections 2, 3, 7, and 8.[101]

Administration of Section 7 from 1914 until its amendment in 1950 was primarily in the hands of the Federal Trade Commission. The degree to which the new provision of law was successful in supplementing the Sherman Act will now be considered.

[101] 38 *U.S. Stat. at L.* (1914), 730–740. As they were created, several other administrative agencies were given the responsibility of administering these Clayton Act provisions for corporations under their jurisdiction.

3. Federal Trade Commission Administration of Section 7 Prior to Judicial Interpretation

In addition to administration by the Justice Department, the Clayton Act provided in Section 11 for administration of Sections 2, 3, 7, and 8 by the Federal Trade Commission for violations by any corporations engaged in interstate commerce, other than those corporations subject to the jurisdiction of the Interstate Commerce Commission or the Federal Reserve Board. It set forth the general procedures to be followed and the powers available to the Federal Trade Commission for enforcing these sections of the Clayton Act.[1]

Section 11 provided that the commission should serve notice on a party complained of, if it believed that a violation of the section had occurred. After a hearing, the commission was empowered to order divestiture of illegally held stock if it found a violation of the law. The respondent was given the right to appeal the order to a Circuit Court of Appeals. If the respondent failed to comply with the order of the commission, then the commission could appeal to a circuit court. In either instance, the court was given the authority to review the order of the commission. Section 11 provided that the court had to uphold the findings of fact

[1] For the text of Section 11 of the Clayton Act, see appendix.

of the commission, if supported by evidence. If the court upheld the commission, it could issue its own order forcing the respondent to comply under the threat of contempt proceedings. An order of the commission would have no force until so enforced by a court.[2] Appeal could be made to the Supreme Court by either the respondent or the commission.

Under the procedures followed by the Federal Trade Commission in the first few years, a Section 7 case would originate with an "application for complaint," which might result from information supplied by an interested party or from investigations by the staff of the commission. Either way there would be a preliminary inquiry before the commission would docket the matter as an application for complaint. After a case reached the stage of an application for complaint, there would be a hearing before a board of review consisting of two lawyers and one economist on the staff of the commission.[3] If this hearing indicated that the law might have been violated, the commission would issue a formal complaint, setting forth the allegations and serving notice on the respondent that the commission would hold a formal hearing. At this point in the procedure, the commission would make its findings of fact and, if it found that an illegal stock acquisition had taken place, issue an order of divestiture of the stock.[4]

Federal Trade Commission Cases Resulting in Orders

During the first fifteen and a half months of its existence—from its organization on March 16, 1915, until the end of the 1916 fiscal

[2] The Wheeler-Lea Amendment to the Federal Trade Commission Act (1938) gave force to an F.T.C. order issued under Section 5 of the F.T.C. Act without the necessity of an appeal by the commission to the circuit court, but this amendment did not apply to orders issued under Section 11 of the Clayton Act. See 52 *U.S. Stat. at L.* (1938).

[3] *F.T.C. Annual Report, 1922,* p. 4.

[4] These rules were later changed so that the formal complaint would be issued immediately after the preliminary inquiry and prior to a hearing by a board of review. *F.T.C. Annual Report, 1928,* p. 19.

year—the commission considered two hundred forty-six applications for the issuance of complaints, but only four were concerned with violations of Section 7 of the Clayton Act.[5] The first formal complaint alleging violation was not issued until early in 1918.[6] From then until the end of the 1926 fiscal year, the commission issued thirty-eight complaints under Section 7.[7] By the end of that period—just before the first Supreme Court decisions interpreting the act—the commission had dismissed twenty-three complaints. Nine complaints were still pending at the end of the 1926 fiscal year, but eight were later dismissed. The other one resulted in an order at a later date. By the end of the 1926 fiscal year, the commission had issued orders of divestiture in only six of the thirty-eight cases.[8]

The Aluminum Company Case—The first order under Section 7 was issued in 1921—six and a half years after the passage of the act—against the Aluminum Company of America.[9] In the complaint, issued on February 6, 1919, the commission alleged that the Aluminum Company had acquired a large part of the stock of the Aluminum Rolling Mill Company and that the effect of the acquisition

> . . . may be, and is to substantially lessen competition between the respondent . . . and the Aluminum Rolling Mill Co., or to restrain such commerce, as aforesaid, in certain sections and communities, or tend to create a monopoly in such line of commerce.[10]

In its findings of facts, the commission stated that from 1915 until the acquisition in 1918 the Cleveland Metal Products Company had owned and operated an aluminum rolling mill, of whose

[5] *F.T.C. Annual Report, 1916*, p. 5. No information is available concerning the facts or opinions of the commission in cases of applications for complaints during these early years, since each matter was considered confidential until a formal complaint was issued by the commission. Such information on applications considered during a later period was released, however, to the Temporary National Economic Committee and is analyzed in a later section of this chapter.

[6] *F.T.C. Annual Report, 1918*, p. 63.

[7] *F.T.C. Annual Reports, 1918–1926.*

[8] *Ibid.*

[9] *Federal Trade Commission* v. *The Aluminum Company of America*, 3 F.T.C. 302 (F.T.C. Docket No. 238, March 9, 1921).

[10] 3 F.T.C. 302, 303.

output 27 per cent was fabricated by the Cleveland company and 73 per cent was sold on the open market. Other than Alcoa, no other company in the United States sold sheet aluminum wider than thirty inches. The commission found also that the Cleveland company was in competition with Alcoa in the sale of aluminum cooking utensils.[11] Alcoa and the Cleveland company had jointly organized a third corporation, the Aluminum Rolling Mill Company, which had acquired the rolling mill from the Cleveland company. Alcoa had received two-thirds and the Cleveland company one-third of the stock of the new company. As a result of Alcoa's acquisition of the controlling stock interest, the Cleveland company ceased the purchase of aluminum ingot, and the American market for foreign ingot almost completely disappeared. The Cleveland company continued to fabricate sheet aluminum, but ceased manufacturing and selling sheet aluminum as a result of the acquisition, according to the findings of the commission. The commission concluded that the setting up of the third corporation to acquire the rolling mill

> . . . was a device for the accomplishment of the purpose of the respondent to obtain control of the said rolling mill and business in its products instead of the direct acquisition of stock in the Cleveland Metal Products Co., and was in effect equivalent thereto; the result of the use of this device, as completely as though the respondent had obtained a controlling stock interest in the Cleveland Metal Products Co., was to eliminate the actual existing competition between the respondent and the . . . [Cleveland company] in the manufacture and sale . . . of sheet aluminum and aluminum cooking utensils, to prevent the Aluminum Rolling Mill Co. from becoming a competitor [in sheet] . . . and tended to and did create in the respondent a monopoly in the manufacture and sale in interstate commerce of sheet aluminum.
>
> The acquisition . . . tended to and did bring about a complete monopoly in the respondent of the production and sale of sheet aluminum of certain much-used and important sizes manufactured in the United States and tended to bring about complete monopoly in the respondent of the sale, in interstate commerce, of all sizes of sheet aluminum manufactured in the United States.[12]

[11] 3 F.T.C. 302, 307.

[12] 3 F.T.C. 302, 310–311.

The commission, concluding that the acquisition violated Section 7 of the Clayton Act, ordered Alcoa to sell the stock to someone completely unconnected with Alcoa or its subsidiaries.[13]

The order of the commission was upheld by the United States Circuit Court of Appeals for the Third Circuit in 1922.[14] The Supreme Court denied a writ of *certiorari*.[15] After the Federal Trade Commission order was sustained, Alcoa disposed of its part of the stock to the Cleveland company. The Rolling Mill Company, however, became insolvent and ceased operations. It owed Alcoa $600,000 for purchases of aluminum ingot, and Alcoa proposed to sue and buy the assets of the Rolling Mill Company at the sheriff's sale. The Federal Trade Commission thereupon petitioned the Circuit Court to modify its decree so as to enjoin Alcoa from acquiring any of the assets of the Rolling Mill Company on the grounds that the debt was fraudulent and that the sale would defeat the intent of Section 7. The Circuit Court held that the debt was not shown to be fraudulent and that in the absence of fraud the decree could not be modified, because the lessening of competition was no longer involved since at that time neither the Rolling Mill Company nor the Cleveland company were engaged in the aluminum business.[16]

Thus, the first Section 7 case resulted in the prevention of the continuation of intercorporate stock ownership between the two firms, but it allowed, instead, the acquisition of the assets of one of the companies by the other. Insofar as the statute was intended to prevent, in their incipiency, merely the holding company and the evils incident thereto, this case was one of successful administration of the law. If it is assumed that the market conditions placed this acquisition in a category that might result in a substantial lessening of competition or a tendency toward monopoly

[13] 3 F.T.C. 302, 312.

[14] *Aluminum Company of America* v. *Federal Trade Commission* (1922), 284 Fed. Rept. 401 (C.C.A., 3d Cir.). The economic reasoning implicit in the opinion of the court as well as of the commission is discussed later in this chapter.

[15] 261 U.S. 616 (1923).

[16] *Federal Trade Commission* v. *Aluminum Co. of America* (1924), 299 Fed. Rept. 361 (C.C.A., 3d Cir.).

in any line of commerce, then the law proved ineffective in preventing the adverse effect on competition.

Whether the acquisition in this instance might have the effect of substantially lessening competition was of secondary importance in the litigation, as the form of the acquisition was the chief point at issue. The commission's order was based on the assumption that competition was lessened substantially between the two companies, since both companies had sold the same product—sheet aluminum wider than thirty inches—in a common market, and the acquisition of two-thirds of the stock of the Rolling Mill Company gave Alcoa control of a formerly competing business. The commission considered that the effect of the acquisition was shown to be not only a tendency toward monopoly, but monopoly in fact, when it had determined that the number of firms selling the product decreased from two to one. The commission did not entertain the question of the degree of control over the price of the product by the remaining one firm. Nothing in the record indicated that the commission inquired into whether the product, sheet aluminum, should be considered a "line of commerce."

The Meat-Packing Cases—In the fiscal year following the issuance of the complaint against Alcoa, the commission issued three complaints that later resulted in orders of divestiture against meat-packing firms. The commission charged Armour and Company with using

> . . . unfair methods of competition by acquiring the capital stock of E. H. Stanton Co. engaged in a similar business to that of respondent, and prior to such acquisition directly in competition with respondent, with the effect of substantially lessening competition between these two companies, restraining commerce in certain sections of the United States, and tending to create a monopoly in the purchase of live stock and sale of meat and meat products, in alleged violation of section 7 of the Clayton Act.[17]

In its complaint against Swift and Company, the commission charged that the

[17] *F.T.C. Annual Report, 1920,* pp. 124–125. The commission used the words "unfair methods of competition," but did not charge a violation of Section 5 of the F.T.C. Act in this complaint.

. . . respondent purchased 956 shares of the total 966 shares of the capital stock of the Moultrie Packing Co., a competitor, causing the same to be transferred on the books of the company to officers and employees of the respondent, who at a stockholders meeting of said company [were] elected as directors . . . for the transfer of property of the said company to respondent; that it purchased all the capital stock of the Andalusia Packing Co., a competitor, and acquired the business of the company by a procedure similar to that employed in acquiring the Moultrie Packing Co. . . . and that the result of such acquisitions is the elimination of competition theretofore existing between the above-mentioned companies and the respondent and the creation of conditions which tend to create a monopoly, in alleged violation of section 5 of the Federal Trade Commission Act and section 7 of the Clayton Act.[18]

The third complaint charged that the Western Meat Company

. . . acquired all of the capital stock of the Nevada Packing Co., which acquisition resulted in the elimination of competition theretofore existing between respondent and said Nevada Packing Co., and the creation of a monopoly in meat and its by-products in communities adjacent to Reno, Nev., in violation of section 5 of the Federal Trade Commission Act and Section 7 of the Clayton Act.[19]

In its findings of fact in the Armour case, the commission stated that Armour and Company had been engaged in many parts of the nation, both in the business of purchasing and slaughtering of livestock and the business of selling meat and meat products. Prior to the acquisition, Armour had no packing plants in the Pacific Northwest, but it had sold meat and meat products in the states of Washington, Idaho, Montana, and Oregon. The operations of the E. H. Stanton Company had been more restricted geographically. It had owned and operated a packing plant in Spokane, Washington, and engaged in the sale of meat and meat products in the states of Washington, Montana, Idaho, and Oregon.[20]

After giving statistics indicating that Armour and Company had had sales of about two million dollars per year in the four-

[18] *Ibid.*, p. 133.

[19] *Ibid.*, p. 134.

[20] *Federal Trade Commission* v. *Armour & Company*, 4 F.T.C. 457, 459–460 (F.T.C. Docket No. 351, May 15, 1922).

state area for the three years prior to the acquisition, the commission stated that

. . . at the date of acquisition of the capital stock of the E. H. Stanton Co. by Armour & Co., competition existed between said E. H. Stanton Co. and Armour & Co., particularly in the City of Spokane, and other cities, in what is known as the "Inland Empire" including the cities Coeur d'Alene, Idaho, Lewiston, Idaho, Spirit Lake, Idaho, St. Maries's, Idaho, and Butte, Montana; that salesmen of both Armour & Co. and E. H. Stanton Co. solicited orders for meat and meat products from the same trade in that territory in those states in competition with each other, and that during the year 1916, and until May, 1917, the E. H. Stanton Co. sold about 75 per cent of the meat and meat products sold in the City of Spokane, Washington, and the territory around that city within a radius of 50 miles therefrom, which includes a portion of Northern Idaho commonly known as the "Coeur d'Alene country." [21]

The commission thus satisfied itself that competition had existed *between* the acquiring and the acquired corporations. They had each been selling several products in the general class known as "meat and meat products" to common customers in a common geographical area—an area large enough to include parts of more than one state. The finding of the commission gave no consideration to the question of the degree to which other firms shared this market.

On May 24, 1917, Armour and Company had acquired most of the stock of E. H. Stanton Company from E. H. Stanton with an agreement that he would not engage in the packing business in the Pacific Northwest for a period of ten years. In October of that year, the title to the packing plant was transferred to Armour and Company, but the Stanton corporation was not dissolved.[22] The commission issued the complaint *after* the transfer of the property.[23]

The commission concluded that the effect of the acquisition of the stock

(1) was and is to totally suppress and destroy the existing and prospective competition in the meat-packing industry and trade between the E. H.

[21] 4 F.T.C. 457, 461.

[22] 4 F.T.C. 457, 460–462.

[23] *F.T.C. Annual Report, 1920,* pp. 124–125.

> Stanton Company . . . and respondent, Armour & Company . . . and (2) was and is to restrain commerce in that section of the United States known as the Pacific Nothwest . . . in the purchase and sale of meat and meat products, commonly known as the meat packing industry and trade, and (3) was and is to tend to create a monopoly in respondent, Armour & Company, in the meat-packing industry and trade *in that section of the United States commonly known as the Pacific Northwest* [italics mine], including the States of Washington, Oregon, Idaho and Montana, and such acquisition, with each of said effects, constituted and is a violation of the provisions of Section 7 of the Act of Congress approved October 15, 1914. . . .[24]

The commission also concluded that the part of the stock purchase contract stipulating that Stanton would not engage in the meat-packing business in the area for ten years was unlawful. The commission said that the contract, in connection with the purchase of the stock, had the same effect as the acquisition and was therefore in violation of Section 7.[25]

With respect to the transfer of the property the commission concluded that it

> . . . was a mere paper transfer of the property covered, done in furtherance of the unlawful purposes, for which the respondent acquired the said capital stock and in connection with the acquisition of said capital stock, the effect thereof (1) was and is totally to suppress the prior and prospective competition between E. H. Stanton Company and respondent, and (2) was and is to tend to create a monopoly therein, in that section of the United States known as the Pacific Northwest . . . and as a result flowing from the acquisition by the respondent of the capital stock of the E. H. Stanton Company, the said transfer constitutes and is a violation of Section 7.[26]

The commission ordered Armour and Company to cease and desist from violating Section 7, and specifically to divest itself of the stock of the Stanton Company and to include the packing plant in the divestment.[27]

These commission actions and the reasoning behind them disclose the interpretation of Section 7 in this period. It is important to note the commission interpretation of the criterion of illegality

[24] 4 F.T.C. 457, 463.
[25] 4 F.T.C. 457, 463.
[26] 4 F.T.C. 457, 464.
[27] 4 F.T.C. 457, 464.

of the statute. The act prohibited an acquisition of stock having, or possibly having, any of three effects—to substantially lessen competition *between* the two corporations, to restrain commerce *in any section or community*, or to tend to create a monopoly in any line of commerce.

The commission faced the problem of giving specific content to the general language of the statute. In its findings as to the facts, the commission interpreted the first of the three parts to mean that an acquisition is prohibited if there exists prior to the acquisition "substantial competition," and if the acquisition transfers control of the business to the acquiring company. In this case the prior existence of "substantial competition" was established without giving any consideration at all to the degree of competition existing in the markets for the products in question. It sufficed to show that both firms sold common products to the same customers in a specified geographical area. That is, the commission concerned itself exclusively with the relationships *between* the two parties.

The commission did not confine itself, however, to the first of the three parts of the criterion. It also concluded that the acquisition had resulted in a restraint of commerce in a section or community. The section of the country was well defined, but the commission gave no indication of why it considered that commerce had been restrained in the Pacific Northwest market for meat and meat products. Apparently it considered that commerce had been shown to have been restrained merely because, in its view, competition had been substantially lessened between these two firms.

The commission, also without apparent reason, included the effect of a tendency toward monopoly *in a section* of the country among the other illegal effects allegedly resulting from the acquisition. The phrase "in any section or community" had been explicitly stricken out of that part of Section 7 in the Senate. Apparently, the commission felt that it was not necessary to show, as it had attempted to do in the Aluminum Company case, that the acquisition had the effect of tending to create a monopoly in a national market. Since no consideration was given to the structure of the market for meat and meat products even in the area in question, it appears that the commission reasoned that the lessening of competition *between* two firms operating in a particular geographical location was tantamount to a tendency to create a monopoly in that section of the country.

In terms of the development of Federal Trade Commission and judicial policy on the administration of Section 7, the most important feature of this case was the inclusion in the order of the requirement that the respondent had to dispose of the physical property as well as the stock of the Stanton Company which it had acquired. The commission was attempting to carry out the function of an administrative agency to implement and give specific content to a general statement of policy laid down by Congress in the statute. The commission reasoned that if the acquiring and holding of the controlling stock interest in a formerly competing corporation is against the public interest because of the effect of lessening competition, then the effect denounced in the law could not be remedied merely by the divestment of the stock of a corporation that had become an empty shell. At the time this order was issued, the commission had not yet met defeat in a similar attempt to prevent the Aluminum Company of America from acquiring the assets of a corporation after having been forced to divest itself of stock control. This and several other subsequent cases involving asset acquisitions differed from the Alcoa case in that the latter hinged on the issue of fraud.

Three months after the order was issued in the Armour case, the commission issued a similar order against Swift and Company.[28] In its findings of fact, the commission indicated that the acquisitions by Swift were similar to those in the Armour case. A relatively large meat-packing company, operating throughout the nation, acquired packing plants in a particular section of the country where it had previously marketed its products, but had not operated a packing plant.

Most of the report of this case concerns the details of the manner of acquisition used, with little attention being given to the market conditions existing before and after the acquisitions. The

[28] *Federal Trade Commission* v. *Swift & Company*, 5 F.T.C. 143 (F.T.C. Docket No. 453, Aug. 3, 1922).

commission found that, before the acquisitions, the Moultrie Packing Company, the Andalusia Packing Company, and Swift and Company had all sold a similar line of meat products in several cities in Georgia, Alabama, and Florida. The acquisition of control of the businesses of the two former companies by the latter had resulted, therefore, in the "total suppression of competition" between the two companies acquired and between each of them and Swift.[29]

The commission quoted that part of Section 7 which sets forth the standard of illegality, and found that the actions set forth in its findings constituted a violation of Section 7 as well as of Section 5 of the Federal Trade Commission Act, but no specific statement was made about restraint of commerce or a tendency toward monopoly. The commission merely held that "total suppression of competition" between the firms constituted a violation of the two sections.

As in the Armour case, the assets had been transferred before the instigation of the case by the Federal Trade Commission. The commission ordered Swift and Company to "cease and desist from further violating Section 7 of the Clayton Act," and to "cease and desist from further engagements in unfair methods of competition." It specifically ordered that Swift divest itself of the stock acquired and retain none of the "fruits of such acquisitions." Swift was ordered to cease controlling or operating the former business or property of the two acquired companies.[30]

The Western Meat Company case differed in several respects from the Armour and Swift cases.[31] The commission found that the management of Swift and Company controlled the Western Meat Company's policies. Swift's officers and stockholders owned 45 per cent of the stock of the Western Meat Company, and the officers of Armour and Company, Morris and Company, and Cudahy Packing Company jointly owned another 30 per cent. The commission found that Louis F. Swift, president of Swift,

---

[29] 5 F.T.C. 143, 149–169.

[30] 5 F.T.C. 143, 170–171.

[31] *Federal Trade Commission* v. *Western Meat Company,* 5 F.T.C. 417 (F.T.C. Docket No. 456, Feb. 2, 1923).

was instrumental in causing Western to acquire all the capital stock of the Nevada Packing Company.[32]

At the time of the acquisition of the stock in December, 1916, both the Western Meat Company and the Nevada Packing Company were engaged in the sale of meat and meat products in the California-Nevada area. Both companies were also engaged in the purchase and slaughter of livestock. The commission found that the two companies were in competition with each other in both lines of commerce. In this case the commission gave even less information on the structure of the markets in question. The findings of the commission were merely that

> . . . buyers of live stock for the Nevada Packing Company and the Western Meat Company endeavored to purchase live stock from the same producers in the States of Nevada and California and other States; and salesmen of both the Nevada Packing Company and the Western Meat Company solicited orders for meat and meat products from the same trade in the States of Nevada and California and other States in competition with each other.[33]

It was established to the satisfaction of the commission that the acquisition substantially lessened this previously existing competition between the companies and also restrained commerce in the California-Nevada section of the country.

> Par. 6. From December 30, 1916, to the date of the taking of testimony in this case in June, 1920, respondent Western Meat Company has operated the packing plant of the Nevada Packing Company, and, connected with the business of such operation, has continuously purchased and shipped to said plant from various points in the States of Nevada and California and adjacent States live cattle, calves, hogs, sheep, and lambs, and after slaughtering same, sold and shipped the meat and meat products resulting therefrom to various purchasers in the States of Nevada and California and elsewhere, and still continues so to do, and as a part of its said business respondent serves substantially all of the trade that was served by Nevada Packing Company while it was in business in competition with respondent as hereinbefore set out.
>
> Par. 7. The effect of the acquisition . . . was and is the entire elimination and suppression of the competition which had theretofore existed . . . and was and is to restrain commerce in the purchase and sale of meat and

[32] 5 F.T.C. 417, 420.
[33] 5 F.T.C. 417, 421.

meat products commonly known as the meat packing industry in the States of Nevada and California.[34]

The commission implies, as it did in the Armour case, that to substantially lessen competition between two corporations is equivalent to a restraint of commerce in an area, and that these effects can be ascertained to have resulted without examining the market structure of the products involved. In this case, as in the Swift case, the commission decided as well that the same facts were grounds for the conclusion that the acquiring company had engaged in an unfair method of competition within the meaning of Section 5 of the Federal Trade Commission Act.[35]

The commission anticipated the possibility that the assets might be transferred before the divestment of the stock.[36] It ordered the Western Meat Company to cease and desist from violating the two statutes

> . . . and particularly to so divest itself absolutely of all capital stock of the Nevada Packing Company as to include in such divestment the Nevada Packing Company's plant and all property necessary to the conduct and operation thereof as a complete, going packing plant and organization, and so as to neither directly or indirectly retain any of the fruits of the acquisition of the capital stock of said Nevada Packing Company, a corporation.[37]

The Thatcher Manufacturing Company Case—In the fiscal year following the issuance of the complaints in the meat-packer cases, a complaint issued in a similar case also resulted in an order by the commission. In 1921 the commission charged the Thatcher Manufacturing Company with violations of Section 7.[38] A cease and desist order was issued June 26, 1923.[39]

The commission found that from 1905 until the time of this case the Thatcher Manufacturing Company had held the exclusive rights to use the patented machines of the Owens Bottle Com-

[34] 5 F.T.C. 417, 421–422.

[35] 5 F.T.C. 417, 422.

[36] The property, in fact, was transferred later. See pp. 105–107.

[37] 5 F.T.C. 417, 423.

[38] *F.T.C. Annual Report, 1921,* p. 140.

[39] *Federal Trade Commission* v. *Thatcher Manufacturing Company,* 6 F.T.C. 213 (F.T.C. Docket No. 738, June 26, 1923).

pany to manufacture milk bottles in the United States. Until about 1916 or 1917 the Thatcher company was the only manufacturer of milk bottles produced with a completely automatic process. In 1916 or 1917 the Hartford-Fairmont Company patented a rival automatic process, the use of which was licensed to several milk bottle manufacturers. After a series of stock transactions, the Thatcher Manufacturing Company acquired control of these companies and, consequently, the exclusive rights to use both the available processes for automatic manufacture of milk bottles. All the assets of the Lockport Glass Company, the Essex Glass Company, and the Travis Glass Company were transferred to Thatcher Manufacturing Company; and the corporations were dissolved. The common stock of the Woodbury Glass Company, which had been engaged primarily in non-milk-bottle manufacturing, was acquired in the same transaction, but was retained without a transfer of assets.[40]

The commission, in this case, examined the conditions in the market for the product in question, but it gave no consideration to definition of the "product" for purposes of ascertaining the degree of control over the market resulting from the acquisitions. It considered the volume of sales of milk bottles, before and after the acquisition, but ignored the extent to which the potential competition of types of containers other than milk bottles might have limited the monopoly power of the Thatcher company. The commission stated:

> In the year 1919 prior to the acquisition . . . the respondent produced and sold in commerce about 40 per cent of all milk bottles manufactured in the United States. During the year 1920 the respondent produced and sold in commerce about 70 per cent of all the milk bottles manufactured in the United States.[41]

The commission found that, in connection with a proposed bond issue, the president of the Thatcher company had stated:

> The Thatcher Manufacturing Company will have the exclusive right to make milk bottles by the only successful bottle-making machines devised,

[40] 6 F.T.C. 213, 222–229.
[41] 6 F.T.C. 213, 240.

and will manufacture and sell about 90% of all the milk bottles manufactured in the United States.[42]

The commission concluded that the acquisition of the stock was in violation of Section 7 and the transfer of assets was

> . . . an artifice and subterfuge of the respondent to evade the provisions of said act of Congress and to escape the penalties thereof. By such acquisition, artifice, and subterfuge, the respondent secured, and now retains and enjoys, the fruits, benefits, and advantages of an illegal acquisition of the stock or share capital of competing corporations engaged in commerce.[43]

The report of the commission states that the effect of the acquisitions was

> . . . (a) to eliminate all competition in commerce in the milk bottle business between the Essex Glass Company, the Travis Glass Company, the Lockport Glass Company, the Woodbury Glass Company and the Thatcher Manufacturing Company, and also between each company and each other of said companies; (b) to restrain commerce in the milk bottle business in the sections or communities of the United States in which . . . [the several companies] were engaged in commerce on and prior to August 28, 1919; and (c) to tend to create a monopoly in commerce in the milk bottle business in the Thatcher Manufacturing Company.[44]

The commission ordered the Thatcher Manufacturing Company to divest itself of all the assets, properties, and rights acquired through its acquisition of the stock of the Essex, Travis, and Lockport companies, and to divest itself of the stock of the Woodbury Company.[45]

Although this case and the three meat-packer cases indicate the manner in which the commission interpreted the standard of illegality provided in the statute, they are distinguished primarily as cases that pointed up for judicial interpretation the question of the meaning of Section 7 with respect to its applicability to acquisitions of physical assets in addition to capital stock. In all four cases, the commission decided that it was authorized by the Clayton Act to prevent mergers achieved by means of stock con-

[42] 6 F.T.C. 213, 240.
[43] 6 F.T.C. 213, 240.
[44] 6 F.T.C. 213, 240.
[45] 6 F.T.C. 213, 242–243.

trol rather than merely to prevent the continued existence of a holding company relationship.

The International Shoe Company Case—The sixth Section 7 complaint to result in an order by the Federal Trade Commission during the first eleven years of its administration of the Clayton Act brought to focus for judicial determination the question of the meaning of the standard of illegality. In a complaint issued during the 1923 fiscal year, the commission charged that the International Shoe Company had violated Section 7 by acquiring almost all the common stock of W. H. McElwain Company, a corporation engaged in the manufacture and sale of shoes.[46]

The commission found that, at the time of the acquisition and prior thereto, the International Shoe Company was engaged in the manufacture and sale of a full line of leather shoes for men, women, and children. It found that

> . . . the trade territory of the respondent was practically all of the United States. The shoes manufactured by it were sold largely to retail dealers in small cities and towns in the various states outside New England. Respondent made some sales of its shoes in New England, and also to wholesale and retail dealers in some of the larger cities throughout the United States.[47]

Before the acquisition, International owned shoe factories manufacturing more than seventy thousand pairs of shoes per day. The W. H. McElwain Company owned shoe factories with a capacity of more than forty thousand pairs of shoes per day. According to the findings of the commission, the McElwain Company manufactured and sold leather shoes for men, boys, and misses.

> The shoes manufactured by W. H. McElwain Company were sold by it direct from its factories to jobbers and wholesalers and to large retailers in cities among the several States and to retail dealers throughout the United States generally. It also sold its shoes direct from its branches or distributing houses to retail dealers among the several States adjacent to such branches or distributing houses. . . . The larger part of its product was sold in the cities, but it also sold its shoes direct to retailers in small cities and towns in

[46] *F.T.C. Annual Report, 1923*, p. 196.

[47] *In the Matter of International Shoe Company*, 9 F.T.C. 441, 445 (F.T.C. Docket No. 1023, Nov. 25, 1925).

at least thirty-five States of the United States. In 1920 it made more dress welt shoes for men and boys than any other manufacturer in the world, and was the largest manufacturer of shoes in the New England States.[48]

The commission thus found that the two companies were both relatively large concerns engaged in the same general line of business in market territories including most of the nation. The commission, however, was primarily concerned with whether, prior to the acquisition, substantial competition existed *between* the two concerns. It found that International Shoe Company was engaged primarily in selling a more durable grade of shoes in small towns in areas other than New England, whereas McElwain sold dress shoes primarily in the larger cities and primarily in New England. The commission, therefore, felt it necessary to show that a substantial degree of competition had existed between the two companies.

Apparently the commission interpreted "competition between two firms" to mean that the two firms were engaged in the sale of almost completely homogeneous products in the same geographical areas to the same classification of customers at approximately the same prices. This was obviously not true of *all* the sales of the two firms. The commission, therefore, sought to ascertain if it were true of enough of the sales to constitute substantial competition. The report states:

The shoes produced by W. H. McElwain Company in 1921 and for some time prior thereto were sold to retail dealers at about $6 to $9 per pair. At the same time the International Shoe Company produced a line of men's dress shoes known as the "Patriot" brand, and of that brand ten styles of low shoes and twenty-two styles of high shoes were similar in style, comparable in price, and equal or superior in quality to the men's high and low dress shoes produced by W. H. McElwain Company. The "Patriot" shoes manufactured and sold by respondent were sold to retailers at about the same price per pair as the shoes manufactured and sold by W. H. McElwain Company. Both companies made and sold medium priced dress shoes and sold such shoes to retail dealers in the same States, and in many of the same cities and towns, and in some instances to the same dealers. On and prior to May 11, 1921, both companies were engaged in manufacturing and

[48] 9 F.T.C. 441, 445–446.

selling leather dress shoes in commerce among the several States and the District of Columbia, in competition with each other, and with others similarly engaged. The competition in commerce between the two companies was substantial.[49]

Just prior to the acquisition, which was initiated by the McElwain Company, the sales of that company had dropped to the point that only a part of its capacity was in use, whereas the International Company had to cancel orders for lack of sufficient capacity to fill them. The commission found that, although the officers of W. H. McElwain Company were apprehensive of the company's financial condition, the company was not insolvent and had not failed.[50]

The commission concluded:

By the acquisition of the stock or share capital of W. H. McElwain Company the respondent gained control of the largest manufacturer of street and dress welt shoes for men and boys and eliminated from the field of competition respondent's largest competitor in the sale of men's dress shoes, and secured immediate entrance into the sales territory of the New England States, and accomplished a nation-wide distribution of its products.[51]

In the opinion of the commission the effect of the acquisition was:

(a) To substantially lessen competition in commerce between International Shoe Company and W. H. McElwain Company in the sale of dress shoes for men.

(b) To restrain commerce in the shoe business and especially in that part of such business relating to the sale of dress shoes for men in various sections or communities of the United States in which International Shoe Company and W. H. McElwain Company were engaged in commerce.

(c) To restrain commerce in the shoe business in sections or communities of the United States including Columbus, Ohio; Kansas City, Mo., and San Francisco, Calif., and in other sections or communities adjacent thereto.[52]

---

[49] 9 F.T.C. 441, 446.

[50] 9 F.T.C. 441, 447.

[51] 9 F.T.C. 441, 452–453.

[52] 9 F.T.C. 441, 453–454. Commissioners Nugent and Thompson dissented from the failure to conclude that the effect had also been "to tend to create in International Shoe Company a monopoly in commerce of the shoe business," according to p. 462 n. 1, of the report.

After the commission had issued its complaint, International Shoe Company attempted to avoid further proceedings in the case by ostensibly divesting itself of the stock after acquiring the assets of the McElwain Company. The commission held that International had not really disposed of the stock and that the assets were acquired as a result of an illegal stock acquisition. This question was of only secondary importance in the review of the case by the courts.

The commission ordered International Shoe Company to divest itself of all the stock and all the property acquired from the W. H. McElwain Company.[53]

Commissioner Humphrey, with the concurrence of Commissioner Hunt, dissented from the order of the commission on the grounds that it was not in the public interest, since competition was not substantially lessened by the acquisition. He pointed out that International Shoe did not decrease the quality or increase the price of shoes as a result of the acquisition. He maintained that, if the acquisition had not taken place, the McElwain Company would have become bankrupt and competition wiped out.[54]

Cases in Which Complaints Were Dismissed

The policies of the Federal Trade Commission are revealed by its actions and the reasons stated therefor in the cases of complaints that were issued and then dismissed after trial, as well as in the cases of complaints that resulted in orders of divestiture.

Of the thirty-eight complaints issued before the close of the 1926 fiscal year, twenty-three had been dismissed by that date. Nine involved the commission's interpretation of the standard of illegality. Four complaints were dismissed because of its interpretation of its power over asset acquisitions. Two complaints were dismissed because of action taken by the Justice Depart-

[53] 9 F.T.C. 441, 462–463.

[54] 9 F.T.C. 441, 463–465. The results of the judicial review of the commission's order are considered in chap. 4.

ment against the same firms.[55] The commission dismissed four complaints for miscellaneous reasons that were unimportant from the standpoint of disclosing its policies.[56] Three complaints were dismissed with no reasons given in the orders of dismissal or in any other source.[57] The commission dismissed one complaint because the "proof [was] not sufficient to sustain allegations of the complaint." [58]

Dismissals Involving Asset Acquisitions—The first of the four dismissals on the ground that assets had been acquired was in the matter of the Victor Electric Corporation.[59] After answer but before trial, the complaint was dismissed "without reasons assigned." [60] Information from the files of the commission, included in the exhibits submitted to the Temporary National Economic Committee in 1939,[61] showed that the chief counsel had

---

[55] These fifteen complaints are discussed subsequently herein.

[56] Complaint No. 450 against Wilson and Company was dismissed because the acquired stock had been disposed of when the matter came to trial. See 10 F.T.C. 425, 426 (1926).

Complaint No. 451 against Cudahy Packing Company was dismissed because the acquisition had taken place prior to the passage of the Clayton Act. See *Federal Trade Commission Report on Monopolistic Practices in Industries,* in *T.N.E.C. Hearings,* part 5-A, p. 2365.

Complaint No. 452 against Armour and Company was dismissed because the acquisition of Morris and Company had been made with the approval of the secretary of agriculture under the Packers and Stockyards Act, approved August 15, 1921 (32 *U.S. Stat. at L.* 2, 159). See *T.N.E.C. Hearings,* part 5-A, p. 2365.

Complaint No. 1305 against the Continental Baking Corporation was dismissed in order to include its allegations in a new complaint, since nine or more new acquisitions had been made. See 10 F.T.C. 424 (1925).

[57] Complaint No. 449 against Wilson and Company was dismissed March 29, 1926. See 10 F.T.C. 433 (1926). Complaint No. 573 against Owens Bottle Machine Company was dismissed May 13, 1925, with Commissioners Nugent and Thompson dissenting, but with no assignment of reasons. See 9 F.T.C. 497 (1925). Complaint No. 1022 against Hygrade Lamp Co. was dismissed in 1924 with no assignment of reasons. See 8 F.T.C. 525 (1924).

[58] *Atlantic Ice and Coal Corporation,* 1 F.T.C. 539 (F.T.C. Docket No. 93, Sept. 7, 1918).

[59] Complaint No. 160, issued June 10, 1918. The commission alleged that the respondent had violated Section 7 by acquiring all of the stock of other companies in the X-ray machine business. See *F.T.C. Annual Report, 1918,* p. 73.

[60] *The Victor Electric Corporation,* 1 F.T.C. 539 (F.T.C. Docket No. 160, March 10, 1919).

[61] F.T.C. Exhibit No. 168.

recommended dismissal because of the discovery that the respondent had acquired all the property of the various corporations in exchange for its own stock. The acquired corporations then owned no property and were not engaged in business when a small amount of stock was issued to protect the respondent against the use of the various corporate names by other persons.[62]

In the 1920 fiscal year, the commission issued two complaints against Armour and Company. In addition to Complaint No. 455, which resulted in an order of divestiture, Complaint No. 531 charged Armour with violating Section 7 by acquiring the stock of three corporations that it organized for the purpose of acquiring the business and property of three competitors in cottonseed oil products and leather goods.[63] On January 30, 1926, after answer and trial, the commission dismissed the complaint on the grounds that the elimination of competition resulted from the purchase of the property of the original competing companies, rather than from the subsequent acquisitions of the stock of the newly created corporations organized to take over the businesses.[64]

In 1923 the commission had charged the Illinois Glass Company with violating Section 7 by acquiring all the assets and stock of three other companies.[65] In 1925 the complaint was dismissed after trial upon the recommendation of the trial attorney and the chief counsel with Commissioners Nugent and Thompson dissenting.[66] The reasons for the dismissal were reported in F.T.C. Exhibit No. 168. It was the judgment of the trial attorney that the Illinois Glass Company had not acquired the stock of the Cumberland Manufacturing Company, but had acquired, instead, its plants and assets, which included the stock of two subsidiary corporations. These subsidiaries were held not to be engaged in

---

[62] F.T.C. Exhibit No. 168, pp. 3–4.

[63] *F.T.C. Annual Report, 1920,* p. 141.

[64] *Armour & Co.,* 10 F.T.C. 427 (F.T.C. Docket No. 531, Jan. 30, 1926). Commissioners Nugent and Thompson dissented to the dismissal of two of the four counts of the complaint.

[65] Complaint No. 1009. *F.T.C. Annual Report, 1923,* p. 193.

[66] *Illinois Glass Co.,* 9 F.T.C. 516 (F.T.C. Docket No. 1009, Oct. 14, 1925).

interstate commerce, since they merely manufactured glass bottles sold by the parent corporation.[67]

The informal record also indicated that the Board of Review had opposed the issuance of the complaint on the ground that no stock had been acquired, but that Commissioner Gaskill had voted with Nugent and Thompson for the issuance of the complaint in 1923. The complaint was dismissed after William E. Humphrey replaced Gaskill on the commission in 1925. The matter had been delayed by a tie vote, between Nugent and Thompson on the one hand and Van Fleet and Hunt on the other, until Humphrey cast the deciding vote in favor of dismissal.[68]

The fourth dismissal on the grounds that assets had been acquired was that of the complaint against the Midland Steel Products Company, which charged that the company had carried out the purposes of its organization by acquiring the stock and assets of two firms in the auto-frame and frame-parts industry.[69] The complaint was dismissed in 1926 "without assignment of reasons," [70] but the *Federal Trade Commission Report on Monopolistic Practices in Industries* said that the dismissal was based on the discovery that the respondent had acquired the assets of the two firms by the exchange of its own stock without at any time acquiring the stock of the acquired firms.[71]

Thus it appears that, by the end of the 1926 fiscal year, the commission's policy was to dismiss complaints if there was no acquisition of stock, or if an acquisition of stock was preceded by the acquisition of the assets, property, and business of the corporation whose stock was later acquired. During this period no complaints were dismissed on the ground that the assets were acquired, if the asset acquisition followed a stock acquisition.

---

[67] F.T.C. Exhibit No. 168, p. 44.

[68] *Ibid.* The Federal Trade Commission has always been composed of five members appointed for staggered seven-year terms by the President with the consent of the Senate.

[69] Complaint No. 1291. See *F.T.C. Annual Report, 1925,* p. 253.

[70] *Midland Steel Products Company,* 10 F.T.C. 429 (F.T.C. Docket No. 1291, Feb. 6, 1926).

[71] *T.N.E.C. Hearings,* part 5-A, pp. 2367–2368.

Dismissals Involving the Standard of Illegality—The disposition of the first complaint issued by the commission alleging violation of Section 7 hinged upon the commission's interpretation of the standard of illegality provided in the statute.[72] The commission found that the stock acquisition had been made and that the stock was still held at the time of the trial. It concluded that Section 7 had not been violated because it found that, prior to the acquisition, the two corporations had not been engaged in purchasing raw materials in the same markets as they operated in separate cities. The commission apparently was not concerned with the effect of the acquisition on competition in the markets for the products sold, perhaps because the allegation of unfair methods of competition related to the purchase of raw materials.[73]

Whether Section 7 contemplated only substantial preëxisting competition rather than potential competition was the issue in the disposition of a complaint against Standard Oil Company of New York.[74] The complaint was dismissed after answer and trial in 1920 with "no reason assigned." [75] One issue raised in the pleading was whether the statute applied to the Magnolia company, a Texas joint stock company rather than a corporation: but the issue apparently more important in determining the disposition was whether the statute applied to an acquisition involving two

[72] Complaint No. 79 against the American Agricultural Chemical Co. and the Brown Co. charged both companies with violating Section 5 of the Federal Trade Commission Act by purchasing raw materials used in manufacturing fertilizer and in refining animal fats at prices so high as to prohibit small competitors from continuing in the same business and by causing their trucks to collide with those of their competitors. It also charged that the acquisition of the stock of the Brown Co. by the American Agricultural Chemical Company was a violation of Section 7 of the Clayton Act. A cease and desist order was issued on the Section 5 allegations, but no action was taken on the Section 7 allegation.

See *Federal Trade Commission* v. *American Agricultural Chemical Co. and the Brown Co.* (*Inc.*), 1 F.T.C. 226 (F.T.C. Docket No. 79, Oct. 8, 1918).

[73] 1 F.T.C. 226, 233.

[74] Complaint No. 92, issued April 15, alleged that the acquisition of a large part of the capital stock of the Magnolia Petroleum Company constituted a violation of Section 7. See *F.T.C. Annual Report, 1918*, p. 64.

[75] *Standard Oil Co. of New York*, 2 F.T.C. 465 (F.T.C. Docket No. 92, May 20, 1920).

corporations not previously engaged in active competition with each other, even though the acquired firm was an expanding, healthy concern.[76]

A complaint was issued in 1918 against the Tobacco Products Corporation.[77] Included in the charges were allegations of violations of Section 5 of the Federal Trade Commission Act and Sections 2, 7, and 8 of the Clayton Act. The case is important, because the commission apparently accepted the idea that the degree of competition in the market is more important than the degree of lessening of competition between the firms. The complaint was dismissed "without prejudice," with no reasons being assigned.[78] In discussing the dismissal, however, the "Digest of Formal Complaints under Sections 7 & 8 of the Clayton Act" says:

> The opinion of the Commission's Chief Counsel was that the effect of the acquisition would tend to maintain and stimulate competition in the interest of the public against the larger and more powerful concerns, and that the courts would not find an ability or tendency to restrain trade on the part of a concern having less than 10% of the trade in an industry where there were far more powerful and larger concerns in the same industry. The respondent controlled only ½ of 1% of the smoking tobacco business of the country and 2.3% of the other tobacco business.[79]

The recommendation of the chief counsel resulted in rescinding an order of divestment and dismissing a complaint in another case a few months later.[80] The chief counsel was of the opinion

---

[76] F.T.C. Exhibit No. 168, p. 2.

[77] Complaint No. 205, issued Oct. 18, 1918. See *F.T.C. Annual Report, 1919*, p. 72.

[78] *Tobacco Products Corporation, et al.*, 4 F.T.C. 484 (F.T.C. Docket No. 205, Nov. 8, 1921).

[79] F.T.C. Exhibit No. 168, pp. 4–5.

[80] Complaint No. 250, against Bordens Farm Products Company, had been issued February 6, 1919, charging violation of Section 7 by the acquisition of all the capital stock of Alexander Campbell Milk Company, Brooklyn, New York. On May 24, 1922, the commission directed that an order of divestment be served and referred the matter to the chief counsel for his approval. After Chief Counsel Fuller had expressed the opinion that the record would not support an order, the commission, on June 23, 1922, rescinded the order and ordered dismissal with "no reasons assigned." Murdock dissented. See *Bordens Farm Products Co., Inc.*, 5 F.T.C. 482 (F.T.C. Docket No. 250, July 3, 1922), and F.T.C. Exhibit No. 168, pp. 7–10.

that the statute had not been violated because substantial competition had not existed between the two firms. He pointed out that the Borden Company and the Campbell Company had not competed in the purchase of milk because they purchased in different geographical areas and the Campbell Company sold its product only in the immediate vicinity of Brooklyn. F.T.C. Exhibit No. 168 said:

> The opinion was advanced that in order for there to be a violation of the statute, both corporations must be, in a substantial sense competitive. . . . In his opinion, a mere negligible portion of competition would not be sufficient unless there was an attempt to monopolize and control the market.[81]

Evidently, the chief counsel felt that, in the absence of evidence of *intent* to monopolize, the law was not violated unless it could be shown that *both* the acquiring and the acquired company had been selling a substantial portion of the quantity of product sold in the market. The market must be interstate in character. This interpretation of the law implies that, if the acquired company has had a small quantity of sales relative to the quantity of sales of all other firms selling the same product in the same geographical area (which must be interstate and larger than the vicinity of Brooklyn), then the acquisition is not illegal no matter how large the acquiring firm may be.

It was not until 1925 that another dismissal resulted from considerations of the effect on competition of an acquisition. In May, 1925, the commission dismissed a complaint against Austin, Nichols and Company, Inc., charged with violating Section 7 by acquiring the capital stock of three corporations engaged in various branches of the wholesale grocery business.[82] All three acquired corporations had been subsidiaries of Wilson and Company, Inc., and the original complaint was issued in the belief that Wilson and Company was ostensibly getting out of the wholesale grocery business, while in fact retaining control of the

---

[81] F.T.C. Exhibit No. 168, p. 9.

[82] *Austin, Nichols & Co., Inc.*, 9 F.T.C. 170 (F.T.C. Docket No. 745, May 14, 1925).

three subsidiaries through control of Austin, Nichols and Company. After taking testimony, the commission concluded that this was not the fact, but tried the case in order to ascertain whether the acquisitions had lessened competition. The commission found that competition had not existed between Austin, Nichols and Company and any of the three acquired companies or between any of the acquired companies. The commission's examiners took testimony from several persons in Cincinnati and New York, but they were unable to establish that the various firms involved in this case had either bought from or sold the same products *to the same firms* prior to the acquisitions.[83] All the firms were engaged in the same general line of commerce throughout the whole country, but their business was but a small part of the total volume of business, and they dealt in only a small part of the many products included within the line of commerce.

On December 19, 1925, the commission dismissed a complaint against Swift and Company and its subsidiary, the United Dressed Beef Company, "without assignment of reasons." [84] The J. J. Harrington Company, a partnership, had engaged in direct competition with Swift in the New York metropolitan area in the sale of meat products. A corporation, J. J. Harrington Company, Inc., was formed to acquire the business of the partnership. Through a subsidiary, Swift acquired all the stock of the new corporation. According to its minutes, the commission dismissed the case on the ground that competition had not previously existed between Swift and the acquired corporation, since the *corporation* had not previously engaged in business.[85] Apparently the commission did not consider whether the acquisition might tend to create a monopoly in the line of commerce in which the firms were engaged. Commissioners Nugent and Thompson dissented, but their reasons were not revealed.

Insufficient preëxisting competition was the basis for dismiss-

---

[83] See 9 F.T.C. 170, 176–179, and F.T.C. Exhibit No. 168, pp. 38–39.

[84] *Swift & Co. and United Dressed Beef Co.*, 10 F.T.C. 423 (Docket No. 454, Dec. 19, 1925).

[85] F.T.C. Exhibit No. 168, pp. 23–24.

ing a complaint against Standard Oil Company of New Jersey.[86] The Federal Trade Commission digest of Section 7 complaints submitted to the Temporary National Economic Committee said this about the case:

. . . Counsel for the Commission in his brief concluded . . . that the corporations were both engaged in commerce at the time of the acquisition and that the effect of the acquisition was to eliminate the competition, actual and potential, between the corporations. It further appears that the respondent itself did not engage in the production of petroleum but it does own stock in subsidiary corporations engaged in the production of crude oil. One of these is the Standard Oil Company of Louisiana, which is engaged in producing oil in Louisiana and Arkansas, with refineries at Baton Rouge and with marketing stations in Louisiana, Tennessee, and Arkansas. It has sold some products in Texas and other states. The Humble Oil and Refining Company is a large producer of crude oil, with plants, refineries, pipe lines, etc. located primarily in Texas, some in Oklahoma, Arkansas, and Louisiana. There is some evidence in the record of competition between the Standard Oil Company of Louisiana and Humble Oil Company. . . .

Shortly prior to the dismissal of the complaint, Commissioner Humphrey filed a memorandum in which he stated that he found there was no competition in the "legal" sense between the respondent or its subsidiary, the Standard Oil Company of Louisiana, and the Humble Oil and Refining Company. He reasoned that if there be no substantial competition, there could be no substantial reduction of competition as a result of the acquisition. "The proposition that there can be a substantial reduction of an unsubstantial thing is a proposition that is too ethereal for my mind to grasp." He indicated in his memorandum that the courts had had the same difficulty.[87]

The view here expressed by Commissioner Humphrey implies that the statute was not designed to achieve the positive goal of enforcing conditions in which competition would be encouraged, but, instead, to achieve the negative effect of preventing any substantial reduction in the degree of competition prevailing. The expression of such a policy by the commission in a case

[86] *The Standard Oil Company of New Jersey,* 10 F.T.C. 426 (F.T.C. Docket No. 964, Jan. 26, 1926). The complaint had been issued in 1921 charging that the acquisition of 60 per cent of the stock of the Humble Oil Company constituted a violation of Section 7. The formal record gives no reasons for dismissal or dissent. Commissioners Nugent and Thompson dissented.

[87] F.T.C. Exhibit No. 168, pp. 42–43.

against the Standard Oil Company of New Jersey seems ironic: one of the causes of the climate of opinion in which the Clayton Act was enacted—and particularly the "holding company section"—was the disclosure of Standard Oil practices, brought before the public as a result of the 1911 Sherman Act case. The Senate changed the language of Section 7 by substituting "may be" for "is" in the phrase "where the effect may be to substantially lessen competition." This change was made on the grounds that the standard of illegality would otherwise be weaker than that of the Sherman Act, since in the Northern Securities case the Supreme Court had said that the creation of the power to restrain trade was illegal, even if there were no actual restraint.[88] The commission, in this case, understood that the Clayton Act prohibition against holding companies applies only if there is reduction of actual competition, rather than potential competition.

The absence of competition appears to have been the reason for dismissing another complaint a few weeks later.[89] The commission dismissed the complaint

> . . . for reasons based upon the report of the trial examiner and upon the recommendations of the trial attorney and the chief counsel as set forth in memorandum of December 10, 1925, from the trial attorney and memorandum of December 16, 1925, from the chief counsel. Commissioners Nugent and Thompson dissenting.[90]

F.T.C. Exhibit No. 168 said that copies of the two memoranda were not contained in either the formal docket or the confidential file. It said, however, that the Holly Sugar Company had urged dismissal on the ground that its production of beet sugar was less than 5 per cent of the total production in the United States.[91] In its report on another case, which charged the same corporations with violation of Section 8 of the Clayton Act, the commission said that the complaint was being dismissed

[88] See chap. 2.

[89] Complaint No. 1181, against Holly Sugar Corporation, was issued May 17, 1924, charging that Section 7 had been violated by the acquisition of three other California sugar companies. See *F.T.C. Annual Report, 1924,* p. 234.

[90] *Holly Sugar Corporation,* 10 F.T.C. 430, 431 (F.T.C. Docket No. 1181, March 3, 1926).

[91] F.T.C. Exhibit No. 168, p. 52.

> . . . for the same reason that the complaint against the Holly Sugar Corporation, Docket 1181, was dismissed, namely, that, due to natural conditions, there was no competition in interstate commerce, or prospect of it between the corporations respondent, and that to prosecute the proceeding would be futile and of no public benefit; and on other grounds. . . .[92]

Apparently the commission interpreted the Clayton Act to require not merely that the corporations involved in an acquisition be engaged in interstate commerce, but that the required amount of preëxisting competition must be of an interstate character.

The ninth case of dismissal on the grounds that an acquisition failed to come within the purview of the standard of illegality of Section 7 throws much light on the development of Federal Trade Commission policy. In 1916 the Fisk Rubber Company acquired 51 per cent of the stock of the Federal Rubber Company. More than eight years later, in December, 1924, the commission issued a complaint against Fisk Rubber Company alleging the stock acquisition and the subsequent transfer of assets of the acquired company to Fisk in 1921 constituted a violation of Section 7 because it had the effect of substantially lessening competition between the two corporations, both engaged in the manufacture and sale of automobile tires, tubes, and other rubber products.[93] No testimony was taken in the case. On March 16, 1926, a motion was filed requesting dismissal of the complaint. The Federal Trade Commission reported to the Temporary National Economic Committee that neither the formal docket nor the confidential file contained the reasons for the dismissal.[94] When the complaint was issued, however, Commissioner Van Fleet filed a memorandum of dissent, subsequently printed in its entirety in the report of the case.[95] The commission issuing the complaint was composed of Vernon W. Van Fleet, Charles W. Hunt, John F. Nugent, Huston Thompson, and Nelson B. Gaskill. When the

[92] *Holly Sugar Corporation, et al.,* 10 F.T.C. 451 (F.T.C. Docket No. 1180, April 16, 1926).

[93] Complaint No. 1248, issued Dec. 9, 1924, against Fisk Rubber Co. See *F.T.C. Annual Report, 1925,* p. 247 and F.T.C. Exhibit No. 168, pp. 57, 58.

[94] F.T.C. Exhibit No. 168, p. 58.

[95] *Fisk Rubber Company,* 10 F.T.C. 433, 433–436 (F.T.C. Docket No. 1248, April 2, 1926).

complaint was dismissed in April, 1926, Commissioner Gaskill had been replaced by William E. Humphrey.[96] The opinions expressed in Van Fleet's dissent represented what was to become the attitude of a majority of the commission's members toward the interpretation of Section 7 after February 25, 1925, when Humphrey joined the commission and changed the balance of power. After that date, only two members serving had been appointed by President Wilson—Nugent and Thompson.

Commissioner Van Fleet's dissenting memorandum set forth in detail his interpretation of the meaning of the standard of illegality and criticized the majority interpretation:

> The complaint alleges that the companies were in competition but the extent thereof is not alleged, nor is it directly alleged that this competition was of a "substantial" nature or amount. The competition between the companies may have been very small and unsubstantial, yet it would not only be "substantially lessened" but in fact entirely eliminated. The whole being greater than the part, where there is any competition at all between two combining companies, it is *always* substantially lessened in the sense given the statute by the majority.
>
> I am convinced from all the facts before us that it cannot be shown that the competition between the companies was of a substantial nature, the elimination of which would be offensive to the spirit of the antitrust laws, including the Clayton Act. But the theory of the case as maintained by the majority of the Commission is that the amount of competition is not material. It is maintained that if there was *some* competition, the amalgamation of the companies "substantially lessened" it because, of course, it entirely eliminated it. . . . If in this section "substantially" refers to "lessen," and means only quantity or amount, the theory of the majority is correct, and grammatically it does, because it is an adverb. But not all statutes are grammatical and they are never construed by the courts according to their strict grammatical construction when to do so would lead to absurd or palpably unjust results, which it never could be presumed the legislature intended. . . . Why use the word "substantially"? The use of this word is significant. If the position of the majority is correct it might well have been omitted and the act read: where the effect of such acquisition may be to lessen competition between the corporations.[97]

Apparently, Commissioner Van Fleet was judging the intent of Congress solely on the basis of the wording of the statute itself,

[96] See 8 F.T.C. ii.

[97] 10 F.T.C. 433, 434.

rather than its legislative history. As was pointed out previously, the section as it passed the House of Representatives contained the phrase "to eliminate or substantially lessen." The words "eliminate or" were stricken out in the Senate, not in order to make the standard stricter, but because it was thought that they were surplusage: if competition is eliminated, it is obviously lessened.[98] Without debate, the Senate accepted an amendment to strike out "substantially," but it was put back in by the conference committee.[99] In the debates on the floor of the Senate on the adoption of the conference report, Senator Walsh expressed the opinion that the word was of no importance to the meaning of the section and noted that in the Union Pacific–Southern Pacific case the Supreme Court had held that a combination violated the Sherman Act even though the traffic affected amounted to only "eighty-eight one-hundredths of 1 per cent of the total tonnage of the Southern Pacific."[100]

In his dissenting memorandum, Commissioner Van Fleet went on to say:

> Under the construction placed on the act by the majority the word [substantially] is superfluous. In my opinion it is not superfluous but it was used by Congress in the sense of unreasonable and means to prohibit such acquisitions when they unreasonably lessen competition. At the time the Clayton Act was passed, the Supreme Court in the Standard Oil and Tobacco cases had declared the rule of reason to be applicable to the Sherman Act, and I believe Congress had this in mind and intended to express the same idea in the use of the word "substantially."[101]

As was pointed out in chapter 2, it is impossible to know what Congress explicitly intended. The legislative record discloses, however, that, at least among those members of Congress whose opinions are on record, there was a strong feeling that passing the Clayton Act represented an effort to counteract the enunciation of the rule of reason by the court. It may well be that the bill was passed because many members of Congress thought that

[98] See pp. 38–39.
[99] See pp. 41–42.
[100] See p. 48.
[101] 10 F.T.C. 433, 434–435.

it would be interpreted as Commissioner Van Fleet interpreted it.

In his dissent, Van Fleet pointed out that the courts, in the Aluminum and the Western Meat cases, which by then had been decided by the Circuit Court of Appeals, had taken into account the degree of preëxisting competition, although the question had not been directly raised. With respect to the market conditions in the Fisk case, Van Fleet said:

> . . . In 1923, there were in the United States 528 establishments engaged primarily in the manufacture of rubber products and 160 such concerns engaged primarily in the manufacture of rubber tires. . . .
>
> Four of respondent's competitors are larger in production and sales than it, two twice as large, and one more than three times as large. There is keen competition in the business. If the respondent is torn apart, will it help competition in the business? Plainly not. The result will be only to cripple one of the competitors of the others.
>
> . . . There being no monopolistic or unfair practices alleged against the corporation since the stock was acquired, the case presents a situation similar to that presented in the case of *United States* v. *United States Steel Corporation,* 251 U.S. 417. . . .
>
> It was found that the original consolidation of the constituent companies forming the corporation was offensive to the Sherman Act. The court pointed out the difference between the case at bar and those cases in which it had decreed dissolution, those cases being where the offense was a continuing one and the restraint of competition and trade had continued. In the Steel case no such condition existed as the corporation, since its organization had in nowise offended by any oppressive or monopolistic practices.
>
> The case is parallel to this case.[102]

Commissioner Van Fleet was thus unwilling to consider the acquisition itself as an offense condemned by the policy of the antitrust laws in the absence of a continuing series of monopolistic practices, unless the acquiring corporation had achieved "a monopoly" by the acquisition. He was explicitly applying the Sherman Act criterion to Section 7 cases.

Dismissals on Other Grounds—The commission dismissed two Section 7 complaints because of action taken by the Department of Justice. A complaint had been issued against the Cement Securities Company in 1920 alleging violation of Section 7 by the

[102] 10 F.T.C. 433, 435–436.

acquisition of stock in three cement manufacturing companies.[103] Although the formal docket gave no reasons for the dismissal, the file contained a memorandum from the chief counsel indicating that dismissal was based on the fact that the United States District Court of Colorado had decreed the Cement Securities Company to be a combination in violation of the Sherman Act. The court had issued a decree of dissolution and an injunction which the chief counsel thought would remedy the situation brought about by the alleged violation of Section 7 of the Clayton Act.[104]

A complaint against the Continental Baking Corporation was dismissed in 1926 on the ground that the same charge was covered by a Justice Department case in which a consent decree was entered.[105] While the commission was in the process of taking testimony in the case, the Department of Justice, on February 8, 1926, filed a petition in the United States District Court in Baltimore against the Continental Baking Corporation, and several other companies, charging violations of the Sherman Act as well as violations of Section 7 of the Clayton Act. The allegations in the Justice Department case against Continental Baking Corporation were essentially the same as those made by the commission.[106] The Federal Trade Commission dismissed its complaint on April 7, 1926, after answer and trial, with Commissioners Nugent and Thompson dissenting. The reasons given were as follows:

> Upon the recommendation of the chief counsel for a dismissal of the complaint herein to take effect when the decree in the case of United States of America, Petitioner *v.* Ward Food Products Corporation and others, defendants, In Equity No. 1073 in the District Court of the United States for the District of Maryland is entered, and it further appearing that said de-

[103] Complaint No. 549, issued Sept. 4, 1920. See *F.T.C. Annual Report, 1920,* p. 144, and *Cement Securities Co.* 9 F.T.C. 504 (F.T.C. Docket No. 549, June 24, 1925).

[104] F.T.C. Exhibit No. 168, pp. 31–32.

[105] Complaint No. 1358 was issued Dec. 19, 1925, alleging violation of Section 7 by the acquisition of the stock of twenty-five corporations. An earlier complaint (No. 1305), which alleged only sixteen of the acquisitions, was dismissed the same day. See *Continental Baking Corporation,* 10 F.T.C. 436, 439 (F.T.C. Docket No. 1358, April 7, 1926).

[106] 10 F.T.C. 436, 439–440.

cree was entered on April 3, 1926, in the District Court of the United States for the District of Maryland.

It is now ordered in consideration of said decree that the complaint herein be and the same is hereby dismissed.[107]

In their dissent from the order, Commissioners Nugent and Thompson related at great length the history of the case. They stated that the chief counsel of the commission, Bayard T. Rainer, conferred with the Attorney General and worked out a plan for the handling of the case. On April 2, 1926, the chief counsel informed the commission about a proposed consent decree that had been worked out by the chief counsel, the representatives of the Justice Department, and the defendants in the Justice Department suit. The proposed decree had been agreed to by the defendants on the condition that the Federal Trade Commission complaint be dismissed effective with the entry of the decree. In the dissent, Commissioners Nugent and Thompson said:

At no time was he [the chief counsel] authorized by the *Commission* to confer with the Attorney General *and the attorneys for the defendants* in the suit instituted by the Department of Justice . . . for the purpose of assisting in preparing or agreeing upon a decree to be entered in that suit, or for any other purpose.[108]

At the meeting of the commission on April 2, Commissioner Thompson being absent "on official business," the chief counsel made a brief oral statement and presented his memorandum and a copy of the proposed consent decree. Chairman Nugent requested that the consideration of the matter go over until the next meeting on April 5, but his request was denied. The memorandum of dissent says:

. . . Commissioner Humphrey then moved that the Commission's case against Continental "be dismissed in consideration of the decree, on the entry of this decree, in accordance with the memorandum of the chief counsel." The motion prevailed by the votes of Commissioners Hunt, Humphrey, and Van Fleet. Chairman Nugent voted "No," and asked that his dissent be noted and stated for the record:

"Let the record show that I dissent particularly from the action of the

[107] 10 F.T.C. 436, 436–437.

[108] 10 F.T.C. 436, 443.

majority members of the Commission in railroading this matter through within about fifteen minutes, without giving me an opportunity, which I requested, to examine the memorandum of the chief counsel and the proposed consent decree, notwithstanding I stated I would be ready to act tomorrow. The proposed decree upon which the order of the majority is based has not even been read for the information of the Commission."

Commissioners Van Fleet and Humphrey thereupon insisted that the decree be read. It is true that the memorandum of the chief counsel, which was read by the secretary, set out what purported to be a *portion* of the consent decree but as said matters were not quoted, it did not appear whether they were his interpretations of the provisions of said decree, or otherwise. Unless Commissioners Hunt, Humphrey, and Van Fleet had seen the decree, prior to the Commission meeting on April 2, they had not even read it before they dismissed the complaint. Thus without consideration, discussion or explanation, Commissioners Hunt, Humphrey, and Van Fleet dismissed the complaint against Continental.[109]

The consent decree was entered in the court on the day following the vote of the commission to dismiss its complaint. According to the dissenting opinion of Commissioners Nugent and Thompson,

Paragraph 13 of said consent decree reads as follows:

"It appears that the charge contained in the petition herein that the acquisition and holding by the defendant, the Continental Baking Corporation, of the stocks and other share capital of alleged competing baking companies is in violation of section 7 of the Clayton Act, *was included in a complaint filed by the Federal Trade Commission* against the Continental Baking Corporation on December 19, 1925:

"*Wherefore, the petition is dismissed* as to that charge without prejudice to the right of the United States to again raise the issue in any other proceeding. (Italics ours.)"

The only reasonable inference that can be drawn from that language and, unquestionably, the inference that it was *intended* should be drawn therefrom, is that said charge was dismissed for the reason a complaint involving the same subject matter was then pending, and undetermined before the Federal Trade Commission. It is mere camouflage. The consent decree was signed by the judge of the Federal District Court at Baltimore and entered on *Saturday, April 3,* and the Federal Trade Commission, at a regular meeting held on *Friday morning, April 2,* was informed by its chief counsel that the entry of said decree was *subject* to the *dismissal by the Commission* of its case against the Continental.[110]

---

[109] 10 F.T.C. 436, 444.

[110] 10 F.T.C. 449.

Thus both the Justice Department civil suit and the Federal Trade Commission complaint charging violations of Section 7 against the Continental Baking Corporation were dismissed on the ground that the other agency was administering the law.

Section 5 of the Federal Trade Commission Act

In the period from the establishment of the Federal Trade Commission until the end of the 1926 fiscal year, the commission, in several complaints concerning stock or asset acquisitions, alleged violation of Section 5 of the Federal Trade Commission Act.[111]

In sixteen of the thirty-eight complaints issued in this period under Section 7 of the Clayton Act, the same acquisitions were used as the basis of allegations of violation of Section 5.[112] The disposition of all these sixteen complaints appears to have been made on the basis of the standard of illegality set forth in Section 7 and the authority given the commission by Section 11 of the Clayton Act. In none of these cases did the commission issue an order based on Section 5 of the Federal Trade Commission Act after finding insufficient evidence to support the allegation of violation of Section 7 of the Clayton Act.

Apparently the commission, in alleging violation of both stat-

[111] 38 *U.S. Stat. at L.* (1914), 717–724. Section 5 of this act, which created the Federal Trade Commission and defined its powers, said "that unfair methods of competition in commerce are hereby declared to be unlawful" and set forth the procedure for the enforcement of this provision. The enforcement procedure was essentially the same as that set forth in Section 11 of the Clayton Act. See p. 38 n. 53.

[112] Complaints No. 449 against Wilson & Co.; 451, Cudahy Packing Co.; 452, Morris & Co.; 453, Swift & Co.; 454, Swift & Co. and United Dressed Beef Co.; 455, Armour & Co.; 456, Western Meat Co.; 457, Western Meat Co. and Nevada Packing Co.; 531, Armour & Co.; 549, Cement Securities Co.; 578, Swift & Co. and Libby, McNeill & Libby, *et al.* See *F.T.C. Annual Report, 1920,* pp. 132–134, 141, 144, and 149, respectively. Complaints No. 738, Thatcher Manufacturing Co.; 745, Austin, Nichols & Co. See *F.T.C. Annual Report, 1921,* pp. 140, 141. Complaint No. 835, Famous Players-Laskey Corp. See *F.T.C. Annual Report, 1922,* p. 131. Complaint No. 1009, Illinois Glass Co. See *F.T.C. Annual Report, 1923,* p. 193. Complaint No. 1291, Midland Steel Products Co. See *F.T.C. Annual Report, 1925,* p. 253.

utes in these sixteen complaints, was merely interpreting Section 7 of the Clayton Act to be the specification by Congress of a particular business practice that should be considered an unfair method of competition. As pointed out in the previous chapter,[113] Section 5 was added to the Federal Trade Commission Act by the Senate Interstate Commerce Committee, which considered it a substitute for the substantive provisions of the Clayton Bill, assigned to the Judiciary Committee.

This interpretation of the commission's actions is supported by the fact that, of the remaining twenty-two complaints issued under Section 7 before the end of the 1926 fiscal year, eleven were reported by the commission in its *Annual Reports* as complaints alleging "unfair methods of competition," even though violation of Section 5 was not charged.[114] In two other complaints, violation of Section 5 was alleged along with violation of Section 7, but the former allegation in these two cases was based on practices other than the acquisitions in question.[115] No apparent difference in the circumstances of the other nine complaints would indicate that the commission had any particular reason for not considering those acquisitions also to be unfair methods of competition and violations of Section 5 of the Federal Trade Commission Act.

In the 1915 to 1926 period, several instances of acquisitions of assets resulted in complaints alleging violation of Section 5 of the Federal Trade Commission Act, but not of Section 7 of the Clayton Act. In the 1922 fiscal year, the commission charged Bethle-

---

[113] See p. 55.

[114] Complaint No. 93 against Atlantic Ice and Coal Corporation. See *F.T.C. Annual Report, 1918*, p. 64. Complaint No. 351, Armour & Co. See *F.T.C. Annual Report, 1920*, pp. 124–125. Complaints No. 964, Standard Oil Company of New Jersey; 1022, Hygrade Lamp Co. See *F.T.C. Annual Report, 1923*, pp. 187, 196. Complaints No. 1215, Motor Wheel Corporation; 1219, Hayes Wheel Co.; 1247, Allied Chemical & Dye Corporation; 1248, Fisk Rubber Co.; 1298, Wickwire-Spencer Steel Corporation. See *F.T.C. Annual Report, 1925*, pp. 243, 247, 254. Complaints No. 1350 and 1358 against the Continental Baking Corporation. See *F.T.C. Annual Report, 1926*, pp. 124–126.

[115] Complaint No. 79 against American Agricultural Chemical Corporation and the Brown Co. See *F.T.C. Annual Report, 1918*, p. 63. Complaint No. 205 against the Tobacco Products Corporation, *et al.* See *F.T.C. Annual Report, 1919*, p. 72.

hem Steel Corporation and the Lackawanna Steel Company with unfair methods of competition

. . . in that the respondents, by entering into an agreement to combine or consolidate their respective properties, businesses, and interests into a common enterprise whereby the properties, assets, and business of respondent Lackawanna Steel Company . . . are to be acquired by said Bethlehem Steel Corporation, itself in control of a number of subsidiary corporations, will thereby effect a combination which will control substantial percentages of the production of certain iron and steel products in the United States and especially in the state of Ohio and all territory north of the Potomac River and east of the said State, which said merger of consolidation will have a dangerous tendency to hinder and lessen competition and restrain trade and commerce, the agreement constituting an attempt to monopolize certain interstate trade and commerce, in alleged violation of the Federal Trade Commission act. . . .[116]

Although violation of Section 7 was not adduced, the allegation was worded so as to bring the acquisition within the standard of illegality of the Clayton Act. Section 5 was used alone in this case, apparently because of the absence of any stock acquisition. The complaint was dismissed after answer and before trial "without prejudice" with no reasons assigned.[117]

The commission brought another complaint in 1923, which was still pending in 1926, against Bethlehem Steel Corporation and several other steel companies, whose assets Bethlehem had acquired, saying:

Unfair methods of competition in commerce are charged in that the respondents by uniting under a common ownership and management and thereby effecting control of the iron and steel products originating in their respective territories tend to substantially lessen potential and actual competition, contrary to the public policy expressed in section 7 of the Clayton Act and in alleged violation of section 5 of the Federal Trade Commission act, to unduly hinder competition in the iron and steel industries in said territory and unreasonably restrict competition so as to restrain trade contrary to the public policy expressed in sections 1 and 3 of the Sherman Act and in alleged violation of section 5 of the Federal Trade Commission act.[118]

[116] *F.T.C. Annual Report, 1922,* p. 139. This was Complaint No. 891.

[117] *Bethlehem Steel Corporation and Lackawanna Steel Co.,* 5 F.T.C. 488 (F.T.C. Docket No. 891, Feb. 5, 1923).

[118] *F.T.C. Annual Report, 1923,* p. 187.

This complaint apparently included all the allegations of the previous one, as well as allegations concerning other acquisitions. The commission issued the complaint under the authority given to it by Section 5 of the Federal Trade Commission Act to prevent unfair methods of competition. The commission was saying that an action contrary to the public policy expressed in the Clayton Act or the Sherman Act is an unfair method of competition and, therefore, subject to its jurisdiction. When it alleged that the acquisition of assets by Bethlehem were contrary to the public policy expressed in Section 7, the commission assumed that Congress had intended to set forth the policy that *any* action tending to lessen competition is undesirable, rather than a policy concerned merely with the evils of the holding company.

In the 1925 fiscal year, the commission issued a complaint charging violation of Section 5, but not Section 7, against the Certain-Teed Products Corporation, which was alleged to have acquired the capital stock of one competitor and the assets of two other competitors, "thereby tending to eliminate competition, restrain trade, and create a monopoly." [119] There is no indication in the record of why the commission failed to allege violation of Section 7, as one of the three acquisitions was of stock. The complaint was dismissed within a year of its issuance after answer without assignment of reasons. Commissioners Nugent and Thompson dissented from the dismissal.[120]

The commission issued but one order as a result of a complaint based on the allegation that an acquisition violated only Section 5 of the Federal Trade Commission Act. In the 1923 fiscal year, it issued a complaint against Eastman Kodak Company.[121] The complaint alleged that Eastman had purchased three laboratories equipped for manufacturing positive motion-picture prints from motion-picture negatives and had conspired with other such manufacturers to refrain from operating the three plants so long

[119] *F.T.C. Annual Report, 1925*, p. 220.

[120] *Certain-Teed Products Corporation*, 9 F.T.C. 502 (F.T.C. Docket No. 1259, June 17, 1925).

[121] See *Eastman Kodak Company, et al.*, 7 F.T.C. 434 (F.T.C. Docket No. 977, April 18, 1924).

as the other companies bought all their supplies of film from American film manufacturers. The commission concluded that:

> The acts of the respondents, as set forth in the foregoing paragraphs, constitute a conspiracy or combination in restraint of trade, in interstate and foreign commerce, and had, and continue to have, the effect of retaining, maintaining and extending the monopoly of the Eastman Kodak Company in the manufacture and sale of positive raw cinematograph film, and of substantially lessening competition in the sale of such film, in interstate and foreign commerce; of hindering, restraining and preventing competitors and prospective competitors of Eastman Kodak Company from establishing enterprises for the manufacture and sale of positive raw and cinematograph film; and of substantially lessening competition in the manufacture and sale of positive prints of cinematograph films, in interstate and foreign commerce.[122]

The commission concluded that Section 5 of the Federal Trade Commission Act had been violated, and it issued an order requiring the respondents to "cease and desist from conspiring, combining, confederating, agreeing and cooperating" to restrain competition in several specified ways. The commission also ordered Eastman Kodak Company to sell the three film laboratories to disinterested parties.[123]

The commission found that the effect of the acquisitions and the other practices associated with them was the same as the effects prohibited by the Sherman Act and the Clayton Act. The Federal Trade Commission, having no jurisdiction over Sherman Act violations, and having no jurisdiction under the Clayton Act except regarding a stock acquisition, interpreted Section 5 of the Federal Trade Commission Act to include the types of practices found in this case. The judicial review of the order will be discussed subsequently along with the judicial interpretation of Section 7.[124]

[122] 7 F.T.C. 434, 457–458.
[123] 7 F.T.C. 434, 459–460.
[124] See pp. 112–118.

Conclusions

The conclusions that can be drawn about the commission's policies in administering Section 7 prior to its interpretation by the Supreme Court can be conveniently divided into two parts: (1) consideration of the policy of the commission regarding the application of Section 7 to acquisitions involving the transfer of assets instead of, or in addition to, the transfer of capital stock; (2) consideration of the policy of the commission in interpreting the standard of illegality set forth in the statute.

Federal Trade Commission Policy with Respect to Asset Acquisitions—In its 1916 *Annual Report,* the commission issued several conference rulings:

These rulings are published for the information of business men engaged in interstate commerce and others interested in the work of the Commission. They are not decisions in formal proceedings, but merely expressions of the opinion of the Commission on applications for the issuance of complaints and informal inquiries with regard to particular facts which involve the interpretation and construction of the Federal Trade Commission Act and of those sections of the Clayton Act with the enforcement of which the Commission is charged.[125]

In one of these rulings, the commission set forth its views on its jurisdiction in cases in which a corporation acquires the business of another corporation.

. . . On inquiry as to the right of one manufacturer to buy out a competitor in the same line of business: *Held,* That the only jurisdiction of the Commission in respect of such transactions is to enforce the provisions of section 7 of the Clayton Act prohibiting the acquisition by any corporation engaged in interstate commerce of the capital stock, in whole or in part, of another corporation thus engaged, where the tendency of such acquisition may be to substantially lessen competition between such two corporations, or to restrain interstate commerce, or to create a monopoly; and also possibly to enforce section 5 of the Federal Trade Commission Act, if such purchase either of property or of capital stock in connection with other circumstances might constitute an unfair method of competition. *Held, also,* That the

[125] *F.T.C. Annual Report, 1916,* p. 52.

mere purchase of such competitor other than capital stock is not prohibited by the Clayton Act or the Federal Trade Commission Act.

As to the validity of such purchase of property or capital stock under the Sherman Act, the Commission expressed no opinion.[126]

During the following ten years, this policy was followed and worked out in more detail as cases came before the commission. The review of the commission's actions in cases both in which complaints were dismissed and in which orders were issued discloses that it interpreted the Clayton Act as giving it no power over acquisitions involving no transfer of stock. In cases of acquisition of stock of the acquired corporation, the commission concluded that the Clayton Act gave it power to order the divestment of the stock and the *property* of the acquired corporation. If a corporation had acquired control of another corporation by means of a stock acquisition and had then transferred the assets, the commission's policy was to order divestment of the assets in order to remedy what it considered to be the evils of the stock acquisition—that is, the lessening of competition. This policy applied even though the assets had been transferred prior to the issuance of the complaint.

In several instances the commission utilized the authority, which it interpreted the Federal Trade Commission Act as giving it under Section 5, to issue complaints in cases in which assets were acquired prior to or in the absence of stock acquisition. Only one order of divestment of assets resulted, however, and that was against the Eastman Kodak Company, which had acquired the assets, according to the findings of the commission, as part of a conspiracy to thwart competition, rather than merely as an extension of its operations.[127]

In deciding to order divestment of assets acquired after and as a result of stock acquisition, the commission interpreted Section 7 to mean that Congress had intended to prevent the lessening of competition resulting from the acquisition of stock. The commission thus placed the emphasis on the lessening of competition, as if it were a general prohibition qualified merely by the provi-

[126] *Ibid.*, pp. 53–54.
[127] 7 F.T.C. 434.

sion that it must have resulted from a stock acquisition. The legislative history of Section 7, however, indicates that Congress intended, instead, to prohibit the creation of a holding company with the qualification that the holding company must be such as probably to lessen competition. The difference between these two points of view is subtle, but it played a highly important part in the administration of Section 7 and in its amendment.

Federal Trade Commission Policy on the Standard of Illegality —Consideration of the actions and reasoning of the commission in the six cases in which orders were issued and in the cases in which complaints were dismissed shows that during this early period no clearly defined and consistent policy was developed on the meaning of the standard of illegality set forth in Section 7 by Congress. Throughout 1915 to 1926, the commission interpreted the criterion to require the existence, *prior* to an acquisition, of a substantial degree of competition *between* the acquiring and the acquired corporations. Substantial competition was required for a substantial lessening of competition to follow. The substitution of "may be" for "is" by Congress in the phrase "where the effect may be to substantially lessen competition" had no effect on the interpretation of the standard of illegality by the commission. There must have been actual—not just potential—competition prior to the acquisition. Nor was it sufficient that each of the corporations be engaged in interstate commerce: it was necessary that the competition be interstate in character.

The commission's test of whether substantial competition had existed prior to an acquisition differed from case to case. Throughout the period the commission intermixed two types of approaches to the question. In some cases it gave consideration to the structure of the market for the products sold or bought by the acquired and acquiring firms. In other cases it ignored completely the market as a whole and concentrated on the marketing of the products only by the firms in question.

In the Aluminum and the Thatcher cases the commission supported its conclusion that the law had been violated by its findings that the proportion of total national sales of the product in question made by the combined firm was 100 per cent in the case of Alcoa and about 70 per cent in the case of Thatcher.[128] Similarly, the commission considered the structure of the national market for the products in the Tobacco Products Corporation case, in which the complaint was dismissed due to the finding that the combined firm made only one-half of 1 per cent of the smoking tobacco sales and only 2.3 per cent of other tobacco sales in the national market.[129] No consideration was given in any of these cases to definition of the product. It was not recognized that the percentage of sales attributable to a particular firm of an arbitrarily defined product is not necessarily related to the degree of control held by the firm over the price at which it will sell its product. The commission gave no consideration to the effect that the existence in the market of other products might have on the price elasticity of demand for the product of the firm in question, if the products are substitutable to some degree.

In all three of these cases, the commission gave only secondary consideration to the relationship between the acquired and the acquiring firms. In other cases, however, the commission's decision to issue an order or to dismiss the complaint depended almost entirely on the relationship of the acquiring and acquired firms to each other, rather than to the market.[130] In these cases the commission limited itself to consideration of whether there had existed, prior to the acquisition, "substantial competition between the firms." For there to be "competition between the firms," the commission required that the two firms must have sold an almost completely homogeneous product in the same market—that is, in the same geographical areas, to the same customers or class of customers, and at approximately the same prices. This policy was most clearly enunciated in the three meat-packer cases that resulted in orders and in the International Shoe case.[131]

[128] See pp. 59–60, 71–72.

[129] See p. 81.

[130] See the previous discussions of the cases against Armour, Swift, Western Meat, and International Shoe companies, against which orders were issued; and the cases against American Agricultural Chemical, Standard Oil Co. of New York, Bordens Farm Products, Austin, Nichols & Co., Swift & Co. and United Dressed Beef, Standard Oil of New Jersey and the Holly Sugar Company, in which the complaints were dismissed.

[131] See pp. 62–70, 73–76.

The commission had thus adopted a policy of requiring, as a prerequisite of the illegality of an acquisition, the existence of a set of circumstances closely resembling what later came to be considered by economists to be the conditions of pure competition.[132] Thus, if each of the corporations had previously achieved sufficient monopoly power by operating in markets to some extent distinct from other firms, then their merger was considered not to lessen competition, irrespective of the relative position of each of the firms in the market for the general product-group.[133] It was not considered necessary that these conditions of homogeneity exist for all the products of the two corporations, nor for all the sales of any particular product. It was necessary merely that the preëxisting competition between the firms be substantial.[134]

In no case did the commission clearly exhibit how it decided whether, prior to the merger, competition between the firms was substantial. It apparently had not developed any definite criterion. Each member decided in each case according to his subjective judgment and frequently followed the advice of whoever was the chief counsel at the time. The differences of opinion among the five commissioners appear to have centered on this point. The result was a large number of dissents by the minority members, both on the issuance of orders and on the dismissal of complaints.

Although the commission had developed no consistent policy, several points of consideration were decisive in the various cases that came before it. In one case the chief counsel had expressed the opinion that the courts would not uphold an order unless each of the two corporations controlled more than 10 per cent of the sales of the industry.[135] In another case the commission acted on

---

[132] Ordinarily, of course, the term "pure competition" is used to describe the conditions of a market, whereas the commission limited its consideration to the conditions under which only the two firms sold to common customers.

[133] See pp. 80–82.

[134] It was only on the meaning of the word "substantial" that the commission's interpretation of the standard of illegality differed from the Supreme Court's in its review of the International Shoe case (*International Shoe Company* v. *Federal Trade Commission* [1930], 280 U.S. 291). See pp. 123–136.

[135] See p. 81.

the basis of the chief counsel's opinion that the law required that *both* corporations must have sold a large proportion of the total amount sold in a particular market, which had to be interstate in character.[136] In general, however, the commission issued an order if it could find several cities in more than one state in which both corporations sold the same or a very similar commodity to the same customers,[137] and dismissed the complaint if this could not be established.[138]

Thus the record of the administration of Section 7 by the Federal Trade Commission, before the initial Supreme Court test, indicates that the commission had developed a definite policy regarding its jurisdiction in cases involving asset acquisition, and therein had given specific content to the general statement of policy laid down by Congress. Having gone beyond the intent of Congress, however, it developed a policy soon to be rejected by the Supreme Court.[139]

The commission failed in its function, as an expert body, to implement and give specific content to the general language of the standard of illegality of the statute. In its all-important initial interpretation of Section 7 during these early years, the Federal Trade Commission developed no consistent, workable criteria for distinguishing between those stock acquisitions that were or were not in the public interest. As will be shown in the following chapter, the Supreme Court combined the various diverse policies of the commission itself into so narrow an interpretation of the standard of illegality that the commission found it impossible to administer Section 7 in the public interest.

---

[136] See p. 82.
[137] For example, the meat-packer cases and the International Shoe case.
[138] For example, the complaint against Austin, Nichols and Company.
[139] See pp. 109–111.

4. Judicial Interpretation of Section 7

The Supreme Court of the United States is the final arbiter of the meaning of the substantive provisions of the federal antitrust statutes. The Federal Trade Commission administered Section 7 of the Clayton Act for more than a decade before the Supreme Court interpreted the language of the statute. From 1926 through 1934, the court reviewed the decisions of the commission in several cases and established the policy followed by the commission in enforcing Section 7 until its amendment in 1950.

The impetus for the amendment came primarily from the Supreme Court decision that the commission was without power to order divestment of assets acquired as a result of an illegal stock acquisition. The court's interpretation of the standard of illegality of the statute was sufficient, in itself, to render Section 7 impotent as a means of supplementing the provisions of the Sherman Act in respect to corporate mergers.

Federal Trade Commission Jurisdiction over Asset Acquisitions

In a series of cases beginning with three decisions rendered together on November 23, 1926,[1] and ending with the Arrow-Hart

[1] *Federal Trade Commission* v. *Western Meat Co., Thatcher Manufacturing Co.* v. *Federal Trade Commission, Swift & Co.* v. *Federal Trade Commission* (1926), 272 U.S. 554.

and Hegeman case in 1934,[2] the Supreme Court reviewed the policy on acquisitions of assets, which the commission had developed during its first eleven years of administration of Section 7.

The Swift, Western Meat, and Thatcher Decisions—In 1922 and 1923 the commission had ordered in four cases the divestment of assets acquired, or about to be acquired, as a result of stock acquisitions.[3] The respondents in three cases appealed the order to a Circuit Court of Appeals, and the commission applied for enforcement in the fourth case.[4]

The Western Meat Company appealed to the Circuit Court of Appeals, Ninth Circuit. On September 2, 1924, that court upheld the commission in every particular.[5] In its opinion, the court did not discuss whether the commission had acted within its authority in ordering the divestment of the property as well as of the stock of the acquired company.

The Western Meat Company petitioned the court for a rehearing, which was granted. On February 17, 1925, the court modified its earlier decision by ordering the elimination from the Federal Trade Commission order of the prohibition against the transfer of the property of the acquired company to Western Meat Company.[6] In this opinion the court said:

> Section 11 empowers the Commission when convinced that any of the provisions of the act have been violated to order the persons so violating the same "to cease and desist from such violations *** in the manner and within the time fixed by said order." Thus is clearly expressed in the Clayton Act the evil which so far as concerns the present case is intended to be

[2] *Arrow-Hart & Hegeman Electric Company* v. *Federal Trade Commission* (1934), 291 U.S. 587.

[3] The four orders were against Armour & Co., Swift & Co., Western Meat Co., and Thatcher Manufacturing Co. See pp. 62–73.

[4] In the case of Armour & Co., the court granted a petition by the company to have the commission rehear the case for additional evidence. The court then granted a suspension of the case to await the decision by the Supreme Court in the Swift case. After that decision, the petition for review was dismissed and the commission rescinded its order on March 11, 1927. See *F.T.C. Annual Report, 1927*, p. 76.

[5] *Western Meat Company* v. *Federal Trade Commission* (1924), 1 Fed. Rept., 2d Ser., 95 (C.C.A., 9th Cir.).

[6] *Western Meat Company* v. *Federal Trade Commission* (1925, 4 Fed. Rept., 2d Ser., 223 (C.C.A., 9th Cir.).

remedied, namely, the holding by one corporation of stock in another corporation engaged in commercial business where the effect thereof is substantially to lessen competition, restrain competition, or tend to create a monopoly, and no enlargement of the Commission's power is contained in the authority given it to fix a time and prescribe the manner of ceasing and desisting from such violation.[7]

The Ninth Circuit Court thus construed the statute as prohibiting only the acquiring and holding of stock. It held that, although Section 11 gave the commission the power to prescribe a remedy, its power was limited to prescribing for the evil condemned in the law—the acquisition and ownership of *stock* under the specified conditions.

Because the commission had found the acquisition to be an unfair method of competition in violation of Section 5 of the Federal Trade Commission Act, and because this finding had been upheld by the circuit court in its first opinion, it remained for the court to decide whether the order of the commission was within the authority given the commission in that act. The opinion of the court said:

Nor is any authority given by the Federal Trade Commission Act to require the petitioner here to do more than to divest itself of its stock in the Nevada Packing Company. Section 5 of the Federal Trade Commission Act directs the Commission to prevent persons, partnerships or corporations from using unfair methods of competition, and it provides that such persons, partnerships or corporations complained of shall have the right to appear and show cause why they shall not be required "to cease and desist from the violation of the law so charged in said complaint." And in dealing with such unfair methods the power of the Commission is limited to an order requiring such person, partnership or corporation to cease and desist from using such unfair method of competition. There is in the Federal Trade Commission Act no expansion of the Trade Commission's powers, beyond the powers conferred by the Clayton Act, to deal with the petitioner here. Said the court in *Federal Trade Commission v. Beech-Nut Co.*, 257 U.S. 441, 453: "That act declares unlawful 'unfair methods of competition' and gives the Commission authority after hearing to make orders to compel the discontinuance of such methods." [8]

[7] 4 Fed. Rept., 2d Ser., 223, 224.
[8] 4 Fed. Rept. 2d Ser., 223, 224.

The court thus decided that Section 5 gave the commission no authority to order anything more than the divestment of stock. It substantiated that interpretation by referring to the Supreme Court decision in the Beech-Nut case; however, in the sentences directly following the foregoing quote in the circuit court opinion, the Supreme Court opinion read:

What shall constitute unfair methods of competition denounced by the act is left without precise definition. Congress deemed it better to leave the subject without precise definition, and to have each case determined upon its own facts, owing to the multifarious means by which it is sought to effectuate such schemes. The Commission, in the first instance, subject to the judicial review provided, had the determination of practices which come within the scope of the act.[9]

The circuit court explicitly ruled on the authority given the commission to order divestment of property. It was, however, implicitly reviewing the initial interpretation of Section 5 by the commission on whether the acquisition and continued ownership of property acquired through stock acquisition is an unfair method of competition. The circuit court implicitly answered the latter question in the negative when it ruled that Section 5 of the Federal Trade Commission Act did not authorize the commission to order divestment of stock so as to include assets, but gave no reasons for this ruling in its opinion.[10]

Circuit Judge Ross, who wrote the first opinion in the case, dissented from the modification:

---

[9] *Federal Trade Commission* v. *Beech-Nut Packing Co.* (1922), 257 U.S. 441, 453. The case centered on whether a scheme of retail price maintenance was in violation of Section 5 of the Federal Trade Commission Act.

[10] It is not surprising that the court made this construction without giving any reasons whatsoever for overruling the commission, when it is observed that, in its original decision in this case, the court upheld the commission's conclusion that the *stock* acquisition violated Section 5 of the Federal Trade Commission Act with this statement: "If the evidence sufficiently sustained the findings of fact made by the Commission, we are also of the opinion that the conclusion of the Commission, that the acts committed by the petitioner also constituted a violation of Section 5 of the *Sherman Act* [italics mine], was also proper. See *Standard Oil Co.* v. *United States,* 221 U.S. 1; *United States* v. *American Tobacco Co.,* 221 U.S. 179, and the numerous cases there cited." See 1 Fed. Rept., 2d Ser., 95, 98.

It is, I think, in effect leaving the theretofore active and substantial competition between the parties entirely eliminated, with the return of stock worth only the paper on which it is printed.[11]

His reasoning is not made explicit, but apparently Judge Ross was willing to interpret the *Clayton Act* as giving the commission power to order asset divestiture, without relying on the more general language of Section 5 of the Federal Trade Commission Act.

Swift and Company appealed the order against it to the Circuit Court of Appeals, Seventh Circuit, and on February 16, 1925, that court upheld the commission in every particular.[12] Section 5 of the Federal Trade Commission Act was not mentioned at all in the opinion, even though the order of the commission was based on a finding of violation of both Section 5 and Section 7.[13] Nor was the authority of the commission to order the divestment of property as well as stock questioned by the respondent. Swift and Company had based its petition only on the question of the commission's interpretation of the standard of illegality.

When the commission applied to the Third Circuit Court for enforcement of its order against the Thatcher Manufacturing Company, the company based its case on the claims that it had never acquired the stock of the three corporations in question, but had acquired their assets, the stock having been acquired by the president of the corporation as an individual, and that the commission did not have the power to order a divestment of property other than stock.[14] The court, on the first claim, ruled that the company had acquired the stock, although indirectly.[15] On the second, the opinion of the court said:

. . . we hold that the Act is remedial, not punitive. . . . Therefore the sole purpose of a valid order of the Commission must be to remedy, how-

---

[11] 4 Fed. Rept., 2d Ser., 223, 225.

[12] *Swift & Co.* v. *Federal Trade Commission* (1925), 8 Fed. Rept., 2d Ser., 595 (C.C.A., 7th Cir.).

[13] See p. 68.

[14] *Federal Trade Commission* v. *Thatcher Manufacturing Company* (1925, 5 Fed. Rept., 2d Ser., 615 (C.C.A., 3d Cir.).

[15] Judge Buffington dissented on the grounds that the original plan was for the acquisition of all the property of the acquired companies, and that it merely had the appearance of a stock acquisition plan. See 5 Fed. Rept., 2d Ser., 615, 622.

ever, the Commission must meet the situation as the offending corporation has made it. If it created the situation so as to defeat the statute, the offending party can not be heard to say that thereby the Commission is helpless and the law unenforcible. The familiar principal [*sic*] that a person cannot profit by his own unlawful act applies. Not in every case can the Commission reach property acquired through stock acquisition, but where, as in this case, the offending corporation has stripped the stock of its value and where, accordingly, the mere divesting itself of the stock would leave the corporation in full possession of the entire fruits of the forbidden transaction, we are of the opinion that the statute empowers the Commission to carry out its purpose by extending its hand to the property.[16]

Thus there were divergent opinions among three Circuit Courts of Appeals on the question of the authority of the commission to order divestment of assets, as well as stock, where it was agreed that the stock acquisitions constituted violations of Section 7 of the Clayton Act. The Ninth Circuit Court, on rehearing the petition of the Western Meat Company, ruled that neither the Clayton Act nor the Federal Trade Commission Act gave the commission authority for such an order. The Seventh Circuit Court approved such an order against Swift without giving explicit consideration to the question. And the Third Circuit Court, without considering the Federal Trade Commission Act, upheld the commission's interpretation of the Clayton Act—that it gave the commission authority to order divestment of any property acquired as a result of an illegal stock acquisition.[17]

The Supreme Court granted a writ of *certiorari* in all three cases and considered them jointly. On November 23, 1926, the Supreme Court rendered its opinion.[18] Regarding the power of the commission to order the divestment of physical property, the Supreme Court reversed the decisions of *each* of the lower courts.

[16] 5 Fed. Rept., 2d Ser., 615, 621.

[17] The Third Circuit Court had previously denied a petition of the commission to amend its order in the Aluminum case so as to enjoin Alcoa from acquiring the assets of the Aluminum Rolling Mill Company, of whose stock it had divested itself on the order of the commission, but in that case the commission had based its petition on the claim that the assets were being acquired by means of foreclosure on a fraudulent debt. The court held that the commission had not substantiated the claim of fraud. *Federal Trade Commission* v. *Aluminum Company of America* (1924), 299 Fed. Rept. 361 (C.C.A., 3d Cir.). See p. 61.

[18] 272 U.S. 554.

The court, in an opinion delivered by Justice McReynolds, distinguished between a situation in which the commission orders divestment of stock so as to include plant and property not yet transferred to the acquiring firm and a situation in which the transfer of plant and property had been made prior to the issuance of a complaint by the commission.

In discussing the Western Meat case, the opinion said:

> Without doubt the Commission may not go beyond the words of the statute properly construed, but they must be read in the light of its general purpose. Preservation of established competition was the great end which the legislature sought to secure.
>
> The order here questioned was entered when respondent actually held and owned the stock contrary to law. The Commission's duty was to prevent the continuance of this unlawful action by an order directing that it cease and desist therefrom and divest itself of what it had no right to hold. Further violations of the act through continued ownership could be effectively prevented only by requiring the owner wholly to divest itself of the stock and thus render possible once more free play of the competition which had been wrongfully suppressed. The purpose which the lawmakers entertained might be wholly defeated if the stock could be further used for securing the competitor's property. And the same result would follow a transfer to one controlled by or acting for the respondent.
>
> . . . Divestment of the stock must be actual and complete and may not be effected, as counsel for respondent admitted was intended, by using the control resulting therefrom to secure title to the possessions of the Packing Company and then to dissolve it. Properly understood, the order was within the Commission's authority, and the court below erred in directing the elimination therefrom of the above quoted words.[19]

With respect to the circuit court decision in the Thatcher Manufacturing Company case, the Supreme Court opinion stated:

> The court further ruled in effect, that as the stocks of the remaining three companies were unlawfully obtained and ownership of the assets came through them, the Commission properly ordered the holder so to dispossess itself of the properties as to restore prior lawful conditions. With this we cannot agree. When the Commission institutes a proceeding based upon the holding of stock contrary to Section 7 of the Clayton Act, its power is limited by Section 11 to an order requiring the guilty person to cease and desist from such violation, effectually to divest itself of the stock, and to

[19] 272 U.S. 554, 559–560.

make no further use of it. The act has no application to ownership of a competitor's property and business obtained prior to any action by the Commission, even though this was brought about through stock unlawfully held. The purpose of the act was to prevent continued holding of stock and the peculiar evils incident thereto. If purchase of property had produced an unlawful status a remedy is provided through the courts. . . . The Commission is without authority under such circumstances.[20]

The decision in the Swift case was almost identical to that in the Thatcher case. The opinion stated:

As all property and business of the two competing companies were acquired by the petitioner prior to the filing of the complaint, it is evident that no practical relief could be obtained through an order merely directing petitioner to divest itself of valueless stock. As stated in No. 213 [the Thatcher case], we are of opinion that under Sections 7 and 11 of the Clayton Act the Commission is without authority to require one who has secured title and possession of physical property before proceedings were begun against it to dispose of the same, although secured through an unlawful purchase of stock. The courts must administer whatever remedy there may be in such situation.[21]

Justice Brandeis wrote a dissenting opinion in which Chief Justice Taft and Justices Holmes and Stone concurred. Justice Brandeis said:

In my opinion, the purpose of Section 7 of the Clayton Act was not, as stated by the court, merely "to prevent continued holding of the stock and the peculiar evils incident thereto." It was also to prevent the peculiar evils resulting therefrom. The institution of a proceeding before the Commission under Section 7 does not operate, like an injunction, to restrain a company from acquiring the assets of the controlled corporation by means of the stock held in violation of that section. If, in spite of the commencement of such a proceeding, the company took a transfer of the assets, the Commission could, I assume, require a re-transfer of the assets, so as to render effective the order of divestiture of the stock. I see no reason why it should not, likewise, do this although the company succeeded in securing the assets of the controlled corporation before the Commission instituted a proceeding. Support for this conclusion may be found in Section 11, which provides for action by the Commission whenever it "shall have reason to believe that any person is violating *or has violated* any of the provisions" of the earlier sections. (Italics ours.)[22]

[20] 272 U.S. 554, 561.

[21] 272 U.S. 554, 563.

[22] 272 U.S. 554, 563–564. The apparent contradiction in the majority's reason-

The authority of the commission under Section 5 of the Federal Trade Commission Act was not considered in either the opinion or the dissent. In spite of the fact that in both the Western Meat and the Swift cases the commission had concluded that the acquisitions constituted a violation of Section 5, and in spite of the fact that the circuit court had ruled in the Western Meat case that the commission did not have the authority under Section 5 to order asset divestment, the Supreme Court said that Section 5 "is not presently important; the challenged orders sought to enforce obedience to Section 7 of the Clayton Act." [23]

This failure to consider whether the acquisition of assets by means of an illegal stock acquisition constitutes an unfair method of competition in violation of Section 5 of the Federal Trade Commission Act, and, if so, whether the commission has the authority to order divestment of assets so acquired, may be accounted for: the point had come up in the circuit court opinions only in the Western Meat case. This was the case in which the Supreme Court upheld the commission on the authority granted by the Clayton Act. Apparently the commission, hoping for a favorable interpretation of the Clayton Act, failed to press the issue of unfair methods of competition in the Swift case.

The Eastman Kodak Case—The question of whether the Federal Trade Commission could consider an asset acquisition as an unfair method of competition in violation of Section 5 of the Federal Trade Commission Act was directly raised for judicial determination when Eastman Kodak petitioned the Second Circuit Court of Appeals to revise an order of the commission.[24]

---

ing pointed out by Brandeis was removed in the Arrow-Hart & Hegeman case, subsequently considered in this section, wherein the court ruled that the commission could *under no conditions* order divestment of physical property.

[23] 272 U.S. 554, 557.

[24] The commission had held both the acquisition of three film laboratories and an agreement not to use them to be unfair methods of competition and had ordered Eastman Kodak to cease and desist from such agreement and also to divest itself of the three plants. *Eastman Kodak Company, et al.*, 7 F.T.C. 434 (F.T.C. Docket No. 977, April 18, 1924). See pp. 96–97.

The opinion of the court summed up the findings of the commission:

> . . . It is plain that what it all amounts to is this—One who by early arrival in the field, excellence of product and marketing skill, makes and sells over 90% of the native raw material, has no legal right to embark on the new business of finishing his own raw material. This is the first half of what has been done, and half of the proposition laid down by the Commission. The other half is this—if two sets of men are equipped to make pictures and one of them is equipped also to make raw film—it is unlawful for them to agree to divide the field of business, so that the raw film maker shall make all the film, and the other men shall make all the pictures.
>
> With the first proposition we do not agree, and hold that since corporate power exists, it was not and is not unlawful for Eastman Kodak Company to equip itself for or to enter upon the business of making pictures; but it was and is unlawful for the Commission to order that Company to divest itself of the factories or laboratories so lawfully acquired.[25]

Thus the court held that the commission had erred in finding the acquisition of the plants to be an unfair method of competition. It might be presumed that this would not apply to acquisition of assets under any and all circumstances and that the same court might consider an acquisition of assets by means of stock acquisition, where the effect has been shown to be a substantial lessening of competition, to be an unfair method of competition. This possibility, however, was made irrelevant by the fact that the court entertained the question of the commission's authority to issue an order of divestiture of assets aside from the other question. It held that the commission, not being a court but an administrative agency, could not exercise the judicial power of ordering "a citizen to sell property acquired in the course of business," in the absence of any express statutory grant of such power.

Circuit Judge Manton dissented. He said that the purchase of the laboratories was not a mere extension of the legitimate business of Eastman Kodak, but

> . . . was used as a powerful club by which the business of the members of the Association would be diminished or destroyed in case the agreement

[25] *Eastman Kodak Company et al.* v. *Federal Trade Commission* (1925), 7 Fed. Rept., 2d Ser., 994, 996 (C.C.A., 2d Cir.).

was violated. Both the purchase and holding of the laboratories in the manner described, coupled with the agreement entered into, was such action as amounted to a hindrance with free competition if, indeed, it did not create a monopoly. . . .

. . . The function of the Commission is to preserve competition and protect competitive business from further inroads by monopoly by preventing the use of unfair methods of competition before any act should be done or condition arise violative of the Anti-Trust Act. . . .

While the Commission is not a court and exercises no judicial power, it has the power in the proper case, to order a respondent to dispose of property acquired by it which it is found using as a means to unfair competition in trade. Indeed, it may order the disposing of the plant or property which it uses in part or whole in creating a monopoly. (*Federal Trade Commission v. Thatcher,* decided April, 1925, C. C. A.-3.)[26]

The Supreme Court granted a writ of *certiorari* on petition of the commission and rendered a decision a few months after the decision in the Swift, Western Meat, and Thatcher cases.[27] In an opinion delivered by Justice Sanford, the court affirmed the judgment of the circuit court. The opinion stated that it was not necessary to consider whether the commission was correct in concluding that the acquisition was an unfair method of competition. It focused attention on the question of the power of the commission to issue an order of divestment of the property, even if the acquisition and ownership did constitute an unfair method of competition.

The proceeding before the Commission was instituted under section 5 of the Federal Trade Commission Act, and its authority did not go beyond the provisions of that section. By these the Commission is empowered to prevent the using of "unfair methods of competition" in interstate and foreign commerce, and if it finds that "any unfair method of competition" is being used, to issue an order requiring the offender "to cease and desist from using such method of competition." The Commission exercises only the administrative functions delegated to it by the act, not judicial powers. . . . It has not been delegated the authority of a court of equity. And a circuit court of appeals on a petition to review its order is limited to the question whether or not it has properly exercised the administrative authority given it by the act, and may not sustain or award relief beyond the authority of

[26] 7 Fed. Rept., 2d Ser., 994, 998.

[27] *Federal Trade Commission* v. *Eastman Kodak Co. et al.* (1927), 274 U.S. 619.

the Commission; such review being appellate and revisory merely, and not an exercise of original jurisdiction by the court itself.

The question here presented is in effect ruled by *Federal Trade Commission v. Western Meat Co.*, 272 U.S. 554, 561, 563, in which the decisions in *Federal Trade Commission v. Thatcher Mfg. Co.* (C.C.A.), 5 F. (2d) 615, and *Swift & Co. v. Federal Trade Commission* (C. C. A.), 8 F. (2d) 595, that were relied upon by the Commission for the writ of certiorari, were reversed by this court. . . .

So here, the Commission had no authority to require that the Company divest itself of the ownership of the laboratories which it had acquired prior to any action by the Commission. If the ownership or maintenance of these laboratories has produced any unlawful status, the remedy must be administered by the courts in appropriate proceedings therein instituted.[28]

In a dissenting opinion in which Justice Brandeis joined, Justice Stone pointed out that in the Swift, Western Meat, and Thatcher decisions, the court had expressly limited its consideration to the power given the commission by the Clayton Act. Justice Stone then said:

It was not held that the Commission under no circumstances could compel the sale of physical property, and there was in fact a clear intimation in the opinion that under section 7 of the Clayton Act the acquisition of the property after a complaint had been filed against the corporation for illegal stock purchases would not find the Commission powerless.

. . . The Commission is directed upon finding that the method of competition under investigation is prohibited by the Act, to issue its order "requiring such person, partnership, or corporation to cease and desist from using such method of competition."

The powers thus broadly given sharply contrast with the specific enumeration of sections 7 and 11 of the Clayton Act. . . .

The comprehensive language of section 5 neither invites nor supports a narrow construction. It is general in terms, and in the authorized prevention of unfair methods of competition the Commission is not limited to any particular method of making its orders effective. . . . Nor does the fact that the Commission is not a court of equity lessen the power conferred upon it by the statute. It is of course essentially an administrative agency. . . . But it is likewise true that it cannot be denied powers granted by Congress merely because its orders resemble in form familiar equitable decrees. To make its want of equity powers ground for limiting those expressly conferred by the statute is to condemn all the orders ever made by the Commission. . . .

[28] 274 U.S. 619, 623–625.

> The conclusion seems to me unavoidable, therefore, that this case cannot be disposed of without determining whether the acquisition and retention of the film laboratories by the Eastman Co., under the circumstances disclosed by the record, constituted in itself or was a part of or a step in an unfair method of competition. Until that is determined we cannot say that the Commission was without power under section 5 to make any appropriate order to prevent the use of such methods.[29]

Thus, except in these dissenting opinions of Judge Manton and Justice Stone, the members of the judiciary were unwilling to grant that the commission might have the power to order divestment of physical property even if the acquisition and holding of such property comes within the meaning of "unfair methods of competition." The confusion and contradictions indicated in the judicial determination of the question may be attributed, perhaps, to the hesitancy on the part of the judiciary to recognize the quasi-judicial aspects of the functions of an administrative commission such as the Federal Trade Commission, and to the failure of its legal staff to present effectively its case.

In commenting on the Supreme Court decisions in the Eastman Kodak case, the *Annual Report* of the Federal Trade Commission said:

> This case and the three immediately preceding cases [Swift, Thatcher, and Western Meat] seem to very definitely decide that the commission is without authority under any circumstances to direct a divestiture of physical properties. The fact that the commission issues its complaint either under section 5 of the Federal Trade Commission act or under section 7 of the Clayton Act before the actual transfer of properties is made confers upon the commission no jurisdiction or gives it no authority to direct a disposition of physical properties that it does not have under the statutes. There is nothing in either statute which would indicate that the commission has the authority in one instance and not in the other.[30]

The majority opinions in these cases certainly did not contain anything that would indicate that the commission had the power under one statute and not under the other, and this was borne out in the Arrow-Hart and Hegeman case, considered later. There was, however, in the minority opinion of Judge Manton and in the

[29] 274 U.S. 619, 626–628.
[30] *F.T.C. Annual Report, 1927,* p. 67.

minority opinion of Justice Stone in the Eastman Kodak case a clear statement of the difference between the powers conferred by the two statutes. The Clayton Act specifically authorized the commission to order divestment of illegally held *stock*. The Federal Trade Commission Act, however, authorized the commission to make the initial determination of what constitutes an "unfair method of competition," and to issue an order requiring a respondent to "cease and desist from using such method of competition."

In the Gratz case, the Supreme Court had taken unto itself the power ultimately to determine which practices were to be included in the meaning of the words "unfair methods of competition." The majority opinion of the court said:

> They are clearly inapplicable to practices never before regarded as opposed to good morals because characterized by deception, bad faith, fraud or oppression, or as against public policy because of their dangerous tendency unduly to hinder competition or create monopoly.[31]

In a case in which the Supreme Court accepted the commission's findings that the union of the control of two corporations by means of acquisition of stock constituted a substantial lessening of competition, the commission could have made a strong case that the accomplishment of the same result by means of acquisition of assets would have a "dangerous tendency unduly to hinder competition or create monopoly." If the commission had not attempted to extend beyond the intent of Congress the authority granted it by the Clayton Act, and had attempted, instead, to obtain the court's approval of an interpretation of Section 5 as including the prohibition of some asset acquisitions, it might have succeeded. Rather than focusing on the nature of an administrative commission and its differences from a court of equity, the courts might have focused on the substantive provisions of the two statutes. In the Swift case, for example, the commission might have obtained approval of its order of divestment of assets, if it had argued that the asset transfers constituted a violation of Section 5. If the Supreme Court had agreed with

[31] *Federal Trade Commission* v. *Gratz* (1920), 253 U.S. 421.

that interpretation, then the power of the commission to order asset divestment would have been looked for in Section 5 rather than in Section 11.

The court at no time considered the question of whether an acquisition of assets could violate Section 5. In the Eastman Kodak case it considered the powers of the commission to be inadequate to deal with such an acquisition as a result of its earlier interpretations of Section 11 of the Clayton Act.

As was pointed out,[32] the Senate Committee on Interstate Commerce, which added Section 5 to the Federal Trade Commission Act, considered the provision to be a substitute for the specific prohibitions of the Clayton Bill. Section 5 was intended to be a broad and general statement of policy. In my opinion, it would not have been an unreasonable interpretation of the intent of Congress for the commission and the court to have declared an asset acquisition to be an unfair method of competition under circumstances such as those presented in the Eastman Kodak case, or in cases in which assets were acquired by means of an illegal stock acquisition.

The Arrow-Hart and Hegeman Case—In 1934 in a five to four decision, the Supreme Court dealt the apparent death blow to Section 7 of the Clayton Act by holding that even though a complaint was issued prior to the acquisition of properties, the commission could not order the divestment of the properties.[33]

In October, 1927, the Arrow-Hart and Hegeman Company, Inc., was organized as a holding company for the purpose of acquiring all the voting stock of the Arrow Electric Company and the Hart and Hegeman Manufacturing Company. Both corporations had been doing a nation-wide business in manufacturing and selling a full line of electrical wiring devices. According to the commission, Arrow-Hart and Hegeman, as a result of the acquisition, became the "largest producer of electrical wiring devices in the United States and all competition which had theretofore existed between the two operating companies was eliminated." The commission therefore issued a complaint in March,

[32] See pp. 54–56.
[33] 291 U.S. 587.

1928.[34] Before the commission had taken any testimony on this complaint, two new holding companies were organized and the stock of the two operating companies was assigned to these new holding companies, and the original holding company was dissolved. On or about December 31, 1928, the two operating companies and the two holding companies were merged under the laws of Connecticut. In June, 1929, the commission issued a supplemental complaint against the new firm, the Arrow-Hart and Hegeman Electric Company, Inc.[35]

The commission concluded that Section 7 had been violated and ordered the Arrow-Hart and Hegeman Electric Company to divest itself of the stock and manufacturing plants of either the Arrow company or of the Hart and Hegeman Company so as to retain none of the fruits of the merger.[36] The company petitioned the Second Circuit Court of Appeals to set aside the order of the commission. In an opinion delivered by Judge Manton, the court affirmed the order of the commission.[37]

> Congress intended to prevent, by section 7, a corporate control which could be concentrated by prohibited acquisition of stock. Wrongful acquisition of the stock facilitates a merger or consolidation of assets. When ordered to divest itself of stock, the utmost good faith should be used by a corporation in order to remove as far as possible the corporate concentration of ownership caused by the wrongful acquisition of stock. . . .
>
> But if the merger by transfer of assets is completed before the Federal Trade Commission filed its complaint, it cannot be attacked under the Clayton Act. Thatcher Mfg. Co. v. Federal Trade Commission (272 U.S. 554).[38]

Judge Manton observed, however, that after the original complaint had been issued, Arrow-Hart and Hegeman, Inc., "dictated and controlled the formation" of the consolidated company, the Arrow-Hart and Hegeman Electric Company. On the basis of the

[34] *F.T.C. Annual Report, 1932*, pp. 75–76.

[35] *Ibid.*

[36] *In the Matter of Arrow-Hart & Hegeman, Inc., and the Arrow-Hart & Hegeman Electric Company*, 16 F.T.C. 393, 421–423 (F.T.C. Docket No. 1498, July 6, 1932).

[37] *Arrow-Hart & Hegeman Electric Co.* v. *Federal Trade Commission*, 65 Fed. Rept., 2d Ser., 336 (C.C.A., 2d Cir.).

[38] 65 Fed. Rept., 2d Ser., 336, 338–339.

Supreme Court decision in the Western Meat case, he concluded that the commission had the authority to issue the order requiring divestment of property.[39] Judge Augustus Hand concurred in the majority opinion, but Judge Swan dissented on the grounds that the commission had exceeded its authority.[40]

In an opinion delivered by Justice Roberts, the Supreme Court reversed the circuit court decision. Justice Stone wrote a dissenting opinion with which Chief Justice Hughes, Justice Brandeis, and Justice Cardozo concurred.[41] The majority opinion said:

> The Commission is an administrative body possessing only such powers as are granted by statute. It may make only such orders as the act authorizes; may order a practice to be discontinued and shares held in violation of the act to be disposed of; but, that accomplished, has not the additional powers of a court of equity to grant other and further relief by ordering property of a different sort to be conveyed or distributed, on the theory that this is necessary to render effective the prescribed statutory remedy. Compare *Federal Trade Commission v. Eastman Kodak Co.*, 274 U.S. 619, 623.[42]

The Court thus held explicitly that the commission could under no circumstances order the divestment of physical property. This ruling was reconciled with the Western Meat decision in the following manner:

> Where shares acquired in violation of the act are still held by the offending corporation an order of divestiture may be supplemented by a provision that in the process the offender shall not acquire the property represented by the shares. *Federal Trade Commission v. Western Meat Co.*, 272 U.S. 554. In the present case the stock which had been acquired contrary to the act was no longer owned by the holding company when the Commission made its order.[43]

This interpretation of the powers of the commission had the effect of requiring that the commission proceed with such haste as to be able to issue an order, rather than merely a complaint, before the acquiring company can use the acquired stock to com-

[39] 65 Fed. Rept., 2d Ser., 336, 339.
[40] 65 Fed. Rept., 2d Ser., 336, 340.
[41] *Arrow-Hart & Hegeman Electric Company* v. *Federal Trade Commission* (1934), 291 U.S. 587.
[42] 291 U.S. 587, 598–599.
[43] 291 U.S. 587, 599.

plete the acquisition of the physical properties and then dissolve the acquired corporation.

The four dissenting justices, however, gave a much broader interpretation to the purpose of the legislation and also to the jurisdiction of the commission, as had the majority of the circuit court judges. Justice Stone said:

> While this proceeding was pending before the Federal Trade Commission to compel a holding company to divest itself of the controlling common stock of two competing corporations which it had acquired in violation of Section 7 of the Clayton Act, that stock was used to effectuate a merger of the competing corporations. It is now declared that, however gross the violation of the Clayton Act, however flagrant the flouting of the Commission's authority, the celerity of the offender, in ridding itself of the stock before the Commission could complete its hearings and make an order restoring the independence of the competitors, leaves the Commission powerless to act against the merged corporation. . . .
>
> . . . It is true that the Clayton Act does not forbid corporate mergers, but it does forbid the acquisition by one corporation of the stock of competing corporations so as substantially to lessen competition. It follows that mergers effected as they commonly are, through such acquisition of stock necessarily involve violations of the act, as this one did. . . .
>
> . . . an examination of the legislative history of the Clayton Act, and that of the earlier Sherman Act, can leave no doubt that the former was aimed at the acquisition of stock by holding companies not only as itself a means of suppressing competition but as the first and usual step in the process of merging competing corporations by which a suppression of competition might be unlawfully perpetuated. . . . It seems plain, therefore, that the illegality involved in acquiring the common stock of the competing companies, which was the first step toward the merger, was neither lessened nor condoned by taking the next and final steps in completing it.[44]

The minority of the Supreme Court thus held that the purpose of the section was more than merely to remedy the ill effects resulting from the continued holding of acquired stock. They considered the purpose of the legislation to include the remedying of the ill effects resulting from the use of the stock for the short period in which it was held. The question remained, however, of deciding whether Congress had provided the commission with the authority to achieve the latter remedy. The majority opinion

[44] 291 U.S. 587, 599–601.

had stated that the commission could under *no* circumstances order the divestment of physical properties already acquired. The minority opinion said:

> It is true that the holding company divested itself of the stock of the two competing operating companies before the Commission had an opportunity to make its order; but it does not follow that it had done all that the Commission could command and that thus the statute was satisfied. Mere divestment of the stock is not enough. The manner of divestment is likewise subject to the requirements of the Clayton Act. This Court has recognized that the purpose of the act is to restore the competition suppressed by the acquisition of the stock and has specifically held, over objections such as are now made, that the Commission has power not only to order divestment but to prescribe that it shall be done in a manner that will restore competition. *Federal Trade Commission* v. *Western Meat Co.*, 272 U.S. 554. . . .
>
> Just as in that case we upheld the Commission's order directing the surrender of one of the fruits of the wrongful stock ownership—the power to place a competing unit under the offender's combination—so should we now sustain the order commanding relinquishment of another of the fruits of that ownership—the accomplished merger.
>
> . . . In this, as in most schemes for regulation by administrative bodies, there must be a balance between the general and the particular. When courts are faced with interpretation of the particular, administration breaks down and the manifest purpose of the legislature is defeated unless it is recognized that, surrounding granted powers, there must be a penumbra which will give scope for practical operation.[45]

In answer to the argument that the commission was without authority to order divestment of physical property because of its administrative character, the minority opinion stated:

> It is true that the Commission is an administrative body, and not a court. But it exercises many of the powers conventionally deemed judicial. It is authorized to bring offenders before it to determine whether they are violators of the act and, if so, "to enforce compliance" by commanding that the violation cease. There is as much reason to believe that Congress did not intend to deny to the Commission the authority to exercise effectively the granted power, and thus to preserve its jurisdiction until its function could be executed, as there would be were similar powers extended to a court of inferior jurisdiction. . . . Recognition of its authority involves neither departure from accepted principles nor any risk of abuse.[46]

---

[45] 291 U.S. 587, 601, 606–607.

[46] 291 U.S. 587, 606–607.

In view of this well-reasoned minority opinion, concurred in by four of the nine Supreme Court justices, and in view of the fact that this acquisition was finally carried out as a statutory merger, it seems likely that in later years, if other cases had been brought to the Supreme Court, the court would have followed the minority opinion, especially in cases in which one corporation bought the stock of another and then transferred the assets after the issuance of a complaint by the commission. As will be seen in the following chapter, however, the commission accepted its defeat as final and concentrated on having the act amended rather than on attempting to have the court reverse its decision.

Judicial Construction of the Standard of Illegality

The Supreme Court reviewed the commission's interpretation of the meaning of the standard of illegality of Section 7 in only one case—the International Shoe Company case in 1930.[47] Before that decision in several cases, and afterward in two cases, the circuit courts reviewed the commission's policy.

Initial Circuit Court Review—In its review of the commission's order against the Aluminum Company of America, the Third Circuit Court of Appeals held that a lessening of competition is not necessarily synonymous with a tendency toward monopoly.[48] The latter might result even without lessening of competition between the acquiring and the acquired corporation. The court also held that it was not necessary for competition actually to have existed between the two corporations for the result to be a substantial lessening of competition, since the law contemplated potential as well as actual competition. Judge Buffington dissented in the aluminum case, maintaining that the law required that two corporations must have competed prior to the acquisition for the acquisition to be illegal.[49]

[47] *International Shoe Company* v. *Federal Trade Commission* (1930), 280 U.S. 291.

[48] *Aluminum Company of America* v. *Federal Trade Commission* (1922), 284 Fed. Rept. 401 (C.C.A., 3d Cir.).

[49] 284 Fed. Rept. 401, 409.

As was seen in the last chapter, the commission did not take advantage of the liberal interpretation given by the majority of the circuit court in this case. The commission's policy, as exemplified in the findings of fact and conclusions drawn in the meatpacker and the Thatcher cases following this decision, was to accept the necessity of showing the existence of actual competition between the acquired and the acquiring firms prior to the acquisitions. The commission also frequently treated a lessening of competition and a tendency toward monopoly as synonymous. Thus in the succeeding instances of judicial interpretation of the standard of illegality, the circuit courts were reviewing orders of the commission based on a much more restrictive interpretation of the language of the statute than that of the circuit court in the Aluminum case. The result was that, even though the commission won the victory of having its interpretation upheld, it later found its range of action narrowly circumscribed.

In the Western Meat Company case, the Ninth Circuit Court of Appeals agreed with the commission's findings that there had been preëxisting, active, and substantial competition between the Western Meat Company and the Nevada Packing Company, and the acquisition had the effect, therefore, of substantially lessening that competition.[50]

In its review of the commission's order against the Thatcher Manufacturing Company, the Third Circuit Court of Appeals did not review the evidence concerning the effect of three of the four acquisitions, but merely said that the evidence sustained the finding that the effect was such as was contemplated by the statute.[51] However, the acquisition of the Woodbury Company, the court pointed out, did not have the effect of substantially lessening competition, restraining commerce, and tending to create a monopoly, since that company had produced only a small quantity of milk bottles compared to national production. Its primary business had been in fruit juice, condiment, and soft-

---

[50] *Western Meat Company* v. *Federal Trade Commission* (1924), 1 Fed. Rept., 2d Ser., 95 (C.C.A., 9th Cir.).

[51] *Federal Trade Commission* v. *Thatcher Manufacturing Company* (1925), 5 Fed. Rept., 2d Ser., 615 (C.C.A., 3d Cir.).

drink bottles, and fruit jars, whereas the acquiring company was primarily engaged in the milk bottle business. Thus the court followed the commission's own definition of the product in question—that is, milk bottles rather than glass containers in general. It also followed the commission's policy of requiring that the acquiring and the acquired corporations must have been in substantial competition with each other prior to the acquisition. It differed only in its interpretation of what constitutes "substantial" preëxisting competition. Neither the commission nor the court considered whether the Woodbury Company might have *potentially* competed to a greater extent in the sale of milk bottles. Nor was consideration given to the degree to which the expansion of Thatcher's operations into the manufacture and sale of other types of bottles might tend to create a monopoly.

In its petition to have the order against it set aside, Swift and Company based its case in part on the argument that Section 7 was unconstitutional unless the court read into it the rule of reason—that is, unless the court interpreted the standard of illegality to mean that preëxisting substantial competition was required along with an effect injurious to the public interest.[52] The Seventh Circuit Court of Appeals, which in this case interpreted the Clayton Act broadly enough to give the commission power to order asset divestiture, interpreted the standard of illegality much as had been done in the Aluminum case. It said that lessening of competition, restraint of trade in a section, and tendency to create a monopoly were separate and alternative standards, although the commission itself had not made this explicit. The court unambiguously stated that the standard set forth in the Clayton Act was separate from and less stringent than the Sherman Act criterion. The court, however, did not deny the necessity of showing that substantial competition must have existed prior to the acquisition. It merely accepted the judgment of the commission that, even though the acquired companies slaughtered only 1 per cent of the total number of hogs and cattle slaughtered in the United States, there was preëxisting substantial

[52] *Swift & Co.* v. *Federal Trade Commission* (1925), 8 Fed. Rept., 2d Ser., 595 (C.C.A., 7th Cir.).

competition, since the acquired companies were the only competitors of the "big four" meat packers in the southeastern section of the United States.

The International Shoe Company Case—From the standpoint of the judicial interpretation of the standard of illegality, the International Shoe Company case was by far the most important. The commission had found the acquisition by International of the McElwain Shoe Company to be in violation of the Clayton Act and had ordered International to divest itself of the stock and assets of the acquired company.[53] The International Shoe Company petitioned the First Circuit Court of Appeals to review the order of the commission, and the court sustained the commission.[54]

The company argued that "no such case of monopoly or damage to the public interest is made out as would ground a case under the Sherman Act." [55] In the opinion of the court, this argument was answered by the fact that the case was brought under the Clayton Act, and the two acts have different standards. The company did not dispute the findings of the commission, but it maintained that the commission had drawn incorrect inferences from the facts. The court ruled that the conclusions of the commission were fully supported by testimony. The commission had maintained that there had been substantial competition between the two concerns prior to the acquisition; the court held this to be a fair inference from the testimony. Thus, whether the statute required substantial competition prior to the acquisition was again not in contention. In its petition the company maintained

> . . . that the McElwain Company was then insolvent, in the sense that "it was unable to pay its debts as they came due," and that therefore it was no longer a potential or prospective competitor.[56]

The court held that this contention was not well founded since the several alternative outcomes of the financial plight of the

---

[53] See pp. 73–76.

[54] *International Shoe Company* v. *Federal Trade Commission* (1928), 29 Fed. Rept., 2d Ser., 518 (C.C.A., 1st Cir.).

[55] 29 Fed. Rept., 2d Ser., 518, 523.

[56] 29 Fed. Rept., 2d Ser., 518, 521.

McElwain company would have kept it operating and in competition with International, if the acquisition had not taken place. The opinion suggested that the bank creditors might have carried the concern, that competition under the management of receivers might have been even greater, or that the preferred stockholders might have assumed the management, if bankruptcy actually had occurred.[57]

The International Shoe Company was granted a writ of *certiorari* by the Supreme Court, which reversed the circuit court.[58] The principal grounds on which the company assailed the order were that there had not been substantial competition between the two companies prior to the acquisition, and therefore no possibility of a substantial lessening of competition, and that the financial condition of the McElwain Company at the time of the acquisition necessitated sale or liquidation, making the prospect of future competition or restraint impossible. The court held that these grounds were determinative and, therefore, found it unnecessary to consider any other issues.[59]

The commission itself, in spite of the liberality of the initial interpretation of the section by the circuit court in the Aluminum case, had evolved a policy that recognized the necessity of establishing preëxisting substantial competition, and that placed emphasis on the relationship between the two corporations in those cases where it appeared that the conditions of the market for the products of the two corporations would make the acquisition significant in that market structure.[60] The commission was, therefore, in this case in no position to argue that the law did not require proof of preëxisting substantial competition. Nor could the commission deny the relevancy of considering the over-all market structure for the products in question due to its own policies in *other* cases. The court was thus in the position of being able to use the very policy that the commission had developed. The issue was merely whether the subjective judgment of the

[57] 29 Fed. Rept., 2d Ser., 518, 521.

[58] *International Shoe Company* v. *Federal Trade Commission* (1930), 280 U.S. 291.

[59] 280 U.S. 291, 294.

[60] See pp. 100–103.

court on the substantialness of the preëxisting competition between the two firms would agree with the subjective judgment of the commission. The court, unlike the commission, attempted to give a legal rationalization of its judgment.

It is true that both companies were engaged in selling dress shoes to customers for resale within the limits of several of the same States; but the *markets* [italics mine] reached by the two companies within these States, with slight exceptions hereinafter mentioned, were not the same.[61]

The court was here saying that if the two companies were not engaged in selling in the same markets, then competition could not exist between them, and, therefore, could not be lessened substantially. What did the word "market" mean to the court? The answer is given explicitly.

Certain substitutes for leather were used to some extent in the making of the McElwain dress shoes; and they were better finished, more attractive and modern in appearance, and appealed especially to city trade. The dress shoes of the International were made wholly of leather and were of a better wearing quality; but among the retailers who catered to city or fashionable wear, the McElwain shoes were preferred. The trade policies of the two companies so differed that the McElwain Company generally secured the trade of wholesalers and large retailers; while the International obtained the trade of dealers in the small communities. When requested, the McElwain company stamped the name of the customer (that is the dealer) upon the shoes, which the International refused to do; and this operated to aid the former company to get, as generally it did, the trade of the retailers in the larger cities. As an important result of the foregoing circumstances, witnesses estimated that about 95 per cent of the McElwain sales were in towns and cities having a population of 10,000 or over; while about 95 per cent of the sales of the International were in towns having a population of 6,000 or less. . . . An analysis of the sales of the International for the twelve months preceding the acquisition of the McElwain capital stock, discloses that in 42 States no men's dress shoes were sold to customers of the McElwain company; and that in the remaining six States during the same period a total of only 52$\frac{5}{12}$ dozen pairs of such shoes had been sold to sixteen retailers and three wholesalers who were customers of the McElwain company. This amounted to less than one-fourth of the production of dress shoes by the International for a single day. . . .[62]

[61] 280 U.S. 291, 295.
[62] 280 U.S. 291, 301–302.

Thus the court was saying that for substantial competition to exist between two firms, they must be selling in a market characterized by most of the conditions of *pure competition*—that is, the two firms must be selling a homogeneous product that must account for somewhat more than 5 per cent of the sales of each of the two firms, if the firms sell more than one product. In addition to these requirements, the previously quoted part of the opinion implies that the degree of competition can be measured by the degree to which the two firms sell to the *same customers.* According to this reasoning, it is relevant to inquire not only into the degree to which the products of the two firms are undifferentiated and therefore are *capable* of satisfying the same wants of all consumers, but also to inquire into the degree to which the same customers *actually* purchase products from both firms. The idea that competition exists to some extent between two firms if some marginal portion of the demand for the general type of product can be satisfied by either of the two firms was foreign to the reasoning of the court.

Needless to say, the court also ignored the possibility that competition might be lessened by the removal from the market of a firm that has the potential capacity to offer for sale a product with characteristics and price such that a significant proportion of the customers of the acquiring firm might have shifted their purchases to the acquired firm. The court was not even willing to concede that the McElwain Company might potentially compete with International Shoe to the same extent that it had in the past. The court held that its financial condition would make the probability of continued operation very small.[63]

The majority of the Supreme Court concluded:

> Thus it appears that in respect of 95 percent of the business there was no competition in fact and no contest, or observed tendency to contest, in the market for the same purchasers; and it is manifest that, when this is eliminated, what remains is of such slight consequence as to deprive the finding that there was substantial competition between the two corporations, of any real support in the evidence.[64]

---

[63] 280 U.S. 291, 301–302.

[64] 280 U.S. 291, 297.

Having accepted the commission's interpretation of Section 7 as requiring the showing of preëxisting substantial competition, and having set forth the meaning of "competition between the firms," on what basis did the court decide that the amount of such competition was insubstantial? At this point the court relied upon the Sherman Act test—the rule of reason—saying:

> Section 7 of the Clayton Act, as its terms and the nature of the remedy prescribed plainly suggest, was intended for the protection of the public against the evils which were supposed to flow from the undue lessening of competition.
>
> Mere acquisition by one corporation of the stock of a competitor, even though it result in some lessening of competition, is not forbidden; the act deals only with such acquisitions as probably will result in lessening competition to a substantial degree . . . that is to say, to such a degree as will injuriously affect the public. . . . If it be conceded that the entire remaining 5 percent of each company's product (although clearly it was materially less than that) was sold in competitive markets, it is hard to see in this, competition of such substance as to fall within the serious purposes of the Clayton Act.[65]

This conclusion of the majority of the court was supported by the addition of the following statement, which discloses the problems encountered in the interpretation by the court, rather than by an expert administrative agency, of a statute concerned with the legal framework in which economic institutions are to be allowed to develop:

> In addition to the circumstances already cited, the officers of the International testified categorically that there was in fact no substantial competition between the companies in respect of these shoes, but that at most competition was incidental and so imperceptible that it could not be located. The existence of competition is a fact disclosed by observation rather than by the processes of logic; and when these officers, skilled in the business which they have carried on, assert that there was no real competition in respect of the particular product, their testimony is to be weighed like that in respect of other matters of fact. And since there is no testimony to the contrary and no reason appears for doubting the accuracy of observation or credibility of the witnesses, their statements should be accepted.[66]

[65] 280 U.S. 291, 297–299.

[66] 280 U.S. 291, 299.

Justice Stone, in a dissenting opinion with which Justices Holmes and Brandeis concurred, expressed the view that the majority were preëmpting the function of the commission.

Under sec. 11 . . . the findings of the Commission "if supported by testimony" and the inferences which it may reasonably draw from the facts proved or admitted, are conclusive upon us. . . . Congress has thus forbidden the substitution of the judgment of the courts for that of the Commission where it is founded upon evidence. Conforming to this requirement I cannot say that its conclusions here lack the prescribed support. Even without such statutory limitation this court will not set aside the findings of an administrative board or commission, upheld, as in the present case, by the reviewing court below, unless the record establishes that clear and unmistakable error has been committed.[67]

Justice Stone also recognized that some element of logic must enter into the determination of the existence of substantial competition. He disagreed with the logical reasoning process by which the majority interpreted the facts, saying:

The opinion of the court and the general testimony of petitioner's officers of their conclusions that there was no competition between the two corporations . . . seem to proceed on the assumption that manufacturers, each engaged in marketing a product comparable in price and adapted to the satisfaction of the same need, do not compete if they do not sell to the same distributors.

Without stating it in detail there appears to me to be abundant evidence that the competitive products made by two of the largest shoe manufacturers in the world, reached the same local communities through different agencies of distribution; the one, of petitioner, through sales directly to retailers throughout the United States, the other, of the McElwain company, through sales in thirty-eight States, chiefly to wholesalers located in cities, who in turn sold to the retail trade. From detailed evidence of this type the Commission drew, as I think it reasonably might, the inference that the rival products, through local retailers, made their appeal to the same buying public and so were competitive. . . .

. . . The inference from this evidence seems irresistible that . . . the competing products were not only offered through different systems of distribution to the same retailers, but were by them offered and sold to the ultimate consumers in their communities. Both products being made and suitable for the same use, the fact that each presented some minor ad-

[67] 280 U.S. 291, 303.

vantages over the other, it might reasonably be inferred, would tend to increase, rather than diminish the competition.[68]

Thus the minority was unwilling to interpret Section 7 to require preëxisting substantial *pure* competition. Justice Stone indicated that he interpreted the law to require substantial competition between the acquired and the acquiring firms prior to the acquisition, if the conclusion is to be drawn that competition might be substantially lessened by the acquisition; but he interpreted substantial competition to mean the existence of a situation in which the two firms are offering for sale products of the same general type, capable of satisfying similar uses, to the same general group of potential customers. A market situation characterized by the conditions of monopolistic competition, particularly if the acquired and the acquiring firms are among the largest firms in the market, would appear to satisfy the requirement of preëxisting substantial competition.

Justice Stone was not willing to agree with the majority view on the financial straits of the McElwain Company. He said that testimony supported the commission's conclusion on the probability of the company continuing to compete with International.[69] The commission, the majority of the court, and the minority appear to have accepted without question the proposition that, if the acquired company had been in such financial straits as to preclude it from continuing in operation, then the acquisition would not substantially lessen competition, restrain trade in a section, or tend to create a monopoly of a line of commerce. Aside from whether such an interpretation of the Clayton Act would be desirable public policy, a further question must be raised: can a policy of excepting such an acquisition reasonably be defended on the ground that it could not possibly have the condemned effect?

Such an interpretation of the criterion of illegality appears to involve a contradiction. The court held that for an acquisition to have the effect of substantially lessening competition, it must be

[68] 280 U.S. 291, 303–305.
[69] 280 U.S. 291, 306.

shown that it would probably result in lessening competition in the industry to a substantial degree—that is, to such a degree as will injuriously affect the public. This means that, even with respect to the first part of the criterion dealing with the relationship between the two corporations, the degree of competition in the market must be considered. If, however, the acquired firm can be shown to be on the verge of leaving the market anyway, then the effect of the acquisition is considered irrelevant, even though the acquisition may result in a lessening of competition.

This interpretation of the standard of illegality to preserve for the firm the right in failing circumstances to make the most profitable disposition of its property can be attributed, perhaps, to the tendency of the court to interpret the law in such a way as to cause a minimum infringement of the rights of property. In the discussions of the amendment to Section 7 in 1950, Congress accepted and reiterated this statement of policy by the Supreme Court.[70] It may be desirable public policy to resolve a conflict between the goals of maintenance of competition and maintenance of property rights by exempting such acquisitions from the prohibitions of Section 7. One cannot logically conclude, however, that a merger under such circumstances necessarily will not lessen competition between the firms or in the markets in which the firms have operated.

The question of the probable effect on competition of an acquisition by one corporation of a corporation in financial distress can be answered only by comparing the circumstances that probably would result if the acquisition were allowed to the circumstances that probably would result if it were prohibited. Conceivably, the market conditions may be such that a particular acquisition may increase or have no effect on competition. On the other hand, if entry into a market is difficult, and if the demand for the product is considerably less than perfectly elastic, then the merger of two of several firms in the market might result in less competition than had previously existed. If the only alternative to merger for the acquired firm is to withdraw from the

---

[70] See p. 266.

market, then the acquisition would result in no less competitive a situation than would exist if the acquisition were prohibited.

In such an instance, however, several alternatives—albeit, not as profitable to the acquired firm—could be expected to result in more competition than if the acquisition were allowed. For example, in a dynamic economy with the passage of time, the firm might recover from its precarious financial position and continue as a factor in the market. The failing firm might be reorganized and continue as an independent firm. Competition might be decreased less, or even increased, if the failing firm were to be acquired by another firm in the market, but a firm with less power than the one attempting to make the acquisition. The financial distress of the firm in question might provide a means of easy entry into the market for an outside firm. The financial condition of the acquired firm thus appears to be only one of many important factors to be considered in ascertaining the probable effect of an acquisition.[71]

In the International Shoe case, the financial plight of the McElwain Company was only incidental in the reasoning of the court, which undoubtedly would have ruled against the commission even if the acquired firm had been operating profitably. The argument of the majority of the court regarding financial distress, however, became as much a part of the law as if it had been included by Congress.

The Supreme Court decision in this case placed on the ability of the Federal Trade Commission to administer Section 7 a restriction that was equally as great, if not greater, than the restriction resulting from the Arrow-Hart and Hegeman case. Indeed, even if the court had recognized the authority of the commission to order the divestment of physical property acquired as a result of an acquisition of stock, it is doubtful that the commission would have been able to bring any case to a successful conclusion without a change in the interpretation of the standard

---

[71] See chap. 9.

of illegality rendered by the court in the International Shoe case.[72]

The opinion of the Supreme Court said, in effect, that, if two firms have previously achieved sufficient monopoly power by a location advantage or by differentiation of product, then substantial competition did not exist between them and therefore cannot be substantially lessened, nor can commerce be restrained in the sections in which they operate. If the two firms had been selling the bulk of their products in the same geographical areas and if their products were homogeneous, then the test becomes that of whether the acquisition has had the effect of injuring the public —that is, by unreasonable restraint of trade. The Sherman Act test would thus be applied. If many other firms sell a considerable proportion of the same homogeneous product, then the acquisition would be deemed not to injure the public, even though competition *between* the firms would have been established as having existed prior to the acquisition and would have been completely eliminated.

With this interpretation of the standard of illegality, the only condemned acquisition would be an acquisition by a relatively large firm of another relatively large firm where there were few other firms in the industry and where the two firms sold completely homogeneous products in the same geographical areas to the same customers. If such an acquisition were to take place, however, the test applied under Section 7 of the Clayton Act would be the same as that applied if violation of the Sherman Act had been charged.

After the International Shoe Company decision in 1930, Sections 7 and 11 of the Clayton Act served merely to give the Federal Trade Commission jurisdiction over stock acquisitions, with less power to remedy the ill effects than existed under the Sher-

[72] See chap. v for a discussion of the administration of Section 7 by the commission subsequent to the court interpretation.

The 1950 Amendment of Section 7 (64 *U.S. Stat. at L.* 1134) changed the language of the standard of illegality. See chap. 7. In addition, the Supreme Court reinterpreted the original statute in *United States* v. *E. I. du Pont de Nemours and Co. et al.* (1957), 353 U.S. 586. See chap. 8.

man Act. Yet in achieving this result by its interpretation of Section 7, the Supreme Court had added nothing essentially different to the policy evolved by the commission itself.

Later Circuit Court Cases—Within two years after the International Shoe decision by the Supreme Court, two other cases involving the interpretation of the standard of illegality were decided by circuit courts on petition by the respondents for review of the orders of the commission.[73]

On October 11, 1928, the commission issued a complaint against the Temple Anthracite Coal Company alleging that the acquisition in 1924 by the respondent of all the capital stock of the Temple Coal Company and of 98 per cent of the outstanding stock of the East Bear Ridge Colliery Company had an effect that "may be and is to substantially lessen competition between said Temple Coal Co. and East Bear Ridge Colliery Co." in violation of Section 7 of the Clayton Act.[74]

The commission found that the two acquired firms had been engaged in mining and selling the same grades and sizes of anthracite coal. The two companies were thus selling a homogeneous product. Both companies sold about 25 per cent of their output to customers in the state of Pennsylvania. The remainder was sold to customers in other states, Canada, and the District of Columbia. The commission set forth in detail the volume and destination of the sales of each company during three years. The Temple company sold all its output through or to Thorne, Neale and Company, Inc., a sales agency. The East Bear Ridge company sold all its output to or through Madiera, Hill and Company, another sales agency. The commission found that the two sales companies competed with each other, selling the same kinds and sizes of coal in the same geographical areas and in some instances to the same customers.[75] The commission had thus established that there had existed, prior to the acquisitions, competition between

[73] *Temple Anthracite Coal Company* v. *Federal Trade Commission* (1931), 51 Fed. Rept., 2d Ser., 656 (C.C.A., 3d Cir.), and *V. Vivaudou, Inc.*, v. *Federal Trade Commission* (1931), 54 Fed. Rept., 2d Ser., 273 (C.C.A., 2d Cir.).

[74] *In the Matter of Temple Anthracite Coal Co.* (1930), 13 F.T.C. 249, 250–251 (F.T.C. Docket No. 1537, March 8, 1930).

[75] 13 F.T.C. 249, 251–260.

the two firms within the meaning of "competition" as set forth in the International Shoe decision. Without examining the market as a whole for the product, however, the commission concluded that the acquisition had substantially lessened the competition between the two firms.[76] It therefore ordered the holding company to divest itself of the stock of one or the other of the two acquired corporations.[77]

Commissioner Humphrey dissented from the order on the grounds that the complaint did not allege nor did the commission conclude "that the acquisition of the stock referred to by the respondent in any way tended to restrain commerce, tended to create a monopoly, or was or may be injurious to the public." [78] Commissioner Humphrey correctly stated:

> Under the decision of the United States Supreme Court in the recent case of the International Shoe Co., an order to cease and desist made by the Federal Trade Commission, based on the statute involved, cannot be sustained until it is alleged and proven, and found by the Commission as a fact, that by the acts complained of competition will probably be lessened to "such a degree as will injuriously affect the public." In the instant case the complaint was purposely drafted as to omit such allegation.[79]

Commissioner Humphrey stated that the use by Congress of the words "may be to substantially lessen competition between such corporations or any of them"

> . . . is a use of words without any meaning. To contend that Congress meant what the words say is to attribute to it lack of ordinary understanding. . . . But what Congress meant by the words "to substantially lessen competition" has been settled by the only power that could settle it. The Supreme Court of the United States has said in the International Shoe Co. case that what Congress meant by that phrase was that the acquisition, whatever effect it might have on the competition existing between the corporations whose stock was acquired, must tend to lessen competition in "such a degree as will injuriously affect the public." In other words, as the Supreme Court interprets the statute, Congress meant that the word "or" as used in this section of the Clayton Act, should be changed to "and," so that it would read, "Where the effect of such acquisition may be to sub-

[76] 13 F.T.C. 249, 260.
[77] 13 F.T.C. 249, 261.
[78] 13 F.T.C. 249, 262.
[79] 13 F.T.C. 249, 262.

stantially lessen competition between such corporations and to restrain such commerce in any section or community, or tend to create a monopoly in any line of commerce." [80]

When the commission had found a violation of Section 7 by the International Shoe Company, Commissioner Humphrey had dissented on these same grounds and had thus anticipated the action of the Supreme Court in that case.[81] In the Temple Anthracite case the circuit court also adopted the view expressed in Humphrey's dissent.

The company petitioned the Third Circuit Court of Appeals to set aside the order of the commission. In a two to one decision, the court concluded that the finding of the commission—the acquisitions had substantially lessened competition—was not supported by evidence.[82] The majority opinion of Judge Thompson, concurred in by Judge Buffington, stated:

> There are no facts found and we find no evidence produced before the Commission to show the relation between the percentage of coal mined and sold by the Temple Coal Co. and its subsidiaries and that sold by the East Bear Ridge Colliery Co. to the total output of anthracite coal of the same kind and quality in the whole anthracite region. From the facts found as to the value of the annual output of the respective mines, it is quite apparent that the percentage of these mines to the total output cannot be consequential. Therefore, if competition were lessened, its effect upon the whole interstate trade in anthracite coal would not tend to create a monopoly through substantially lessening competition.[83]

The opinion also stated that no evidence indicated any direct competition between the two acquired mining companies. The commission had found that two acquired companies competed indirectly, since they sold through two wholesalers who competed with each other. The court was of the opinion that the two wholesalers had continued to distribute the coal of the two acquired corporations and that the competition between them

[80] 13 F.T.C. 249, 264.

[81] See 9 F.T.C. 441, 463; and see p. 76.

[82] *Temple Anthracite Coal Company* v. *Federal Trade Commission* (1931), 51 Fed. Rept., 2d Ser., 656 (C.C.A., 3d Cir.).

[83] 51 Fed. Rept., 2d Ser., 656, 660.

had not been affected by the union of the two mining companies by the holding company.[84]

Circuit Judge Woolley dissented from the judgment of the court on the ground that the case merely involved the allegation that the acquisitions may have the effect of substantially lessening competition between the two corporations, since the monopoly and restraint of trade provisions of the statute had not been invoked. He said:

> In arriving at the conclusion that the evidence sustains the order of the Commission I have kept in view the fact, at different times lost sight of in this case, that we are not concerned with the lessening of competition between these two companies and other companies in the industry, but are concerned with the lessening of competition between the two companies themselves.[85]

Judge Woolley concluded that the power to lessen competition between the two companies was achieved by the holding company when it gained the power, through the acquisitions, to decide when each of the companies would accept and when they would refuse orders—a power that had previously been exercised by each of the firms independently. In this opinion Judge Woolley recognizes the word "competition" to be a term connoting the degree to which a firm has the power to refuse orders unless the terms of sale are agreeable. Since any firm can always refuse to sell if it so pleases, the point at issue is whether the holding company will be in a position to refuse orders that the two companies acting independently would have chosen to accept. If so, then one could maintain that the portion of the total sales of anthracite coal sold by these two companies was being sold after the merger under conditions of less competition.

That is, if the merger resulted in a combined firm that viewed the demand schedule for its own product to be less elastic than was the case with the two independent firms prior to the acquisition, then competition can be considered to have been lessened. Judge Woolley was on sound ground from the standpoint of

[84] 51 Fed. Rept., 2d Ser., 656, 660–661.
[85] 51 Fed. Rept., 2d Ser., 656, 662.

economic analysis when he recognized the issue to be the effect of the acquisition on the willingness of the company to fill orders under given terms. He held that the acquisition had substantially lessened competition between the two firms, since, in deciding whether to accept an order, either company would no longer be influenced by the potential actions of the other. In effect, he was saying implicitly that prior to the merger the elasticity of demand for the product of company A was affected by the existence of company B as an alternative source of supply. With A and B no longer independent, the demand for the product of both firms will become less elastic, *ceteris paribus.*

The degree to which the merger decreases the elasticity of demand for the product of either firm, however, cannot logically be considered to be completely independent of the existence or absence of sources of the product alternative to both firms in question. Under conditions of pure and perfect competition, with "many" firms selling a homogeneous product in a homogeneous geographically defined market, the merger of any two firms would have a negligible effect on the elasticity of the demand function faced by any one firm. Under such conditions the degree of competition in the market could not reasonably be said to have been *substantially* lessened even though all competition *between* the firms would have been eliminated. If a succession of such mergers took place, however, a situation might result in which the demand functions faced by the various firms were no longer perfectly elastic. Perhaps this is what Congress meant by the desire to prevent monopolies in their incipiency. It appears, however, that, as Congress obviously did not intend to prevent all stock acquisitions between corporations in the same line of business, the minority opinion that the market conditions could be completely ignored would result in the prohibition of many mergers that might very well increase the degree of competition in a particular market and that Congress did not intend the law to prohibit.

Unless one *assumes* that the degree of competition in the market for a product is directly related to the number of firms in the industry, it is possible to conceive of a situation in which a merger will result in an increase in competition in the industry. For example, the combination of the bargaining power of two of the least powerful firms in an industry with only a half-dozen firms might effect a change from a situation of price leadership, with a price output adjustment close to that which would result from a single firm in the industry, to an oligopoly situation with a price-output adjustment close to that which would result from the conditions of pure and perfect competition. It must be kept in mind, however, that the difference between the elasticity of the demand function faced by a single firm and that faced by each of "many" firms may be negligible, if the industry demand function is close to being perfectly elastic—a situation possible if the "product" is defined so narrowly that there are many closely substitutable products available as alternatives to the buyers.[86]

All the court opinions dealing with the interpretation of the meaning of the standard of illegality of Section 7 approach the question from the legal point of view, and little progress was made by any of them in formulating a logically consistent and administratively workable concept of the standard to be applied. Judge Woolley's dissenting opinion, however, at least hinted at the real issues involved. He at least was unwilling to follow the majority of the Supreme Court in the International Shoe case in considering competition as a simple matter of fact involving no logical questions of definition. In this case, as well as the others involving the same question, the attempt to give a simple definitive meaning to the general policy statement of Congress resulted in the court splitting into two groups, neither of which had a satisfactory solution to what particular acquisitions are undesirable. Inevitably, each group chose an interpretation that would make practically all acquisitions legal or practically all acquisitions illegal.

The Federal Trade Commission voted to seek a writ of *certiorari* in order to have the Supreme Court review the Temple

[86] See chap. 9 for more discussion of the questions of economic analysis raised by the attempt to frame policy with respect to mergers in terms of the effect on competition.

Anthracite case, but the solicitor general of the United States decided against such an application.[87]

A few months later, the Second Circuit Court rendered a similar opinion in the review of the commission's order against V. Vivaudou, Inc.[88] On May 27, 1927, the commission issued a complaint against V. Vivaudou, Inc., charging that the acquisition by that company of the capital stock of two other companies constituted a violation of Section 7.[89] This case differed from the Temple case in that the acquiring and the acquired firms were engaged in the manufacture and sale of lines of cosmetics which were highly advertised, differentiated products. The complaint charged that the effect of each of the acquisitions was to restrain commerce and tend to create a monopoly, as well as to substantially lessen competition.

The three corporations had engaged in the sale of several complete lines of toilet articles including perfumes, toilet waters, talcum and face powders, and cosmetics. The commission's findings of fact included the dollar volumes of sales of each of several products by each of the three companies during two years prior to the acquisitions. Each company had total annual sales of from two million to three million dollars.[90] Without considering the market structure in the industry, the commission concluded that each firm had been "one of the important factors in the industry in which it is engaged." [91] Each of the companies sold its various lines of cosmetics throughout the United States to the retail and jobbing trade and to department stores. The commission concluded that all the allegations of the complaint were supported by the testimony and issued an order of divestment of the stock and assets of both the acquired companies.[92] Commissioner

[87] *F.T.C. Annual Report, 1932*, p. 114.

[88] *V. Vivaudou, Inc.*, v. *Federal Trade Commission* (1931), 54 Fed. Rept., 2d Ser., 273 (C.C.A., 2d Cir.).

[89] *In the Matter of V. Vivaudou, Incorporated* (1930), 13 F.T.C. 306 (F.T.C. Docket No. 1464, April 28, 1930).

[90] 13 F.T.C. 306, 310–317.

[91] 13 F. T. C. 306, 310, 312, 317.

[92] 13 F.T.C. 306, 320–321.

Humphrey dissented on the same grounds as in the International Shoe case and the Temple Anthracite Coal case.[93]

In an unanimous opinion delivered by Judge Manton and concurred in by Judges Augustus Hand and Chase, the Second Circuit Court of Appeals reversed the order of the commission.[94] The opinion said:

> We must consider the extent of the trade carried on by the three companies and compare it with the volume of business carried on by their competitors previous to the period of ownership of the stock, and endeavor to ascertain whether the public interest has been affected.[95]

In reviewing the record, the court found testimony to the effect that the total annual volume of sales in the industry was about one hundred and twenty-five million dollars. The court held:

> There can be no monopolistic tendency in acquiring control of properties which added 5 million dollars to the petitioner's already 3 millions volume of business, when the total of the country's similar business, amounting to at least 125 millions, is considered.[96]

The opinion also pointed out that there were from three hundred to five hundred different manufacturers of perfumes and cosmetics as well as three thousand manufacturers of face powders in the United States. The court found no evidence of increase in prices, curtailment of production, or division of territory. The court also considered the testimony that the different firms involved had had their largest sales in different products, the acquisitions being made in order to increase the sales of the respondent in those parts of the general lines of toilet articles in which its sales were small.[97]

The market structure in this industry could aptly be described as one characterized by monopolistic competition with many firms. In the light of the International Shoe case, it would have been difficult for the circuit court to have come to any other con-

[93] 13 F.T.C. 306, 321–322.
[94] 54 Fed. Rept., 2d Ser., 273.
[95] 54 Fed. Rept., 2d Ser., 273, 275.
[96] 54 Fed. Rept., 2d Ser., 273, 275.
[97] 54 Fed. Rept., 2d Ser., 273, 275–276.

clusion than to reverse the commission. The information about the character of the markets involved, obtained in the course of the proceeding, indicates that the public interest probably was best served by allowing the merger to stand, but the decision of the circuit court was based on an interpretation of the law which might well have resulted in the permitting of some mergers that would tend to increase monopoly power. The mere fact that the merged firm's volume of business was eight million dollars and the total volume of such business in the nation was one hundred and twenty-five million dollars does not necessarily rule out the possibility that competition was substantially lessened in the markets for some of the products in some sections of the country.

The commission voted against making application for a writ of *certiorari* in this case.[98]

Conclusions

From 1926 to 1934, the Supreme Court reviewed the policies of the Federal Trade Commission with respect to Section 7 of the Clayton Act. Of the court's interpretation of the statute, the *Federal Trade Commission Report on Monopolistic Practices in Industries* said:

> By judicial interpretation many limitations other than those inherent to Section 7 have been imposed upon the Commission's authority to act thereunder; in fact, it is believed that the effectiveness of this section has been completely emasculated as the result of court decisions.[99]

In the previous chapter it was shown that the commission evolved a policy of attempting to make use of Section 7 to prevent and remedy not only the acquiring and holding by a corporation of a competitor's stock, but also the acquiring and holding of a competitor's assets, if the asset acquisition was preceded and achieved by means of a stock acquisition. The effectiveness of the Clayton Act in achieving this goal was undoubtedly emasculated by the

[98] *F.T.C. Annual Report, 1932,* p. 115.
[99] *T.N.E.C. Hearings,* part 5-A, p. 2379.

series of Supreme Court decisions in which the court reviewed the commission's policy on this question.

The court initially indicated in the Western Meat decision[100] that the commission might legally order divestment of stock so as to include assets or divestment of assets already acquired, if the acquisition of the assets had not already taken place at the time of the issuance of the complaint by the commission. In the decision in the Arrow-Hart and Hegeman case,[101] however, the court held that the commission lacked the power to order divestment of physical property under any circumstances. The possibility of the commission using the authority given it under Section 5 of the Federal Trade Commission Act to achieve the goal of preventing asset acquisitions was eliminated by the decision in the Eastman Kodak Case.[102]

The responsibility for this limitation on the effectiveness of Section 7 rests primarily with Congress and the courts, since Congress failed explicitly to authorize the commission to make such an order, and since the courts tended to interpret the statutes strictly on the question of the power of an administrative agency to exercise what was considered to be the normal functions of a court of equity.

If the limitation placed by the court on the power of the commission to order asset divestment were the only limitation imposed by the judicial review, the effectiveness of Section 7 would not have been emasculated. The section might have remained effective in preventing the use of the holding company device as a method of uniting competing corporations and in preventing the evils incident thereto. The Supreme Court's interpretation of the standard of illegality of Section 7 in the International Shoe case[103] did undoubtedly remove the effectiveness of Section 7. Even if the power of the commission to order asset divestment had been upheld, the standard of illegality was interpreted in such a way that Section 7 would have provided no effective supplementation of the Sherman Act.

[100] 272 U.S. 554 (1926).
[101] 291 U.S. 587 (1934).
[102] 274 U.S. 619 (1927).
[103] 280 U.S. 291 (1930).

The responsibility for this fundamental emasculation of the section does not appear to rest, however, entirely with the Supreme Court. The problem originated with the way in which Congress worded the standard of illegality. By qualifying the prohibition in terms of the effect that an acquisition of stock may have on competition *between* the acquiring and the acquired corporations, Congress presented the commission and the courts with the problem of choosing between the interpretation of the statute to mean that either (1) an acquisition resulting in complete control of the acquired corporation completely eliminates and, therefore, substantially lessens competition between the two firms, or (2) an acquisition completely eliminating the competition between the two firms does not substantially lessen competition between the two firms unless the competition is substantial. It appears from the legislative history of Section 7 that Congress intended the first interpretation.[104] The Federal Trade Commission, however, chose the second interpretation. The commission adopted the policy of requiring as a prerequisite to an order of divestment the existence, prior to the acquisition, of substantial competition between the acquiring and the acquired firms. The commission failed to develop any objective criterion for determining whether the preëxisting competition had been substantial. In the International Shoe decision[105] the Supreme Court merely set forth the basis on which this latter question must be answered —the preëxisting competition is to be considered substantial only if its elimination would constitute a Sherman Act violation.

Congress had written Section 7 in such a way that, if it had been accepted at face value by the court, almost every acquisition of a controlling stock interest in another corporation would have been unlawful, since all probable competition between the two firms would have been eliminated. Not wishing to go to this extreme in interpreting the statute, the court avoided the responsibility of giving specific content to the statute by reverting to the Sherman Act test of illegality. Twenty years later, Congress plugged the "asset loophole" by including asset as well as stock

[104] See pp. 46–49.
[105] 280 U.S. 291 (1930).

acquisitions among the prohibitions of Section 7 and by specifically authorizing the commission to order asset divestment in Section 11. In so doing, the language in which the standard of illegality is stated was also amended, thus requiring new interpretation and removing the effect of the International Shoe decision as well as that of the Arrow-Hart and Hegeman decision.[106]

[106] See chap. 8.

5. Federal Trade Commission Administration of Section 7 Subsequent to Judicial Interpretation

During the period from the initial Supreme Court interpretation of Section 7 of the Clayton Act in 1926[1] until the amendment of the section in 1950,[2] the Federal Trade Commission continued to inquire into the legality of corporate acquisitions, although the degree of activity of the commission in administering Section 7 was sharply curtailed after 1930. Table 1 indicates the approximate number of preliminary inquiries instituted, applications for complaints docketed, complaints issued, and cease and desist orders issued in each fiscal year for which such information was published by the commission in cases arising under Section 7.

In this second phase of administration of Section 7, the Federal Trade Commission no longer had the opportunity to render initial interpretation of a general statement of Congressional policy. The commission's function became that of administering the statute in conformity with its interpretation by the Supreme Court. The implications of that Supreme Court interpretation are

[1] *Federal Trade Commission* v. *Western Meat Co., Thatcher Manufacturing* v. *Federal Trade Commission, Swift & Co.* v. *Federal Trade Commission* (1926), 272 U.S. 554. See pp. 109–112.

[2] 64 *U.S. Stat. at L.* 1125 (1950).

evident in the policies adopted by the commission during this period. This chapter attempts to describe and evaluate Federal

TABLE 1

FEDERAL TRADE COMMISSION INQUIRIES, APPLICATIONS FOR COMPLAINTS, COMPLAINTS, AND ORDERS INSTITUTED YEARLY UNDER SECTION 7 OF THE CLAYTON ACT, 1927–1950 FISCAL YEARS *

Fiscal Year	Preliminary Inquiries Instituted	Matters Docketed as Applications for Complaints	Complaints Issued	Orders Issued
1927	[a]	[b]	2	1
1928	[a]	[b]	3	0
1929	228	[b]	5	0
1930	98	11	6	2
1931	67	6	1	0
1932	52	2	1	0
1933	53	2	1	1
1934	45	0	1	1
1935	23	2	1	0
1936	39	0	2	0
1937	18	1	1	0
1938	26	1	1	0
1939	13	0	0	0
1940	18	3	3	0
1941	5	1	0	0
1942	1	0	0	0
1943	0	0	0	0
1944	1	0	0	0
1945	[a]	0	1	0
1946	1	0	2	0
1947	5	5	0	0
1948	[a]	1	0	0
1949	[a]	[a]	0	0
1950	[a]	[a]	0	0
Total	693	35	31	5

* SOURCE: *F.T.C. Annual Reports, 1927–1950.*

[a] Information not published.

[b] From 1927 to 1929 the commission dismissed inquiries or issued complaints after preliminary inquiry in order to take formal action against stock acquisitions before assets could be transferred.

Trade Commission policies by considering (1) the few cases in which it issued complaints, (2) preliminary inquiries in which the commission found that the probable effect on competition was insufficient to warrant a complaint, (3) inquiries in which it found that statutory merger or asset acquisition had occurred, and (4) the recommendations of the commission for changes in the Clayton Act.

The record of the administration of Section 7 during this second phase discloses that the law, as interpreted, had become a "dead letter." The Federal Trade Commission chose to seek Congressional amendment of the statute rather than reinterpretation by the Supreme Court. In advocating such amendment, the commission was primarily concerned with the so-called "assets loophole," and failed to utilize its experience in dealing with acquisitions to formulate a proposal for an economically meaningful standard of illegality.

Cases in Which Complaints Were Issued

Although the commission inquired into about seven hundred corporate acquisitions between 1927 and 1950, only thirty-one complaints were issued; and of these, only four resulted in cease and desist orders. No orders were issued after the Supreme Court decision in the Arrow-Hart and Hegeman case on March 12, 1934.[3] In the latter part of 1926, the Federal Trade Commission issued an order against Armour and Company directing the divestment of acquired stock and all properties acquired subsequent to the acquisition of the stock of two corporations.[4] As a result of the Supreme Court decision in the Swift case,[5] the order was rescinded a few months later on March 11, 1927.[6] In 1930 the commission issued orders against V. Vivaudou, Inc., and Temple Anthracite Coal Company. On appeal by the respondents, the

[3] 291 U.S. 587.
[4] *F.T.C. Annual Report, 1927,* p. 131.
[5] 272 U.S. 554.
[6] *F.T.C. Annual Report, 1927,* p. 76.

circuit courts reversed both orders.[7] In the 1933 fiscal year the commission issued the order against Arrow-Hart and Hegeman, which the Supreme Court refused to uphold.[8]

The last order to be issued by the commission under the original Section 7 was that issued just before the Supreme Court decision in the Arrow-Hart and Hegeman case[9] against the Vanadium-Alloys Steel Company on February 3, 1934.

The Vanadium-Alloys Steel Company Case—The complaint against the Vanadium-Alloys Steel Company had been issued September 19, 1929, alleging that the acquisition in 1928 by the Vanadium Company of all the common stock of Colonial Steel Company had the effect of substantially lessening competition between the two firms, restraining commerce in various sections and communities, and tending to create a monopoly in alloy and other forms of steel.[10]

The commission concluded that, even though the effect of the acquisition was not to restrain commerce or tend to create a monopoly, substantial competition had existed between the two firms in the production and sale of various types of tool steels, and this competition had been substantially lessened. In a closely reasoned opinion reviewing the facts of the case, taking into account the legislative history of Section 7 and the prior court opinions in Section 7 cases, the commission enunciated a new policy on the meaning of the standard of illegality of the Clayton Act. An attempt was made to undo some of the damage done by the International Shoe decision, which had applied the Sherman Act criterion to Section 7 cases.[11] In this case, the Federal Trade Commission ruled that Section 7 was violated if the effect of the acquisition was to substantially lessen competition between the firms, even though the effect was *not* to restrain commerce in a section or to tend to create a monopoly. It further held that competition was substantially lessened between the firms be-

[7] See pp. 138–144.

[8] 291 U.S. 587. See pp. 118–123.

[9] *In the Matter of Vanadium-Alloys Steel Company*, 18 F.T.C. 194 (F.T.C. Docket No. 1694, Feb. 3, 1934).

[10] 18 F.T.C. 194, 196–198.

[11] See pp. 123–136.

cause, prior to the acquisition of all the common stock of one company by the other, the bulk of the sales of each firm had been of competing products.

In its opinion, the commission defined the product, in the sale of which the firms were held to have been in substantial competition, as "tool steel." [12] This constituted, however, a category that included several different and distinct types of high-grade steel made from carbon or alloys for use primarily in the manufacture of tools. In addition to the differentiation among the various types of tool steels produced by each firm, the various brands produced by Vanadium were differentiated to a greater or lesser degree from the comparable brands of Colonial. Prior to the acquisition, the Vanadium company had practically confined its business to tool steels. Colonial produced other steels as well. About 40 per cent of its output for the year ending June 30, 1928, was of steel products other than tool steel.[13]

The commission carefully examined the record of sales of the two companies during the 1928 fiscal year in order to ascertain the proportion of total sales by each company of brands of tool steel for which the other company offered a comparable brand considered to be "competitive." According to the commission's opinion:

> Respondent contends . . . that so-called comparability is in itself no evidence of true competition between the brands. Comparability, it says, refers primarily to steels having the same composition or like physical properties. To be competitive the brands must be usable for the same purposes, possess a like quality and sell at about the same price.[14]

Counsel for the commission contended, however, that the comparable brands of the two firms were competitive within the meaning of Section 7. The opinion stated:

> In behalf of that contention, they rely not so much upon evidence as to trade significance attached to the concept of "comparability," as upon the fact that these brands come into actual competition in the market. Thus they introduced evidence that salesmen of both companies solicited the

[12] 18 F.T.C. 194, 198.
[13] 18 F.T.C. 194, 199.
[14] 18 F.T.C. 194, 200.

same class of trade and even the same customers, that warehouses were maintained in comparable consuming regions, and that these comparable brands were used by customers for the same purposes.[15]

Vanadium's largest selling brand in 1928 was called "Red Cut Superior," which was listed at seventy cents per pound and accounted for more than half of their total sales. Colonial's largest selling brand had been a brand called "Beaver High Speed," listed at sixty-five cents per pound, accounting for about 15 per cent of Colonial's total sales. Testimony established that after the merger the salesmen of both companies had at times urged customers to buy Vanadium's Red Cut Superior in place of Colonial's Beaver High Speed. By counting the volume of sales of these brands along with the sales of several other brands found to be competitive, the commission concluded that "about 82.5 per cent of Vanadium's sales and about 77.7 per cent of Colonial's tool steel sales were of competitive products." [16] The opinion of the commission stated:

> Nor can we close our eyes to the fact that similarity with reference to (1) types of tool steel, (2) determining elements, and (3) price, characterizes all these brands of tool steel. . . . Thus taking a viewpoint of competition, fully in accord with the analyses of competitive products made in *International Shoe Company* v. *Federal Trade Commission,* 280 U.S. 291, we find that there was substantial competition in tool steel production between the Vanadium company and the Colonial company.
>
> These percentage values give a true concept to the term "competition." Though there may be at the moment no willingness on the part of customers to take one brand instead of another because of a multitude of difference . . . products that at the beginning may only be "comparable" quickly become "competitive" as salesmen become active, markets limited, and manufacturers mould quality and price to meet variant desires.[17]

The commission was thus returning to the interpretation that the law forbade an acquisition if the effect was to substantially lessen competition *between* the two firms, irrespective of the effect of the acquisition on the degree of competition in the markets for the products of the firms.

[15] 18 F.T.C. 194, 200.
[16] 18 F.T.C. 194, 201.
[17] 18 F.T.C. 194, 201.

The opinion states that there were approximately twenty-four domestic and seven foreign manufacturers of tool steel selling their products in the same market with the respondent. The commission estimated that in 1929, after the combination of Vanadium and Colonial, the combined firm accounted for only about 12 per cent of the sales of tool steel in the United States by the fifteen largest manufacturers. From this finding the commission concluded:

> The resultant increases in the production of the two companies as a result of the stock acquisition did not, in the judgment of the Commission, so substantially increase the respondent's production in its relation to the whole as to enable it to restrain in any section or community the line of commerce in which the two companies were engaged, and did not tend to create a monopoly in the line of commerce in which the two corporations were engaged. Nevertheless, there having been substantial competition between the two companies, the lessening of this competition was *pari passu* substantial and one whose elimination was a matter of concern to the consuming public.[18]

If the effect of the acquisition on the markets for the products of the two firms is to be ignored in determining whether the acquisition is illegal, then on what grounds can it be maintained that the acquisition "was a matter of concern to the consuming public"? The commission's opinion answered this question:

> The reduction in the number of leading manufacturers in a product, especially where the number of such manufacturers is comparatively small, may have consequences the import of which is so subtle that it is only fully determinable after the passage of such time as will allow for the new industrial unit to occupy its place in the changed industrial competitive structure thus created.[19]

The commission seems to have been assuming that the degree of competition in a market is necessarily directly related to the number of firms in the market. It is conceivable, however, that the changed industrial structure created by the acquisition may be one that is more conducive to competition than had existed before, particularly if only a relatively small number of firms are in

[18] 18 F.T.C. 194, 203–204.

[19] 18 F.T.C. 194, 204.

the market. Since the equilibrium price-output adjustment under conditions of oligopoly may very closely approximate that of either competition or monopoly, depending on the reaction of the various entrepreneurs to the actions of each other, the effect of the change in market structure may be to create conditions such that the equilibrium adjustment is closer than before to that of perfect competition. This could occur, for example, if the acquisition resulted in an addition to the number of "dominant" firms in the market. In a market characterized by four approximately equally powerful firms, which are setting the price pattern by tacit agreement among themselves, and twenty smaller firms, which are following the price leadership of the large firms, the combination of two of the smaller firms might result in a less stable oligopoly adjustment, if it creates a fifth large firm with which the four previously dominant firms must contend.

The commission was deciding, in effect, that in a situation in which it is impossible to know whether the final result will be more or less monopoly power, it is better to minimize the risk of permitting an acquisition that should be prohibited, even though such a policy may result in a higher risk of prohibiting an acquisition that should have been permitted. The consequence of either error is injury to the consuming public.

Even if this policy of the commission did not suffer from the disadvantage of possibly prohibiting an acquisition that might actually increase competition in the markets for the products in question, it is open to criticism on another ground. There is an inherent inconsistency in a policy based on the percentage of sales of each of the competing companies. These percentages, which the commission deemed to give a "true concept of the term 'competition,'" have very little, if any, relation to the degree of competition or monopoly power in the markets for the products in question. Two very small firms each producing a single product like that of the other would be prohibited from merging under this criterion, while the two firms that account for the largest percentage of the sales of the product might be found not to be competitors, if they produce many other dissimilar products.

In this case the respondent also had an important inconsistency in his argument. In ascertaining the relative position of the respondent in the market after the acquisition, the commission compared the respondent's output of tool steel with the total output of tool steel by the fifteen largest firms, which produced the bulk of that line of products. The respondent contended that, in ascertaining whether the acquisition tended to create a monopoly, the commission should define the product more broadly so as to include the output of all carbon, alloy, and electric furnace steel by the combined firm with the total output of such steel in the United States. It was maintained that these other types of steel products by proper treatment could be placed in direct competition with the products of Colonial and Vanadium. Thus, at this point in its argument, the company was maintaining that it had not acquired too much monopoly power, since it would still have to contend with the threat of direct competition from the producers of related products. The company had argued at another point, however, that it had not competed prior to the acquisition with Colonial, because there were very slight differences in the types of tool steel produced by the two firms. The commission did not rule on this question, as it decided that there was no tendency to create a monopoly under either measure of relative market shares.[20]

Undoubtedly, the interpretation of the standard of illegality of Section 7 by the Supreme Court in the International Shoe case had made it almost impossible for the commission to find any acquisition of stock illegal unless the acquisition would have constituted a violation of the Sherman Act. This was because of the ruling of the high court that competition between two firms is not substantial, and therefore cannot be substantially lessened,

[20] 18 F.T.C. 194, 203. There had been a general tendency for advocates of stronger legislation against mergers to stress the competition between merging firms that produce differentiated products, while denying the adequacy of competition from substitute products, in discussing the administration of the Sherman Act. On the contrary, the opponents of stringent standards of illegality have generally stressed the absence of competition between merging firms producing differentiated products, while denouncing the strengthening of the Sherman Act criterion of what constitutes a "monopoly" for ignoring the great amount of competition faced by a single firm in an industry from the products of related industries.

unless its elimination injures the public, the injury being judged by the relative market position of the combined firm. The devastating effect of this ruling was not attributable, however, to the fact that the court eliminated from the law as written by Congress the relevancy of the degree of competition *between* the two firms, but, instead, to the fact that the court applied the Sherman Act criterion to ascertain whether or not the effect on the market for the product was to create a monopoly in the legal sense.[21] In its attempt to reëstablish a separate and less stringent criterion of illegality under Section 7 than under the Sherman Act, in order to be able to carry out what it considered to be the intent of Congress in enacting the Clayton Act, the commission chose to base its argument on a grammatical interpretation of Section 7, which explicitly states that competition *between* the acquiring and the acquired firm is relevant. The ill effects of the International Shoe decision might have been remedied without resorting to an attempt to carry out the letter of the statute. Congress had been unable to clearly define a concept of workable competition. In order to attack monopoly in its incipiency, however, it wanted to provide a criterion less stringent than that of the Sherman Act as interpreted by the Supreme Court at that time. Congress had provided in the Clayton Act that an acquisition would be illegal if the effect *might* be to restrain commerce *in a section or community*, or to *tend* to create a monopoly. The commission would have been on sounder economic ground if it had chosen to assert its authority to implement the Clayton Act by attempting to get the Supreme Court to uphold an interpretation basing the criterion on the effect of an acquisition on the degree of competition and monopoly *in the market* and yet not requiring

[21] The test of illegality under the Sherman Act was, of course, not set forth explicitly in that statute, which was couched in the language of the common law. The test applied by the Supreme Court in cases of merger or combination changed from case to case. From 1911 to 1945, however, it was necessary in such Sherman Act cases to show either that *intent* to restrain trade or to monopolize was present, or that the *effect* of a merger was *in fact* the creation of a monopoly with power that had been utilized to injure the public. For an excellent discussion of the meaning taken on by the Sherman Act over the years, see *Report of the Attorney General's National Committee to Study the Antitrust Laws*, U.S. Dept. of Justice (Washington: 1955), pp. 1–64.

the equivalent of proof of a Sherman Act violation. Such an interpretation could have been based on the provision that explicitly states that restraint of commerce is to be judged within market geographically more limited than the whole nation, and the provision condemning a *tendency* to monopolize as opposed to the actual creation of a legal monopoly or an attempt to monopolize. The Clayton Act provided an opportunity for the commission to develop a standard of illegality based upon the *effect* of an action by entrepreneurs without regard to their *intent*, while at the same time not requiring proof of the achievement of what the courts had come to recognize as a "monopoly" or an "unreasonable restraint of trade."

The order of the commission against Vanadium-Alloys Steel Company was never tested in the courts, since the decision in the Arrow-Hart and Hegeman case was rendered within a few days after the issuance of the order, and the company took advantage of that decision to by-pass the order of the commission by acquiring the assets of Colonial Steel.[22]

Thus the Supreme Court's interpretation of the commission's authority over asset acquisitions made it very difficult, if not impossible, for the commission to develop a new standard of illegality under Section 7. The concern of the commission with the inadequacy of the law on the asset question is understandable, but it is doubtful whether Section 7 would have been effective even if it had not allowed the "asset loophole," as neither the court nor the commission had developed a satisfactory standard of illegality. The importance of the standard of illegality was usually ignored in the discussions of the necessity of a change in the act to "plug the loophole," as will be seen in the following analysis of the administration of Section 7 by the commission and its efforts to have the statute amended.

Dismissed Complaints—The Federal Trade Commission dismissed twenty-seven of the thirty-one Section 7 complaints issued between 1927 and 1950. Twelve of the complaints were dismissed on the grounds that the testimony would not support a finding that the effect of the acquisition might be to substantially lessen

[22] *T.N.E.C. Hearings*, part 5-A, p. 2370.

competition, restrain commerce, or tend to create a monopoly within the meaning of the statute as interpreted by the Supreme Court in the International Shoe case. Three complaints were dismissed on the grounds that the acquisition of assets had ousted the commission of jurisdiction. The commission reported no reasons for dismissing the other twelve complaints.[23]

Before the Supreme Court decision in the International Shoe case in 1930, the commission dismissed a complaint against the Continental Sugar Company for almost the same reasons that the court used in reversing the commission in the shoe case. On March 2, 1928, the commission had issued a complaint against Continental Sugar as a result of its acquisition of the Holland–St. Louis Sugar Company. Both firms were engaged in the production of beet sugar. On June 23, 1928, before any testimony had been taken, the commission dismissed the complaint upon the report of a board of review, on the basis that the acquisition did not substantially lessen competition. The two companies produced only about 5 per cent of the nation's beet sugar. In addition, the board's majority held that the corporations had not been competing because the acquired firm was on the verge of bankruptcy.[24]

A few days after the International Shoe decision, the commission on January 22, 1930, dismissed a complaint against the Consolidated Cigar Corporation, which had acquired the stock of two other cigar manufacturing companies. The commission found that the acquired firms were small compared to the industry as a whole and concluded that the acquisitions were not illegal, "although the respondent was a very substantial concern, with factories in a number of states." [25]

The Purity Bakeries Corporation had acquired several baking companies located in Michigan, Minnesota, Kentucky, and Tennessee. The commission issued a complaint in 1929 charging vio-

[23] The reasons for dismissing complaints were not usually reported by the commission, but information from its files on some complaints was included in the *Federal Trade Commission Report on Monopolistic Practices in Industries, T.N.E.C. Hearings*, part 5-A, pp. 2368–2372.

[24] F.T.C. Exhibit No. 168, p. 70.

[25] *T.N.E.C. Hearings*, part 5-A, p. 2368.

lation of Section 7, but the complaint was dismissed in December, 1930, as a result of the International Shoe decision, on the grounds that there had not been substantial competition between the various acquired companies.[26]

A complaint issued in 1929 against the Continental Steel Corporation was dismissed in 1931 as a result of a finding by the commission that less than 1 per cent of the business of each of the firms had been in competition with the other firms.[27]

One of the most important complaints to be dismissed as a result of the International Shoe decision was that issued against McKesson and Robbins, Inc., in 1930. The respondent had acquired a large number of wholesale drug firms located throughout the United States. The various acquired firms, however, had been operating in geographically distinct markets and were not considered to have been in substantial competition with each other. The acquisitions gave the respondent a substantial share of the sales of its line of products in the national market. Under the interpretation of the statute by the Supreme Court, the commission could not find a tendency toward monopoly, since the acquired firms had not been competing substantially with each other prior to the acquisitions.[28] In 1932 the commission again based a dismissal on a lack of preëxisting substantial competition between the acquiring and the acquired firms or between the two acquired firms. The commission dismissed a complaint against Borg-Warner Corporation even though the acquisitions resulted in a dominant market position for the respondent, according to the commission.[29]

In 1931 the commission dismissed complaints against Philip Morris Consolidated, Inc., and against National Pastry Products Corporation because of lack of evidence showing that the acquisitions might have the ill effects denounced in the statute as interpreted by the Supreme Court. In 1937 the same reasons resulted

[26] *Ibid.*, p. 2370.
[27] *Ibid.*
[28] *Ibid.*
[29] *Ibid.*, p. 2371.

in the dismissal of a complaint against Sterling Products, Inc., which had acquired the R. L. Watkins Company.[30]

In accordance with the opinion of the court in the International Shoe case that the acquisition of a corporation in failing financial condition would not have the effect of lessening competition, the commission dismissed a complaint against Charles Freshman Company, Inc., in 1930, because of the precarious financial position of the acquired corporation.[31] In 1936 the commission dismissed a complaint against the Van Kannel Revolving Door Company because of the poor financial condition of both the acquiring and the acquired company. The commission believed that an order of divestment would have forced the respondent out of business, and therefore would not have prevented a lessening of competition.[32]

In 1934 the merger by stock acquisition of the Crown Willamette Paper Company and the Zellerbach Corporation resulted in a complaint against the Crown Zellerbach Corporation. The commission dismissed the complaint in 1935 on the ground that no monopoly was created. The commission report to the Temporary National Economic Committee stated that the decision was influenced by the "adverse economic conditions in the paper industry on the Pacific coast" as a result of the competition from Swedish firms, although there was also a question of whether there had been preëxisting substantial competition.[33]

Before the decision in the Arrow-Hart and Hegeman case, the commission in 1931 dismissed a complaint against the Crown Overall Manufacturing Company because the assets of the company, the stock of which had been acquired, were also acquired soon after the commission issued its complaint but before the commission had issued an order of divestment of stock.[34] In 1936 the commission dismissed a complaint against Laird and Com-

[30] *Ibid.*, pp. 2370–2371.
[31] *Ibid.*, p. 2371.
[32] *Ibid.*
[33] *Ibid.*
[34] *Ibid.*, p. 2370.

pany for similar reasons on the authority of the Arrow-Hart and Hegeman case.[35]

In disposing of a complaint against the American Smelting and Refining Company, the commission limited itself to consideration of whether the acquisition was of stock or assets. The respondent had set up and acquired the stock of a subsidiary corporation in exchange for bonds of the respondent and certificates representing quantities of various metals. These bonds and certificates were then transferred to Federated Metals Corporation in exchange for all its assets, which included the capital stock of the Missouri Zinc Corporation.[36] The complaint alleged that American Smelting and Refining Company and the Federated Metals Corporation had been in competition with each other prior to the acquisition, but it did not specifically charge that American Smelting had competed with the Missouri Zinc Company. The respondent rested its case before the commission entirely on the contention that the transaction was an acquisition of assets and, therefore, not within the jurisdiction of the commission in the light of the Arrow-Hart decision. The commission held that the acquisition by the subsidiary corporation was legally an acquisition by the parent and was of assets. It rejected the contention of the counsel for the commission that the acquisition of the stock of the subsidiary was legally the same as an acquisition of the stock of the Federated company and therefore illegal. The commission stated in its opinion that the ruling was without prejudice to the propriety of another complaint, based on the fact that the respondent had acquired the stock of the Missouri Zinc Company, but it issued no such complaint.[37]

It is clear from this review of the formal complaints issued from 1927 through 1950 that the commission's administration of Section 7 of the Clayton Act in that period did not prevent or

[35] *Ibid.*, p. 2371.

[36] *In the Matter of American Smelting & Refining Company*, 19 F.T.C. 94, 99 (F.T.C. Docket No. 2102, June 25, 1934). This is the only one of the twenty-seven complaints dismissed from 1927 to 1950 for which the opinion of the commission was reported in the *Federal Trade Commission Decisions*.

[37] 19 F.T.C. 94, 99–106.

dissolve any mergers, though it may have affected the form in which some combinations were organized.

Inquiries Dismissed Because of the Standard of Illegality

In order better to define the policies of the Federal Trade Commission and to evaluate the adequacy of the statute as interpreted by the court, it is useful to examine the facts concerning several of the acquisitions inquired into by the commission which did not result in the issuance of a complaint. Although the general policy of the commission has been to release no information on investigations prior to the issuance of a formal complaint, in its report to the Temporary National Economic Committee[38] it used information from its files as a basis for a brief review of the reasons for the failure of the commission to take further action after 121 informal investigations of acquisitions during the 1932 to 1938 period. A complete digest of all these cases was filed with the Temporary National Economic Committee, but was not made a part of the printed record of that committee's investigations.[39]

With respect to these 121 dismissals of preliminary investigations, the report of the commission said:

> There are several reasons why the Commission lacked authority to act in the situations mentioned. These reasons will be discussed later in this memorandum, and cases will be cited therewith. The most important one, and one concerning which the Commission has repeatedly urged an amendment to the section, is that the acquisition was of assets rather than of stock.[40]

Examination of the available facts concerning these 121 acquisitions leads to the conclusion that the commission overemphasized the importance of the "assets loophole." The commission neglected to stress the failure of itself and the courts to develop a workable interpretation of the standard of illegality. It also failed

[38] *T.N.E.C. Hearings*, part 5-A.
[39] F.T.C. Exhibit No. 192.
[40] *T.N.E.C. Hearings*, part 5-A, p. 2373.

to stress the need for Congressional amendment of that part of Section 7.

The commission's report to the Temporary National Economic Committee classified what it considered to be the limitations placed upon its ability to prevent mergers into (1) "Substantive Restrictions of Section 7 by Legislative Intent," (2) restrictions due to the International Shoe decision, (3) restrictions due to the Swift and Thatcher cases, and (4) restrictions due to the Arrow-Hart and Hegeman case. About the first category, the report said:

> In 57 cases one of the principal reasons for the Commission's dropping the matter after a preliminary investigation was the fact that the assets, and not the stock, of the acquired companies were purchased. Section 7 does not prohibit acquisition of physical assets and properties. The reason the section was never intended to prohibit such asset acquisition was undoubtedly that the usual method of acquisition at the time Section 7 was enacted was through obtaining control of the capital stock. By reason of this limitation a way has been left open to accomplish the same result which the section sought to prohibit.[41]

The third category of limitations on the commission's ability to prevent mergers was a primary reason for dismissal in nine cases —stock had been acquired, but a transfer of assets had taken place prior to the issuance of a complaint by the commission. In nine other cases, mergers had taken place under the provisions of state laws providing for consolidation of corporations, and the cases were dropped in accordance with the Arrow-Hart and Hegeman case. In 92 of these 121 preliminary inquiries, the commission carried the investigation far enough to conclude that the given conditions removed the acquisition from the condemnation of Section 7, irrespective of the question of asset or stock acquisition.

Cases of Firms Selling the Same Products—Following the interpretation of Section 7 given by the Supreme Court in the International Shoe Company case, the commission attempted to ascertain whether there had been substantial competition between the acquiring and the acquired firms, or between two or

[41] *Ibid.*, p. 2377.

more acquired firms, prior to the acquisition. Many preliminary inquiries disclosed that competition prior to an acquisition had not been substantial, even though the companies had been selling the same products.

In several cases substantial competition was found to have been lacking because the markets of the firms were geographically distinct. For example, the Bartlett Frazier Company owned and operated grain elevators in Illinois and Wisconsin and sold grain primarily in the Chicago grain market. It acquired the Trans-Mississippi Grain Company, which operated elevators in Iowa, Nebraska, and Missouri and sold primarily in the Kansas City and Omaha grain markets. It was held that the two companies had been in competition in neither buying nor selling grain.[42] The C. H. Sprague and Son Company was engaged in selling tidewater coal—that is, coal mined in southern coal fields, shipped by rail to Hampton Roads ports, and shipped by water to New England. Sprague and Son acquired T. A. D. Jones and Company, Inc., which was also engaged in the sale of tidewater coal. The acquiring company, however, sold its product in the northern section of the New England states, whereas the acquired company sold almost entirely in Connecticut and the southern part of western Massachusetts.[43] The City Ice and Fuel Company, the largest distributor of ice in the United States, acquired the Detroit City Service Company, which sold ice within Detroit only. The two companies were considered as not having been in competition even though the City Ice and Fuel Company did operate in the outskirts of Detroit.[44]

In ascertaining whether two companies operating in different geographical areas competed with one another, the commission appears to have ignored the effect on the elasticity of demand to one firm of the potentiality of marginal market penetration of the other firm. That is, the commission ignored the effect that a price increase of one firm might have on the geographical extension of the operations of the other firm. One very important factor deter-

[42] File No. 17–7–801, F.T.C. Exhibit No. 192, p. 809.
[43] File No. 17–7–826, F.T.C. Exhibit No. 192, pp. 42–43.
[44] File No. 17–7–848, F.T.C. Exhibit No. 192, pp. 81–82.

mining the degree of monopoly power of any firm is the ease of entry of other firms into the market in which it operates. The acquisition of a firm in the same line of business in an adjacent geographical area might be a highly effective way of preventing the entry into one firm's market of the firm that could most easily make such entry. The commission took the same position in cases in which the firms had sold the same product to different customers. The fact that two firms have habitually sold their product to distinct groups of customers does not mean that they have not been in competition in the economic sense. Particularly in instances in which there is not concomitance between producer and purchaser of a product, the existence of another firm producing the same product, even though it sells to different customers, can serve to limit the control that the first firm is able to exercise over its own prices. The acquisition of the second firm can be an effective means of removing this source of demand elasticity and of forestalling entry by the acquired firm into direct competition for customers. An example of such a situation is the acquisition of the Sunlight Electrical Manufacturing Company by Delco Products Corporation, a wholly owned subsidiary of General Motors. Delco had been selling washing-machine motors to three firms, none of which ever bought the product from Sunlight. Sunlight had been selling 75 per cent of its output to thirteen washing-machine manufacturers, none of which were at any time customers of Delco. The commission held that the two companies had not been in substantial competition with each other.[45]

Many of these acquisitions, which, after preliminary inquiry, were held not to have had the effect of lessening competition, involved one or more multiproduct firms, with each firm selling a common product. In such cases, if the proportion of the sales of the common product to the total sales of either firm was small, the commission held that substantial competition had not existed. For example, the General Household Utilities Company was formed with the acquisition by United States Radio and Television Corporation of the Grunow Corporation. The acquiring company sold radios and refrigerators. The acquired company had

[45] File No. 17-7-802, F.T.C. Exhibit No. 192, pp. 10–12.

been organized to sell radios and refrigerators, but had sold no radios prior to the acquisition. In 1932, the acquiring firm sold over two million dollars' worth of radios and only forty-six thousand dollars' worth of refrigerators. Competition was considered to be not substantial between the firms.[46]

The Eaton-Detroit Metal Company was formed with the acquisition by Eaton Manufacturing Company of the Detroit Metal Specialties Company. The Eaton company manufactured and sold an extensive line of automobile parts. One per cent of its sales were of hubcaps. The acquired company manufactured a line of stamped metal products. Twenty-five per cent of its sales were of hubcaps. This was considered sufficient evidence that the companies had not been in competition with each other.[47]

With respect to the acquisition by Continental Can Company, Inc., of the Columbia Can Company, Saint Louis, Missouri, the digest of the file on the inquiry said:

> It is reported that about 63% of the total sales of the Columbia Can Company for 1934 consisted of cans of a type not manufactured by the East St. Louis plant of the Continental Can Company. In the can making industry it appears that equipment suitable for the production of one style of container cannot always be used for the manufacture of another. Also, due to prohibitive freight rates, a plant engaged in the production of medium and large size cans is compelled to sell more or less locally, and cannot compete with producers of similar cans located any appreciable distance away.[48]

Prior to its consolidation with the Arden Salt Company, the Leslie-California Salt Company produced refined vacuum salt, dried processed salt, and crude wet salt. Only 15 per cent of its sales were reported to be of crude wet salt; the Arden Salt Company had produced only crude wet salt.[49] Apparently the commission failed to consider the possibility that the demand for the whole line of products of the acquiring firm might have been a function of the price charged by the acquired firm. The elimination of independent price-output decisions by the management

[46] File No. 17–7–807, F.T.C. Exhibit No. 192, pp. 16–18.
[47] File No. 17–7–815, F.T.C. Exhibit No. 192, pp. 25–26.
[48] File No. 17–7–860, F.T.C. Exhibit No. 192, p. 99.
[49] File No. 17–11–2416, F.T.C. Exhibit No. 192, pp. 229–230.

of the Arden company might have substantially increased the monopoly power of the Leslie-California Salt Company. Possibly, the percentage of a firm's sales of the common product is relevant to the degree of lessening of competition brought about by an acquisition. If the Leslie-California Salt Company, for example, had produced only crude wet salt and no other products, then 100 per cent of its sales would have been in competition with the Arden company and vice versa, on the assumption that the markets of the products of the two firms were not otherwise differentiated. Is the degree to which competition is lessened by the acquisition any smaller merely because the acquired company produced other types of salt in addition to crude wet salt?

If all the sales of the acquiring and acquired companies were in competition with each other, the commission still would not necessarily conclude that the law had been violated, since the International Shoe decision would require that it ascertain whether the acquisition had injuriously affected the public. That is, it would have to look to the market as a whole to ascertain whether the acquisition had *substantially lessened* the substantial competition between the two firms. The policy of the commission was to examine the market as a whole in such cases, only because of what it considered to be a restriction on its administration of Section 7 resulting from the International Shoe decision. In its report to the Temporary National Economic Committee, the commission's spokesman said:

> The court was of the opinion that mere acquisition by one corporation of the stock of a competitor, even though it resulted in the lessening of some competition, is not forbidden; that the act deal [sic] only with such acquisitions as would probably result in lessening competition in the industry to a substantial degree, that is, to such a degree as will *injuriously affect the public*. Such a decision applies no more than the Sherman Law test, and the test of competition between the two companies is disregarded.[50]

The report goes on to say:

> In the *Temple Anthracite Coal Company Case* Justice [*sic*] Wooley, in a dissenting opinion, gave the best criticism of the test of competition laid down in the *International Shoe Company Case* in a statement in which he

[50] *T.N.E.C. Hearings,* part 5-A, p.p 2379–2380.

said, "In arriving at the conclusion that the evidence sustains the order of the Commission, I have kept in view the fact, at different times lost sight of in this case, that we are not concerned with the lessening of competition between these two companies and other companies in the industry, but are *concerned with the lessening of competition between the two companies themselves.*" [51]

The Supreme Court's interpretation of the standard of illegality did place undue restrictions on the Federal Trade Commission. In the first place, it required that the commission find evidence that the acquiring and the acquired companies had been in competition with each other in the sense that they were each selling the same product or products in the same markets. A substantial proportion of the sales of each firm were required to be of the common product. To this restriction, the commission raised no objection. In the second place, the court required that the probable effect of the acquisition must be to injure the public by substantially lessening competition in the industry. The most important restriction was that the court required that proof of the latter be essentially the same as the proof required for a Sherman Act violation. The commission appears to have not objected merely to the stringency of the Sherman Act test, but to the consideration of the effect on competition in the market as relevant to a Section 7 violation. The record of the commission's administration of Section 7 subsequent to the 1930 International Shoe decision reveals no attempt to formulate a less stringent criterion for determining the effect of an acquisition on competition *in a market.* It appears to have been operating with the traditional legal concept of a "monopoly"—that is, a single firm selling some particular line of products.

Several of the acquisitions about which preliminary inquiries were made in this period involved firms that had engaged in selling the same product or products in the same market in competition with each other, but that had not, after the merger, obtained complete control of the market in question. For example, the report on the inquiry into the acquisition of Twentieth Century

[51] *T.N.E.C. Hearings,* part 5-A, p. 2380. Italics supplied in the report of the F.T.C.

Pictures, Inc., by the Fox Film Corporation said that the facts showed preëxisting competition, but that "due to the large number of motion picture producers, there is no tendency toward monopoly." [52] With respect to the acquisition of A. B. See Elevator Company, Inc., by Westinghouse Electric and Manufacturing Company, the report of the inquiry said:

The available facts indicate that Westinghouse and A. B. See were in substantial competition with each other in the sale and installation of elevators, elevator machinery, and equipment. No tendency toward monopoly is noted, however, due to the large companies engaged in this business, notably Otis Elevator Company, which company enjoys practically 70% of such business.[53]

The commission found preëxisting competition in the sale of heavy chemicals between Monsanto Chemical Company and the Atlantic Chemical Company in its investigation of the acquisition of the latter by the former. It concluded, however, that the "acquisition will not tend toward monopoly, because of the fact that there are a large number of concerns in the United States engaged in the manufacture and sale of heavy chemicals." [54]

Cases of Firms Selling Different Products—In addition to the inquiries into acquisitions involving firms deemed to be engaged in the sale of the same product or products, there were many inquiries from which the commission concluded that the acquiring and the acquired firms were sellers of different products. Acquisitions of this second general type can conveniently be divided into four categories on the basis of the various relationships between the products.

One category, termed "vertical backward integration," includes those acquisitions in which the product of the acquired firm was a factor of production of the acquiring firm. For example, the National Standard Company manufactured a line of garage equipment including wire braid and steel cable. It acquired the Worchester Wire Works, Inc., a manufacturer of wire of various kinds, with facilities for drawing wire from rods. The commission

[52] File No. 17–8–8550, F.T.C. Exhibit No. 192, p. 130.
[53] File No. 17–11–2968, F.T.C. Exhibit No. 192, p. 251.
[54] File No. 17–8–8549, F.T.C. Exhibit No. 192, p. 128.

found no substantial competition between the firms, since they sold different products, and no tendency toward monopoly, since many other firms were manufacturing similar products.[55] Similarly, Bird and Son, Inc., which manufactured and sold a large variety of paper, roofing, and building products, some of which were produced with asphalt, acquired the Berry Asphalt Company, which owned and operated crude asphalt properties and refineries.[56]

In at least one case the acquisition involved two firms, the product of each of which was a factor of production of another finished product. The American Wringer Company, Inc., a manufacturer of rubber rolls and rubber-covered rolls for washing machine wringers, industrial wringers, and printing presses, acquired the Chamberlain Corporation, a manufacturer of metal wringer frames. The examiner concluded that the two firms had not been in competition with each other since:

> The wringer units sold by Chamberlain were fitted with American rolls, and the wringer units sold by American were fitted with Chamberlain frames. The bulk of the production of metal wringer frames by the Chamberlain Corporation was purchased by the American Wringer Company, Inc.[57]

There were also cases of a firm acquiring another firm that used the product of the acquiring firm as a factor of production—vertical forward integration. In such cases the commission held that competition could not be lessened, since the firms were considered not to have been in competition with each other prior to the acquisition. For example, American Commercial Alcohol Corporation, which operated distilleries for production of commercial alcohol, acquired the Kesler Chemical Company, which made solvents from alcohol, and Noxon, Inc., which made cleaners, polishes, insecticides, and similar products, in the production of which commercial alcohol was used.[58] A similar situation was disclosed in the inquiry into an acquisition by the E. I. du Pont de Nemours and Company, Inc., manufacturers of explosives used

---

[55] File No. 17-7-827, F.T.C. Exhibit No. 192, pp. 44–45.
[56] File No. 17-7-868, F.T.C. Exhibit No. 192, pp. 115–116.
[57] File No. 17-7-861, F.T.C. Exhibit No. 192, p. 102.
[58] File No. 17-7-803, F.T.C. Exhibit No. 192, pp. 13–15.

in the production of ammunition products. Explosives accounted for one-third of du Pont's sales in 1932. du Pont was the largest United States powder manufacturer; it acquired the largest producer of ammunition products in the United States, the Remington Arms Company, Inc. The commission considered that competition had not been lessened.[59]

The commission again ruled that competition was not substantial, and therefore could not be substantially lessened, in its consideration of the proposed acquisition by Republic Steel Corporation of the stock of Truscon Steel Company.

> Its [Republic Steel's] activities include all important steps in steel making, from the mining of ore and other raw materials to the manufacture of a diversified line of finished products. The company is reported to convert a greater percentage of its steel output into highly finished products and manufactured articles than any other of the large steel companies. . . .
>
> The fact that Truscon is really a fabricator of steel products, utilizing in such fabrication the finished steel products of steel manufacturing companies, places this company in a sphere of activity different from that engaged in by Republic . . . but is a customer of Republic, purchasing a large portion of its finished steel requirements from the latter company.
>
> In view of the circumstances above described, the contemplated capital stock acquisition of Truscon by Republic would not fall within the provisions of Section 7 of the Clayton Act.[60]

Working within its limited concept of competition between the firms involved, the commission in these cases ignored the possibility that such vertical integration might reduce competition in the market for the products of either the acquired or the acquiring firm. Removing the transfer of the basic commodities to the fabricator from the category of a market transaction might conceivably place the acquiring, integrated firm in a position to threaten the remaining fabricating firms with sufficiently high prices for a necessary factor of production that the fabricating firms would be forced to follow the price leadership of the integrated firm or suffer the possible consequences of higher prices

[59] File No. 17–7–819, F.T.C. Exhibit No. 192, pp. 31–32. In the 1957 du Pont–General Motors case, the Supreme Court reinterpreted the original Section 7 to prohibit just such a vertical forward integration. See chap. 8.

[60] File No. 17–7–847, F.T.C. Exhibit No. 192, pp. 78–80.

for the product of the integrated firm, accompanied by lower prices of a competing fabricator newly acquired by the producer of the basic commodity. Such a "squeeze" on the fabricating firms, of course, could not take place if there were independent alternative sellers of the basic commodity. It would not be necessary, however, for the acquiring firm to be the only firm in the market, since a small number of integrated firms might tacitly agree to such a price policy by the acquiring firm. The important point is that the Federal Trade Commission did not consider such possibilities, but merely concerned itself with the degree of competition between the acquiring and the acquired firms and, in some cases, with the question of whether there were any other firms in the industry.

By far the most numerous type of acquisition inquired into by the commission during this period involved the addition of new items to a general "line of products." The commission obtained little information regarding the degree of interrelationship of the demand functions for the products of the acquiring and the acquired firms, but apparently this varied considerably from case to case. The commission was using a very narrow definition of the "product" in ascertaining whether the firms were engaged in the sale of the same or of different products.[61] This narrowness of definition, as well as the variation in the degree of interrelationship between the demands for the products of the combining firms, is revealed in the following examples of acquisitions considered by the commission not to substantially lessen competition.

The Cord Corporation acquired a controlling stock interest in the Columbia Axles Company, the L. G. S. Devices Corporation, the Smith Engineering Company, Stinson Aircraft Corporation, Lycoming Manufacturing Company, and the Checker Manufacturing Corporation. These companies produced, respectively, automobile axles, automobile freewheeling devices, airplane propellers, aviation and automobile engines and heaters, and taxicabs.[62]

---

[61] The Supreme Court had followed a similar policy in the International Shoe Company case. See chap. 4.

[62] File No. 17–7–813, F.T.C. Exhibit No. 192, pp. 13–15.

Bristol-Myers Company, which sold an extensive line of drug and cosmetic products, acquired the Minit-Rub Corporation, producer of Minit-Rub salve, and the Rubber and Celluloid Products Company, a producer of shaving brushes and paint brushes.[63] Dictograph Products Company, Inc., which manufactured and sold Acousticon Hearing Aids and motor Dictographs, was considered not to have been in competition with Ampliphone Products Company, Inc., producers of interior office communication systems.[64]

A manufacturer of a complete line of couplings, pipe, and miscellaneous products for use in the construction and repair of pipe lines, S. R. Dresser Manufacturing Company, acquired the Bryant Heater and Manufacturing Company, a producer of gas fire boilers, warm air furnaces, and other products connected with house heating and air conditioning.[65] The Ludlum Steel Company, which manufactured high-grade carbon and alloy tool steels, and heat and wear-resisting special purpose steels, was considered not to have been in competition with the Wallingford Steel Company, which manufactured open hearth steel in the form of cold strips, according to the report of the inquiry into the acquisition of the latter by the former company.[66] The commission considered the Swann Corporation to be a producer of products complementary to those of the Monsanto Chemical Company, which was reported to produce over one hundred and fifty different types of fine and medicinal chemicals and heavy chemicals. The acquired company engaged in the electrolytic production of phosphoric acid and its derivatives.[67]

The degree to which the legal staff of the commission inquired into the economic aspects of the question of competition in such cases as these is indicated by the summary of the investigation into the acquisition by the Superheater Company of the stock of the Air Preheater Corporation. The summary of the file stated:

[63] File No. 17-7-845, F.T.C. Exhibit No. 192, pp. 73–74.
[64] File No. 17-11-2429, F.T.C. Exhibit No. 192, pp. 231–232.
[65] File No. 17-7-822, F.T.C. Exhibit No. 192, pp. 35–36.
[66] File No. 17-8-8556, F.T.C. Exhibit No. 192, pp. 133–134.
[67] File No. 17-7-821, F.T.C. Exhibit No. 192, pp. 33–34.

It is officially reported, and inquiry appears to indicate, that the Superheater Company was not engaged in the manufacture or sale of air preheaters, the principal business of the Air Preheater Corporation.

The basic differences in the functions of the products of the two companies are, to a degree, expressed in their names, air preheaters and superheaters. The distinction is a technical one, but inquiry reveals that the two have definite meanings in engineering circles. . . .

Although the acquisition was of the capital stock of the company, the Chief Examiner and the Chief Counsel find that there is no cause for action, since the facts show that the two companies were not engaged in competition.

Disposition: On April 23, 1934, the Commission, in accordance with the recommendation of the Chief Examiner, as concurred in by the Chief Counsel in a memorandum of April 19, closed the matter.[68]

Throughout this whole period, it appears that the economic staff of the commission took no part in the preliminary investigations of Section 7 matters. An example of the manner in which these investigations were conducted is provided by the investigation into the merger of Parker-Wylie Carpet Manufacturing Company and the General Carpet Corporation. Photostatic copies of papers of an evidentiary nature from the file in this as well as some of the other investigations were submitted to the Temporary National Economic Committee along with the summary of the files in all the cases. It appears that the investigation consisted of the writing of a letter to the merged corporation asking for details on the manner in which the acquisition was effected and also asking if the two corporations had been in competition with each other prior to the acquisition. The legal firm representing the corporation replied with the details of the financial transactions involved and with a statement that the two firms had not been in competition. This was supported with an account of the dollar value of the sales of the various products of the two firms for the year preceding the merger.[69] On the basis of this

[68] File No. 17-7-830, F.T.C. Exhibit No. 192, p. 48.

[69] "Photostatic Copies of Papers from File No. 17-11-2886, General Carpet Corporation," F.T.C. Exhibit No. 191, admitted to the record during hearings held March 1, 1939, by the Temporary National Economic Committee and included within T.N.E.C. Exhibit No. 305, National Archives, Washington, D.C.

information, the chief counsel recommended that the matter be closed without docketing. The summary of the inquiry included no information about the nature of the products produced by the two firms except that supplied in the letter from the legal representative of the firm. The summary stated:

> Prior to the merger herein involved Alva Carpet and Rug Company engaged in the manufacture of *velvet jute* [italics throughout are mine] and *velvet wool* rugs. During the year 1936 sales of velvet jute rugs amounted to approximately $214,000.00 and sales of velvet wool rugs amounted to approximately $53,000.00, total sales amounting to approximately $268,-000.00. . . .
>
> . . . As of date of merger with Alva Carpet and Rug Company, this company [Parker-Wylie Carpet Manufacturing Company] was engaged in the manufacture of *tapestry, Axminster* and *jute* rugs. During the year 1936 the company's sales amounted to approximately $1,500,000.00. . . .
>
> Preliminary inquiry into the matter herein involved discloses that although the constituent corporations merged into the General Carpet Corporation were engaged in the manufacture and sale of a similar line of products, nevertheless the individual products of these corporations were unlike in type and character and non-competitive. The products do not appear to have been sold in competition.[70]

It is quite possible that this merger had a negligible effect on the degree of competition in the market for the general line of products produced by the two firms. If it had been a merger that might substantially lessen competition or tend to create a monopoly in the economic sense, however, the legal concept within which the staff of the commission was working and the manner of conducting the inquiry were such that it seems very unlikely that the commission would have made its decision on the basis of the economically relevant information.

Another example of the tendency of the legal staff of the commission to make its decision on the basis of the physical characteristics of the products rather than on the nature of the demand for them is provided by the inquiry into the acquisition by the Sutherland Paper Company of the Wisconsin National Fibre Can Company. The Sutherland company was found to be the nation's largest manufacturer of paraffined cartons. It also produced other

[70] File No. 17–11–2886, F.T.C. Exhibit No. 192, pp. 248–249.

types of folding containers as well as "paper-board display specialties." The acquired company produced only round paper cans, a type of container not produced by Sutherland. The summary of the file on the case stated:

> Inquiry discloses that the acquisition did not tend to create a monopoly by reason of the fact that no increase resulted in the production of Sutherland manufacturers, since the two organizations in question were not engaged in the manufacture of similar articles prior to the acquisition.[71]

This statement shows that the legal staff of the commission considered an increase in the sales of a firm to be a sign of a tendency toward monopoly, an attitude evident in other cases as well.

Other Types of Cases—In several of these cases the commission followed the ruling of the court in the International Shoe case[72] that the acquisition of a firm in financial distress could not violate Section 7 because, if the acquisition had not taken place, the acquired firm would no longer be offering competition to the acquiring firm. The commission in no case raised the question of the effect on competition of the acquisition of a firm in failing circumstances, but merely accepted the legal judgment of the court on the economic aspects of such an acquisition. For example, Goodyear Tire and Rubber Company, reported to be the world's largest manufacturer of automobile tires and tubes with 1934 sales at one hundred thirty-six million dollars, acquired Kelly-Springfield Tire Company, which had suffered losses for several years prior to the acquisition. The summary of the investigation of the case said:

> From the foregoing statement of facts, it is concluded that the Goodyear Tire and Rubber Company has acquired the entire business of the Kelly-Springfield Tire Company through a bankruptcy proceeding. In the light of the decision of the Supreme Court in the International Shoe case, the Chief Counsel believes that the Commission is without jurisdiction to take any action on the premises.[73]

The chief counsel thus viewed the case as one outside the jurisdiction of the commission and failed to even consider the ques-

[71] File No. 17-7-857, F.T.C. Exhibit No. 192, p. 93.
[72] 280 U.S. 291 (1930). See pp. 126–136.
[73] File No. 17-7-863, F.T.C. Exhibit No. 192, p. 104.

tion of the effect of the acquisition on competition in the market for automobile tires and tubes. Conceivably, if the commission had investigated the case more thoroughly, and if it had found that the acquisition might have the effect of tending to create a monopoly in this line of commerce, the Supreme Court might have upheld the finding. There may have been many alternative plans of reorganization, other than the transfer of the productive capacity of the firm to the largest firm in the industry, which would have provided an equitable settlement to the creditors and stockholders of the corporation, and which might have created market conditions more conducive to competition than those resulting from this acquisition.[74] The fostering of the maximization of the profits of individuals and firms is not always compatible with the public interest that the antitrust law policy of the nation is designed to serve.

In one of these inquiries, the commission held that competition could not have been lessened between the acquiring and the acquired corporations as there had been a community of interest between the two firms prior to the acquisition. Both the New Haven Trap Rock Company and the Connecticut Quarries Company, Inc., were engaged in the production and distribution of crushed rock in New England.

> Since practically all of the outstanding stock of the two old corporations was held by members of the Blakeslee family, it is more or less evident that the two companies would not be in competition with each other.[75]

If this reasoning were to prevail, then any acquisition following the achievement of a community of interest or any form of conspiracy or agreement between firms which eliminated competition would not be considered to lessen competition and would, therefore, be legal.

Many acquisitions among the 121 inquired into by the commission do not fall into any one classification, but could be placed in several. For example, in the acquisition of Corcoran-Brown Lamp Company by Electric Auto-Lite Company, only a small propor-

---

[74] See pp. 132–134.

[75] File No. 17–8–8534, F.T.C. Exhibit No. 192, p. 121.

tion of the sales of each firm were of a product sold by the other firm, since each firm produced tail lights for automobiles and also other products. It represented an extension of Electric Auto-Lite's line of products. In addition, the two companies sold to different customers and many other firms were selling the same products.[76]

It is clear from the preceding review of the disposition of preliminary inquiries that the commission accepted the interpretation given the law in the International Shoe case. This interpretation of the standard of illegality precluded the commission from preventing acquisitions, even if it had had the power to order divestment of assets. The commission made little attempt to achieve a redefinition of the standard of illegality by means of further judicial review of what might have been an economically more meaningful policy.

Inquiries Dismissed Because of the "Assets Loophole"

Although the Federal Trade Commission's report to the Temporary National Economic Committee maintained that the chief limitation placed on its ability to administer Section 7 was the "assets loophole," it failed to question whether any of the acquisitions into which the commission inquired during this period could and would have been prevented even if the so-called loophole had not existed. The commission based this part of its report to the Temporary National Economic Committee on the summary of the material from the commission's files, which was submitted to the committee and made a part of the record, but not printed. This summary discloses that, in all nine cases of mergers made pursuant to state laws, it was concluded that there had *not* been substantial competition between the merged firms prior to the mergers.[77] Thus, even if the Supreme Court, in the Arrow-Hart and Hegeman case, had ruled that a merger made pursuant to state law is subject to Section 7, these nine inquiries would have

[76] File No. 17-7-855, F.T.C. Exhibit No. 192, pp. 90–91.
[77] F.T.C. Exhibit No. 192, appendix, pp. 1–6.

been dismissed for lack of preëxisting substantial competition under the International Shoe interpretation of the standard of illegality.

Acquisitions of Stock and Then Assets—In the nine cases in which a stock acquisition was followed by a transfer of assets and in which the commission's dismissal was attributed to the Swift and Thatcher decisions, the information available from the inquiry indicates that, even if the commission had had the power to proceed against the asset transfer, evidence would quite likely not have sustained a finding of violation of Section 7.

In the case of an acquisition of stock by the Atlas Powder Company, the commission apparently had gone far enough with its inquiry before the assets were transferred to conclude that there had been no substantial competition between the firms.[78] The other eight inquiries were terminated, however, upon finding that transfers of assets had followed the stock acquisitions. In these cases the commission drew no definite conclusions about the effects of the acquisitions. For example, the summary of the file on the inquiry into the acquisition of Thinshell Products, Inc., by the Consolidated Biscuit Company states that "there is evidence that competition did exist" between those two firms, but there is no indication of whether the commission would have held it to have been substantial. The acquiring company was said to be "one of the largest companies" in the manufacture and sale, at wholesale and retail, of crackers and other bakery products, and the acquired company was said to be in "practically the same line of business." [79]

The General American Transportation Corporation, engaged in the leasing of tank cars for transportation of gasoline and other liquids, had acquired the stock and then the assets of the Pennsylvania–Conley Tank Car Company. The file contained no information on the nature of the business of the acquired company, and there is no indication that the acquisition would have been held to be illegal, even if the assets had not been acquired.[80]

[78] File No. 1–6918, F.T.C. Exhibit No. 192, appendix, p. 2.
[79] File No. 17–11–2240, F.T.C. Exhibit No. 192, pp. 219–220.
[80] File No. 17–10–3248, F.T.C. Exhibit No. 192, pp. 167–169.

The commission inquired into the acquisition by the National Gypsum Company of the stock and then the assets of the Universal Gypsum and Lime Company. The acquiring company sold lime, gypsum, and insulation products. The acquired company was engaged in the mining of gypsum, the quarrying of gypsite, and the manufacture of gypsum wallboards and wall plaster. In support of its thesis that the "assets loophole" was the chief limitation on the ability of the commission to prevent mergers, its report to the Temporary National Economic Committee said that National Gypsum was one of the largest companies in the United States in this industry and that, "prior to the acquisition, the two companies involved were in substantial competition in the sale of their products." [81] The summary of the file on the inquiry, however, contains no information on the geographical markets or the extent to which the sales of the two firms were of comparable, competitive products. The chief counsel recommended dismissal on the grounds that the asset transfer precluded the commission from proceeding in the case. Further inquiry might have resulted in a finding of no substantial preëxisting competition.[82]

In only one of these nine inquiries into acquisitions of stock and then assets[83] does the summary of the confidential file reveal that further investigation very likely would have produced sufficient evidence to sustain a finding of violation of Section 7 as interpreted by the court in the International Shoe case, even if the assets had not been acquired. The Phelps Dodge Corporation, the third largest producer of copper in the United States, acquired the stock and then the assets of United Verde Copper Company, the fourth largest domestic copper producer. As a result of the acquisition, Phelps Dodge surpassed Anaconda in productive capacity, becoming second only to Kennecott Copper Company. In the Arizona copper producing region, the acquisi-

[81] *T.N.E.C. Hearings*, part 5-A, p. 2382.

[82] File No. 17–10–2327, F.T.C. Exhibit No. 192, pp. 153–155.

[83] The other five inquiries not here discussed were inquiries into acquisitions of stock and then assets by Atlas Powder Company, File No. 1–6918; Glidden Co., File No. 17–11– . . . 96 (ellipses represent unreadable digits, here and throughout file numbers); Hafleigh & Co., File No. 17–8–8516; Rapid Electrotype Co., File No. 17–11–1996; and Wheeling Steel Corp., File No. 17–7–649.

tion united the first and second largest copper producers. Quite possibly preëxisting substantial competition might have been established and a substantial lessening of competition—resulting in injury to the public—might have been shown to have resulted.[84]

Acquisitions of Assets and Not Stock—In the fifty-seven inquiries into acquisitions initially of assets, the commission frequently terminated the investigations before ascertaining the effect on competition. In at least twenty-four of these cases, however, the files indicate that among the reasons for dismissal was a finding that either there had been no preëxisting substantial competition or the effect was not to create a tendency toward monopoly.[85] Among the remaining thirty-three preliminary inquiries —inquiries in which the commission did not find either an absence of substantial preëxisting competition or no tendency to-

[84] File No. 17–7–867, F.T.C. Exhibit No. 192, pp. 112–114.

[85] F.T.C. Exhibit No. 192, appendix, pp. 1–6. The names of the acquiring companies and the file numbers in these twenty-four inquiries are as follows:

Acquiring Company	*File No.*
Delco Products Corp.	17–7–802
Eaton-Detroit Metal Co.	17–7–815
Le Blond-Schacht Truck Co.	17–11–1873
Sparta Foundry Co.	17–11–1963
Armstrong Cork Co.	17–11–2096
Westinghouse Electric & Mfg. Co.	17–11–2968
Monsanto Chemical Co.	17–8–8549
Continental Can Co., Inc.	17–7–860
Kendall Co.	17–7–834
Ludens, Inc.	17–7–864
General Household Utilities Co.	17–7–807
General Foods Corp.	17–11– . . . 90
City Ice & Fuel Co.	17–7–848
Anchor Cap. Co.	17–11–3207
S. R. Dresser Mfg. Co.	17–7–822
Fox Film Corp.	17–8–8550
Air Reduction, Inc.	17–10–5887
Sherwin Williams Co.	17–11–800
Sutherland Paper Co.	17–7–857
National Standard Co.	17–7–829
American Rolling Mill Co.	17–10–2527
Distillers Corp.–Seagrams, Ltd.	17–11–3082
American Commercial Alcohol Corp.	17–7–803
Century Brewing Assn.	17–11–2440

ward monopoly—it seems probable that further investigation would not have supported a finding of the evil effects denounced by the law as interpreted by the Supreme Court.[86]

The inquiry into the acquisition by United States Steel Corporation of the assets of the Virginia Bridge and Iron Company, for example, was dismissed on the grounds that no acquisition of stock was involved. The investigation disclosed that United States

[86] F.T.C. Exhibit No. 192, appendix, pp. 1–6. These thirty-three inquiries were as follows. In the last fourteen cases listed, one or more asset acquisitions were made, as well as one or more stock acquisitions.

Acquiring Company	*File No.*
Electric Auto-Lite Co.	17–7–839
Bendix Aviation Corp.	17–7–865
Thompson Products, Inc.	17–10–2459
United States Gypsum Co.	17–7–846
United States Gypsum Co.	17–7–866
American Cyanamid & Chemical Corp.	17–11–2784
Metal Package Corp.	17–7–849
Hobart Mfg. Co.	17–7–840
American Cyanamid Co.	17–7–844
General Foods Corp.	17–11–3394
Zapon Brevolite Lacquer Co.	17–11–923
Standard Oil Co. (Indiana)	17–7–8228
Standard Steel Car Corp.	17–7–828
General Shoe Corp.	17–11–2241
United States Steel Corp.	17–8–8609
Republic Steel Corp.	17–11–2807
M. T. Stevens & Son Co.	17–7–836
R. G. Dun-Bradstreet Corp.	17–7–831
P. Goldsmith Sons Co.	17–11–3089
Consolidated Biscuit Co.	17–11–2240
Drug, Inc.	1–5619
Owens-Illinois Glass Co.	17–7–814
Owens-Illinois Glass Co.	17–10–2321
Robert Gair Co.	17–7–843
National Distillers Products Corp.	17–7–853
United Biscuit Co. of America	17–11– . . .
Glidden Co.	17–11– . . . 96
Fibreboard Products Co., Inc.	17–10–2846
Ground Gripper Shoe Co., Inc.	1–5673
Republic Steel Corp.	17–11–2242
Belding Heminway Co.	17–11–2242
Rapid Electrotype Co.	17–11–1997
Consolidated Oil Corp.	17–10–2326

Steel had had no subsidiaries fabricating steel in the south and had made this acquisition to round out its facilities in that area.[87] The assets of the acquired company were reported to be only about three-tenths of 1 per cent as large as those of the acquiring firm.[88] In view of the diversity of operations of United States Steel and its large size compared with the acquired company, further investigation probably would have disclosed that only a very small percentage of the business of the acquiring company was in competition with the acquired company. Were this true, then an order of divestment could not have been upheld under the policies of the commission during this period.

There were several other similar cases of a relatively large firm, with a greatly diversified line of products, acquiring one or more smaller firms engaged in the manufacture and sale of a much more limited number of types of products in a market geographically less extensive than that of the acquiring firm. The United States Gypsum Company, for example, was engaged in the manufacture and sale of many different types of lime, gypsum, asphalt, and allied products. It acquired the assets of the Dittlinger Lime Company, a Texas corporation engaged principally in the manufacture and sale of lime. It also acquired the assets of the Arborite Company, a Maine corporation engaged in the manufacture and sale of wood fibre insulating board. The chief examiner of the commission recommended that the file be closed when it was ascertained that the acquisitions did not involve stock.[89] It appears, however, that further investigation and consideration of the case by the commission would have resulted in a dismissal on grounds of a lack of preëxisting substantial competition, even if the acquisitions had been of stock instead of assets.

The American Cyanamid Company, a large firm with a diversified line of products in the heavy chemicals and explosives fields, acquired the General Explosives Corporation and the Maryland Chemical Company, each of which was a much smaller firm producing a much more limited group of products than the

[87] File No. 17–8–8609, F.T.C. Exhibit No. 192, pp. 137–138.
[88] *Ibid.*, appendix, p. 5.
[89] File No. 17–7–866, F.T.C. Exhibit No. 192, pp. 110–111.

acquiring company.[90] The Electric Auto-Lite Company, one of the largest manufacturers of starting, lighting, and ignition systems as well as storage batteries for automobiles and trucks, acquired the assets of the Owen Dyneto Corporation, which sold a much more limited line of similar products to three automobile firms.[91] Similarly, the Owens-Illinois Glass Company, the world's largest manufacturer of bottles, acquired the assets of the Hemingray Glass Company, a manufacturer of glass insulators, and the O'Neil Machine Company, a manufacturer of vacuum-type bottle-blowing machines.[92]

Other acquisitions in this group of thirty-three inquiries into asset acquisitions probably would not have been held to be unlawful, even if the assets had not been acquired. Several involved the acquisition of a firm producing different types of products in order to further diversify the line of products of the acquiring firm. For example, the General Shoe Corporation, which produced only men's and boys' shoes, acquired the assets of J. K. Orr Shoe Company, 75 per cent of the sales of which were of women's shoes.[93]

In some of the other cases of asset acquisitions, the acquiring and the acquired companies appear to have been engaged in the sale of comparable products in the same geographical areas, but it is unlikely that the courts would have upheld a finding of a substantial lessening of competition and a tendency to create a monopoly in view of the small share of the market controlled by the acquiring firm after the acquisition. The acquisition of the assets of five firms by Robert Gair Company, Inc., was of this type. All the firms were engaged in the sale of various kinds of shipping containers, wallboard, cartons, and other boxboard products.[94] The summary of the file on the investigation said, however:

---

[90] File No. 17-7-844, F.T.C. Exhibit No. 192, pp. 71–72.

[91] File No. 17-7-839, F.T.C. Exhibit No. 192, pp. 62–63.

[92] File No. 17-7-814, F.T.C. Exhibit No. 192, pp. 23–24.

[93] File No. 17-11-2241, F.T.C. Exhibit No. 192, pp. 222–223.

[94] The inquiry included investigation of three other acquisitions that were of stock of firms engaged in the sale of products different from these. File No. 17-7-843, F.T.C. Exhibit No. 192, pp. 68–70.

The acquisition of these several interests since 1932 does not appear to have placed Robert Gair Company, Inc., in a monopolistic position. Inquiry discloses that the corporation's position in the industry is considerably less than 10%, and that the company encounters keen competition from several large organizations similarly engaged, notably Container Corporation of America.[95]

The creation of R. G. Dun-Bradstreet Corporation by the acquisition of Bradstreet Company by the R. G. Dun Corporation was a similar case. The inquiry disclosed that both firms had engaged in very similar lines of business. They had competed with each other for eighty-five years prior to the acquisition. It is doubtful, however, that the commission would have held that the lessening of competition between the two firms was substantial.

There are some competitors who make reports on certain phases or branches of industry who compare favorably with Dun and Bradstreet in volume of business of such phases or branches of industry.[96]

The file was sent to the Justice Department for its consideration of a possible Sherman Act violation and the Attorney General "advised the Commission this transaction had been considered by his department and had been closed as disclosing no violation of the Federal anti-trust laws." [97]

It is impossible, of course, to know what would have resulted from these investigations of acquisitions if the commission had been permitted to proceed under Section 7 against asset acquisitions. The record of these 121 investigations from 1932 to 1938 indicates clearly, however, that the so-called "assets loophole" was not the primary limitation on the commission's ability to prevent mergers; the interpretation given the standard of illegality of Section 7 by the commission and the Supreme Court had prevented action against the acquiring corporation in most of these cases.

The limitation placed on the commission's administration of Section 7 by the International Shoe case might possibly have been

[95] *Ibid.*, p. 70.
[96] File No. 17-7-831, F.T.C. Exhibit No. 192, p. 49.
[97] *Ibid.*

removed if the commission had developed, and if the Supreme Court had approved, a different interpretation of the standard of illegality. Except for the interpretation given the section in the case of the Vanadium-Alloys Steel Company,[98] the commission made no attempt to initiate a reinterpretation of the standard, after its reversal in the V. Vivaudou and the Temple Anthracite cases.[99]

Federal Trade Commission Recommendations to Congress

Not only did the commission fail to work within the administrative and judicial framework to achieve a more meaningful interpretation of Section 7, but it also did little to obtain Congressional redefinition of the standard of illegality. It did, however, persistently attempt to have the Clayton Act amended to extend the authority of the commission to include the power to order divestment of assets as well as stock.

The Federal Trade Commission had first expressed an interest in having Section 7 amended to include asset acquisitions in 1921; its *Annual Report* said:

> On the score of absorption of competing companies by a single unit and other practices tending to lessen competition and to create monopoly, the Commission has handled cases under certain sections of the Clayton Antitrust Act, which are within its jurisdiction. . . . The Commission has found that corporations frequently now absorb competitors, not by acquiring capital shares, but by acquiring the physical assets which the Clayton Act does not forbid. . . . These ineffectual features of the law have been brought to the attention of the Congress.[100]

Not until after the Arrow-Hart and Hegeman decision[101] did the commission begin to make a determined effort to have the statute amended. In its *Annual Report* for the 1935 fiscal year, the commission stated:

---

[98] See pp. 151–158.

[99] See pp. 136–144.

[100] *F.T.C. Annual Report, 1921,* p. 6.

[101] 291 U.S. 587 (1934).

If the section is to accomplish the general purpose of preventing monopoly, it should be amended to prohibit acquisition of assets, not only indirectly through use of stock unlawully [*sic*] acquired but also direct acquisition of assets independently of stock acquisition. The Commission therefore recommends that both the direct and indirect acquisition of assets be prohibited *where the effects are the same as those already prohibited by the section* [italics mine].[102]

Only a few months before the recommendation that asset acquisitions be prohibited under the same conditions as were stock acquisitions in the original Clayton Act, the commission had recommended a more comprehensive amendment of the section in a report on an investigation of chain stores.[103] The commission criticized the International Shoe decision for making the effect on competition in an industry the test of illegality rather than the effect on competition between the acquiring and the acquired corporation, which it considered to be the "vital part of the section."[104] It therefore recommended that the law be amended to include asset as well as stock acquisitions, and also to make such acquisitions illegal when they involve corporations "in competition with" each other, irrespective of the effect on competition within the industry.[105] The commission proposed no basis of judgment on whether two corporations are "in competition with" each other. It recommended further that, were the proposal unacceptable, Congress at least should amend the law so as to make illegal the acquisition of assets by means of an illegal stock acquisition.[106]

In a 1937 report to Congress, the commission recommended amendment of Section 7 to remove the necessity of ascertaining the effects of an acquisition. It would have substituted a criterion based on the percentage of total assets in an industry controlled by a firm after an acquisition, the percentage to be specified by

[102] *F.T.C. Annual Report, 1935*, p. 16.

[103] *Final Report of Chain-Store Investigation, Federal Trade Commission*, U.S. 74th Cong., 2d sess., S. Doc. 4 (1934).

[104] S. Doc. 4 (1934), p. 95.

[105] *Ibid.*, p. 96.

[106] *Ibid.*, p. 95.

Congress in the proposed legislation.[107] The commission said:

Determination of whether the effect in a particular case may be to substantially lessen competition or tend to create a monopoly often requires a judicial process so extended that during the period of litigation the assets of the combined companies may be so commingled that to separate them again is no easy matter. . . . For effective administration, the law should be quickly enforceable; and to this end the proof required to establish a violation should be simplified as much as the nature of the facts permits.[108]

In its 1937 *Annual Report* the commission stressed that it was chiefly concerned with having assets included in the prohibitions of the section, although it renewed the recommendation for changing the criterion of illegality for the sake of easier administration:

. . . The Commission has . . . recommended in earlier annual reports and upon other occasions and now renews its recommendation that the acquisition of assets be declared unlawful under the same circumstances that the acquisition of stock is already so declared.

In its recent report on Agricultural Income . . . the Commission amplified the foregoing recommendation so as to preclude the acquisition of assets where the combined assets would exceed an amount to be specified by Congress. This would have the advantage of a positive legislative standard, defining the limit at which corporate accretions in size and power shall be halted in order to prevent monopoly. The Commission renews that recommendation.[109]

In 1938 the commission suggested the same type of amendment to Congress, but made more specific the proposed change in the standard of illegality. In the report on its inquiry into the agricultural implement and machinery industry, the commission recommended:

That Section 7 of the Clayton Act be amended so as to make it unlawful for any corporation, directly or indirectly, through a holding company, subsidiary, or otherwise, to acquire any of the stock or assets of a competing corporation when either of said corporations is engaged in interstate com-

[107] *Principal Farm Products, Agricultural Income Inquiry,* U.S. 75th Cong., 1st sess., S. Doc. 54 (1937), p. 31.

[108] S. Doc. 54 (1937), p. 30.

[109] *F.T.C. Annual Report, 1937,* p. 15.

merce; provided, this prohibition shall not apply where the corporations involved control, in the aggregate, less than 10 percent of the total output of any industry or branch thereof in the United States, or of the sale of the commodity as to which the corporations are in competition, unless the effect of such acquisition may be to restrain competition or tend to create a monopoly in any line of commerce.[110]

If this proposal had been accepted by Congress, the effect would have been to make the question of whether the acquiring and the acquired corporations are in competition with each other the test of illegality. The effect of an acquisition on competition in a market would have been presumed to be adverse if the combined firm produced or sold more than 10 per cent of the nation's total of the product in question.

In making this type of recommendation, the commission appears to have confessed its inability to improve upon the interpretation of the original Section 7, which had evolved from the policies of the commission itself and the courts. It was seeking some means of avoiding the necessity of carrying out the duties of an administrative agency to implement and give specific content to a general statement of policy by Congress. It was for this type of administration by a continuing body of experts that the commission was created. Little would be gained by having an administrative commission administer the antimerger provisions of the antitrust laws, if the attempt to ascertain the undesirable effects on competition of each individual merger were to be abandoned in favor of an arbitrary statistical test of illegality ignoring such effects.

The 1938 *Annual Report* renewed the recommendation made in the *Report on Agricultural Implement and Machinery Inquiry*, saying of it, as it did a year earlier of the previous recommendation, that such an "amendment would have the advantage of creating a positive legislative standard, defining the limit at which corporate accretions shall be halted in order to prevent monopoly." [111]

---

[110] *Federal Trade Commission Report on Agricultural Implement and Machinery Inquiry*, U.S. 75th Cong., 3d sess., H. Doc. 702 (1938), p. 1038.

[111] *F.T.C. Annual Report, 1938*, p. 19.

The commission's suggestions for amending the standard of illegality of Section 7 thus were based on the desire for ease of administration and the simple assumption that monopoly power is directly related to corporate size. The commission did not request that the standard of illegality of the statute allow it to formulate criteria for determining for each acquisition whether its effect might be to increase monopoly power.

The *Preliminary Report of the Temporary National Economic Committee* in 1939 recommended the amendment of Section 7 of the Clayton Act to include asset as well as stock acquisitions. It also recommended that the law be changed to forbid the acquisition of *one* or more corporations instead of *two* or more, in order to cover a case in which a holding company acquires a corporation that had not been competing with that holding company but with one of its subsidiaries. In addition, the section should be amended to exempt an acquisition of a corporation in failing circumstances, although this had been done, in effect, by the International Shoe decision. No change in the wording of the standard of illegality was recommended.[112]

In its 1939 *Annual Report* the Federal Trade Commission renewed its request that Section 7 be amended to prohibit asset acquisitions:

> As a result of its studies of competitive conditions in many industries during the past few years, the Commission believes that when a considerable proportion of the total output of an industry is brought under one ownership, there is a strong probability that competition will be substantially lessened in the process. It is also believed that the problem created by consolidations and mergers is not merely that of lessening of competition in a particular industry. The progressive enlargement of a few predominant enterprises has already gone so far that, in financial strength and in numbers of persons subject to their control, the largest concerns outrank some State governments. The dangers of such concentration of power are evident whether the power is concentrated in one industry or spread over a number of industries. The Commission believes that there should be limits to growth which can be exercised by the combination.[113]

---

[112] *Preliminary Report of the Temporary National Economic Committee,* U.S. 76th Cong., 1st sess., S. Doc. 95 (1939), pp. 21–22.

[113] *F.T.C. Annual Report, 1939,* p. 15.

This *Annual Report* of the commission then quoted and endorsed the recommendations of the Temporary National Economic Committee and reiterated its recommendations of previous years that acquisitions of assets or stock be prohibited

> . . . when the effect of such acquisition of stock or assets may be to substantially lessen competition between the two corporations or, where from the relative size of the corporation resulting from the merger and the surrounding conditions, the effect of such acquisition may be to restrain competition or tend to create a monopoly in any line of commerce.[114]

The next paragraph makes it clear that the commission no longer wished to have the law specify the particular percentage of sales which would make a merger illegal.

> The permissible percentage of corporate control over an industry should be elastic. A given percentage in one industry might be wholly harmless to the public interest, while the same or even smaller percentage in another industry might be gravely prejudicial. The minimum percentage necessary to effective corporate control of an industry is quite analogous to the minimum percentage of stock ownership necessary to control a corporation. In both cases it varies widely according to circumstances.[115]

This does not indicate what circumstances should be considered in ascertaining whether a merger is prejudicial to the public interest, nor how the limitation placed on the section by the Supreme Court in applying the Sherman Act criterion is to be overcome.

In its *Annual Report* for 1940, the commission reiterated the recommendations made the previous year:

> The Commission again recommends the acquisition of corporate assets be declared unlawful *under the same conditions* [italics mine] that the acquisition of capital stock has been so declared since 1914.[116]

In 1941 the Federal Trade Commission submitted a draft of conclusions and recommendations for the Temporary National Economic Committee to adopt in its final report on Section 7 of

[114] *Ibid.*, p. 16.
[115] *F.T.C. Annual Report, 1939*, p. 16.
[116] *F.T.C. Annual Report, 1940*, p. 13.

the Clayton Act.[117] The commission proposed that the Temporary National Economic Committee conclude that Congress had intended to prevent corporate mergers and consolidations when it enacted Section 7, but inexpert draftmanship had resulted in a failure to effectively prevent the evil, since acquisition of assets had been unknown at that time.[118] The commission would have had the committee conclude that the nation was faced with only two alternatives—either amend Section 7 to prevent corporate concentration by means of mergers, or resort to direct regulation of prices. The latter was considered undesirable but inevitable if Section 7 were not amended.[119] The Federal Trade Commission suggested that the committee recommend that Section 7 be amended in accordance with the committee's *Preliminary Report*.[120] Thus the great evils of corporate concentration attributed to mergers were to be prevented merely by giving the Federal Trade Commission authority over asset acquisitions with a standard of illegality unchanged from that of the original Section 7 as interpreted by the Supreme Court in the International Shoe decision.

The Temporary National Economic Committee, in its *Final Report,* did not accept the draft of the commission as the basis of its recommendations. It recommended that asset as well as stock acquisitions be included in Section 7, but it went further: the law should require prior approval by the Federal Trade Commission of proposed mergers.[121] In its *Annual Report* for each of the years from 1941 through 1945, the commission recommended the enactment of the legislation proposed by the Temporary National Economic Committee.[122]

---

[117] "Drafted Material, for Consideration by the Temporary National Economic Committee for its Final Report, as to Corporate Mergers and Section Seven of the Clayton Act," submitted by the Federal Trade Commission (typewritten, Feb., 1941), National Archives, Washington, D.C.

[118] *Ibid.*, pp. 1–2.

[119] *Ibid.*, p. 12.

[120] *Ibid.*, pp. 15–16.

[121] *Final Report and Recommendations of the Temporary National Economic Committee,* U.S. 77th Cong., 1st sess., S. Doc. 35 (1941), pp. 38–39.

[122] *Annual Reports of the F.T.C., 1941, 1942, 1943, 1944, and 1945,* pp. 12, 9,

The commission was primarily concerned with having Section 7 amended to give it authority over asset acquisitions. At no time, in its *Annual Reports,* special reports, or in its participation in the Temporary National Economic Committee investigations, did the commission focus attention upon the problem of changing the standard of illegality as interpreted in the International Shoe case in order to make it possible for the amended Section 7 to be administered effectively. In spite of the commission's many statements about the evils resulting from mergers, it failed to define how it proposed to prevent them by merely amending the law to include asset acquisitions within its jurisdiction in administering a Section 7 to which the court had applied the Sherman Act test.

Conclusions

In both the Temple Anthracite[123] and the V. Vivaudou case[124] the commission had based its findings of violation of Section 7 on the elimination of competition between the corporations, but only in the latter case did the commission conclude that the acquisition had had the effect of restraining commerce or tending to create a monopoly.[125] In reviewing the orders of the commission in these two cases, the Circuit Courts of Appeals for the Third and Second Circuits, respectively, followed the International Shoe decision by looking to the market structures of the industries for evidence to support a finding of a tendency to create a monopoly under the Sherman Act test. They held that the lessening of competition between the corporations was not substantial.[126]

In the Vanadium-Alloys Steel Company case, the commission attempted to lessen the stringency of the International Shoe in-

9, 9, and 8–9 respectively. See chap. 7 for a discussion of the Federal Trade Commission's recommendations on the various bills considered by Congress in the years just prior to the amendment of Section 7 in 1950.

[123] 13 F.T.C. 249 (1930).

[124] 13 F.T.C. 306 (1930).

[125] *Ibid.,* p. 314.

[126] 51 Fed. Rept., 2d Ser., 656 (1931), and 54 Fed. Rept., 2d Ser., 273 (1931).

terpretation of the standard of illegality by holding that the acquisition had substantially lessened competition between the acquiring and the acquired corporation, while admitting explicitly that the degree of monopoly power of the acquiring firm had not been significantly affected.[127] The courts did not review this interpretation of the law, because the assets of the acquired company were transferred and the commission made no effort to seek enforcement of its order of stock divestment.

After the Vanadium-Alloys case, the commission reverted to the International Shoe case interpretation of the standard of illegality. In deciding to dismiss complaints or to dismiss inquiries without issuing complaints, the commission followed the Supreme Court's interpretation. If the corporations concerned were not engaged almost exclusively in the sale of nearly identical products in the same market, the cases were dismissed on the grounds that preëxisting substantial competition was lacking. On the other hand, if an acquisition met the test of preëxisting substantial competition, the case would be dismissed for a lack of a tendency to create a monopoly under the Sherman Act test. The record of Federal Trade Commission administration of Section 7 after 1930 shows clearly that the International Shoe decision made it impossible for the commission to prevent monopoly "in its incipiency," since it could act only in cases which would be subject to Sherman Act prosecution.

The commission investigated many acquisitions in which (1) only assets were acquired, (2) stock and then assets were acquired, or (3) the corporations were merged under the provisions of state statutes. Clearly, however, the inability of the commission to deal with such cases was not the chief limitation on its ability to prevent incipient monopoly, since there were very few, if any, such cases in which a finding of Section 7 violation could have stood the International Shoe test of illegality.

Although the commission abandoned its attempt to focus on the lessening of competition between the acquiring and the acquired corporations after the Vanadium-Alloys Steel case, it continued to indicate in its reports to Congress that it believed the

[127] 18 F.T.C. 194, 203–204.

public interest to be served by the prevention of mergers between companies, which display a substantial proportion of the business in competition with the other, irrespective of the structure of their markets. This policy appears to have been adopted not from any careful economic analysis of the effect of such mergers on the public, but, instead, from an awareness of the administrative and legal difficulties avoided by having a simple statistical measure as a criterion of illegality. This conclusion is supported by the fact that, on the few occasions when the commission recommended a change in the wording of the standard of illegality of the statute, it framed the alteration in terms of a simple test based on the relative market share of the merged firm.

The policies of the Federal Trade Commission during the whole period of its administration of the original Section 7 were such that, if they had been applied in the absence of any restrictions from judicial review, they would have (1) prohibited many mergers between competitors, even if they might result in an increase in competition in a market, and (2) permitted many mergers involving firms not previously in "substantial competition" with each other, even if they might result in a substantial lessening of competition in a market.

6. Administration of Section 7 by Other Than the Federal Trade Commission from 1914 Through 1950

The primary responsibility for the administration of Section 7 has rested with the Federal Trade Commission. In the Clayton Act, however, Congress gave concurrent authority to the Justice Department to enforce the antitrust sections of the act through equity suits in the United States district courts.[1] Section 11 of the Clayton Act originally provided for enforcement also by the Federal Reserve Board for banking corporations and by the Interstate Commerce Commission for common carriers. When Congress created the Federal Communications Commission and the Civil Aeronautics Authority, it also gave them jurisdiction over the substantive sections of the Clayton Act for corporations under their jurisdictions.[2]

---

[1] 38 *U.S. Stat. at L.* 730–740 (1914). Section 15 provides: "That the several district courts of the United States are hereby invested with jurisdiction to prevent and restrain violations of this Act, and it shall be the duty of the several district attorneys of the United States in their respective districts, under the direction of the Attorney General, to institute proceedings in equity to prevent and restrain such violations."

[2] 15 U.S.C.A. Section 21.

The Clayton Act also provided for private suits to be brought under the antitrust laws, including Section 7. In Section 4 the act provided:

That any person who shall be injured in his business or property by reason of anything forbidden in the antitrust laws may sue therefor in any district court of the United States . . . without respect to the amount in controversy, and shall recover threefold the damages by him sustained, and the cost of suit, including a reasonable attorney's fee.[3]

Section 16 provided for injunctive relief:

That any person, firm, corporation, or association shall be entitled to sue for and have injunctive relief, in any court of the United States having jurisdiction over the parties, against threatened loss or damage by a violation of the antitrust laws, including sections two, three, seven, and eight of this Act.[4]

Although, compared with the administration of Section 7 by the Federal Trade Commission, the enforcement role of the Justice Department, the other administrative agencies, and private litigation between 1914 and 1950 was minor, there were several cases of each of the three types. The most important are discussed in this chapter.

Private Suits under Section 7

In the period from the enactment of the Clayton Act in 1914 until the amendment of Section 7 in 1950, several private suits were brought under Section 7 for the recovery of damages, but the courts upheld no awards. The provisions of the law for private actions appear to have had little deterrent effect on stock acquisitions.

In 1931 the Seventh Circuit Court of Appeals held that treble damages cannot be awarded for injury alleged to have occurred from a violation of Section 7 unless the plaintiff can show not only that the acquisition of stock has violated the law and that he has

[3] 38 *U.S. Stat. at L.* (1914), 730–740.

[4] *Ibid.*

been injured, but also that his injury has resulted directly from the lessening of competition or tendency to create a monopoly rather than merely from the acquisition itself.[5] The plaintiffs had owned 315 shares of the common stock of the Clover Leaf Milk Company. With money supplied by the Borden Company, two other stockholders bought the plaintiffs' shares for five hundred thirty-five dollars each, and then transferred the corporate assets to the Borden Company in exchange for a number of Borden Company shares having a value equal to one thousand dollars per share of Clover Leaf stock. The plaintiffs claimed that the acquisition was in violation of Section 7. The court did not rule on whether the law had been violated, but merely held that the plaintiffs had not shown that their loss was due to any violation that might have occurred.[6]

In several cases, allegation of injury from a violation of Section 7 of the Clayton Act was included with other charges. For example, Raymond E. Beegle brought action against Charles M. Thomson, as trustee of the Chicago and North Western Railway Company, to recover for damages alleged to have been suffered from violation of Section 7 and from patent infringement. The railway company had acquired the Sharon Railway Supply Company, which subsequently manufactured anti-splitting irons for railway ties, which the plaintiff alleged to be an infringement of his patent on a similar product invented while working for the railway. He alleged that the acquisition of the supply company was in violation of Section 7. The district court dismissed the complaint.[7] On appeal, the circuit court held that the acquiring railway company had not been in competition with the acquired company in the sale of the anti-splitting irons, because the supply company did not manufacture them until after the acquisition, and that the acquired company had been in failing condition at the time of the acquisition. The opinion said that, even if this had not been the case, the lower court was right in dismissing the

[5] *Peterson et al.* v. *Borden Co. et al.* (1931), 50 Fed. Rept., 2d Ser., 644 (C.C.A., 7th Cir.).

[6] 50 Fed. Rept., 2d Ser., 664.

[7] *Beegle* v. *Thomson* (1941), 2 Fed. Rules Decisions 84 (D.C., N.D. Ill.).

case, since the plaintiff did not affirmatively show injury to himself from the alleged violation.[8]

The acquisition by Columbia Gas and Electric Corporation of controlling stock interest in the American Fuel and Power Company gave rise to several cases involving Section 7. The first of these was an action brought by Ben Williamson, Jr., trustee of the Inland Gas Corporation, a subsidiary of American Fuel, against Columbia Gas and Electric Corporation for treble damages for injuries sustained by Inland to its business and property by reason of the indirect acquisition of a majority of its stock by Columbia. The district court granted a motion of the defendant to dismiss the complaint on the ground that it failed to state a cause of action under which relief could be granted, because the actions alleged to have injured Inland occurred more than three years prior to the commencement of the action. The court held that the Delaware statute of limitations applied, since the Clayton Act failed to state a limitation.[9] The decision was upheld by the Third Circuit Court of Appeals.[10]

The same acquisition was involved in an appeal from a bankruptcy proceeding in which the question at issue was the position occupied by a majority stockholder and creditor corporation in relation to other stockholders and creditors, where such stockholders acquired stock in violation of Section 7.[11] According to the findings of the court, the American Fuel and Power Company, through several subsidiaries, had been engaged in producing, transporting, and selling natural gas. It had been in financial difficulties that it proposed to overcome by projecting pipelines into Ohio to sell gas to industrial users in competition with the Columbia Gas and Electric Corporation, which was engaged in the same business as American, but theretofore in different geographical areas. Columbia, in order to prevent the entry into its markets of American as a competitor, acquired a controlling stock

[8] *Beegle* v. *Thomson* (1943), 138 Fed. Rept., 2d Ser. 875 (C.C.A., 7th Cir.).

[9] *Williamson* v. *Columbia Gas & Electric Corporation* (1939), 27 Fed. Supp. 198 (D.C., D. Del.).

[10] 110 Fed. Rept., 2d Ser., 15 (1939).

[11] *In re American Fuel & Power Co. and Five Other Cases* (1941), 148 Fed. Rept., 2d Ser., 428 (C.C.A., 6th Cir.).

interest in American. It then stopped the proposed pipeline construction and forced bankruptcy upon American and its subsidiaries. The court held that the acquisition had been in violation of Section 7 of the Clayton Act and that it was not the duty of a court of equity to aid in the achievement of an illegal purpose. It therefore ordered the lower court to fix the claims in the bankruptcy proceeding so as to exclude Columbia completely from claims acquired in violation of Section 7.[12]

Columbia Gas and Electric Corporation, which had not been a party in that proceeding, appealed to the court in an action in which the Securities and Exchange Commission and the Justice Department both intervened. The court then ruled that, although the stock had been acquired in violation of Section 7, the claims of Columbia should be merely subordinated rather than excluded.[13]

Justice Department Administration of Section 7

Between 1914 and 1950 the Justice Department instituted proceedings in equity in four cases, alleging violation of Section 7 of the Clayton Act. Three of the four cases also involved allegations of violation of the Sherman Act. In these three cases it included the Section 7 allegations because the alleged monopolistic practices of the defendants included acquisition of stock of competing corporations.

In 1917 the Justice Department brought a bill of equity to prevent forty corporations and ten individuals engaged in the fresh fish industry from violating the Sherman Act and "acts supplementing that act." The court found that the defendant dealers had violated the Sherman Act by combining "with a view to centralizing and controlling the flow of fish in interstate commerce." [14] The court decided that the acquisition by the Boston

[12] 148 Fed. Rept., 2d Ser., 428.

[13] *Columbia Gas & Electric Corporation* v. *United States et al.* (1946), 151 Fed. Rept., 2d Ser., 461 (C.C.A., 6th Cir.).

[14] *United States* v. *New England Fish Exchange, et al.*, 258 Fed. Rept. 732, 748 (D.C., D. Mass.).

Fish Pier Company of the stock of twenty-five corporations doing business as wholesale fresh fish dealers in Boston and the acquisition by the Bay State Fishing Company of eight corporations constituted in themselves violations of the Sherman Act. In addition to deciding that these acquisitions violated the Sherman Act, the court held that the Clayton Act test of illegality had been met as well.[15] The two corporations were ordered to divest themselves of the illegally acquired stock.[16]

In 1935 the Justice Department attempted to have the International Shoe case interpretation of the Section 7 standard of illegality modified in the same way that the Federal Trade Commission had attempted to have it modified in the Temple Anthracite case[17]—that is, by interpreting the statute to declare an acquisition illegal if the effect is to eliminate competition between the acquiring and the acquired corporations irrespective of the effect of the acquisition on the degree of monopoly in the market. The Justice Department brought suit to enjoin the merger of Republic Steel Corporation and the Corrigan, McKinney Steel Company.[18] Republic had proposed a merger with the Corrigan, McKinney company under which the latter company would be dissolved after transferring its assets to Republic. It was not alleged that the asset acquisition was in itself illegal. The assets of the Corrigan, McKinney company, however, included the controlling stock interest in the Newton Steel Company and the N. and G. Taylor Company.[19]

The government rested its case on the allegation that the stock acquisitions would have the effect of substantially lessening competition between Republic and Newton and between Republic and Taylor. It maintained that it was unnecessary to prove restraint of trade or a tendency to create a monopoly. According to the opinion of the court, the government argued

[15] 258 Fed. Rept. 732, 746, 750–751.

[16] 258 Fed. Rept. 732, 752.

[17] 13 F.T.C. 249 (1930).

[18] *United States* v. *Republic Steel Corporation et al.* (1935), 11 Fed. Supp. 117 (D.C., N.D. Ohio, E.D.).

[19] 11 Fed. Supp. 117, 119.

> . . . that by the clause relied upon, construed in the light of the authorities, Congress has in effect declared that substantial lessening of competition and public injury are synonymous, and urges that Congress did not intend to submit the general question of public injury to the courts.[20]

The court rejected this argument and denied the injunction.

> Careful analysis of the foregoing and of other cases brings conviction that the courts have been unwilling to adopt a construction of the language used in section 7 which warrants an injunction against acquisition of stock in another corporation by one engaged in interstate commerce without affirmative showing of a probable effect to restrain commerce, create a monopoly, or other injurious effect upon public interest. When a statute has been construed by the highest courts having jurisdiction to pass on it, such construction is as much a part of the statute as if plainly written into it originally.[21]

The Sherman Act test was explicitly applied to the case. The opinion said that

> . . . in determining whether given acts amount to unfair methods of competition within the meaning of the Federal Trade Commission Act, or substantially lessen competition and tend to create a monopoly within the meaning of the Clayton Act, the only standard of illegality with which we are acquainted is the standard established by the Sherman Act in the words "restraint of trade or commerce" and "monopolize, or attempt to monopolize," and by the courts in construing the Sherman Act.[22]

The Justice Department included an allegation of violation of Section 7 of the Clayton Act among several allegations of Sherman Act violations in a suit brought against Associated Press. In addition to an injunction requiring Associated Press not to enforce some of its bylaws and agreements, the government sought an order of divestment of stock in Wide World Photos, Inc., which it alleged had been acquired in violation of Section 7.[23]

At the time of the acquisition of Wide World, Associated Press operated a picture service. This service was not offered generally

[20] 11 Fed. Supp. 117, 121.

[21] 11 Fed. Supp. 117, 123.

[22] 11 Fed. Supp. 117, 121.

[23] *United States* v. *Associated Press et al.* (1943), 52 Fed. Supp. 362 (D.C., S.D. N.Y.).

on the market in competition with Wide World, but instead, was offered only to Associated Press members. The court reasoned that the only way in which the two picture services could have been in competition prior to the acquisition was by Wide World diverting Associated Press members from its picture service to Wide World. This was considered not to have been substantial competition, since only seven Associated Press members were found to have subscribed to Wide World's service.[24] In the Supreme Court review of the Associated Press case, the question of Section 7 violation was not at issue.[25]

In 1950 another case was decided in which the Justice Department included an allegation of Section 7 violation along with a Sherman Act allegation.[26] The Justice Department alleged that Celanese acquired the stock and assets of Tubize Rayon Corporation through a merger in 1946 in violation of Section 1 of the Sherman Act and also Section 7 of the Clayton Act. Celanese petitioned the court to dismiss the claim under Section 7 in the complaint either on the ground that it was not a claim under which relief could be granted or by granting a partial summary judgment. The court did the latter.

In the Celanese case the Justice Department sought to have Section 7 reinterpreted by the court so as to prohibit mergers consummated under state statutes rather than merely through direct acquisition of stock. The government advanced the theory that this merger necessarily involved the acquisition of stock indirectly, since

> . . . the interest represented by the shares of stock in the merging corporation (Tubize) passed to the surviving corporation (Celanese); and that the merger represents more than a mere acquisition of assets, which admittedly does not violate Section 7, since the surviving corporation obtains control over the merging corporation's profits and property which its former stock represented.[27]

---

[24] 52 Fed. Supp. 362, 374.

[25] *Associated Press et al.* v. *United States* (1945), 326 U.S. 1.

[26] *United States* v. *Celanese Corporation of America* (1950), 91 Fed. Supp. 14 (D.C., S.D. N.Y.).

[27] 91 Fed. Supp. 14, 15.

The judge reasoned that under this theory a direct acquisition of assets also would have to be considered a stock acquisition, as it, too, would constitute an acquisition of control over profits and property. The court held that, even if there had been an acquisition of stock incident to the merger of the corporations under state statutes, Section 7 would not have been violated because of the Arrow-Hart case. The court said that case removed mergers under state laws from the prohibition provided in Section 7, because the decision had not hinged merely on the power of the Federal Trade Commission to order divestment of assets.[28]

The opinion of the court pointed out that Section 7 was designed primarily to deal with the secret acquisition of stock by a holding company and that strenuous efforts were being made by the government to have the law amended by Congress to apply to corporate mergers.

> This court cannot amend Section 7 by judicial legislation, nor overrule the direct holding on the subject by the Supreme Court. The instrumentality to combat this evil which the government says is a threat to a well-balanced, free, competitive economy, must come from Congress.[29]

The Justice Department played a minor role in the administration of Section 7 from 1914 until 1950. It achieved an order of divestment only in the New England Fish Exchange case, but the order was fully supported by the Sherman Act allegation. The Justice Department did attempt to overcome to some extent the limitations placed on Section 7 by the Supreme Court in the International Shoe case and in the Arrow-Hart and Hegeman case, but the lower courts were unwilling to render decisions clearly in contradiction with the Supreme Court's interpretation of the statute, and appeals were not made to the high court.

Enforcement of Section 7 by Other Administrative Agencies

The administrative commissions other than the Federal Trade Commission were rarely concerned with Section 7 of the Clayton

[28] 91 Fed. Supp. 14, 16.
[29] 91 Fed. Supp. 14, 17.

Act, since they generally had jurisdiction over corporations that, although not immune to antitrust prosecution, were regulated under special legislation. For example, Section 5 of the Transportation Act of 1920 gave the Interstate Commerce Commission authority to approve the acquisition of control of one railroad company of another railroad company by means of purchase of stock. Paragraph 8 of that section provided:

> The carriers affected by any order made under the foregoing provisions of this section and any corporation organized to effect a consolidation approved and authorized in such order shall be, and they are hereby, relieved from the operation of the "antitrust laws" as designated in section 1 of the . . . [Clayton Act].[30]

With the enactment of that legislation, the Interstate Commerce Commission continued to have the responsibility of administering Section 7 of the Clayton Act for corporations under its jurisdiction, but it was vested with the authority to waive the prohibitions of Section 7, if its permission was sought and granted prior to an acquisition of stock.

Section 7 Cases before the Interstate Commerce Commission—In the first Section 7 case before the Interstate Commerce Commission in 1929, the Baltimore and Ohio, the New York Central, and the Nickel Plate railroads were ordered to divest themselves of the capital stock which they had acquired in 1927 in the Wheeling and Lake Erie Railway Company.[31] Each of the three acquiring railroads purchased 17 per cent of the outstanding shares of capital stock of the Wheeling. The commission's complaint alleged that the effect of the acquisition may be to substantially lessen competition between the railroads concerned and to restrain commerce in a section or community. It was not alleged that the acquisition would tend to create a monopoly.[32]

The commission found that, during a representative period, 48.6 per cent of the carloads of freight moved on the Wheeling could have been moved on the Baltimore and Ohio and 29.4 per

[30] 41 *U.S. Stat. at L.* (1920), 482.

[31] *Interstate Commerce Commission* v. *Baltimore & Ohio Railroad Company*, 152 I.C.C. 731 (No. 21012, March 11, 1929).

[32] 152 I.C.C. 721, 723.

cent could have been moved on the New York Central. On one-line routes, 13 per cent of the Wheeling freight could have been moved on the New York Central and 13 per cent could have been moved on the Nickel Plate.[33] The commission considered these percentages to be an indication of the competition between the various acquiring companies and the acquired company prior to the acquisition. It was not satisfied, however, with so simple an analysis of the effect of the acquisition on competition between the firms, saying:

The volume of competitive traffic moving over a carrier's line is not a measure of its competitive influence. The value of its competition is not dependent upon its success in securing traffic. The existence of transportation facilities and the desire on the part of the operator of the facilities to perform the transportation are factors in determining the amount and quality of service and the level of the rates of all lines in position to perform the same or similar service for a section or community. That the Wheeling is an unsuccessful competitor for much traffic that might reasonably be routed over its lines is shown by the testimony of its vice president.[34]

Unlike the Federal Trade Commission and the Supreme Court in the International Shoe case, the Interstate Commerce Commission conceived of competition in terms of the effect on the demand curves of other firms by the removal from independent status of one of the firms that previously served as an actual and potential alternative source of supply for the purchasers in the market for the product in question. With this broad interpretation of the meaning of competition, the commission took cognizance of the effect of the acquisition on the price and service policies of the acquiring firms with respect to coal and other commodities hauled to markets in which competition was encountered from similar commodities hauled over the acquired carrier from *different* points of origin, saying:

Question is raised by counsel for the Central as to the propriety of including so-called market competition of railroads within the term "competition" as used in Section 7. . . . Where different railroads are engaged in hauling the same commodity from different fields to the same consumers, it seems

[33] 152 I.C.C. 721, 726.
[34] 152 I.C.C. 721, 728.

obvious that railroad competition must exist in a very positive form. Adopting an illustration used in argument, if a shipper of sugar to Chicago had a choice of routes through New York or through New Orleans, he would clearly be interested in a proposal of the carriers over one of the routes to secure such interest in the carriers serving the other route as would give control of their service or rates.[35]

The commission recognized the impossibility of accurately measuring the effect on other carriers of the service of Wheeling as an independent line, but it decided that the testimony amply showed the existence of substantial competition. The commission concluded that not only was it probable that competition would be lessened in the future, but that a substantial lessening of competition was in fact accomplished by the acquisition of control.[36] Regarding the allegation that the acquisition restrained commerce, the opinion of the commission stated:

We are not advised of any judicial interpretation of the expression "restrain such commerce," as used in section 7 of the Clayton Act, when applied to the commerce of railway companies. It is perhaps more applicable to relationships between industrial or commercial corporations. However, it seems reasonably clear that control of the Wheeling by other carriers engaged, for example, in the transportation of coal which competes with coal produced on the line of the Wheeling may result in restraint of commerce in that commodity from its producing territory.[37]

A few months after this action, the Interstate Commerce Commission decided another case against the Baltimore and Ohio Railroad, ordering it to divest itself of the controlling stock interest in the Western Maryland Railway Company, which had been acquired in 1927.[38] The commission found that the transportation of bituminous coal constituted about two-thirds of the total freight tonnage of the Western Maryland. Coal from the districts served by the Western Maryland and the districts served by the Baltimore and Ohio was shipped to the same destinations,

[35] 152 I.C.C. 721, 731.
[36] 152 I.C.C. 721, 731–736.
[37] 152 I.C.C. 721, 737.
[38] *Interstate Commerce Commission* v. *Baltimore & Ohio Railroad Company*, 160 I.C.C. 785 (No. 21032, Jan. 13, 1930).

and both carriers served some coal fields. Both carriers also transported merchandise between Baltimore and several wholesale and jobbing centers that they served in common. The export and import freight through the port of Baltimore handled by the Western Maryland was considered to be largely competitive with that handled by the Baltimore and Ohio. The respondent admitted that about 29 per cent of the cars of freight carried by the Western Maryland during a month chosen as typical was of freight solicited by the Baltimore and Ohio.[39]

The vice-president in charge of traffic of the Western Maryland testified that

> . . . rates on all traffic classified as competitive with the respondent, as published by both carriers, were invariably the same, and that the rates on coal from each district served by both the Western Maryland and the respondent to the same destination were invariably equal; that this parity had long been maintained; that any rate reduction on the part of one of the carriers would be immediately followed by the other; and that *any difference in rates would cause loss of tonnage to the carrier endeavoring to maintain the higher rates* [italics mine].[40]

The respondent maintained that in enacting the transportation act in 1920, Congress had declared in favor of a policy of railroad consolidation. In a tentative plan for consolidation, the commission had assigned the Western Maryland to the New York Central system, and the respondent believed that a better assignment would be to the Baltimore and Ohio system. The commission said:

> The application of the law to the facts is clear and leaves no opportunity for speculation as to the general effect upon the public interest of the ultimate disposition of the Western Maryland lines in consolidation proceedings. Increase of traffic and benefits to stockholders are not necessarily accompanied by corresponding benefits to shippers whom the Clayton Act was intended primarily to protect; and in view of the retention of the act it is clear that Congress did not see fit to rely upon our authority under the statutes to afford that protection. Although the consolidation provisions of the act, including paragraph (2) of section 5 [of the Transportation Act of

[39] 160 I.C.C. 785, 787–789.

[40] 160 I.C.C. 785, 788.

1920], clearly contemplate the substantial lessening of competition between particular lines, it is equally clear that acquisitions of control which may have that effect are not to proceed without our authorization.[41]

With three of the eleven members dissenting, the commission ordered the Baltimore and Ohio to cease and desist from violating Section 7 and to divest itself of the stock illegally acquired.[42]

Less than a year later, the Interstate Commerce Commission ordered the Pennsylvania Railroad Company to divest itself of illegally acquired stock in the Lehigh Valley Railroad Company and in the Wabash Railway Company.[43] The Pennsylvania Railroad, through its wholly owned subsidiary the Pennsylvania Company, acquired 48 per cent of the voting stock of the Wabash and 30 per cent of the voting stock of the Lehigh. The Wabash owned 19 per cent of the Lehigh stock, so the Pennsylvania had acquired effective control of both railroads.[44] The record shows that these acquisitions by the Pennsylvania, like the acquisitions in the previous two cases brought by the commission under Section 7, were part of the efforts of the various eastern trunk line railroads to improve their respective positions in the reorganization of the railroad systems, forthcoming under the consolidation plans of the Interstate Commerce Commission under the provisions of the Transportation Act of 1920.[45] The commission appears to have brought these complaints under Section 7 of the Clayton Act in order to prevent consolidation of the various railroads prior to its final disposition of the reorganization problem.

The commission in this case again examined the record of shipments of freight of the acquired companies and found that a significant proportion of it could have been handled by the acquiring company. It also took cognizance of the other freight that the acquired companies could have handled, but which the Pennsylvania had obtained. It also found that the acquiring and the acquired railroads in many instances shipped commodities

[41] 160 I.C.C. 785, 791.

[42] 160 I.C.C. 785, 792.

[43] *Interstate Commerce Commission* v. *Pennsylvania Railroad Company et al.*, 169 I.C.C. 618 (No. 22260, Dec. 2, 1930).

[44] 169 I.C.C. 618, 620.

[45] 41 *U.S. Stat. at L.* (1920), 482 ff.

from different points of origin to the same destinations, where the commodities were sold in competition with each other. The commission rejected the contention of the respondent that the acquisitions had been made solely for investment and were therefore exempt from the prohibitions of Section 7 by the third paragraph of that section.[46] The commission stated that in its opinion the statute required merely the showing that the acquisitions may possibly have the condemned effects; but it found that, even if it were necessary, as the respondent contended, to show that the condemned effects would probably follow, the record would amply meet the additional test.[47]

The Pennsylvania Railroad appealed the order of the commission, and the Third Circuit Court held that it was necessary to show a reasonable probability that the acquisitions would substantially lessen competition. The court found no changes in the policies of the acquired firms since the acquisition and no indication that competition had in fact been lessened. It concluded that there was, therefore, no reason to expect any lessening of competition in the future. The order of the commission was reversed.[48]

These three cases brought under Section 7 by the Interstate Commerce Commission were not part of a continuous policy of application of the law to common carriers as was the Federal Trade Commission's attempt to enforce it in the area of industrial and commercial corporations. The railroads had definitely been included within the prohibitions of Section 7 in 1914, but in 1920 Congress had enunciated a new policy regarding the consolidation of these corporations. Unlike the Federal Trade Commission, the Interstate Commerce Commission had been given the duty of fostering consolidations of the corporations under its jurisdiction. Section 7 had remained applicable to acquisitions by railroads only if the acquisitions were made without prior authorization by the commission. The purpose of these cases was not to

---

[46] 169 I.C.C. 618, 624–627.

[47] 169 I.C.C. 618, 633–638.

[48] *Pennsylvania Railroad Company* v. *Interstate Commerce Commission* (1933), 66 Fed. Rept., 2d Ser. 37 (C.C.A., 3d Cir.).

prevent the lessening of competition between the railroad corporations concerned, but was, instead, to enable the commission better to oversee the lessening of competition which would admittedly result from its own consolidation plans, but which would be in accordance with its view of over-all transportation policy.

The Transamerica Case—The Board of Governors of the Federal Reserve System has initiated only one case under Section 7 of the Clayton Act. In June, 1948, the board issued a complaint against Transamerica Corporation, alleging that the acquisitions of a controlling stock interest in several banks were in violation of Section 7. Rudolph M. Evans, a member of the board, was designated in December, 1948, to serve as hearing officer in the proceeding, and in June, 1951, he rendered a recommended decision to the board. The board issued findings of fact, conclusions, and order on March 27, 1952.[49]

While the hearings in the proceeding were in progress, Transamerica announced the forthcoming transfer of the assets of the acquired banks to the Bank of America. The board petitioned the Ninth Circuit Court of Appeals to enjoin the asset transfer pending the conclusion of its proceedings against the stock acquisitions, on the grounds that the court's jurisdiction in reviewing an order of divestment of stock, if it should be issued by the board, would be ousted by an asset transfer. The court agreed with the contention of the board and, on June 24, 1950, issued an order enjoining the contemplated transfer of assets.[50]

Since this court decision was rendered in 1950, just prior to the amendment of Section 7, it had no effect on the administration of the section by the Federal Trade Commission. It is important to note, however, that the board successfully used a legal procedure, which the Federal Trade Commission failed to use in many similar situations, to prevent a transfer of assets following an illegal acquisition of stock. The courts had never maintained that an acquisition of assets based on an illegal acquisition of stock was legal. They had merely denied that the Federal Trade

[49] *Federal Reserve Bulletin*, 38 (April, 1952), 368–398.

[50] *Board of Governors of the Federal Reserve System* v. *Transamerica Corporation, et al.* (1950), 184 Fed. Rept., 2d Ser., 311 (C.C.A., 9th Cir.).

Commission had the powers of an equity court necessary to prevent such action.[51] The ability of a corporation to acquire the stock of a competitor in violation of the Clayton Act, and then to acquire the assets and dissolve the acquired corporation before the commission could order divestment of the stock, was all that could properly be considered a "loophole" in the statute as interpreted (and this was a "loophole" only if it is assumed that Congress intended to prevent more than the holding company relationship). The Federal Reserve Board found a means of "plugging the loophole" prior to the amendment of the statute. Possibly, of course, the attitude of the courts would have been different at an earlier time, but it seems that this action by the Federal Reserve Board demonstrates that the Federal Trade Commission failed to take available legal steps that might have aided in making administration of the original Section 7 more effective.

Although it was decided after 1950, since the Transamerica case was an action brought under the original Section 7, the case is of considerably less importance than it otherwise would have been in depicting the manner in which the courts were likely to interpret the amended Section 7. The Board of Governors based its conclusion of violation of Section 7 primarily on its findings that Transamerica had continuously followed a policy of expansion by means of acquiring independent banks, and had grown very large. The board found that Transamerica had the power to control, and had used the power to control and direct the major policies and activities of the Bank of America.[52] The board's opinion stated: "The course followed by Transamerica requires the conclusion that so long as it is profitable and advantageous to the group to acquire more banks, this will be done to the extent possible." [53] In order to prevent this continued growth of the Transamerica group, it was necessary for the board to conclude from the testimony that the effect of the acquisitions may be to substantially lessen competition among the acquired banks, and, if the previous judicial interpretation of

[51] See pp. 109–111.

[52] *Federal Reserve Bulletin*, p. 380.

[53] *Ibid.*, pp. 381–382.

the law was to be followed, that the acquisitions tended to create a monopoly to the extent of injuring the public.

The respondent tendered evidence attempting to show the continued existence of effective competition. It maintained that it could not possibly substantially lessen competition because of competition from commercial banks outside the five-state area in which the acquired banks in question were located, and because of competition from nonbanking institutions. The board rejected such evidence, saying:

> These matters have been considered in the light of the fact that this proceeding challenges the lawfulness of respondent's acquisition and use of stock in commercial banks within the five-State area and in the light of the characteristics and functions of commercial banks.[54]

This statement points up the question of the definition of the product or products in the market for which competition was alleged to have been lessened, and the question of the definition of the market. The board considered commercial banks to be engaged in rendering economic services with which nonbanking institutions could not compete. The opinion stated that the money-payment function and the money-creation function are unique to commercial banks and there are no existing alternatives or substitutes for them. Regarding the function of providing short-term business credit, the board said that other financial institutions lacked the knowledge of local conditions to afford a practical substitute for the local commercial banks.[55] The opinion enumerated other services offered by banks, such as the making of real estate and other loans; admitted that the banks faced competition in these services; but concluded that such competition was immaterial to the inquiry, since it provided no substitute for the major banking functions.[56]

In the question of delineating the geographical areas involved in ascertaining the effect of the acquisitions on competition in the market for the major banking services, the opinion of the board was ambiguous. At one point in the opinion, the board said:

---

[54] *Ibid.*, p. 382.
[55] *Ibid.*, pp. 382–383.
[56] *Ibid.*, pp. 383–384.

> Because of the frequency of need for access to one or more of the services of commercial banks, such banks draw their business largely from areas within which customers may conveniently visit the banks as occasion may require. Thus, in this aspect of their customer relations, commercial banks are largely local, and for the usually needed customer services a distant bank cannot adequately serve a customer.[57]

That statement appears to have been made in refutation of the contention that the Transamerica group met competition from outside the five-state area in which it operated. In attempting to show that the acquisitions were in violation of the law, however, the board said:

> In order to consider the effect of the acquisition and use by Transamerica of the stock of banks, as heretofore found, it is necessary to relate the Transamerica controlled banks and their operations to the entire commercial banking structure of the area involved.[58]

This was done by showing the change from 1928 to 1948 of the proportion of such items as the number of banking offices, deposits, and bank loans attributable to the Transamerica group in California, Oregon, Nevada, Arizona, Washington, and in the whole five-state area. The board related none of this information to the particular acquisitions in question.[59]

The findings included several tables showing, for communities in which the Transamerica group operated a single banking office, the number of communities having, as of December 31, 1947, one, two, three, and four banking offices, and for each of these categories, the number of communities in which Transamerica had acquired, since 1904, one, two, three, four, and five banking offices. Again, the information was not related to the acquisitions about which the allegations were made.[60] Although the board appears to have made very little use of this information in drawing its conclusions, it can be ascertained from these tables that on December 31, 1947, the five-state area had 204 communities with only one Transamerica-operated banking office and

[57] *Ibid.*, p. 383.
[58] *Ibid.*, p. 384.
[59] *Ibid.*, pp. 384–389.
[60] *Ibid.*, pp. 385–386.

no other bank. In only 31 communities had Transamerica, since 1904, acquired more than one bank. In 156 communities with two, three, or four banking offices, the Transamerica group operated only one after having acquired from one to five banks since 1904.[61]

The board was not concerned with the degree of competition before and after the acquisitions in the market areas of the acquired banks. This is made explicit in the following statement in the opinion:

> . . . There is also evidence showing that as a result of acquisitions by the Transamerica group, in a large number of communities that had two or more banks, the only banking services now existing are Transamerica controlled. There is opinion testimony by economists as to what constitutes competition and monopoly; and much testimony was proffered by respondent to show that its expansion and methods of expansion and operation have been benign in character and dominated by a wish to make superior services and facilities available to more people. All of these matters have been considered. They are largely immaterial. The controlling facts are that it is clear from the record that by the significant standards—number of commercial banking offices, volume of deposit liabilities, volume of loans, and number of deposit accounts—Transamerica-controlled banks have, in the five-state area, approximately 41 per cent of all banking offices, 39 per cent of all bank deposits, 50 per cent of all bank loans, and 46 per cent of all deposit accounts of individuals, partnerships and corporations . . . that Transamerica has the purpose and the power to continue to expand its occupancy of the market in the five-state area . . . and that the effect of its holding and use of such stocks may be to substantially lessen competition and restrain commerce in commercial banking in the States of California, Oregon, Nevada, Arizona, and Washington, and tend to create a monopoly in such line of commerce in said area.[62]

The board reasoned that the community of interest between Transamerica and the Bank of America was such that a divestment of stock in the latter by the former would be useless, so it ordered Transamerica to divest itself of the stock of all the other banks named in the complaint.[63]

The order of the Board of Governors was appealed to the Third

[61] *Ibid.*

[62] *Ibid.*, pp. 390–391.

[63] *Ibid.*, pp. 391–392.

Circuit Court of Appeals, which set it aside.[64] The court upheld the jurisdiction of the board over such cases, ruling that Section 7 applies to banking corporations, but held that the evidence did not support the finding of violations of the law.

The court agreed with Transamerica's contention about substantial lessening of competition, saying that the board had failed to make findings and had rejected testimony on the present or possible future competition between the individual acquired banks in the communities they served. It pointed out that thirty-eight of the forty-eight acquired banks were not located in communities with other acquired banks.

> The Board's ultimate finding on this score was "that the effect of its [Transamerica] holding and use of such stocks may be to substantially lessen competition and restrain commerce in commercial banking in the States of California, Oregon, Nevada, Arizona, and Washington." This finding is deficient in two respects. It is not directed to competition between the acquired banks, the only competition with which Section 7 is concerned. And it sets up a five-State area of competition for which there is no support in the evidence and which is inconsistent with its own specific finding on this point. . . . So far as concerns the portion of this finding that the effect of these stock acquisitions may be to restrain commerce in commercial banking in the five-State area it is sufficient to say that the Board did not refer to it in this court either in its brief or in oral argument and evidently does not rely on it.[65]

With respect to the finding that the acquisitions may have the effect of tending to create a monopoly, the court said:

> No valid reason is shown for taking five States rather than one, the seven included in the Federal Reserve District, or all 48. The Board's conclusion of a tendency to monopoly in the five-State area, therefore, fails for want of a supporting finding that the five States constitute a single area of effective competition among commercial banks and flies in the face of its own finding that the local community is the true competitive banking area.[66]

The court indicated that it might very well have supported a finding of a tendency to create a monopoly, if the board had

---

[64] *Transamerica Corporation* v. *Board of Governors of the Federal Reserve System* (1953), 206 Fed. Rept., 2d Ser., 163 (C.C.A., 3d Cir.).

[65] 206 Fed. Rept., 2d Ser., 163, 168.

[66] 206 Fed. Rept., 2d Ser., 163, 169.

shown that any of the particular acquisitions had substantially lessened competition in some local area. If the board had taken the acquisitions by communities and handled them as separate allegations, perhaps it could have sustained orders of divestment of stock in those corporations that previously had competed with each other—that is, had been located in the same community—or had competed with other banks controlled by Transamerica. Although it followed the International Shoe case in insisting that competition between the corporations must be shown to have existed prior to the acquisition and also that the effect of the acquisition must be to injure the public by tending to create a monopoly, the opinion indicated that the court would have accepted a finding of preëxisting competition and of public injury where acquisitions united the managements of most of the banks in a particular community.

The Board of Governors apparently made the attempt to obtain support for an order of divestment of the stock in all the forty-eight acquired corporations as a group, because of a belief that Section 7 would be interpreted by the court in the light of the Supreme Court's interpretation of Section 3 of the Clayton Act in the 1949 Standard Oil case, in which it was held that competition is substantially lessened if exclusive dealing contracts involve sales that constitute a substantial share of the total sales in the competitive market area.[67] The court decided that the Board of Governors had failed to show that the five-state area was a competitive market area. In addition, it held that it is not sufficient in a Section 7 case to show that the acquisitions involve firms doing a substantial share of the business in a competitive market area. The court reasoned that an exclusive dealing contract lessens competition *per se,* and it is only necessary to show that the competition is substantial, whereas an acquisition is legal *per se,* and it must be shown that it may lessen competition.[68]

This opinion may be of importance as a precedent for the interpretation of the amended Section 7, since the chief change

[67] *Standard Oil Co.* v. *United States* (1949), 337 U.S. 293.
[68] 206 Fed. Rept., 2d Ser., 163, 170.

in the wording of the standard of illegality was to remove the competition between the corporations and replace it with competition in a line of commerce. In this case the court appears to have interpreted the test of a tendency to create a monopoly in a line of commerce to require the showing of a probability of lessening of competition in a line of commerce in a competitive market area.

Conclusions

The foregoing review of the administration of Section 7 of the Clayton Act by other than the Federal Trade Commission leads to the conclusion that enforcement by these other means was sporadic and incidental to the administration by that commission. It is unlikely that administration by private litigation could ever lead to the development of a positive, continuing policy of enforcement. This type of suit at best can be expected merely to offer a threat of inconvenience and financial loss which would tend to deter acquisitions. Generally, however, it is the consuming public that is injured by reductions in competition. Private suits are ill suited to protection against such injury.

The administration of Section 7 by the more specialized commissions did not and probably could not lead to a continuing policy of enforcement for two reasons: the corporations under their jurisdictions are engaged in specific lines of activity, and they are subject to other, and to some extent conflicting, statements of policy by Congress. The Justice Department failed to follow a policy of systematic investigation of acquisitions with the consequent continuing litigation of Section 7 cases. This appears to have been the result of a deliberate policy of division of labor with the Federal Trade Commission, which has not continued since the 1950 amendment.[69] Administration of the section by the district courts through Justice Department action

[69] See chap. 8.

offers one advantage—widespread use could be made of preliminary injunctions to prevent acquisitions from taking place, pending investigation of their probable effect, where preliminary investigation of proposed acquisitions shows a high probability of law violation.

7. The 1950 Amendment of Section 7: Legislative History

From 1921 until 1949, twenty-one separate bills to amend Section 7 of the Clayton Act were introduced in Congress.[1] The principal amendment effort did not begin, however, until after the Temporary National Economic Committee made its final recommendations.[2] Sixteen bills were introduced between 1943 and 1949 in the Seventy-eighth through the Eighty-first Congresses and received varying degrees of Congressional consideration before the Celler-Kefauver Act was finally enacted on December 29, 1950.[3]

The record of the legislative history of the amendment shows that neither the proponents nor the opponents of the proposals to change the statute focused their arguments on the most important questions—the effect of various types of mergers on the effectiveness of competition in the markets of the economy, and the changes needed in the law in order to increase the probability that mergers that might decrease competition would be pro-

[1] See "Section 7 of the Clayton Act: A Legislative History," *Columbia Law Review*, 52 (June, 1952), 766–781.

[2] *Final Report and Recommendations of the Temporary National Economic Committee*, U.S. 77th Cong., 1st sess., S. Doc. 35 (1941), pp. 38–39.

[3] 64 *U.S. Stat. at L.* (1950), 1125.

hibited. Perhaps because Section 7 had for so long been considered a dead letter, the experience of the commission and the courts in administering the original section was utilized in debates on the amendment only insofar as it threw light on the assets situation. Congress only briefly considered the question of the specific content that the commission and the courts had given to the standard of illegality of the original Section 7 and that might be given to the various bills under consideration, but the amendment adopted made important changes in the standard of illegality.

The Development of the Amendment in Congress

The various bills to amend Section 7 introduced between 1943 and 1949 fall into three categories: (1) proposals following the recommendations of the Temporary National Economic Committee,[4] which would have required the prior approval of stock or asset acquisitions where the corporations involved were larger than some specified absolute size, (2) proposals merely to include asset acquisitions in the prohibitions of the statute under a standard of illegality identical with that of the original Clayton Act, and (3) proposals like the one that was finally adopted to prohibit asset as well as stock acquisitions, but with a change in the standard of illegality.

In 1943 Senator O'Mahoney and Representative Sumners each introduced a bill following the Temporary National Economic Committee recommendations.[5] No action was taken on either bill. In 1945 Senator O'Mahoney reintroduced his bill in the Seventy-ninth Congress and Representative Kefauver introduced a similar bill in the House.[6] A subcommittee of the House Committee on the Judiciary held hearings on Representative Kefauver's bill.[7]

[4] See pp. 192–194.

[5] U.S. 78th Cong., 1st sess., S. 577 and H.R. 1517.

[6] U.S. 79th Cong., 1st sess., S. 615 and H.R. 2357.

[7] *To Amend Sections 7 and 11 of the Clayton Act,* Hearings on H.R. 2357, U.S. Subcommittee of the House Committee on the Judiciary, 79th Cong., 1st sess. (Washington: 1945).

After he reintroduced it twice with slight amendments,[8] the House Committee on the Judiciary approved it unanimously.[9]

Under the provisions of this bill—H.R. 4810—prior approval by the Federal Trade Commission of an acquisition of stock or assets by a corporation subject to the jurisdiction of that commission would have had to be obtained, if the acquisition would have unified the control of corporations, the sales of which had aggregated during the previous calendar year as much as 5 per cent of the total sales in their lines of commerce.[10] The bill provided that the commission should not approve an acquisition unless it found:

(a) that the acquisition will not substantially lessen competition, restrain trade, or tend to create a monopoly (either in a single section of the country or in the country as a whole) in the trade, industry or line of commerce in which such corporations are engaged;

(b) that the size of the acquiring corporation after the acquisition will be compatible with the existence and maintenance of effective competition in the trade, industry, or line of commerce in which it is engaged;

(c) that the acquisition will not so reduce the number of competing companies in the trade, industry, or line of commerce affected as materially to lessen the effectiveness of competition therein;

(d) that the acquiring corporation has not, to induce the acquisition or to eliminate the competition of the corporation sought to be acquired, indulged in unfair methods of competition in violation of the Federal Trade Commission Act, as amended.[11]

Although the standards to be used by the commission in deciding whether to approve an acquisition did not include the test of the lessening of competition between the firms, the bill retained that test in the first two paragraphs of the section. The committee report indicates that there was no intent to change the standard of illegality of the act. The committee was attempting to apply Section 7 to asset acquisitions with a prior approval provision apparently designed to avoid the problems involved in dissolving a merger already accomplished. The House Rules

[8] U.S. 79th Cong., 1st sess., H.R. 4519 and H.R. 4810.

[9] *Amending Sections 7 and 11 of the Clayton Act,* U.S. House Committee on the Judiciary, 79th Cong., 2d sess., H. Rept. 1480 (Washington: 1946).

[10] *Ibid.,* p. 6.

[11] *Ibid.,* p. 7.

Committee refused the bill a rule, and thus the whole House did not consider it. Representative Kefauver later reported that the Rules Committee objected only to the prior approval provision.[12] In an attempt to obtain consideration of some amendment of Section 7, the Judiciary Committee recalled Representative Kefauver's bill and reported unanimously a new version—H.R. 5535—omitting the prior approval provision.[13] In spite of the removal of this provision, the bill was again refused a rule, and it died with the Seventy-ninth Congress. H.R. 5535 would have prohibited asset acquisitions under the *same* conditions as those under which stock acquisitions were prohibited in the original Section 7.[14]

In the first session of the Eightieth Congress, Representative Kefauver reintroduced the same proposal designated as H.R. 515. Senator O'Mahoney, having failed to get consideration of his bill in the previous Congress, also reintroduced his proposal, which was designated S. 104. The O'Mahoney bill retained the prior approval provision, which would have required Federal Trade Commission approval of an acquisition by a corporation whose assets were valued at one million dollars or more of stock or assets of a corporation whose assets were valued at one hundred thousand dollars or more.[15] The bill was not reported by the Senate Committee on the Judiciary.

In the House of Representatives, the Judiciary Committee held extensive hearings on H.R. 515, during which Representative Clifford P. Case objected to the test of lessening of competition between the acquiring and the acquired corporations on the grounds that it would make practically all asset acquisitions il-

[12] *Amending Sections 7 and 11 of the Clayton Act,* Hearings on H.R. 515, U.S. Subcommittee No. 2 of the House Committee on the Judiciary, 80th Cong., 1st sess. (Washington: 1945), p. 6.

[13] *Amending Sections 7 and 11 of the Clayton Act,* U.S. House Committee on the Judiciary, 79th Cong., 2d sess., H. Rept. 1820 (Washington: 1946).

[14] *Ibid.,* p. 8.

[15] A subcommittee of the Senate Committee on the Judiciary held, but did not publish, hearings on S. 104. Part of these hearings were included within *Amending Sections 7 and 11 of the Clayton Act,* Hearings on H.R. 988, H.R. 1240, H.R. 2006, H.R. 2734, U.S. Subcommittee No. 3 of the House Committee on the Judiciary, 81st Cong., 1st sess. (Washington: 1949), pp. 60–94.

legal, even though they might have the effect of increasing competition in the lines of commerce in which the corporations were engaged.[16] To meet this objection, the chief counsel of the Federal Trade Commission, W. T. Kelley, suggested that the wording of the standard be changed to remove all reference to competition between the acquiring and the acquired firms.[17] Representative Kefauver incorporated Kelley's suggestions into a new bill—H.R. 3736—which was approved by the House Committee on the Judiciary.[18] Again the bill did not receive a rule and was not considered by the House of Representatives. Another bill was introduced during the second session of the Eightieth Congress by Representative Kersten, but received no consideration.[19]

In the first session of the Eighty-first Congress, Representative Mansfield introduced a bill that would have amended Section 7 with the standard of illegality unchanged, but with a provision for prior approval.[20] Representatives Jackson, Hobbs, and Celler each introduced bills essentially the same as the bill, approved in 1947 by the House Judiciary Committee, providing for the prohibition of asset acquisitions under a standard of illegality with the acquiring-acquired test removed.[21] The identical bill was introduced in the Senate jointly by Senators Kefauver and O'Mahoney.[22]

After hearings by a subcommittee of the House Committee on the Judiciary,[23] the full committee on August 4, 1949, reported H.R. 2754 favorably with no dissenting views.[24] Representative Celler by-passed the Rules Committee by having the bill debated in the House of Representatives under suspension of the rules,

---

[16] *Hearings on H.R. 515,* p. 23.

[17] *Ibid.*, pp. 115–117.

[18] *Amending Sections 7 and 11 of the Clayton Act,* U.S. House Committee on the Judiciary, 80th Cong., 1st sess., H. Rept. 596 (Washington: 1947).

[19] U.S. 80th Cong., 2d sess., H.R. 7024 (1948).

[20] U.S. 81st Cong., 1st sess., H.R. 1240.

[21] U.S. 81st Cong., 1st sess., H.R. 988, H.R. 2006, and H.R. 2734 (1949).

[22] U.S. 81st Cong. 1st sess., S. 56 (1949).

[23] *Hearings on H.R. 988, H.R. 1240, H.R. 2006, H.R. 2734.*

[24] *Amending an Act Approved October 15, 1914,* U.S. House Committee on the Judiciary, 81st Cong., 1st sess., H. Rept. 1191 (Washington: 1949).

even though such a procedure required a two-thirds majority for passage, and it passed the House without amendments on August 15, 1949, by a vote of 223 to 92 with 117 not voting.[25]

Hearings were not held in the Senate on the bill introduced by Senators Kefauver and O'Mahoney. In September, 1949, and in February, 1950, however, a subcommittee of the Senate Committee on the Judiciary held hearings on H.R. 2734 after the House had approved it.[26] On June 2, 1950, the Senate Committee on the Judiciary reported the bill favorably with Senator Donnell presenting minority views.[27] With only minor changes recommended by the Senate Committee, the Senate passed the bill on December 13, 1950, by a 55 to 22 vote with 19 not voting,[28] and it was approved by President Truman on December 29, 1950.[29]

The Arguments Presented for and against the Amendment

The Federal Trade Commission had been recommending the amendment of Section 7 for many years. It had in these recommendations showed concern almost exclusively with the need for merely including asset acquisitions in the prohibitions of the statute, ignoring the problems inherent in the development of an economically meaningful standard of illegality. The commission had been the moving force behind the recommendations of the Temporary National Economic Committee. It had presented this problem to that committee primarily in terms of the effect of the so-called assets loophole on the concentration of economic power.[30] Throughout the six-year effort to get the amendment passed in the House of Representatives, this same approach was

[25] *Congressional Record,* 95, pp. 11484–11507.

[26] *Corporate Mergers and Acquisitions,* Hearings on H.R. 2734, U.S. Subcommittee of the Senate Committee on the Judiciary, 81st Cong., 1st and 2d sess. (Washington: 1950).

[27] *Amending an Act Approved October 15, 1914 (38 Stat. 730), U.S. Senate Committee* on the Judiciary, 81st Cong., 2d sess., S. Rept. 1775 (1950).

[28] *Congressional Record,* 96, p. 16573.

[29] *Ibid.,* p. 17138. See chap. 8 for a discussion of the changes that this amendment made in Section 7 of the Clayton Act.

[30] See pp. 187–196.

followed by the commission and by the Congressional proponents of the amendment. It was not until the final consideration of H.R. 2734 by the House and Senate Committees that attention was focused on the problem of the standard of illegality. Thus, the amendment was put through Congress by the twofold argument: (1) as a result of corporate mergers, corporate concentration was proceeding at a dangerously increasing rate, and (2) the failure of Section 7 of the Clayton Act to treat asset acquisitions *in the same manner* as stock acquisitions had provided the legal loophole by which corporate mergers were being effected.

The opponents of the amendment were not attempting to achieve a new statement of policy which would enable the commission and the courts to develop an economically meaningful standard for judging which corporate acquisitions were in the public interest. They argued, instead, that the Sherman Act was adequate for preventing monopoly and favored no amendment of the Clayton Act.

The Corporate Concentration Argument—In a letter of submittal of a report to the subcommittee of the House Committee on the Judiciary, which first considered the amendment of Section 7, the Chairman of the Federal Trade Commission, Edwin L. Davis, said:

> . . . The evidence is overwhelming that corporate consolidation is going forward rapidly and that, following the war, there is a grave likelihood of an intensified process of corporate consolidation.
>
> . . . The history of the anti-trust acts and that of industry and commerce has proved that a preventive remedy is essential to the needs of the American public if economic and political freedom are to be maintained.[31]

In this report urging enactment of the amendment, W. T. Kelley, Chief Counsel of the Federal Trade Commission, said "the consolidation of huge economic power into the hands of but few corporations" had continued since the study of the Temporary National Economic Committee. He quoted statistics, which Senator O'Mahoney had previously presented to Congress, showing that several corporations had gross annual revenues, number of

[31] *Report and Comment of the Federal Trade Commission on H.R. 2357* (mimeographed, Washington: 1945), p. 3.

employees, and total assets in excess of many of the states of the Union. Kelley also quoted statements from a Smaller War Plants Corporation report to the effect that small businesses were being "gobbled up" by big corporations.[32]

In 1947 in a statement to the subcommittee holding hearings on this bill to plug the loophole without changing the standard of illegality, Representative Kefauver said:

> Mr. Chairman, the enactment of this bill is in my opinion one of the most important matters Congress will have before it during this session. The approval of this measure is the one most effective thing Congress can do to stop the onrush of monopolistic mergers which is dangerously threatening the competitive enterprize system to which this country is devoted. . . .
>
> We must decide very quickly what sort of country we want to live in. This Nation was founded and built by men who believed in individualism. It has grown under a system carried on largely by individual capital. The increased concentration of economic power is dooming free enterprize. The present trend of great corporations to increase their economic power is the antithesis of meritorious competitive development.[33]

When testifying before the same subcommittee, Federal Trade Commissioner Robert E. Freer expressed similar views about the need to stop corporate concentration:

> . . . The facts of record demonstrate that our economy has been evolving in a manner that increasingly contradicts the economic foundations of our institutions and the basic assumptions of our anti-trust laws. This bill affords an appropriate opportunity to make an effective choice between taking the first step toward changing our law to cope with the changing facts and letting our law against mergers of competing corporations fall further and further behind while concentration of economic power proceeds further and further toward its full fruition in some form of monopolistic industry and strongly centralized government. The factual diagnosis showing the relation of mergers to concentration is as complete and as exact as specialists in the field can make it, and the choice is one between legislative action and continued frustration of our declared public policy against such mergers.
>
> The most recent addition to the factual record on the subject of concentration is embodied in the special report to Congress which the Commission submitted under the date of March 7, 1947.[34]

[32] *Ibid.*, pp. 19–22.

[33] *Hearings on H.R. 515,* pp. 4, 7.

[34] *Ibid.*, p. 13.

In that report[35] the commission attempted to show that corporate acquisitions were taking place in alarming numbers and corporate concentration was thereby being increased to an alarming degree. This argument was based on the number of acquisitions. It was implicitly assumed that the trend toward more corporate mergers would be reversed if the assets loophole were plugged, but the report ignored the thirty-two years' experience of the commission in administering Section 7. This report attempted to use the approximately eighteen hundred acquisitions that had taken place between 1940 and 1947 as evidence of the need for enacting H.R. 515, which would have prohibited asset acquisitions *under the same standard of illegality as the original Section 7.* The description of this merger movement in the commission's report indicated that the mere plugging of the assets loophole would not have provided the commission with statutory authority to act against very many of the acquisitions of the types described, unless the standard of illegality were reinterpreted by the Supreme Court. Commissioner Freer, however, had explicitly stated that the commission favored the retention of the original language in order that the earlier interpretations would be preserved as precedents! [36]

The report stated that few of the acquisitions during the 1940 to 1947 period took place in highly concentrated industries.[37] The commission found that the outstanding characteristic of that merger movement was the predominance of acquisitions by large corporations of small corporations.[38] The report implied that all the mergers were against the public interest and would have been prevented had the asset loophole not existed. The commission classified the eighteen hundred mergers as 60 per cent horizontal, 17 per cent vertical, and 22 per cent conglomerate, saying:

> Each of these three types of acquisition contributes to the increase of economic concentration and to the decline of competition. A major result of

[35] *The Present Trend of Corporate Mergers and Acquisitions,* Federal Trade Commission (Washington: 1947), included in *Hearings on H.R. 515,* pp. 300–317.

[36] *Hearings on H.R. 515,* p. 23.

[37] *Ibid.,* p. 305.

[38] *Ibid.*

horizontal acquisition is to bring together firms producing (1) identical products for similar markets or (2) products which might be substituted for one another. . . . Obviously, many horizontal acquisitions have been instigated by the desire of large concerns to eliminate troublesome competitors producing a similar line of goods.[39]

The history of the administration of the original Section 7 shows clearly that the statute, as interpreted by the commission and the courts, was inadequate to prevent even stock acquisitions involving firms selling identical products in merely similar markets or selling heterogeneous products in identical markets.[40]

About the other two classifications of acquisitions, the report of the commission said:

Vertical integrations have a particularly severe effect upon small business during periods such as the present which are plagued by shortages of raw materials, components, etc. During such periods, large firms frequently reach backward to acquire important suppliers, and in so doing, reduce the amount of supplies available for small independent business. . . .

The third avenue of expansion, the conglomerate acquisition contributes greatly to the concentration of economic power, since it results in the absorption of many small firms in different and often completely unrelated lines of activity.[41]

As long as the statute was worded and interpreted to require the showing of preëxisting substantial competition between the acquiring and the acquired firm, such vertical and conglomerate acquisitions could not be reached by Section 7, irrespective of their effect, if any, on competition.[42]

The arguments of the commission's 1947 special report to Congress were elaborated upon in 1948 with the issuance of another commission report, the stated purpose of which was

---

[39] *Ibid.*, p. 308.

[40] See chaps. iv and v.

[41] *Hearings on H.R. 515*, p. 308.

[42] Fortunately, the amendment to Section 7 was finally fashioned in a way that changed the standard of illegality by removing the acquiring-acquired test. The proponents of the bill, however, did not present this change as a means of providing an economically more meaningful standard. It was presented by the commission somewhat reluctantly to meet objections that the old language would prevent all asset acquisitions since any competition existing between the corporations would be not just substantially lessened, but entirely eliminated by an acquisition of assets. See pp. 242–245.

. . . not merely to add one more to the long list of recommendations made by the Commission for the amendment of this part of the Clayton Act, but rather to bring together in one place the more important legal and economic considerations relating to the proposal and also to describe in some detail the character of the merger movement which has been under way since World War II.[43]

The commission had again emphasized the need for plugging the loophole in the Clayton Act in order to halt the tide of corporate concentration. In discussing the relationship between mergers and economic concentration, the 1948 report rejected the theory that the long-term increase in concentration had been due to internal expansion based on technological requirements, saying:

While it is impossible to measure the importance of internal versus external growth in industry as a whole, what little information there is on the subject suggests that the role of external expansion has been unduly discounted; that, in fact, a very large part of the rise in economic concentration has been due to consolidations, acquisitions, and mergers.[44]

This report implied that it is against the public interest for concentration to be increased and that almost any merger or acquisition increases concentration. The relationship between the concept of concentration and the concepts of monopoly power and market competition was not adequately considered in this report or anywhere in the debates on the amendment. The Federal Trade Commission's concept of concentration is revealed in the 1948 report:

To the extent that . . . [internal] expansion takes place more rapidly in large than in small enterprises, economic concentration is obviously increased. External growth—with which this report is concerned—takes place through the combining together of existing firms by means of acquisitions, mergers, or consolidations, and through the creation of other types of combinations such as trusts and holding companies. To the extent that this process takes the form of the creation of new large enterprises out of existent smaller concerns or the buying up of small concerns by larger enterprises, concentration is, of course, increased.[45]

---

[43] *Report of the Federal Trade Commission on the Merger Movement; a Summary Report* (Washington: 1948), p. v.

[44] *Ibid.*, pp. 22–23.

[45] *Ibid.*, p. 22.

This equating of corporate acquisitions with increasing concentration and of increasing concentration with declining competition was the central theme of the proponents of the amendment throughout its legislative history. Yet the amendment would have continued as the test of illegality the effect of an individual acquisition on competition, rather than the effect on concentration. The Senate Judiciary Committee report on the bill went so far as to consider the prevention of a competition-lessening acquisition as a means to the end of preventing increasing concentration, saying:

The purpose of the proposed bill, H.R. 2734, is to limit future increases in the level of economic concentration resulting from corporate mergers and acquisitions. The bill would accomplish this purpose by enabling the Federal Trade Commission to prevent those acquisitions which substantially lessen competition or tend to create a monopoly.[46]

In his lengthy testimony before the subcommittee of the Senate Judiciary Committee holding hearings on H.R. 2734, Gilbert H. Montague attempted to point out a *non sequitor* in the proponents' arguments about economic concentration:

They talk a good deal about economic concentration, and we had a fine discourse as we always have from Senator O'Mahoney on economic concentration. He failed to tell you that there was not a single thing in this bill which stopped the economic concentration he is talking about. You have found economic concentration discussed in a very voluminous report of the Federal Trade Commission . . . [but] not a single thing in this bill touches it—not a single thing. . . .

The complete adequacy of the Supreme Court interpretation of the Sherman Act, particularly since 1946, makes it a complete remedy against everything that they are talking about here, and the complete remedy, if I may say so, which reaches the completed acquisitions, as well as acquisitions about to be. So that all of this coming before you on the part of the Federal Trade Commission year after year, talking about something which does not in any way touch economic concentrations now existing or which already now are being assailed under recent decisions of the Supreme Court, simmers down to nothing except an effort to get power. Even if this bill is passed, it cannot do anything against economic concentration as it now exists.[47]

---

[46] S. Rept. 1775, p. 3.

[47] *Senate Hearings on H.R. 2734*, pp. 171, 173.

Montague expressed a fear that in associating any acquisition with increasing concentration, the commission was advocating a policy that would have the effect of increasing the monopoly power of existing large enterprises by preventing their small competitors from combining with each other.

Certainly it is questionable to represent that this bill will diminish so-called "economic concentration." Instead, it will perpetuate it, by preventing small and medium-sized companies from achieving by acquisition or merger the size and efficiency of their larger competitors.[48]

In his minority views on H.R. 2734, Senator Donnell argued that the proponents of the bill had not demonstrated a need for the legislation. In reply to the claim that the amendment was needed to halt the rapidly increasing degree of concentration of economic power, Senator Donnell did not challenge the power of the legislation to lessen concentration, but, instead, maintained that corporate acquisitions had in recent years played only a minor role in increasing concentration.[49] To substantiate his position, he relied on the Lintner-Butters article entitled "Effect of Mergers on Industrial Concentration, 1940–47,"[50] in which the authors concluded that in contrast to the earlier merger movements at the turn of the century and in the 'twenties, the merger movement of the 'forties was characterized by acquisitions of small companies by large companies and had had very little effect on corporate concentration.[51]

Senator Donnell and Montague, who better than anyone else presented the case against the enactment of the legislation, failed to convince very many members of Congress. A primary reason for the enactment of the amendment seems to have been a general, though vague, feeling that increasing corporate concentration was a major problem facing the nation and that the inclusion

[48] *Ibid.*, p. 202.

[49] S. Rept. 1775, p. 11.

[50] John Lintner and J. Keith Butters in *The Review of Economics and Statistics*, XXXII (Feb., 1950), reprinted in *Senate Hearings on H.R. 2734*, pp. 371–391.

[51] *Senate Hearings on H.R. 2734*, p. 391. The difference in conclusions between the Federal Trade Commission and the Lintner-Butters study generated a large volume of literature on the general question of corporate concentration and its measurement.

of asset acquisitions in the prohibitions of the Clayton Act would be an effective way of meeting the problem. The discussions, however, did not produce any clear-cut answers to three questions about corporate acquisitions which might well have been raised in the process of formulating public policy: (1) what is the relationship between corporate concentration and the degree of effectiveness of competition in the economy, (2) what is the relationship between corporate acquisitions on the one hand and concentration and the degree of competition on the other, and (3) what will be the effect of the amended Section 7 on corporate acquisitions and thus on concentration and on the degree of competition in the economy? [52]

The Assets Loophole Argument—One of the most important reasons for the willingness of Congress to accept the 1950 amendment to Section 7 with so little discussion of wording to achieve prohibition of acquisitions against the public interest, while permitting those in the public interest, was that, throughout most of its legislative history, the amendment was presented as a bill merely to plug the loophole in the Clayton Act in order to conform to the "original intent" of Congress. It was incorrectly argued that: (1) in 1914 Congress had intended to prohibit mergers, (2) in 1914 asset acquisitions were unknown and were initiated after the enactment of the Clayton Act as a device for avoiding the law, and (3) if the loophole were closed, then most asset acquisitions would be prevented.[53] This concept of the intent of Congress in enacting the original Section 7 and of the nature of the amendment as a mere plugging of a loophole rather than as a substantive change in the antitrust law policy is indicated throughout the record of the legislative history of the amendment. For example, the report of the House Judiciary Committee on H.R. 5535 said:

---

[52] See chap. 9 for a discussion of some aspects of these questions.

[53] The only voice raised against this erroneous interpretation of the purpose of the original Section 7 was that of Gilbert H. Montague. He filed a brief with the subcommittee studying H.R. 515 in which he pointed out that Congress had originally intended merely to prevent the evil of one corporation acquiring control of another secretly and without the consent of the owners of the acquired firm. See *Hearings on H.R. 515*, p. 214.

Section 7 of the Clayton Act was intended to prevent mergers where monopolies would be created but it does not, in specific terms, prohibit the acquisition by one corporation of one or more other corporations, no matter how dangerous the effect as to restraints of competition or as to creation of monopoly, if the acquisition is accomplished through the purchase of physical properties or business assets, rather than through outright purchase of stock. It was not long before the acquisitions of corporations resulting in restraints and monopolies took the form of acquisition of assets to avoid attack under section 7. The same loophole exists today.[54]

In a report to Congress recommending the enactment of H.R. 2357, Chairman Edwin L. Davis and Chief Counsel W. T. Kelley of the Federal Trade Commission argued that the original Section 7 was intended to prevent lessening of competition and tendency toward monopoly resulting from corporate acquisitions. By failing to specify asset as well as stock acquisitions, Congress left a loophole broadened by the Supreme Court's rulings that the commission could not order divestment of property acquired by means of an illegal stock acquisition.[55]

In testifying on H.R. 515 before a House Judiciary Subcommittee, Congressman Kefauver gave a clear statement of this misconception prevailing in the arguments of the proponents of the amendment throughout its Congressional history.

The bill is not complicated. It proposes simply to plug the loophole in sections 7 and 11 of the Clayton Act.

The Clayton Act was passed in 1914 on the theory that it should be the purpose of the Federal Government to prevent monopolistic mergers by making them illegal in the first instance. The purpose was to prevent monopoly rather than merely to punish it after it had taken place. The intent of Congress at the time the Clayton Act was passed is definite and indisputable. An examination of the reports of the House and Senate committees and of the debate fully confirms this point. The Congress which passed the Clayton Act had in mind that monopolistic corporate mergers would be accomplished by one corporation purchasing the capital stock of another. The purchase of capital stock was the way mergers were being consummated at that time. The holding company device was generally used. This is prohibited in section 7. Section 11 of the same act provides that if, after a hearing, the Federal Trade Commission finds that section 7 has been

[54] H. Rept. 1820, pp. 2–3.

[55] *Report and Comment of the Federal Trade Commission on H.R. 2357,* pp. 1–14.

violated the Commission shall issue a cease-and-desist order and direct the divestment of the stock involved.

Within a few years after the passage of the Clayton Act corporations conceived a means of bypassing the plain intent of the act by purchasing the physical assets of their competitors rather than the capital stock. As a practical matter these two sections became a dead letter in 1926 as a result of the Supreme Court decision in the case of *Federal Trade Commission* v. *Western Meat Co.* . . .

The loophole was further widened by the decision of the Court in the case of *Arrow-Hart & Hageman* [*sic*] *Electric Company* v. *Federal Trade Commission.* . . .[56]

This interpretation of the historical development of the means of effecting industrial combinations is most forcibly stated in the 1948 *Report of the Federal Trade Commission on the Merger Movement:*

The question may be asked why Congress did not foresee these potential defects in the law when it originally passed the Clayton Act in 1914. The answer is to be found in the nature of the great consolidation movement of 1897–1905, which formed the economic background behind the passage of the Clayton Act. It is a historical fact that during this period, which witnessed the birth of such huge corporations as the United States Steel Corp., most mergers were effected through the purchase of stock. This predominance of stock acquisitions was based on solid economic reasons. In the first place, it is much easier to purchase stocks than assets. This is especially true in the case of holding companies, which mushroomed during this early movement since the holding company can readily exchange some of its shares for the stock of the company to be absorbed. In the second place, stock acquisitions are peculiarly suitable in any era which is characterized by the flotation of enormous amounts of watered stock. . . . The greater the amount of watered stock, the easier it was to absorb companies through the means of stock transfers.[57]

This statement is subject to question on two grounds. (1) Is it a historical fact that most of the mergers of the 1897–1905 period were effected by means of stock acquisitions? (2) How solid is the reasoning used to explain the alleged facts? On the second question, it appears sufficient to point out that a corporation could have readily exchanged some of its own stock for the *assets* of the company to be absorbed; and in a period in which the state

[56] *Hearings on H.R. 515,* pp. 4–5.

[57] P. 2.

of the securities market will facilitate large new common stock flotations, absorption by means of asset acquisitions is as suitable as absorption by means of stock acquisition. The first question is one of fact, and only an examination of the literature available for the given period can furnish the answer.

The Manner of Effecting Mergers Prior to 1914—It is impossible to obtain from the sources any precise quantitative information on the extent to which the device of asset acquisition was used before 1914, but obviously asset acquisitions were not unknown and the use of stock acquisitions was not the usual and common means of effecting combinations. Writing in 1929, Seager and Gulick described in detail what they considered to be the *usual* procedures followed in the promotion of a combination in the 1897–1902 period:

> . . . [T]he usual method pursued by promoters was first to secure financial backing. In fact, this was so important that not infrequently . . . the promotion was actually engineered by the subsequent underwriting. . . . The initial proposal to them [the businessmen to be brought in] would usually be that they turn over their *properties and business* [italics mine] to the new corporation to be organized in exchange for a fair proportionate share of the stock of such corporation. If the promoter was of the highest type and all the important firms that he desired to combine could be induced to agree to the plan, the allotment of stock might be made on appraisals made by the accountants, so that each would get his exact proportionate share as so determined. Additional stock would, of course, be needed to reward the promoter for his services and to secure from the underwriters any working capital that might be required.[58]

In 1914 Arthur S. Dewing described the method of organization of several of the important combinations formed between 1890 and 1906. A promoter had formed in 1890 the National Starch Manufacturing Company as a corporation. At a meeting of a large number of starch producers, he arranged a plan of amalgamation whereby cash and securities in the new corporation were to be exchanged for twenty manufacturing plants in various parts of the country.[59] On its formation in 1893, the United States

[58] H. R. Seager and C. A. Gulick, Jr., *Trust and Corporation Problems* (New York: Harper & Bros., 1929), p. 65.

[59] Arthur S. Dewing, *Corporate Promotions and Reorganizations* (Cambridge: Harvard University Press, 1914), pp. 52–53.

Leather Company became the industrial corporation with the largest capitalization in the country, and controlled about 58 per cent of the capacity to tan sole leather. Of its formation, Dewing said:

> The leaders of the movement appointed committees to appraise the tanneries and bark lands owned by the interests that had consented to enter the consolidation. . . . The company paid for the tanneries and bark lands by issuing its preferred stock and by giving an equal amount of common stock as a bonus.[60]

The intermixture of asset and stock acquisition during this period is illustrated by the developments in the starch industry. In 1899 the United Starch Company was formed and acquired the *assets* of four starch companies other than the older National Starch Company. In 1900 a new National Starch Company was formed as a holding company to acquire a majority of the stock of the old National Starch Company, the United Starch Company, and the United States Glucose Company.[61] In 1902 the Corn Products Company, by means of an exchange of securities, acquired the controlling stock interest in the new National Starch Company. The Corn Products Company at the same time similarly obtained control by stock acquisition of the Glucose Sugar Refining Company,[62] which had been formed five years earlier by the acquisition of the *plants and inventories* of six companies in exchange for cash and securities.[63] The Corn Products Company was reorganized in 1906 and, by an exchange of stock, obtained the controlling interest in the New York Glucose Company, and also the *assets* of two other companies.[64]

Similar developments were taking place in other industries. In 1899 the National Salt Company was organized. It exchanged its stock for the plants of several companies and immediately began to expand by means of acquisitions of either stock or assets of other corporations.[65] The American Bicycle Company, incor-

[60] *Ibid.*, p. 18.
[61] *Ibid.*, pp. 60–61, 64–65.
[62] *Ibid.*, pp. 87–89.
[63] *Ibid.*, pp. 78–79.
[64] *Ibid.*, pp. 103–104.
[65] *Ibid.*, pp. 206–210.

porated in 1899, exchanged its securities and cash for the *assets* of about forty-eight companies.[66]

Another procedure that appears to have been used in some instances, and played an important part in the later administration of Section 7 of the Clayton Act, is illustrated by the activities of the New Jersey du Pont Company and the Eastern Dynamite Company, a subsidiary. These companies acquired the stock of sixty-four different corporations between 1903 and 1907, and then absorbed the *assets* of the acquired companies.[67]

One of the best sources of information concerning the pre-1914 use of the device of asset acquisitions to achieve combination is the 1901–1902 study made by the Industrial Commission at the very time that the combination movement was well advanced. Its purpose was to inform Congress on the facts as a basis for possible legislation. The report said:

> In the case of the newer combinations in the United States it has been found that practically all of the important ones are put into the form of a single large corporation. In many cases the new corporation buys the individual plants which it seems desirable to combine and thus becomes a single owner of all the establishments.
>
> In other cases, and this is perhaps true especially with reference to the largest combinations, the stock of the constituent members is all bought by the single unifying company. The constituent companies then retain their organization intact, being controlled simply by the central corporation, as a stockholder. . . .[68]

Writing in 1901, in the midst of the movement, Luther Conant, Jr., said:

> Although the organization of these consolidations has been effected largely on a stock basis, a considerable amount of money is needed to provide working capital or to purchase outright plants that can be secured only for cash.[69]

---

[66] *Ibid.*, p. 253.

[67] Lewis Haney, *Business Organization and Combination*, rev. ed. (New York: Macmillan, 1914), p. 245.

[68] *Report of the Industrial Commission—Trusts and Combinations*, U.S. 57th Cong., 1st sess., H. Doc. 182 (Washington: 1901–1902), p. vii.

[69] "Industrial Consolidations in the United States," *Publications of the American Statistical Association*, VII, 53 (March, 1901), 17.

E. S. Meade in 1903 writes that, after the abandonment of the legal trust form of organization, the usual form of organization of combinations was the acquisition of the *plants* of many concerns. Payment was made preferably in stock or, if necessary, in cash.[70]

The generally accepted view that stock acquisition was the common means of effecting corporate mergers before 1914 thus appears to be a fallacy. Careful examination of both the literature on the great merger movement and the legislative history of the Clayton Act[71] shows that *asset* acquisition was a well-known and commonly used device, and Congress deliberately failed to prohibit it in the Clayton Act. The Sherman Act was not supplemented with new *merger* legislation until 1950. The idea that the new legislation would merely "plug the loophole" was accepted by most proponents and opponents of the amendment. As a result, the problem of formulating an economically meaningful standard of illegality received little attention.

Discussions of the Effect of Merely Plugging the Loophole—Most proponents and opponents of the proposals to amend the Clayton Act thought that the prohibition of asset acquisitions under the same conditions as stock acquisitions would prevent otherwise legal mergers. The opponents accepted the idea that, if amended, the statute would prohibit many acquisitions that would not be unlawful under the Sherman Act. They thought such acquisitions would not be against the public interest—particularly acquisition of small firms with no other means of disposing of their assets. Most of the proponents argued that such prevention of mergers would be in the public interest, since the Sherman Act allowed monopolistic mergers. They thought that merely amending Section 7 to prevent asset as well as stock acquisitions would prevent monopolies in their incipiency.

One proponent of the amendment—John D. Clark, member of the President's Counsel of Economic Advisers—recognized that in the past Section 7 had been interpreted very narrowly and thought that the statute, if amended by H.R. 2734, would also

[70] Edward S. Meade, *Trust Finance* (New York: Appleton, 1903), pp. 88–89.

[71] See chap. 2.

be interpreted so as to make no acquisitions illegal that would not otherwise be illegal under the Sherman Act. He advocated enactment of the amendment in order to give the Federal Trade Commission jurisdiction over such acquisitions:

The Clayton Act and the Federal Trade Commission Act established a non-juridical, but very effective administrative method of enforcing antitrust policy, and there is this loophole in that enforcement practice.[72]

With the exception of Clark's testimony, the record indicates that both proponents and opponents of the amendment presumed that the proposals would make unlawful some acquisitions that were not unlawful under the Sherman Act. For example, Chief Counsel W. T. Kelley, in recommending the enactment of H.R. 2357 in 1945, said that the Sherman Act had proved to be inadequate in preventing corporate mergers and acquisitions.[73] To support his contention, he reviewed the major cases under that statute from the E. C. Knight case in 1895 to the United States Steel case in 1920, and concluded:

The degree of usefulness of the Sherman Act as a statute for preventing concentration of economic power through corporate consolidations and acquisitions of stock presents a marked contrast with the proved effectiveness of that Act in breaking up conspiracies and mutual understandings among independent concerns which, if no meeting of the mind eliminating competition were indulged in, would be competitors. This contrast is for the reason that the decisions which we have outlined constitute a body of law in which the Act has been construed to preclude relief from a concentration of power, through stock acquisitions or mergers, irrespective of how huge and preponderant the consolidated concern may be, unless and until its power is abused.[74]

Kelley saw in the proposed amendment to Section 7 a means of bringing the law on corporate consolidations into line with the law on conspiracies, saying:

A statutory provision should be passed of which it cannot be said that "it is against monopoly that the statute is directed, and not against an expectation of it, but against its realization * * *" . . . . H.R. 2357 is clearly di-

[72] *Senate Hearings on H.R. 2734*, p. 355.
[73] *Report and Comment of the Federal Trade Commission on H.R. 2357*, p. 23.
[74] *Ibid.*, p. 29.

rected toward the prevention of proposed corporate consolidations, not only if they are likely to lead to monopoly, but also if they will probably tend to lessen competition.[75]

Kelley failed to point out that the court had applied essentially the same standard of illegality to Section 7 cases as had been applied in the United States Steel case under the Sherman Act. He attributed the failure of Section 7 solely to the assets loophole.

The House Judiciary Committee also ignored the interpretation given by the court and the commission to the standard of illegality of Section 7. In its report recommending the enactment of H.R. 5535 in 1946,[76] the committee attempted to supplement the Sherman Act by merely plugging the assets loophole in Section 7:

The original purpose of the Clayton Act, as stated by the report of the Senate Committee on the Judiciary under date of July 22, 1914, was to make illegal practices producing such results and "to arrest the creation of trusts, conspiracies, and monopolies in their incipiency." The retention of the full language of section 7 as it now stands with respect to the lessening of competition between the acquiring and acquired corporations is as vital as retaining the general provision respecting restraints or tendencies to create a monopoly of any line of commerce. Without language enabling proceedings against lessening of competition tending in the direction of restraints and monopolies, the power to arrest in their incipiency the creation of restraints and monopolies is lost.[77]

The House Judiciary Committee thus appears to have thought that the prohibition of asset acquisitions under the same conditions as stock acquisitions would prevent acquisitions that would not be prohibited under the Sherman Act.

The Origin of the New Standard of Illegality—During the hearings on an identical bill in the following Congress, the spokesman for the commission, Commissioner Freer, also ignored the history of the administration of the original act and assumed that a mere plugging of the loophole would strengthen the antitrust laws on corporate consolidations. In an exchange with Commissioner Freer about the implications of the amendment, Con-

[75] *Ibid.*, pp. 29–30.
[76] H. Rept. 1820.
[77] *Ibid.*, p. 3.

gressman Clifford P. Case, with no reference to the previous interpretations, but on the basis of the language itself, expressed concern that the law would prevent mergers of competitors, no matter how small an effect the merger might have on competition in the market, and at the same time would permit mergers between corporations not directly in competition with each other, even if the effect were to greatly reduce competition in some markets. If the amendment had been enacted with no change in the standard of illegality, and if the commission had continued its previous policies, then the result would most probably have been that anticipated by Case.[78] In answer to these objections, Commissioner Freer said:

I am afraid that the best answer I can make here is that we don't agree, Mr. Case, that such rigidity is one of the bill's purposes. I would say that the Commission supports this bill which repeats the language of the previous act, because that seems the way of embodying that part of the decision law defining the test of what is a substantial lessening of competition tending toward monopoly, or the test of what constitutes restraint of commerce, in any line of commerce or in any community or area, etc.[79]

In a statement to the committee the following week, Chief Counsel Kelley took cognizance of the objections of Representative Case. Kelley pointed out that the Supreme Court had not accepted the effect on competition between the corporations as the only test of the illegality of a stock acquisition, but had applied the Sherman Act test—that is, the effect on competition in the industry. Kelley observed that, if the court were to interpret the amended Section 7 in the same way, many acquisitions that substantially lessen competition in an industry, but do not come within the Sherman Act test, would be permitted; and, on the other hand, if the court were to interpret the language literally, then Case's fears would be realized and some mergers might be prevented which might otherwise have increased competition.[80] Kelley said:

---

[78] See chap. 5.

[79] *Hearings on H.R. 515*, p. 23.

[80] *Ibid.*, pp. 115–116. Kelley did not point out that such a literal interpretation of the acquiring-acquired test might also work the other way to permit mergers between two corporations not in substantial competition with each other, even

Now, the point I am making is that the Sherman law is not an effective remedy and is not adequate, and under its interpretation and enforcement, in a long line of decisions, it has not reached many of these acquisitions that I think are not in the public interest.

On the other hand, under the terms of this bill as it is written, there is a definite standard, all right, and I am much in favor of a definite standard. I do not like legislation without standards, particularly, where they are to be enforced through administrative tribunals and through the courts, but the trouble I find with this bill is that I think the standards are too rigid, and thinking about this, in line with the questions of Congressman Case, I have worked out some language that I am going to lay before you. . . .

If you have 515 before you, I have here, with a view to finding and formulating some acceptable middle ground and solving what might become an irreconcilable difference between two opposing philosophies, I offer the following suggestion. . . .

So I would make it read:

"That no corporation engaged in commerce shall acquire, directly or indirectly, the whole or any part of the stock or other share capital and no corporation subject to the jurisdiction of the Federal Trade Commission shall acquire the whole or any part of the assets of another corporation engaged also in commerce where in any line of commerce or *in any section, community, or trade area* [italics mine], there is reasonable probability that the effect of such acquisition may be to substantially lessen competition or tend to create a monopoly." [81]

With this suggestion for changing the standard of illegality of the proposed amendment to Section 7, the Federal Trade Commission abandoned its attempts to have the test of lessening of competition between the acquiring and the acquired corporation *explicitly* incorporated into the proposed prohibition of asset acquisitions. This was the first time that any spokesman for the commission had recognized the possibility of any middle ground between a standard based on the lessening of competition be-

though the merger might lessen competition in some market or markets. It appears from the record that the commission wanted to retain the old language in the hope that it would be reinterpreted literally and thus provide a definite standard based on preëxisting competition between the acquiring and the acquired firms. At no place in the record of the legislative history of the amendment up to this point, or in the record of the administration of the original Section 7, is there any indication that Kelley or the commission as a whole recognized the economic irrelevancy of the concept of competition between the firms.

[81] *Ibid.*, pp. 117–119.

tween the firms involved in a merger and the standard of the Sherman Act. This proposed standard of illegality, which was substantially the same as that finally adopted, was offered with the expectation that it would prohibit some mergers and acquisitions which would not be condemned by the Sherman Act, while not prohibiting all acquisitions.[82]

Discussions of the Amendment as Finally Proposed—Throughout the various stages of consideration of the proposed amendment, the case against it was most clearly and in most detail presented by Gilbert H. Montague. His chief arguments against the amendment were that the Sherman Act as interpreted in recent cases was adequate for the prevention of asset acquisitions that might injure the public, and that the Clayton Act, if amended, would result in preventing small corporations from competing with the giants. In testifying before a House Judiciary Subcommittee in 1947, Montague took issue with Kelley's statements about the inadequacies of the Sherman Act to prevent monopolistic mergers. Montague said:

> . . . I would like to take up, first, what is the law at the present time governing these subjects, and I am going to call your attention to a case which, in all four hearings which you have had, in which the Federal Trade Commission has been represented; throughout all the discussion of the law, they have never mentioned this case, which every lawyer at the present time regards as absolutely controlling on the subject, but which has never been brought to your attention. It is very singular.
>
> I am referring to the case of the *American Tobacco Company* v. *United States* (328 U.S. 781), decided June 10, 1946. The unanimous decision was rendered by Justice Burton, which absolutely states the law in regard to all concentration of property and assets under existing law, and which, as I have said, neither Mr. Kelley, nor the Department of Commerce, nor Commissioner Freer, or the Federal Trade Commission, or anybody else has ever mentioned here in any of your hearings.[83]

Montague said that the meaning of the case was

> . . . that if any corporation, whether by acquisition of assets or natural growth, has got so powerful that it has the power, if it chose to exercise it,

[82] *Ibid.*, p. 119.
[83] *Ibid.*, p. 136.

to exclude competition . . . even if it does not exercise that power, but if it has it, and the possession of that power is so great that it can exclude competition and raise prices, then it has violated the law.[84]

He said that this not only was now the law, but that it had been in effect for a long time. He cited the Socony Vacuum Company merger case in 1931 and the Appalachian Coals Company case in 1933, wherein the tests were whether there remained effective competition.

Now, that is exactly the same rule that most of us have been applying for the last 10 or 15 years, and I am merely speaking of the previous authority which we had; and in the Aluminum and the American Tobacco cases, this has been expanded by the Supreme Court, going a little further, you understand.

You now don't need to exercise the power, but if you have the power, so that you can raise prices, or exclude competition, then you are violating the law.

Well, such being the present state of the law, what possible use is there for this sort of legislation? And I want to say, it is a deporable situation, for the Federal Trade Commission, charged with the duty of protecting this country, to come before you, as it did 2 years ago, and again this year, and have the Commission tell you there is not now anything to remedy the situation, when if they would have only gone three blocks down the street on Pennsylvania Avenue, they would have found lawyers in the Department of Justice who could have told them exactly what these cases are. It is extremely unfortunate that that condition should exist, in a body as important as the Federal Trade Commission, and I regard that as being by far and away one of the most unfortunate features of the situation. Why try to change the law? The law is there.[85]

Montague attempted to buttress his case by pointing out that the Justice Department had just brought suit seeking to enjoin the purchase of Consolidated Steel Company by Columbia Steel Company.[86]

In discussing the legal effect of the amendment to Section 7 proposed in H.R. 515, Montague maintained that the reading of the Sherman Act test into the Clayton Act by the Supreme Court in the International Shoe case could not be taken as the way in

[84] *Ibid.*, p. 137.
[85] *Ibid.*, p. 140.
[86] *Ibid.*, p. 141.

which Section 7 would be interpreted by the present court. He felt that in any new cases after such an amendment of the act, the court's interpretation would prevent mergers of any corporations previously in competition with each other, no matter how small the degree of competition. He thought the bill would do no harm to big corporations, but would prevent small companies from achieving sufficient size to offer effective competition to the large firms.

Now the little fellows can get together, and give the big fellows competition, and as long as the little fellows don't get so big as to be able to exclude competition, or raise prices, there is no violation under the law. The little fellows are absolutely stopped by this legislation proposed here, from ever getting together with any of their competitors, so that it is a most extraordinary case of a bill being put forward as helping small business, when it is nothing but a handicap to small business, and it does not touch the big companies at all, except to insure them against the possibility that there can be any merger of small competitors, smaller than themselves, so as to build up a company which will be effective against a large company.[87]

With respect to the changes suggested in the bill by Kelley to remove the acquiring-acquired test, Montague thought they would scarcely alter its interpretation. He felt that the court would interpret "in any line of commerce" and "in any section, community, or trade area" to mean that the test of illegality would be whether competition between two firms is substantially lessened. He said that

. . . if a man who had been successful with a filling station in Washington chose to buy out two or three others, there might be some lessening of competition in his immediate trade area; there might be some substantial lessening of competition within a few blocks, and that could be considered in this section as a "trade area," and that man would be violating the law.

Mr. Kelley has merely interjected some language which in effect says, "if you do anything which substantially lessens competition in any area, no matter how small, you are violating the law." [88]

Montague's testimony, which occupies 100 of the 550 pages of the published record of the hearings on H.R. 515, had an important effect on the House Judiciary Committee. The bill with the

[87] *Ibid.*, p. 145.
[88] *Ibid.*, pp. 145–146.

amendments suggested by Kelley was reported favorably as H.R. 3736 by the full Judiciary Committee.[89] The committee, however, deleted the phrase "community or trade area" from the suggested rewording of the bill, making the standard of legality read: "where in any line of commerce in any section of the country, the effect of such acquisition may be substantially to lessen competition, or to tend to create a monopoly." [90]

The majority of the committee rejected Montague's argument that the Sherman Act was adequate, saying:

> The attention of the committee has been called to recent decisions of the Supreme Court, particularly the *American Tobacco Company* v. *United States* (328 U.S. 781), decided June 10, 1946. Opponents of H. R. 3736 say that, under the Sherman Act as now unanimously interpreted by the Supreme Court, any person, firm, or corporation, or group of them, can be dissolved, enjoined, and punished criminally if it or they have the power to raise prices or exclude competition, even though it or they may never exercise such power.
>
> If this be true, Congress, instead of amending the Clayton Act to cover the acquisition of assets, might well repeal that part of the law pertaining to capital stock. For according to the view above expressed, both are equally unnecessary.
>
> However beneficial these decisions may prove to be in the enforcement of the Sherman Act, we do not believe they solve the entire problem. Nor do they convince us that Congress should no longer rely on the Clayton Act or not make attempts to cure its obvious defects.[91]

The majority of the House Judiciary Committee was apparently expressing a desire to amend the antitrust laws so they would go further than the Sherman Act in prohibiting mergers, and also to confer power of administration of the antimerger provisions on the Federal Trade Commission.

Seven members of the Judiciary Committee submitted a minority report in which they concluded that no new legislation was needed.[92] These members accepted the argument that the recent

[89] H. Rept. 596.

[90] *Ibid.*, p. 8.

[91] *Ibid.*, p. 7.

[92] *Ibid.*, pp. 11–16. The seven members concurring in these minority views were Republican Representatives Goodwin, Jennings, Lewis, Chadwick, Graham, and Springer, and Democratic Representative Cravens. Representatives Reed, Repub-

interpretations of the Sherman Act made that statute adequate to cope with the problem of mergers. "While the Commission may lack jurisdiction to proceed in a given case, it is evident that every violation of Section 7 of the Clayton Act can be remedied by application of the Sherman Act." [93] This group expressed fear that the bill, if enacted, "would inject entirely new and indefinite tests of antitrust violations." [94] The minority was not willing to confer new powers on an administrative commission:

> With all due respect for the views of this expert tribunal, there is a lack of complete candor on the part of the Commission. This campaign has been prosecuted more in the manner of a self-seeking advocate as distinguished from the more appropriate role of an impartial agency of the Government concerned with the public interest. . . .
>
> While the Commission has had adequate time over the years to *obtain* such information, it has submitted no evidence or testimony to show the economic effect of the mergers about which it complains. The effect on prices; the effect on production efficiency; the effect on employment; the effect on competition are all pertinent questions to be answered if the Congress is to intelligently appraise the worth of or necessity for this legislation. Such information has not yet been furnished to the Congress.[95]

In the additional minority views, Representatives Reed and Walter proposed that Section 11 of the Clayton Act be amended to authorize the commission to order divestiture of assets acquired as a result of an illegal stock acquisition. These members of the committee were willing to correct the loophole in the law resulting from the Arrow-Hart and Hegeman decision, but were unwilling to "grant new and undefined administrative authority which could have the effect of radically changing our whole economic system." [96]

When H.R. 2734 was reported favorably by the House Ju-

lican, and Walter, Democrat, submitted a second minority report. Representative Case, who instigated the change in the wording of the proposal, and Representative John W. Gwynne, chairman of the subcommittee that held the hearings on H.R. 515 and who was later appointed to the Federal Trade Commission, did not join in the minority reports and apparently supported the bill.

[93] *Ibid.*, p. 13.

[94] *Ibid.*, p. 14.

[95] *Ibid.*, pp. 14–15.

[96] *Ibid.*, p. 18.

diciary Committee in August, 1949, two years later, no minority views were expressed in the committee report, even though five of the nine members who had dissented two years earlier were still on the committee. During the time intervening between the two reports, the Supreme Court had rendered its decision against the government in the Columbia Steel case, proving that such mergers would not be prevented by the Sherman Act.[97] Regarding the adequacy of the Sherman Act, the Judiciary Committee of the House of Representatives in its report on H.R. 2734 said:

> It has been contended that, owing to recent Court decisions, specifically in the Aluminum case decided in 1945 and the Tobacco case in 1946, the Sherman Act is now adequate to meet the economic problem to which this bill is addressed and that therefore the amendment of section 7 of the Clayton Act is not necessary.
>
> What are the facts in the Tobacco case? . . . The Court held that the jury had been correctly instructed and that it was unlawful under Section 2 of the Sherman Act—"for parties, as in these cases, to combine or conspire to acquire or maintain the power to exclude competitors"—when they are —"able, as a group, to exclude actual or potential competition from the field"—and when they have—"the intent and purpose to exercise that power." . . .
>
> Hence, it appears that in the Tobacco case the charge of conspiracy is so interwoven as to be indistinguishable from that of monopoly power, and thus the case fails to provide any clear-cut basis for proceedings against the particular problem with which this bill is concerned. . . .
>
> It is true that the Supreme Court said in the Tobacco case that it welcomed the opportunity to endorse certain statements in the Aluminum case opinion. But the statements that were endorsed were to the effect that a monopoly cannot be disassociated from its power, that its power cannot be disassociated from its exercise, and that if 90 percent of the ingot producers had combined it would have constituted an unlawful monopoly. It is important to note that the Supreme Court did not affirmatively endorse the statement of the special court that 90 percent control by one corporation is enough to make it an unlawful monopoly, per se, or the statement that it was doubtful whether 60 to 64 percent would be enough and that 33 percent is certainly not enough.
>
> On top of these considerations, which in themselves would seem to dissipate the contention that the Sherman Act, as recently interpreted, is clearly sufficient to deal with the problem of acquisitions and mergers, there are the further considerations that (a) the Department of Justice,

[97] *United States* v. *Columbia Steel et al.* (1948), 334 U.S. 495.

which administers the Sherman Act, has maintained that in addition to the Sherman Act there is need for the amendment of the Clayton Act in order to deal adequately with the merger problem and (b) the Supreme Court, in a decision subsequent to the Aluminum and Tobacco decisions, held that the acquisition of the largest steel fabricator on the west coast (which itself is a subsidiary of the largest steel producer in the Nation) did not violate the Sherman Act.[98]

The House Judiciary Committee thus made quite clear that it intended the bill to reach acquisitions that would be considered legal under the Sherman Act. The Senate Judiciary Committee, in its report on H.R. 2734, also rejected the argument that the Sherman Act was adequate to prevent mergers considered to be against the public interest.

The present wording of H.R. 2734 is intended to cover more than is prohibited by the Sherman Act. . . .

The committee wish to make it clear that the bill is not intended to revert to the Sherman Act test. The intent here, as in other parts of the Clayton Act, is to cope with monopolistic tendencies in their incipiency and well before they have attained such effects as would justify a Sherman Act proceeding.[99]

In his dissenting views on the report on H.R. 2734, Senator Donnell argued against a need for amendment of Section 7, as he felt that the court's interpretation of the Sherman Act was sufficient to prevent mergers either that tend to create a monopoly or that substantially lessen competition in any line of commerce in any community. He reviewed several cases to show that Section 2 of the Sherman Act was adequate for mergers that substantially lessen competition. He argued that the Consolidated Steel decision had clearly depicted that an asset acquisition would be considered to be a contract in restraint of trade in violation of Section 1 of the Sherman Act, if an unreasonable lessening of competition were proved.[100]

The strongest opposition to the amendment of Section 7 was based on the argument that the recent Supreme Court interpretations of the Sherman Act had made amendment unnecessary.

---

[98] H. Rept. 1191, pp. 9–11.
[99] S. Rept. 1775, pp. 4–5.
[100] *Ibid.*, pp. 13–16.

This argument was accepted by one proponent of the amendment —Dr. John D. Clark—who favored the proposal because it would give the Federal Trade Commission jurisdiction in merger cases. Most Congressional committee members who considered the measure rejected the argument that the Sherman Act was adequate and passed a bill intended not only to confer jurisdiction on the Federal Trade Commission in asset acquisition cases, but also intended to declare a standard of illegality more stringent than that of the Sherman Act.

Conclusions

The Celler Amendment to Sections 7 and 11 of the Clayton Act was the culmination of twenty-nine years of spasmodic efforts by the Federal Trade Commission to plug the assets loophole. The 1950 amendment was the last in a long line of bills proposed and considered by the Congress subsequent to the recommendations of the Temporary National Economic Committee. The bills at first proposed amendment of the Clayton Act to make asset acquisitions unlawful under the same conditions as stock acquisitions and to require prior approval by the Federal Trade Commission for mergers of large firms. Objections to the prior-approval provisions by the House Rules Committee led to a series of bills which merely would have added asset acquisitions to the Clayton Act prohibitions. The bill finally adopted changed the standard of illegality as well.

The Federal Trade Commission was the moving force behind the amendment of the Clayton Act. It carried on a concerted campaign over a period of many years to have Section 7 amended. At no time did the commission center its discussions on the economic question of the effect of particular mergers under various sets of circumstances, or on the legal question of the effect of the various proposals for amendment on the legality of mergers under various sets of circumstances. Instead, the campaign of the commission and its Congressional proponents was based primarily on the general argument that corporate mergers, by increasing economic concentration, were undermining the free enterprise system. The ability of corporations to achieve the alleged drastic results in spite of the existence of the antitrust laws was attributed to the loophole. The existence of the Sherman Act and the Justice Department to administer it was ignored until the opponents of the amendment, with the very capable guidance of Gilbert H. Montague, pressed the issue. The failure of the Justice Department to win its case against Columbia Steel was of paramount importance in the conclusion by Congress that the Sherman Act was inadequate to cope with combinations of firms brought about by complete fusion of control in the same manner that it could cope with conspiracies and loose agreements.

8. The 1950 Amendment of Section 7: Its Implications

The Celler-Kefauver Amendment of the Clayton Act, like most other parts of the Federal antitrust statutes, is couched in general language, the meaning of which the Supreme Court must ultimately determine. Before such interpretation, it is possible to ascertain only within broad limits the implications of the legislation by analyzing the changes made in the language of Section 7 in the light of (1) the statements of Congressional intent found in the committee reports, (2) recent Supreme Court interpretations of related provisions of antitrust law, and (3) the record of administration of the new statute since 1950.

The Changes Made in the Wording of the Statute

The Celler-Kefauver amendment changed the wording of the original Section 7 by including asset acquisitions for corporations subject to the jurisdiction of the Federal Trade Commission, and by changing the standard of illegality. Also, several ancillary procedural revisions were made in the statute by changes in Section 11 as well as Section 7.

Procedural Revisions—The following paragraph was added to Section 7:

Nothing contained in this section shall apply to transactions duly consummated pursuant to authority given by the Civil Aeronautics Board, Federal Communications Commission, Federal Power Commission, Interstate Commerce Commission, the Securities and Exchange Commission in the exercise of its jurisdiction under section 10 of the Public Utility Holding Company Act of 1935, the United States Maritime Commission, or the Secretary of Agriculture under any statutory provision vesting such power in such Commission, Secretary, or Board.[1]

This provision was included in order that the bill would not have the effect of amending the existing statutes administered by these agencies. It was explicitly stated in the Senate Judiciary Committee's report on the bill that with the inclusion of this paragraph it was "not intended that . . . any . . . agency included in this category . . . shall be granted any authority or powers which it does not already possess."[2] The report on the bill by the House Judiciary Committee, however, said:

The last paragraph of section 7 is new. It simply provides that provisions of the bill should not apply to *corporations coming under the jurisdiction of* [italics mine] ICC, CAA, FCC, FPC, SEC, and the Secretary of Agriculture. These agencies already have jurisdiction over these corporations, and there is no disposition to change the present arrangement regarding them.[3]

This statement taken alone would indicate that a large group of corporations that are in some manner regulated by any of these agencies are exempt from Section 7. The act, itself, however, exempts only "transactions duly consummated pursuant to authority given by" these agencies "under statutory provision vesting such power in such Commission, Secretary, or Board." Because the language of the statute appears unambiguous and because the Senate report was rendered subsequently to the House report, the Supreme Court will probably rule that an acquisition by a corporation under the jurisdiction of any of these

[1] 64 *U.S. Stat. at L.* (1950), 1125, 1126.

[2] *Amending an Act Approved October 15, 1914* (*38 Stat. 730*), U.S. Senate Committee on the Judiciary, 81st Cong., 2d sess., S. Rept. 1775 (1950), p. 7.

[3] *Amending an Act Approved October 15, 1914,* U.S. House Committee on the Judiciary, 81st Cong., 1st sess., H. Rept. 1191 (1949), p. 6.

agencies, unless specifically authorized by the agency, will be subject to Justice Department action or complaint by the appropriate administrative agency, if it violates Section 7. The first paragraph of Section 11 empowers the Interstate Commerce Commission, the Federal Communications Commission, the Civil Aeronautics Board, and the Federal Reserve Board to enforce compliance with all the four substantive sections of the Clayton Act by persons subject to the jurisdiction of these agencies. The Federal Trade Commission is given jurisdiction "where applicable to all other character of commerce."[4]

Thus it appears that the Federal Trade Commission has authority over acquisitions by corporations subject to the jurisdiction of the Federal Power Commission, the Securities and Exchange Commission, and the Secretary of Agriculture, if such acquisitions are not authorized by such agency under some statutory provision. Such acquisitions would thus be covered by the law even if they are effected through asset purchases. The asset provision does not apply, however, to acquisitions involving corporations under the jurisdiction of the Interstate Commerce Commission, Federal Communications Commission, Civil Aeronautics Board, or the Federal Reserve Board. The Interstate Commerce Commission, Federal Communications Commission, and Civil Aeronautics Board, under other statutes, can approve and authorize acquisitions by common carriers. They also can issue complaints under Section 7 against common carriers that make unauthorized *stock* acquisitions. Section 7 prohibits banking corporations from making stock acquisitions but not asset acquisitions. The Federal Reserve Board can issue complaints against banking corporations, if it finds a stock acquisition to be in violation of Section 7.

Section 11 was amended to require that any complaint issued by any administrative agency under Sections 2, 3, 7, or 8 of the Clayton Act must be served on the Attorney General, who was given the right to intervene in such proceedings.[5] This provision was added to the Clayton Act in order to achieve better coördina-

[4] 64 *U.S. Stat. at L.* (1950), 1125, 1126–1127.
U.S. Stat. at L. (1950), 1125, 1127.

tion between the Justice Department and the various commissions in the administration of the act.

The original language of Section 11 provided for appeal to the circuit courts with the provision that "the findings of the Commission or Board as to the facts, if supported by testimony, shall be conclusive." The amendment substituted "substantial evidence" for "testimony." This change was made so that the reenactment of Section 11, as subsequent legislation, would not have the effect of amending the Administrative Procedure Act. The Senate report said:

> The courts have interpreted the language of §11 as equivalent to the requirement of substantial evidence, and the Administrative Procedure Act requires that findings as to facts shall be supported by reliable, probative, and substantial evidence. The intent of the present bill is not to introduce new standards of proof, but to reaffirm existing standards.[6]

The Celler-Kefauver Act also amended Section 11 to authorize the Federal Trade Commission to order divestment of assets, as well as stock, acquired in violation of Section 7.[7]

Substantive Revisions—The most important changes made in the Clayton Act by the amendment in 1950 were the changes in the wording of the first two paragraphs of Section 7. The Celler Amendment changed those paragraphs by striking out the words written in italics below and by adding the words enclosed in brackets, as follows:

> That no corporation engaged in commerce shall acquire, directly or indirectly, the whole or any part of the stock or other share capital [and no corporation subject to the jurisdiction of the Federal Trade Commission shall acquire the whole or any part of the assets] of another corporation engaged also in commerce, where [in any line of commerce in any section of the country,] the effect of such acquisition may be *to* substantially [to] lessen competition *between the corporation whose stock is so acquired and the corporation making the acquisition, or to restrain such commerce in any section or community,* or [to] tend to create a monopoly *of any line of commerce.*
>
> No corporation shall acquire, directly or indirectly, the whole or any part of the stock or other share capital [and no corporation subject to the juris-

[6] S. Rept. 1775, p. 6.

[7] 64 *U.S. Stat. at L.* (1950), 1125, 1127.

diction of the Federal Trade Commission shall acquire the whole or any part of the assets] of *two* [one] or more corporations engaged in commerce[,] where [in any line of commerce in any section of the country,] the effect of such acquisition, [of such stocks or assets,] or [of] the use of such stock by the voting or granting of proxies or otherwise, may be *to* substantially [to] lessen competition *between such corporations, or any of them, whose stock or other share capital is so acquired, or to restrain such commerce in any section or community,* or [to] tend to create a monopoly *of any line of commerce.*[8]

In the original Section 7, the first two paragraphs dealt with two distinct types of acquisitions: (1) acquisition by a corporation engaged in commerce of the stock of another corporation also engaged in commerce, and (2) acquisition by any corporation, whether or not engaged in commerce, of the stock of *two* or more corporations engaged in commerce. The second paragraph was designed to deal with the problem of a pure holding company. The distinction was important so long as the standard of illegality was written in terms of competition between corporations. Congress originally used the word "two" in the second paragraph, apparently because a lessening of competition between one corporation engaged in commerce and another corporation not engaged in commerce, was considered impossible. The amendment changed the second paragraph to cover also the acquisition by any corporation of the stock of only *one* corporation engaged in commerce and the acquisition by any corporation subject to the jurisdiction of the Federal Trade Commission of the assets of one corporation engaged in commerce, where the prescribed effect may occur. The Temporary National Economic Committee had recommended this change and all the proposals for amendment retained it. With it, and with the removal of the acquiring-acquired test, it appears that the first paragraph is surplusage, since the second paragraph is now worded so as to prohibit any acquisition prohibited by the first. The committee reports on the final version of the proposal to amend Section 7 do not mention the difference between the two paragraphs or the necessity of both of them.

---

[8] 38 *U.S. Stat. at L.* (1914), 730, 731–732, and 64 *U.S. Stat. at L.* (1950), 1125.

The original Section 7 contained three separate phrases to describe the illegal effect: (1) to substantially lessen competition, (2) to restrain commerce, and (3) to tend to create a monopoly. Each of these was qualified by other phrases. The lessening of competition referred to competition between two or more corporations involved in the acquisition. The criterion of restraint of commerce was qualified by "in any section or community." The phrase "tend to create a monopoly" was qualified by "in any line of commerce."

The 1950 amendment changed the wording of the standard in several ways. The phrase "to restrain such commerce" was deleted, but the geographical modifier was retained in part. The word "community" was deleted, but the qualifying phrase "in any section of the country" was used to refer to both the remaining parts of the standard, although in the original bill the geographical modifier referred neither to the lessening of competition nor to the tendency to create a monopoly. The phrase concerning competition between the corporations was removed completely, and in its stead "in any line of commerce" was applied to modify the substantial lessening of competition part of the new criterion.

The net result of these changes is a standard of illegality containing the concepts of substantial lessening of competition and tendency to create a monopoly. Both parts of the new criterion are modified by "in any line of commerce in any section of the country." These two parts of the act's standard of illegality are separate and alternative criteria.

Thus, the new Section 7 prohibits acquisitions of stock or, for corporations subject to the jurisdiction of the Federal Trade Commission, assets of one or more corporations engaged in commerce by any corporation, whether or not engaged in commerce, if the effect of the acquisition may be substantially to lessen competition in any line of commerce in any section of the country, or if the effect may be to tend to create a monopoly in any line of commerce in any section of the country.

It is apparent that the amendment has changed the standard of illegality. The new Section 7 as well as the old one, however, employs language that has no clear and unambiguous meaning, either in law or in economics. The legal meaning and economic implications must be sought elsewhere than in the language of the statute itself.

Some implications of the changes in the wording are evident from the specific statements included in the committee reports on H.R. 2734, in which Congress attested its intent to change the standard. The attitude of the Supreme Court toward antitrust policy has changed considerably since its last interpretation of Section 7 in the 1930's. Recent interpretation of the original Section 7, as well as decisions of the Supreme Court in some recent cases under other provisions of the antitrust statutes, afford some evidence of the manner in which the new Section 7 might be interpreted. Although no case had reached the Supreme Court by the end of 1958, the record of the administration of Section 7 during its first eight years also provides information on what can be expected from the Celler-Kefauver Act.

The Intent of Congress

In an apparent attempt to provide the courts with a lucid legislative history of Congressional intent, both the House and the Senate Judiciary Committees made specific statements about the meaning of the bill. The committee reports were designed also to achieve enactment of the bill by Congress, so some ambiguities resulted.

On the basic question of whether the bill was intended to provide a standard of illegality stronger than that of the Sherman Act and the original Clayton Act, the report of the House Judiciary Committee said:

> Acquisitions of stock or assets by which any part of commerce is monopolized or by which a combination in restraint of trade is created are forbidden by the Sherman Act. The present bill is not intended as a mere reenactment of this prohibition. It is not the purpose of this committee to recommend duplication of existing legislation.
>
> Acquisitions of stock or assets have a cumulative effect, and control of the market sufficient to constitute a violation of the Sherman Act may be achieved not in a single acquisition but as the result of a series of acquisi-

tions. The bill is intended to permit intervention in such a cumulative process when the effect of an acquisition may be a significant reduction in the vigor of competition, even though this effect may not be so far-reaching as to amount to a combination in restraint of trade, create a monopoly, or constitute an attempt to monopolize. Such an effect may arise in various ways: such as elimination in whole or in material part of the competitive activity of an enterprise which has been a substantial factor in competition, increase in the relative size of the enterprise making the acquisition to such a point that its advantage over its competitors threatens to be decisive, undue reduction in the number of competing enterprises, or establishment of relationships between buyers and sellers which deprive their rivals of a fair opportunity to compete.

. . . Thus, it would be unnecessary for the Government to speculate as to what is in the "back of the minds" of those who promote a merger; or to prove that the acquiring firm had engaged in actions which are considered to be unethical or predatory; or to show that as a result of a merger the acquiring firm had already obtained such a degree of control that it possessed the power to destroy or exclude competitors or fix prices.[9]

Perhaps because of unawareness of the extent to which the International Shoe decision read the Sherman Act test into the Clayton Act, the committee in another part of the report endorsed that decision. In answer to whether the bill would hinder competition by preventing small firms from merging, thus offering more competition to larger firms, the House Committee said that this bill is less restrictive than the original Section 7, and the original Section 7 had not been interpreted so as to prevent acquisitions of stock involving small corporations. The report stated:

. . . The Supreme Court has only applied the present language of Section 7, even in the case of stock acquisitions, to large transactions which would substantially lessen competition or tend to create a monopoly. In the case of *International Shoe Company* v. *Federal Trade Commission*, supra, decided January 26, 1930, the International Shoe Co., having a Nation-wide business, purchased the stock of McElwain Co., a smaller shoe company also having a Nation-wide business. As to part of the business of the two corporations, they were not in direct competition. The Federal Trade Commission sought to order a divestiture of the stock and prevent the merger. The Supreme Court held that the merger was not of sufficient size or importance, even though there was some competition between the two corporations, to substantially lessen competition or to create a monopoly. The Court has this to say:

[9] H. Rept. 1191, p. 8.

"Mere acquisition by one corporation of the stock of a competitor even though it results in some lessening of competition, is not forbidden; the act deals only with such acquisitions as probably will result in lessening competition to a substantial degree, *Standard Fashion Co.* v. *Magrane-Houston Co.* (258 U.S. 346, 357); that is to say, to such a degree as will injuriously affect the public."

The language in the amendment it will be noted follows closely the purpose of the Clayton Act as defined by the Supreme Court in the International Shoe case.[10]

This endorsement of the International Shoe decision implies that the new Section 7 is intended to be no more restrictive, and perhaps less restrictive, than the original section *as interpreted by the Court;* yet in another part of the report the Committee said that the new bill would cover *vertical and conglomerate* mergers.[11]

The statements of the Senate Judiciary Committee were much less ambiguous and, being part of a subsequent report, probably would have greater weight with the Supreme Court as evidence of Congressional intent, if the court were to look beyond the language of the statute itself in interpreting its meaning. The Senate Committee report said:

The present wording of H.R. 2734 is intended to cover more than is prohibited by the Sherman Act and yet to stop short of the stated test of the present section 7 of the Clayton Act. Section 7 of the Clayton Act was originally written to reach effects beyond those prohibited by the Sherman Act, extending to the reduction of the competition which had previously existed between the acquiring and acquired companies. This latter feature, namely the effect on competition between the acquiring and the acquired corporations, has been regarded as the distinctive "Clayton Act test," insofar as it relates to section 7 of the Act.

The purpose of H.R. 2734 was to make this legislation extend to acquisitions which are not forbidden by the Sherman Act. But here a problem presented itself. While on the one hand it was desired that the test be more inclusive and stricter than that of the Sherman Act, on the other hand it was not desired that the bill go to the extreme of prohibiting all acquisitions between competing companies. The present wording of H.R. 2734, but beginning with H.R. 515, introduced on April 24, 1947, represents an

[10] *Ibid.*, p. 7.

[11] *Ibid.*, p. 11.

attempt to solve this problem. Several steps have been taken in order to achieve a solution. . . .

The committee believe that the excessive sweep that has been given to section 7 of the Clayton Act by these two features [the acquiring-acquired test and the use of the word "community"] of that section has been largely responsible for the tendency of the courts in cases under that section to revert to the Sherman Act test. By eliminating the provisions of the existing section that appear to reach situations of little economic significance, it is the purpose of this legislation to assure a broader construction of the more fundamental provisions that are retained than has been given in the past. The committee wish to make it clear that the bill is not intended to revert to the Sherman Act test.[12]

In addition to these general statements regarding the intent of the 1950 amendment to the Clayton Act, these committee reports contained important information on several specific questions that will arise in the administration of the act.

The House Committee obviously considered the bill to contain two separate and alternative standards. Its report said: "Under H.R. 2734 a merger or acquisition will be unlawful if it may have the effect of either (a) substantially lessening competition or (b) tending to create a monopoly." [13] Neither report, however, delineates the difference between the concept of lessening competition and the concept of tending to create a monopoly.

The meaning of the phrase "in any line of commerce in any section of the country" was explicitly discussed in both reports. The House Committee said:

The test of substantial lessening of competition or tending to create a monopoly is not intended to be applicable only where the specified effect may appear on a Nation-wide or industry-wide scale. The purpose of the bill is to protect competition in each line of commerce in each section of the country.[14]

The Senate Committee made clear that the term "section" was to have a meaning different from "community":

As the bill originally stood, it was to be violated if, among other things, competition was substantially lessened "***in any community***" of the

[12] S. Rept. 1775, p. 4.

[13] H. Rept. 1191, p. 8.

[14] *Ibid.*

country. The use of this word raised a storm of controversy, centering around the possibility that the act, so worded, might go so far as to prevent any local enterprise in a small town from buying up another local enterprise in the same town. As a consequence, the word "community" was dropped from the subsequent versions of the bill.[15]

The Senate report pointed out that in the amendment, unlike the original Section 7, the phrases "in any line of commerce" and "in any section of the country" applied to both a lessening of competition and a tendency to create a monopoly. With respect to the meaning of the former phrase, the Senate report said:

It is intended that acquisitions which substantially lessen competition, as well as those which tend to create a monopoly, will be unlawful if they have the specified effect in any line of commerce, *whether or not that line of commerce is a large part of the business of any of the corporations involved in the acquisition* [italics mine].[16]

Should this statement of the intent of Congress be recognized by the court when interpreting the new law, it will be very important in establishing an economically meaningful criterion, since it would be impossible for a merger having a substantial detrimental effect in some particular market to escape condemnation of the law because the corporations involved are sufficiently large and varied in their operations that only a small part of their business is in the market concerned.

The Senate Committee considered in more detail the meaning of "in any section of the country," saying:

Although it is, of course, impossible to define rigidly what constitutes a "section of the country," certain broad standards reflecting the general intent of Congress can be set forth to guide the Commission and the courts in their interpretation.

What constitutes a section will vary with the nature of the product. Owing to the differences in the size and character of markets, it would be meaningless, from an economic point of view, to attempt to apply for all products a uniform definition of section, whether such a definition were based upon miles, population, income, or any other unit of measurement. A section which would be economically significant for a heavy, durable

[15] S. Rept. 1775, p. 4.

[16] *Ibid.*, p. 5.

product, such as large machine tools, might well be meaningless for a light product, such as milk.[17]

The Senate Committee then endorsed the Supreme Court's definition in the Standard Stations case[18] of the relevant section in terms of the area of effective competition.[19] The report then elaborated upon the means of defining such an area, saying:

> In determining the area of effective competition for a given product, it will be necessary to decide what comprises a significant segment of the market. An appreciable segment of the market may not only be a segment which covers an appreciable segment of the trade, but it may also be a segment which is largely segregated from, independent of, or not affected by the trade in that product in other parts of the country.
>
> It should be noted that although the section of the country in which there may be a lessening of competition will normally be one in which the acquired company or the acquiring company may do business, the bill is broad enough to cope with a substantial lessening of competition in any other section of the country as well.[20]

The removal of the acquiring-acquired test and these clear statements of Congressional intent regarding the meaning of the phrase "in any line of commerce in any section of the country" reveal clearly that one of the most important implications of the 1950 amendment of Section 7 is a complete change in the direction in which the commission and the courts must look for the effect of an acquisition. Under the new law, the investigation must be centered on a market, in the economic sense, rather than on the relationship between the acquiring and the acquired firms.

In determining whether an acquisition violates the law, the commission and the courts must base their decisions on the effect of the acquisition on the degree of competition in a market. It is not necessary, however, to find that undesirable consequences have occurred. The words "may be" were retained in the new statute, and, according to the Senate report, Congress intended to

[17] *Ibid.*, pp. 5–6.

[18] *Standard Oil Co.* v. *United States* (1949), 337 U.S. 293.

[19] The importance of this case in indicating the possible attitude of the Supreme Court on the meaning of Section 7 is discussed in a later section of this chapter.

[20] S. Rept. 1775, p. 6.

retain the meaning that the Supreme Court had given to them in the interpretation of the original Clayton Act. The report stated:

> The use of these words means that the bill, if enacted, would not apply to the mere possibility but only to the reasonable probability of the prescribed effect, as determined by the commission in accord with the Administrative Procedure Act.
>
> The words "may be" have been in section 7 of the Clayton Act since 1914. The concept of reasonable probability conveyed by these words is a necessary element in any statute which seeks to arrest restraints of trade in their incipiency and before they develop into full-fledged restraints violative of the Sherman Act. A requirement of certainty and actuality of injury to competition is incompatible with any effort to supplement the Sherman Act by reaching incipient restraints.[21]

The legislative history of the 1950 amendment also indicates clearly that Congress did not intend to change the meaning of the Section 7 application to acquisitions arising from the financial distress or imminent bankruptcy of the acquired firm. The House report on H.R. 2734 said:

> The argument that a corporation in bankrupt or failing condition might not be allowed to sell to a competitor has already been disposed of by the courts. It is well settled that the Clayton Act does not apply in bankruptcy or receivership cases.[22]

The Senate Committee report said:

> The committee are in full accord with the proposition that any firm in . . . [a failing or bankrupt] condition should be free to dispose of its stock or assets. The committee, however, do not believe that the proposed bill will prevent sales of this type. . . .
>
> It is expected that, in the administration of the act, full consideration will be given to all matters bearing upon the maintenance of competition, including the circumstances giving rise to the acquisition.[23]

The House Committee anticipated and answered one other question that may arise in the administration of the statute:

> The bill retains language of the present statute which is broad enough to prevent evasion of the central purpose. It covers not only purchase of

[21] *Ibid.*

[22] H. Rept. 1191, p. 6.

[23] S. Rept. 1775, p. 7

assets or stock but also any other method of acquisition, such as, for example, lease of assets. It forbids not only direct acquisitions but also indirect acquisitions, whether through a subsidiary or affiliate or otherwise.[24]

By the enactment of the original Section 7 of the Clayton Act in 1914, Congress intended to supplement the Sherman Act with provisions of law designed to cope with intercorporate stockholding and the particular evils incident thereto. The 1950 amendment served much more than plugging a loophole in that part of the antitrust law. It constituted a major substantive change in antitrust policy on corporate mergers and acquisitions of all types. The procedural and substantive provisions of the law regarding asset acquisitions and statutory mergers were made to conform to the law with respect to stock acquisitions (except for corporations excluded from the jurisdiction of the Federal Trade Commission). In addition to being an amendment of the Clayton Act, the Celler-Kefauver Act was, in effect, an amendment of the Sherman Act, which previously had been the statute setting forth policy on asset acquisitions. The amendment changed the standard of illegality by which both types of acquisitions are to be judged. An important characteristic of the Sherman Act standard is the emphasis it places on intent and monopolistic practices. The original Section 7 standard was framed in terms of the effect of stock acquisitions, but the wording focused the attention of the commission and the courts on the relationship between the corporations involved. The legislative history of the 1950 amendment indicates that Congress intended to change the law on corporate acquisitions of all types so as to make illegal all acquisitions manifesting a reasonable probability of the *effect* of a substantial lessening of competition or a tendency toward the creation of a monopoly *in the market for any commodity,* irrespective of the existence of a conspiracy, or of an intent to monopolize or to restrain trade.

[24] H. Rept. 1191, pp. 8–9.

Recent Supreme Court Cases under Related Provisions of Law

Some intimation of the manner in which the Supreme Court will apply this new legislative standard for judging the legality of corporate mergers and acquisitions can be obtained from its opinions in recent cases under other provisions of the antitrust laws.

In administering the new statutory provision, the commissions and the courts must ascertain the probable effect of a corporate merger or acquisition in order to determine whether it may substantially lessen competition in any line of commerce in any section of the country, or whether it may tend to create a monopoly in any line of commerce in any section of the country. Similar language is used in Section 3 of the Clayton Act. The Sherman Act alone would make a corporate merger illegal, if it were found by the court to be a contract or combination in restraint of trade, or if it were found to have resulted in a monopoly or to have been an attempt to monopolize, or a combination or conspiracy to monopolize any part of commerce.[25] It is quite clear that, in amending Section 7, Congress intended the Clayton Act to reach some mergers and acquisitions that would not be prohibited by the Sherman Act. Both statutes are general statements of policy that must be implemented and reinterpreted in each case. An examination of some recent Supreme Court opinions in Sherman Act cases should reveal what might be called the upper limit on the range of interpretation which the court can be expected to give to the new Section 7.

Some Recent Sherman Act Cases—In the Columbia Steel Company case,[26] the Supreme Court dealt explicitly with the applica-

[25] 26 *U.S. Stat. at L.* (1890), 209. The first two sections of the Sherman Act provide:

Sec. 1. Every contract, combination in the form of trust or otherwise, or conspiracy, in restraint of trade or commerce among the several States, or with foreign nations, is hereby declared to be illegal. . . .

Sec. 2. Every person who shall monopolize, or attempt to monopolize, or combine or conspire with any other person or persons, to monopolize any part of the trade or commerce among the several States, or with foreign nations, shall be deemed guilty of a misdemeanor. . . .

[26] *United States* v. *Columbia Steel Co., et al.* (1948), 334 U.S. 446.

tion of both Sections 1 and 2 of the Sherman Act to a single corporate acquisition. The United States sued under Section 4 of the Sherman Act to enjoin the acquisition by Columbia Steel Company, a subsidiary of United States Steel, of the assets of the Consolidated Steel Corporation. The government alleged that this acquisition would violate both Sections 1 and 2 of the Sherman Act. The acquisition would constitute a contract in restraint of trade, as all other steel producers would be excluded from the business of supplying Consolidated with rolled steel products, and existing competition between Consolidated and United States Steel in the sale of structural fabricated products and pipe would be eliminated. The government also alleged that, in the light of previous acquisitions by United States Steel, this acquisition would constitute an attempt to monopolize a part of interstate trade.[27]

The government contended that the acquisition would constitute a restraint of trade which is illegal *per se,* since United States Steel's competitors in the sale of rolled steel products would be foreclosed from an "appreciable" amount of commerce. It argued that the Supreme Court opinion in the Yellow Cab case[28] the previous year had declared vertical integration to be illegal *per se,* and it was therefore unnecessary to prove by an examination of the market that the restraint would be unreasonable.[29] The majority opinion rejected this argument, answering that the court had not declared vertical integration to be illegal *per se.*[30] The opinion said that the court had applied the rule of reason in the

[27] 334 U.S. 446.

[28] *United States* v. *Yellow Cab Co.* (1947), 332 U.S. 218.

[29] 334 U.S. 446, 519–521.

[30] There appears to have been some sentiment in the court in 1948 for declaring vertical integration to be illegal *per se.* In the majority opinion in *United States* v. *Paramount Pictures, Inc., et al.* (1948), 334 U.S. 131, 173–174, Justice Douglas said: "Exploration of these phases of the cases would not be necessary if, as the Department of Justice argues, vertical integration of producing, distributing and exhibiting motion pictures is illegal *per se.* But the majority of the Court does not take that view."

In his dissenting opinion in *Standard Oil Company of California, et al.* v. *United States* (1949), 337 U.S. 293, 318 n. 6, Justice Douglas said that in the Paramount case "a majority of the Court could not be obtained for holding illegal *per se* the vertical integration in the motion picture industry."

Yellow Cab case, but it had been unnecessary to show that the business involved was a substantial proportion of the total market in question because of a clear showing of intent to monopolize. The court said that where a "complaint charges such an unreasonable restraint as the facts of the *Yellow Cab* case show, the amount of interstate trade affected is immaterial." [31]

The majority of the court in the Columbia Steel decision interpreted Section 1 of the Sherman Act as providing three distinct criteria of illegality. A restraint may be illegal "because it falls within the class of restraints which are illegal *per se*." There are two other types of illegal restraints. The opinion said:

> When a combination through its actual operation results in an unreasonable restraint, intent or purpose may be inferred; even though no unreasonable restraint may be achieved, nevertheless a finding of specific intent to accomplish such an unreasonable restraint may render the actor liable under the Sherman Act.[32]

In the Columbia Steel case, the majority found no evidence of specific intent:

> Granting that the sale will to some extent affect competition, the acquisition of a firm outlet to absorb a portion of Geneva's rolled steel production seems to reflect a normal business purpose rather than a scheme to circumvent the law.[33]

In a dissenting opinion concurred in by Justices Black, Murphy, and Rutledge, Justice Douglas said:

> However the acquisition may be rationalized, the effect is plain. It is a purchase for control, a purchase for control of a market for which United States Steel has in the past had to compete but which it no longer wants left to the uncertainties that competition in the west may engender. This in effect it concedes. It states that its purpose in acquiring consolidated is to insure itself of a market for part of Geneva's production of rolled steel products when demand falls off.
>
> . . . The competitive purchases by Consolidated are over $5,000,000 a year. I do not see how it is possible to say that $5,000,000 of commerce is immaterial, it plainly is not *de minimis*. And it is the character of the

[31] 334 U.S. 446, 522.
[32] 334 U.S. 446, 525.
[33] 334 U.S. 446, 533.

restraint which § 1 of the act brands as illegal, not the amount of commerce affected.[34]

Having rejected the argument that a vertical integration is illegal *per se* and having found no specific intent to achieve an unreasonable restraint of trade, the majority of the court allowed the question of the legality of the Steel company acquisition to rest on the unreasonableness of the result. In deciding, the court treated the horizontal and vertical aspects of the merger separately:

. . . We conclude that the so-called vertical integration resulting from the acquisition of consolidated does not unreasonably restrict the opportunities of the competitor producers of rolled steel to market their product. We accept as the relevant competitive market the total demand for rolled steel products in the eleven-state area; only 3% of that demand, and if expectations as to the development of the western steel industry are realized, Consolidated's proportion may be expected to be lower than that figure in the future, [is affected by the acquisition]. . . .

The same tests which measure the legality of vertical integration by acquisition are also applicable to the acquisition of competitors in identical or similar lines of merchandise. It is first necessary to delimit the market in which the concerns compete and then determine the extent to which the concerns are in competition in that market. If such acquisition results in or is aimed at unreasonable restraint, then the purchase is forbidden by the Sherman Act. In determining what constitutes unreasonable restraint, we do not think the dollar volume is in itself of compelling significance; we look rather to the percentage of business controlled, the strength of the remaining competition, whether the action springs from business requirements or purpose to monopolize, the probable development of the industry, consumer demands, and other characteristics of the market. We do not undertake to prescribe any set of percentage figures by which to measure the reasonableness of a corporation's enlargement of its activities by the purchase of the assets of a competitor. The relative effect of percentage command of a market varies with the setting in which that factor is placed.

We conclude that in this case the Government has failed to prove that the elimination of competition between Consolidated and the structural fabricating subsidiaries of United States Steel constitutes an unreasonable restraint. . . . To hold this does not imply that additional acquisitions of fabricating facilities for structural steel would not become monopolistic.[35]

[34] 334 U.S. 446, 537.

[35] 334 U.S. 446, 527–529.

The court considered separately the allegation that the acquisition would be a violation of Section 2 of the Sherman Act. The opinion stated that the trial court had interpreted Section 2 too narrowly, because Section 2 may be violated even if no unreasonable restraint of trade is found under Section 1, if a specific intent to monopolize is shown. The court found no such specific intent in this case.[36]

The meaning of Section 2 of the Sherman Act was elaborated on further by the court in *United States* v. *Griffith*,[37] which was decided at about the same time. The majority opinion said:

> Anyone who owns and operates the single theatre in a town, or who acquires the exclusive right to exhibit a film, has a monopoly in the popular sense. But he usually does not violate § 2 of the Sherman Act unless he has acquired or maintained his strategic position, or sought to expand his monopoly, or expanded it by means of those restraints of trade which are recognizable under § 1. For those things which are condemned by § 2 are in large measure merely the end products of conduct which violates § 1. But this is not always true. Section 1 covers contracts, combinations, or conspiracies in restraint of trade. Section 2 is not restricted to conspiracies or combinations to monopolize but also makes it a crime for any person to monopolize or to attempt to monopolize any part of interstate or foreign trade or commerce. So it is that monopoly power, whether lawfully or unlawfully acquired, may itself constitute an evil and stand condemned under § 2 even though it remains unexercised.[38]

In the Paramount Pictures case, the court considered the legality of a vertical integration, but distinguished less clearly between Sections 1 and 2 of the Sherman Act.

> In the opinion of the majority the legality of vertical integration under the Sherman Act turns on (1) the purpose or intent with which it was conceived, or (2) the power it creates and the attendant purpose or intent. First, it runs afoul of the Sherman Act if it was a calculated scheme to gain control over an appreciable segment of the market and to restrain or suppress competition, rather than an expansion to meet legitimate business needs. . . . Second, a vertically integrated enterprise, like other aggregations of business units . . . will constitute monopoly which, though un-

[36] 334 U.S. 446, 531–532.

[37] 334 U.S. 100 (1948).

[38] 334 U.S. 100, 106–107.

> exercised, violates the Sherman Act provided a power to exclude competition is coupled with a purpose or intent to do so. . . . Likewise bearing on the question whether monopoly power is created by the vertical integration, is the nature of the market to be served . . . and the leverage on the market which the particular vertical integration creates or makes possible.[39]

Congress directed that the criterion of illegality under the amended Section 7 of the Clayton Act should be stronger than the Sherman Act standard. That standard, as recently set forth by the Supreme Court, has several facets. A merger may be deemed illegal under Section 1 of the Sherman Act, if a specific intent to restrain trade is shown. In the absence of specific intent, it may still be illegal if an examination of the relevant competitive market shows that the merger will unreasonably restrict the opportunities of competitors to continue to sell their products, or that the merger increases the percentage of business controlled by the acquiring firm so much that no effective competition remains. The court declined to give a definite percentage criterion. Furthermore, recent opinions of the court suggest that the court would hold a merger to violate Section 2 if a specific intent to monopolize is proven, even if the merger does not result in the achievement of monopoly. Even without a specific intent to monopolize, a merger may be held to violate Section 2 if it results in the power to exclude competitors or to raise prices, if this power is coupled with the intent to use it.

Recent Interpretation of Section 3 of the Clayton Act—A possible interpretation that the Supreme Court may give to the new Section 7 can be obtained from an examination of the reasoning of the court in a recent case brought under Section 3 of the Clayton Act. The Justice Department sought to enjoin the Standard Oil Company of California from enforcing or entering into exclusive dealing contracts with independent dealers. The government alleged that the contracts were in violation of Section 1 of the Sherman Act and Section 3 of the Clayton Act. In an opinion written by Justice Frankfurter, the court upheld a lower court

[39] 334 U.S. 131, 174.

that had found the contracts to be in violation of Section 3 of the Clayton Act.[40]

The standard of illegality under Section 3 resembles the standard provided in the 1950 amendment of Section 7 more than the original Section 7, since Section 3 provides that it shall be unlawful for any person to make a contract for the sale of goods on the condition that the purchaser not deal in the goods of a competitor "where the effect of such . . . contract . . . may be to substantially lessen competition or tend to create a monopoly in any line of commerce."[41] Although this criterion does not contain the phrase "in any section of the country," the court said: "It is clear, of course, that the 'line of commerce' affected need not be nationwide, at least where the purchasers cannot, as a practical matter, turn to suppliers outside their own area."[42] The standard of illegality in Section 3 thus appears to be about the same as in the amended Section 7, which declares an acquisition to be illegal "where in any line of commerce in any section of the country, the effect of such acquisition may be substantially to lessen competition, or to tend to create a monopoly."[43]

In discussing the meaning of Section 3, the opinion of the court said:

> The issue before us, therefore, is whether the requirement of showing that the effect of the agreements "may be to substantially lessen competition" may be met simply by proof that a substantial portion of commerce is affected or whether it must also be demonstrated that competitive activity has actually diminished or probably will diminish.[44]

A majority of the court interpreted Section 3 as requiring proof only that a substantial portion of commerce was affected. The court held that requirements contracts affecting fifty-eight million dollars of gross business—6.7 per cent of the total business in a seven-state area—constituted a substantial proportion of the volume of sales in the line of commerce in the area of effective com-

---

[40] *Standard Oil Company of California, et al.* v. *United States* (1949), 337 U.S. 293.

[41] 38 *U.S. Stat. at L.* (1914), 730, 731.

[42] 337 U.S. 293, 299 n. 5.

[43] 64 *U.S. Stat. at L.* (1950), 1125.

[44] 337 U.S. 293, 299.

petition, and the contracts thus were illegal.[45] The court held that the nature of requirements contracts meant that competition was substantially lessened *per se,* because the contracts affected a substantial proportion of the sales in the market. In justifying this interpretation of the statute, the majority opinion of the court said that

> . . . to demand that bare inference be supported by evidence as to what would have happened but for the adoption of the practice that was in fact adopted or to require firm prediction of an increase of competition as a probable result of ordering the abandonment of the practice, would be a standard of proof, if not virtually impossible to meet, at least most ill-suited for ascertainment by courts.[46]

Although the difference between mergers and requirements contracts probably would lead these same justices to view Sections 7 and 3 differently, the following statement, appended in a footnote, seems to be equally applicable to Section 7:

> The dual system of enforcement provided for by the Clayton Act must have contemplated standards of proof capable of administration by the courts as well as by the Federal Trade Commission and other designated agencies. . . . Our interpretation of the Act, therefore, should recognize that an appraisal of economic data which might be practicable if only the latter were faced with the task may be quite otherwise for judges unequipped for it either by experience or by the availability of skilled assistance.[47]

There were two dissenting opinions in this case, and both have a direct bearing on the interpretation the court might give to the new Section 7. In a dissenting opinion concurred in by Chief Justice Vinson, and Justice Burton, Justice Jackson rejected the majority's declaration that exclusive dealing arrangements are illegal *per se.* He said:

> . . . It is indispensable to the Government's case to establish that either the actual or the probable effect of the accused arrangement is to substantially lessen competition or tend to create a monopoly.
>
> I am unable to agree that this requirement was met. To be sure, the contracts cover "a substantial number of outlets and a substantial amount of products, whether considered comparatively or not." . . . But that fact does

[45] 337 U.S. 293, 305.

[46] 337 U.S. 293, 309–310.

[47] 337 U.S. 293, 310 n. 13.

not automatically bring the accused arrangement within the prohibitions of the statute. The number of dealers and the volume of sales covered by the arrangement of course was sufficient to be substantial. That is to say, this arrangement operated on enough commerce to violate the Act, provided its effects were substantially to lessen competition or tend to create a monopoly. But proof of their quantity does not prove that they had this forbidden quality; and the assumption that they did, without proof, seems to me unwarranted. . . .

I regard it as unfortunate that the Clayton Act submits such economic issues to judicial determination. It not only leaves the law vague as a warning or guide, and determined only after the event, but the judicial process is not well adapted to exploration of such industry-wide, and even nation-wide, questions.

But if they must decide, the only possible way for the courts to arrive at a fair determination is to hear all relevant evidence from both parties.[48]

Although Justice Douglas also dissented, he would have interpreted even the Sherman Act as declaring mergers of a vertical type to be illegal *per se*. His dissent from the decision of the court was based on the argument that, because the court had failed to declare vertical integration to be a *per se* illegal restraint of trade, the outlawing of the exclusive dealing arrangement might lead to an even greater lessening of competition by encouraging a return to the agency device or outright acquisition of the independent stations by Standard Oil and other oil companies. He said:

When the choice is thus given, I dissent from the outlawry of the requirements contract on the present facts. The effect which it has on competition in this field is minor as compared to the damage which will flow from the judicially approved formula for the growth of bigness tendered by the Court as an alternative. Our choice must be made on the basis not of abstractions but of the realities of modern industrial life.[49]

The decision in this case, of course, will not serve as a precedent in the interpretation of Section 7 of the Clayton Act. Unlike tying contracts, mergers are presumed to be legal, and the court is bound to draw a distinction between the two.

The du Pont–General Motors Case—In June, 1957, for the first time since 1930, the Supreme Court rendered a decision in a case

[48] 337 U.S. 293, 321–322.

[49] 337 U.S. 293, 320.

arising under the original Section 7 of the Clayton Act.[50] In 1949 the Department of Justice brought a civil action in a district court alleging that du Pont's ownership of stock in the General Motors Corporation constituted a violation of Sections 1 and 2 of the Sherman Act and Section 7 of the Clayton Act, because it gave du Pont an unlawful preference in purchases of materials by General Motors. After a long trial which centered on the Sherman Act allegations, the district court decided against the government.[51] The Supreme Court made no decision on the Sherman Act allegations, but held that du Pont's acquisition from 1917 to 1919 of 23 per cent of the common stock of General Motors violated Section 7 of the Clayton Act and remanded the cause to the district court for determination of the appropriate equitable relief.

This case may serve to revitalize the original Section 7 for stock acquisitions made before 1950. Its relevance to the interpretation that the court will give to the amended Section 7 is lessened by the fact that it was decided by a four to two division among only six participating justices[52] and involved the original Clayton Act, but the opinion of the court, along with the dissenting opinion, provides some clue to the court's approach to cases arising under the new law.

The court held that the facts justified a conclusion that the stock acquisition was not made solely as an investment, but that it constituted sufficient control of General Motors to influence its purchases. The court, viewing the case as a vertical acquisition, questioned whether the original Section 7 applies to such acquisitions. The majority held that

> . . . any acquisition by one corporation of all or any part of the stock of another corporation, competitor or not, is within the reach of the section whenever the reasonable likelihood appears that the acquisition will result

[50] *United States* v. *E. I. du Pont de Nemours and Co. et al.* (1957), 353 U.S. 586.

[51] *United States* v. *E. I. du Pont de Nemours and Co. et al.* (1954), 126 Fed. Supp. 235 (D.C., N.D. Ill.).

[52] Justices Clark, Harlan, and Whittaker did not participate; Justices Burton and Frankfurter dissented.

in a restraint of commerce or in the creation of a monopoly of any line of commerce. Thus, although du Pont and General Motors are not competitors, a violation of the section has occurred if, as a result of the acquisition, there was at the time of suit a reasonable likelihood of a monopoly of any line of commerce.[53]

The Supreme Court thus overruled the International Shoe case interpretation of the standard of illegality of the original Section 7. It said that the original statute's statement about a tendency to create a monopoly in any line of commerce is separate from the criterion of substantial lessening of competition *between* the acquiring and the acquired firm, but that a tendency to create a monopoly must be judged in terms of whether the threatened monopoly is one that will *substantially* lessen competition *in a market*. Substantiality must be determined in terms of the market affected. The court concluded:

The record shows that automobile finishes and fabrics have sufficient peculiar characteristics and uses to constitute them products sufficiently distinct from all other finishes and fabrics to make them a "line of commerce" within the meaning of the Clayton Act.[54]

The brief of General Motors had stated that du Pont's 1947 sales to General Motors of finishes and fabrics constituted only 3.5 per cent and 1.6 per cent, respectively, of the total sales in the markets for those products. The court defined the products more narrowly and found both that the market affected was substantial and that the acquisition foreclosed competitors from a substantial share of that market. This conclusion was based on the assumption that General Motors' purchases amounted to about 40 per cent of all purchases of automotive finishes and fabrics, since General Motors produces about half of the automobiles, and on the fact that du Point supplied the largest part of General Motors' requirements of these two products. The reasoning is very similar to that used by the court in the Standard Stations decision. The court gave no consideration to the market position of the other firms that compete with du Pont in the automotive finishes and fabrics markets. But this may have been a result of the court's

[53] 353 U.S. 586, 592.
[54] 353 U.S. 586, 593–594.

judgment that du Pont and General Motors were such large factors in those two markets that no detailed inquiry was necessary. It is not at all certain that the four justices who constituted the majority in this case would accept the reasoning used in the Standard Stations case, as applicable to Section 7, if the relative size of the firms involved were as small as in that case. Justice Frankfurter, who wrote the opinion in the Standard Stations case, joined the dissent of Justice Burton in this case.

The dissenting opinion takes issue with the majority's contentions that vertical acquisitions are included in the prohibitions of the old law and that the time at which the suit is brought, rather than the time of the acquisition, is controlling in determining whether the effect of the acquisition may be that stated by the law. The dissenting opinion implies, however, that the amended Section 7 applies to vertical acquisitions.[55] The minority opinion also appears to agree with the majority view that a vertical acquisition should be evaluated on the basis of the principle that Section 7 is violated when there is a reasonable probability that the acquisition is likely to have the effect of foreclosure of competitors of the acquiring corporation from a substantial share of the relevant market. Justice Burton disagreed on the application of this principle: he did not think the record had established the existence of a reasonable probability that General Motors' trade was foreclosed to du Pont's competitors. He concluded that, even if the record had established such foreclosure, it did not establish that the foreclosure involved a substantial share of the relevant market. He would judge the substantiality of the market share on the basis of whether its foreclosure "significantly limits the competitive opportunities of others trading in that market." [56]

The diversity of opinion of the members of the Supreme Court in the Standard Stations and the du Pont–General Motors cases implies that uncertainty about the meaning of the new Section 7 will continue at least until a case reaches the Supreme Court.

As Congress clearly directed the court not to revert to the Sherman Act test, and as it is not necessary under the Clayton

[55] 353 U.S. 586, 615–616.

[56] 353 U.S. 586, 627.

Act even *to infer* an intent to restrain trade or to monopolize, the court might adopt a criterion very similar to that used in the du Pont case—that is, intermediate between the tests applied in the Standard Stations and the Columbia Steel cases. If so, the court will agree with Justice Jackson that it is necessary to show a probable lessening of competition, and yet accept as proof of such an effect evidence that would not be adequate to prove a Sherman Act violation in the absence of specific intent.

The interpretation the court will give to the new Section 7 would thus differ from that given the Sherman Act in the Columbia Steel case only in the subjective evaluation made from the evidence: the nature of the evidence considered relevant would be of the same general character. The court would judge the effect of the acquisition on the degree of competition in one or more markets. The markets would be defined in terms of both the product and geography on the basis of what is considered the area of effective competition. Quantitative evidence of the degree of participation in the market in the past by the firms involved in the merger would be given great weight, but the decision would not be based on a simple numerical formula. The court would consider the structure of the market, both before and after the merger, as well as the particular business practices characteristic of the market and of the firms in question.

The initial interpretation of the amended Section 7 by the lower courts and by the Federal Trade Commission in several cases tend to corroborate this view of the meaning of the new statute.

Legal Proceedings under the Celler-Kefauver Act

Since the amendment of Section 7 of the Clayton Act in 1950, the Federal Trade Commission and the Department of Justice have issued a number of complaints under the new law. One important private suit has also been brought charging violation of Section 7 as amended by the Celler-Kefauver Act.

The Hamilton Watch Company Case—One of the first cases

under the amended law was a private suit by the Hamilton Watch Company against the Benrus Watch Company.[57] After the Benrus Watch Company acquired a minority stock interest in the Hamilton Watch Company, Hamilton brought suit seeking a preliminary injunction and a permanent injunction to prevent Benrus from voting the stock. The suit also sought a permanent injunction to restrain Benrus from acquiring additional shares and an order requiring divestment of the shares already acquired. The district court granted the preliminary injunction to prevent the exercise of the voting rights of the acquired stock, and thus the election of several directors, while the case proceeded. The district court judge held that the acquisition violated Section 7 and irreparable injury to Hamilton would have resulted if the injunction were not granted.[58]

The court held that acquisition of stock insufficient to carry control could constitute a violation of Section 7

> . . . in cases in which there is a showing that the acquisitions were made pursuant to a plan or purpose to obtain control the achievement of which at the time the acquisitions were made, was reasonably probable and which, if achieved, would probably have had the effect to substantially lessen the competition which the amended Act sought to preserve.[59]

The court further held that, even if such a plan or purpose to obtain control were absent, the control of a minority of the board of directors of Hamilton would constitute a violation, since it would afford an opportunity to bring about a relaxation of the "full vigor of Hamilton's competitive effort." [60]

The Circuit Court of Appeals pointed out that the findings of the lower court were temporary, because the hearings were on the temporary injunction rather than the order of divestment. As the findings of the trial judge were not clearly erroneous, the circuit court affirmed the granting of the injunction. With respect to the meaning of the amended Section 7, the court said: "Although we

[57] *Hamilton Watch Company* v. *Benrus Watch Company, Inc.* (1953), 114 Fed. Supp. 307 (D.C., D. Conn.), affirmed 206 Fed. Rept., 2d Ser., 738 (C.C.A., 2d Cir.).

[58] 14 Fed. Supp. 307, 317.

[59] 14 Fed. Supp. 307, 316.

[60] 14 Fed. Supp. 307, 316.

now indulge in no ultimate conclusion, we believe the amendment of Section 7 in 1950 certainly casts doubt on decisions . . . interpreting that section as it stood previously."[61] The temporary injunction was later vacated after Benrus sold the stock of Hamilton.

The Pillsbury Case—In June, 1952, the Federal Trade Commission issued a complaint against Pillsbury Mills, Inc., alleging that its acquisitions of the assets of Ballard and Ballard Company in June, 1951, and of the assets of the Duff's Baking Mix division of American Home Foods Corporation in March, 1952, violated Section 7 of the Clayton Act.[62] The preliminary inquiry disclosed and the complaint alleged that, prior to the acquisitions, all three firms were engaged in the sale of family flour, bakery flour, and prepared flour-base mixes, as well as other products. According to the complaint, during a twelve-month period in 1949/50, seven companies, including Pillsbury and Duff, made about 70 per cent of the total national sales of prepared flour-base mixes. Pillsbury had ranked as the nation's second largest seller of this product with about 16 per cent of the total sales, and Duff had ranked fourth with about 6 per cent.[63]

In the southeastern section of the United States—the area "generally lying east of the Mississippi River and south of the Ohio and Potomac Rivers"[64]—both Pillsbury and Ballard were alleged to have been leaders in the sale of family flour, bakery flour, and prepared flour-base mixes.[65] The complaint alleged that in the southeast in 1950 in the sale of family flour, Pillsbury ranked fifth with 3.66 per cent of total sales and Ballard ranked third with 4.65 per cent. In the sale of bakery flour, Pillsbury ranked third with 4.93 per cent and Ballard ranked ninth with 3.62 per cent. In the sale of prepared flour-base mixes, Pillsbury ranked first with 22.7 per cent, Ballard third with 12.0 per cent, and Duff fifth with 10.2 per cent. Thus in 1950 the three firms

[61] 206 Fed. Rept., 2d Ser., 738, 741.

[62] *In the Matter of Pillsbury Mills, Inc., Complaint,* mimeographed (F.T.C. Docket No. 6000, June 16, 1952).

[63] *Ibid.*, pp. 1–3.

[64] *Ibid.*, p. 2.

[65] *Ibid.*, p. 4.

combined sold 44.9 per cent of the prepared flour-base mixes in the southeast.[66]

The complaint said that these acquisitions were part of a general tendency toward concentration of ownership and control in the flour-milling industry. In 1945 the nine largest flour-milling companies controlled about 32.7 per cent of the nation's capacity. By 1950 this had increased to 38.1 per cent. It was stated that in recent years the consumer demand for family flour had decreased while the demand for prepared flour-base mixes had increased rapidly.[67]

After the issuance of the complaint, testimony was taken in support of it by a hearing examiner in Minneapolis, Louisville, Cincinnati, New York, and many cities in the southeastern states. At the close of the taking of testimony, Pillsbury's counsel filed a motion for dismissal on the ground that the commission had failed to establish *prima facie* proof that the acquisitions had violated Section 7. On April 8, 1953, the hearing examiner denied the motion, but allowed the counsel in support of the complaint only until July 1, 1953, to obtain, by court action if necessary, reliable evidence on production and sales of Pillsbury and other major firms both before and after the acquisitions. The counsel in support of the complaint refused to comply with that ruling and filed a motion for reconsideration, in which they argued that the information in the record was sufficient, unless successfully rebutted, to prove violation of the law. The hearing examiner denied the motion for reconsideration, and dismissed the complaint on April 22, 1953.[68]

Subpoenas had been served on officials of Pillsbury in an attempt to obtain sales and production figures for periods of time before and after the acquisitions, but the respondent had failed to supply such information. During the preliminary inquiry, the respondent had supplied its "best estimates" of sales and production of itself and the acquired companies and their competitors

[66] *Ibid.*

[67] *Ibid.*, pp. 4–5.

[68] *In the Matter of Pillsbury Mills, Inc., Initial Decision: Order Dismissing Complaint without Prejudice*, by Everett F. Haycraft, Hearing Examiner, mimeographed (F.T.C. Docket No. 6000, April 22, 1953).

for the 1949/50 fiscal year. In his opinion, the hearing examiner said:

> The record does not contain, however, any figures with respect to the volume of sales of the competitive products manufactured and sold by the respondent after it had acquired the assets of Ballard and Ballard Company and Duff's Baking Mix Division of American Home Products Corporation. Furthermore, the record does not contain any authentic or reliable production or sales figures with respect to family flour and bakery flour or of flour-base mixes or commercial feeds of competitors of the respondent in the Southeastern territory of the United States. No attempt was made to get such authentic sales figures from these competitors, counsel in support of the complaint relying upon estimates by respondent officials and others in the trade, surveys made by newspapers and other independent agencies such as chain stores in specific market areas surrounding such consuming centers as New Orleans, Louisiana, Birmingham, Alabama, Atlanta, Georgia, and Jacksonville, Florida.[69]

It is evident from his opinion that Hearing Examiner Haycraft interpreted the amended Section 7 as requiring positive evidence that the acquisitions had, in fact, resulted in an increase in the relative share of the market controlled by the respondent sufficient to constitute the equivalent of an unreasonable restraint of trade. He pointed out that the House Judiciary Committee report had specifically approved of the International Shoe decision,[70] and said that the counsel in support of the complaint were following a theory he considered untenable:

> They do not seem to realize that the language of Section 7 of the Clayton Act has been substantially changed by the recent amendment and that evidence of market position of the respondent as a result of the acquisition, is now necessary to show whether its effect may be "to substantially lessen competition" generally.[71]

The hearing examiner said that even if the standard of illegality used by the Supreme Court in the Standard Stations case were applicable, it would be necessary to have reliable evidence concerning the percentage of the total market sales made by the respondent after the acquisitions. Without expressing an opinion

---

[69] *Ibid.*, p. 2.

[70] See pp. 261–262.

[71] *Initial Decision*, p. 3.

on whether the acquisitions were in fact illegal, the hearing examiner dismissed the complaint on the ground that "the allegations of the complaint are not supported by reliable, probative and substantial evidence in the record as required by the Administrative Procedure Act." [72]

The counsel supporting the complaint appealed the decision to the commission. In their appeal brief they set forth the following as the issues to be decided by the commission:

1. Whether essential allegations of the complaint are supported by reliable, probative and substantial evidence.
2. Whether Congress in amending Section 7 of the Clayton Act renounced the application of the Sherman Act rule of reason test to the Clayton Act.
3. Whether the substantiality test adopted in cases arising under Section 3 of the same Act when applied to an acquisition involving a leading factor in the relevant market is sufficient to satisfy the qualifying clause in Section 7.
4. Whether Section 7 as amended requires not only that quantum of proof which will satisfy the test set forth in paragraph 3 above, but also proof of additional market characteristics.[73]

On the first question, the counsel in support of the complaint argued that actual production and sales figures for the relevant products in the relevant market areas after the acquisitions were impossible to obtain, since there were so many firms and many kept their records in such a manner that comparable figures could not be supplied. They argued further that such evidence is unnecessary to prove violation of the amended Section 7, saying:

> Sections 15 and 16 of this Act provide for the prevention of violations of Section 7. Obviously, actual effects of an acquisition cannot be shown prior to the occurrence of the acquisition, therefore it must be concluded that the test did not envisage a showing of transactions following an acquisition or of any actual results or effects. Such figures will be impossible to produce in a number of cases which will arise under Section 7, such as injunctive proceeding by the Department of Justice or by private parties.[74]

---

[72] *Ibid.*, p. 4.

[73] *In the Matter of Pillsbury Mills, Inc., Appeal Brief*, mimeographed (F.T.C. Docket No. 6000, 1953), p. 3.

[74] *Ibid.*, p. 13.

The appeal brief reviewed the House and Senate Judiciary Committee reports on the Celler Bill to show that Congress had intended that the Sherman Act test should not be applied in cases arising under the amended Section 7. It then argued that the commission should construe the amended Section 7 in the same manner as the Supreme Court had construed Section 3 in the Standard Stations case, as each section is directed against specific acts and practices, provided they have the effect of substantially lessening competition or tending to create a monopoly, and as requirements contracts and acquisitions both have the effect of foreclosing a part of the market.[75] The counsel in support of the complaint said in applying this test

> . . . it is sufficient to establish a prima facie case in the instant proceeding to show:
>
> (1) That the relevant products involved are competitive;
>
> (2) The relevant market;
>
> (3) That the respondent has a substantial share of and is one of the leading factors in the relevant market;
>
> (4) That the acquired companies had a substantial amount of business and were important competitive factors in the relevant markets.[76]

It was argued that the evidence presented had satisfied not only this test, but also the broader and more difficult test of showing that the character of the markets and the nature of competition was such that the acquisitions, "which are substantial in the absolute," increased the relative share of Pillsbury's business in the relevant markets enough to have a reasonable probability of substantially lessening competition. The appeal brief stated:

> In this connection we have satisfied the comparative test by the introduction of respondent's "best estimates" of the competitive market shares for the relevant products. However, we do not concede that in developing the character of the markets it is an absolute necessity to adopt the comparative approach.[77]

The attorneys supporting the complaint considered five products relevant: premium brands of family flour, bakery flour, for-

[75] *Ibid.*, pp. 24–31.
[76] *Ibid.*, pp. 36–37.
[77] *Ibid.*, p. 37.

mula feeds, mill feeds, and prepared mixes. They argued that the urban centers in the southeast constitute a relevant area of effect competition, since the smaller regional firms sold primarily in the rural areas and were unable to compete in the urban premium flour market characterized by large advertising campaigns and customer loyalty to well-known brands. They considered the southeast, in general, as the relevant market area for bakery flour, formula feeds, and mill feeds. Two areas were considered relevant in defining the area of effective competition for prepared mixes: the southeast, in which Pillsbury, Ballard, and Duff had operated, and the whole United States, in which Pillsbury and Duff had engaged in the sale of mixes.[78] Evidence on sales of these products by the three firms prior to the acquisitions in the relevant market areas was offered to show that the absolute amount of commerce involved was substantial. On the basis of the information supplied by Pillsbury and by persons familiar with the markets in question, the attorneys argued that the record proved that all three firms were leading factors in the markets for these products. Although the counsel in support of the complaint argued that no other evidence was necessary to prove violation of Section 7, they offered additional information on the character of the markets for consideration by the commission, were it to reject the applicability of the Standard Stations test.[79]

On the market structure in the milling industry, evidence was offered to show that between 1945 and 1951 the number of flour mills in the United States declined from 2,571 to 1,799 and their total capacity declined 5 per cent. This was attributed to technological changes making larger mills more efficient and to a drop in per capita consumption.

In this same period the number of flour mills in the southeast declined from 750 to 615, and their total capacity declined about 8 per cent. Very few new mills and even fewer new milling companies were established in the Southeast during that period. The attorneys supporting the complaint inferred that opportunity for

[78] *Ibid.*, pp. 37–42.

[79] *Ibid.*, pp. 38–58, and Appendix A, pp. 1–70.

entry was greatly limited. In 1945 the ten largest companies controlled 34 per cent of the nation's flour-milling capacity. In 1951 the same ten companies controlled 40 per cent, with acquisitions accounting for 71 per cent of their increased capacity. The small mills in the Southeast sold primarily in rural areas, whereas Pillsbury and the other national firms sold primarily in urban areas through supermarkets which handle only a few premium brands. The national firms were thus affected very little by competition from the many small firms. Ballard, however, was much more sensitive to such competition, which affected a significant proportion of its sales. Ballard also sold advertised brands in the urban areas in competition with Pillsbury and other national firms. Its elimination would make the few national sellers "immune to competition from below." [80]

On December 28, 1953, the Federal Trade Commission vacated the dismissal order and remanded the matter to the hearing examiner for further consideration.[81] In an opinion written by Chairman Edward F. Howrey, the commission rejected the application of the Section 3 test of illegality, saying that the tests prescribed by the two sections "are to be determined in the light of the purpose of each section." The difference in the purpose of the two sections are described as follows:

> The primary purpose of Section 3 is the protection of buyers and sellers in the marketing process—to guarantee to buyers the right to handle any goods they see fit, and to sellers the opportunity to obtain the business of any buyer whose trade they wish to seek.
>
> Section 7, on the other hand, is directed toward adverse changes in competitive patterns that may result from mergers. It is concerned with the effects of acquisitions on the character of competition, with the maintenance of competition in every market to the end that business rivalry may produce better products at lower costs.
>
> While both sections are designed to protect the competitive process, they reach this goal by different routes—one by protecting the seller and buyer segment of our economy, the other by protecting competition on an over-all basis.
>
> . . . The reason that acquisitions are, under certain circumstances, to be

[80] *Ibid.*, pp. 45–51.

[81] *In the Matter of Pillsbury Mills, Inc., Opinion of the Commission,* mimeographed (F.T.C. Docket No. 6000, Dec. 28, 1953).

regarded as illegal is not because of their effect on buying and selling practices but because of their probable effect on competition.

Moreover, a further distinction can be drawn from the fact that tying and exclusive dealing contracts are frequently coercive, while acquisitions are usually voluntary in nature.[82]

Although the commission refused to apply the "quantitative substantiality" test of Section 3 to Section 7, it explicitly held that this did not mean a return to the Sherman Act test of illegality:

In fact, one of the purposes of amended Section 7 was to re-establish the difference between Sherman Act and Clayton Act violations and to restate the legislative view, largely repudiated by the case law, that the tests of the Sherman Act have no proper place in the application of Section 7.[83]

What, then, is the standard of illegality under Section 7? The opinion of the commission said:

As we see it, amended Section 7 sought to reach mergers embraced within its sphere in their incipiency, and to determine their legality by tests of its own. These are not the rule of reason of the Sherman Act, that is, unreasonable restraint of trade, nor are Section 7 prohibitions to be added to the list of *per se* violations. Somewhere in between is Section 7, which prohibits acts that "may" happen in a particular market, that looks to "a reasonable probability," to "substantial" economic consequences, to acts that "tend" to a result. Over all is the broad purpose to supplement the Sherman Act and to reach incipient restraints.

While these are far from specific standards—specificity would in any event be inconsistent with the "convenient vagueness" of antitrust prohibitions—they can, we believe, be applied on a case-by-case basis. We think the present case is the type Congress had in mind—one that presents a set of facts which would be insufficient under the Sherman Act but nonetheless establishes, *prima facie,* a violation of Section 7 of the Clayton Act.[84]

The commission held that the evidence supplied by the respondent during the preliminary inquiry regarding sales and relative shares of the market prior to the acquisitions should be accepted as reliable, because the respondent had not objected to its admission, because it had used the information as the best

[82] *Ibid.,* pp. 7–8.
[83] *Ibid.,* p. 10.
[84] *Ibid.,* p. 13.

available in its business, and because it had refused to comply with the commission's subpoenas for additional information. The opinion emphasized that the commission was merely holding that a *prima facie* case had been proved, and that Pillsbury would have an opportunity to rebut the evidence.[85]

In elaborating on the commission's reasoning in concluding that the facts so far presented exhibited violation of Section 7, the opinion stated:

> . . . Competition is a complex and constantly changing phenomenon. It has never been sharply defined. Injury to competition, as distinguished from injury to the competitor, is seldom capable of proof by direct testimony and may therefore be inferred from all the surrounding circumstances. . . .
>
> Analysis of the competitive effects of an acquisition should begin, we believe, with the relevant facts concerning the competitive pattern of the industry as a whole and its markets, particularly in the period preceding the acquisition. From such facts, and from information about the specific merger, it should be possible to determine what changes the acquisition can be expected to make in the character of competition in the markets concerned.[86]

The opinion said the record did not suggest that the acquisitions would immediately convert the southeast market from a competitive to a noncompetitive pattern, as several other large firms remained to furnish effective competition to Pillsbury. The commission observed, however, that

> . . . By these acquisitions it [Pillsbury] has substantially increased its milling and production capacity and its market position. In one of the relevant products, namely, mixes, its position in the southeast increased to about 45 percent.
>
> These acquisitions have taken place in an industry which has steadily declined in size and capacity, and in which the big companies have increased their percentage share. This increase has been largely due—71 percent of it—to mergers. In the southeast the number of mills has not only declined but there have been no new entries of any size into the industry. The number of competitors in the southeast, more particularly in the urban markets, has been materially reduced by the acquisitions; in the mix business, for example, Ballard with 12 percent and Duff with 10.2 percent of the market, have been eliminated. . . .

[85] *Ibid.*, pp. 14–15.
[86] *Ibid.*, p. 15.

. . . [In] the urban markets at least, the mergers lead in the direction of what is sometimes called oligopolistic or "monopolistic" competition, that is, to a situation where the remaining competition in the particular market is between big companies.

If, for example, respondent should continue to acquire competitors at the rate it has since 1940, and other large companies should do the same, the urban markets in the southeast may come to be dominated by a few large milling companies. This, of course, has been the trend in other industries. In some of them, under the policy of the Sherman Act, competition between the big companies continues to protect the consumer interest. But, as we understand it, it was this sort of trend that Congress condemned and desired to halt when it adopted the new Clayton Act anti-merger provision.[87]

In this opinion, the Federal Trade Commission interpreted the new law to be different from both the original Section 7 and the Sherman Act, but admitted that it did not know precisely the distinction between the new and the old law.

In December, 1953, just before the commission's decision to reverse the dismissal of the complaint, the Duff Baking Mix Corporation was organized. Pillsbury sold to the new corporation part of the assets that it had acquired from American Home Products Corporation. The physical property—land, plant, and equipment—was not transferred, but the trade name "Duff's," the good will, patents, copyright, formulae, and manufacturing processes incident to the Duff Baking Mix business, were sold and transferred to the newly organized corporation.[88]

The counsel in support of the complaint filed a motion requesting the commission to amend the complaint to join the Duff Baking Mix Corporation as a party respondent in the proceeding and to add to the complaint the facts concerning the transfer of assets. The commission agreed to the inclusion in an amended complaint of the relevant facts, but refused to join the newly formed corporation as a respondent.[89] Commissioners Albert A. Carretta and

---

[87] *Ibid.*, pp. 15–16.

[88] *In the Matter of Pillsbury Mills, Inc., Amended and Supplemental Complaint*, mimeographed (F.T.C. Docket No. 6000, June 30, 1954).

[89] *In the Matter of Pillsbury Mills, Inc., Order Disposing of Motion and Amending and Supplementing Complaint*, mimeographed (F.T.C. Docket No. 6000, June 30, 1954).

Lowell B. Mason interpreted the statute as not authorizing the joining of Duff Baking Mix Corporation as a respondent merely on the grounds that it was a successor to and assignee of Pillsbury without specifically charging that it had violated the law. Commissioners Edward F. Howrey, James M. Mead, and John W. Gwynne left open "the question whether an action may be maintained against the party to whom the interest has been transferred," but all members agreed that, if upon final determination of the case Pillsbury is found to have violated the law, it will be ordered to divest itself of all assets acquired whether or not such assets are then in its possession.[90]

The Crown Zellerbach Case—In February, 1954, the commission issued a complaint against Crown Zellerbach Corporation, charging that its acquisition of the assets of St. Helens Pulp and Paper Company violated Section 7.[91] The complaint alleged that the sales of paper products by the two firms accounted for 85 per cent of the sales of paper products in the western states. According to the complaint, the effect of the acquisition might be to create a monopoly in pulp wood sales, to increase the market dominance of Crown Zellerbach, and to eliminate opportunity for independent market behavior by converters and jobbers. After the issuance of the complaint, the commission authorized the Bureau of Economics—under the authority of Section 6 of the Federal Trade Commission Act—to collect data on market conditions from the customers of St. Helens. The results of this study were presented in evidence by Dr. Irston R. Barnes as an exhibit in conjunction with his testimony before the hearing examiner. The respondent objected to the admission of the results of a survey made by mail questionnaires on the grounds that it was hearsay evidence. On appeal of the hearing examiner's ruling sustaining the objection, the commission decided that the evidence should be admitted, but that the respondent should have ample opportunity to examine the basic materials from which the exhibit was made, insofar as this could be done without disclosing informa-

[90] *In the Matter of Pillsbury Mills, Inc., Special Concurring Opinion by Commissioner Carretta* (F.T.C. Docket No. 6000, June 30, 1954), p. 2.

[91] *In the Matter of Crown Zellerbach Corporation* (F.T.C. Docket No. 6180, Feb. 15, 1954).

tion about specific firms.[92] This case illustrates some of the difficulties arising in the administration of a statute requiring both elaborate economic analysis and proper legal procedure.

In September, 1957, the Federal Trade Commission held that this acquisition may have the effect of substantially lessening competition or tending to create a monopoly in the market for coarse paper in the eleven western states. Crown Zellerbach's share of this market had been about 50 per cent and St. Helens' share added another 10 per cent, giving the combined firm "a predominant share of the market" and removing "an important, fully integrated competitor." Crown Zellerbach was ordered to divest itself of the acquired plants and properties in such a manner as to recreate St. Helens as an independent competitive entity.[93]

Some Other Federal Trade Commission Orders—In 1956, the commission affirmed a hearing examiner's finding that the Farm Journal company's acquisition of *Better Farming* (formerly, *Country Gentleman*) from Curtis Publishing Company violated the law by eliminating one of the two large nation-wide farm magazines. Farm Journal, Inc., was ordered to divest itself of the names "Better Farming" and "Country Gentleman" and of the lists of subscribers and advertisers. In this case, the commission, of course, was unable to force the reëstablishment of *Better Farming* or *Country Gentleman* as a competing magazine.[94]

In June, 1955, the Federal Trade Commission issued a complaint against the Union Bag and Paper Corporation, which had acquired 25,000 shares of stock in Hankins Container Company.[95] The acquisition was a part of a series of agreements between the

---

[92] *In the Matter of Crown Zellerbach Corporation, Order Ruling on Interlocutory Appeal* (F.T.C. Docket No. 6180, May 16, 1955).

[93] *In the Matter of Crown Zellerbach Corporation, Final Order and Opinion of the Commission* (F.T.C. Docket No. 6180, Dec. 26, 1957). See David D. Martin, "The New Clayton Act and the Crown Zellerbach Case," *Washington University Law Quarterly* (1958), 167–175.

[94] *In the Matter of Farm Journal, Inc.* (F.T.C. Docket No. 6388). F.T.C. Annual Report, 1956, p. 29 ff.

[95] *In the Matter of Union Bag and Paper Corporation, et al.* (F.T.C. Docket No. 6391, June 30, 1955). See *CCH Trade Regulation Reporter*, Par. 25,565, and *F.T.C. Annual Report, 1956*, p. 29.

two firms. The commission charged violation of Sections 7 and 8 of the Clayton Act and also Section 5 of the Federal Trade Commission Act. Both firms sold corrugated boxes and sheet in the region east of the Mississippi. Hankins, however, did not manufacture sufficient liner board, a raw material used in the production of boxes and sheets, to supply its own needs. As a result of the agreements, Union became the principal supplier of the material to Hankins. The commission alleged that the effect of the acquisition may be to eliminate competition between the two firms in the sale of corrugated boxes and sheets, to substantially lessen competition in the market for corrugated boxes and sheets, to eliminate Hankins as a competitive element in that market as well as in the market for liner boards, and to enhance Union's competitive advantage over other firms. In 1956, the commission issued an order limiting the amount of stock Union may hold in Hankins.

Another merger affecting the paper industry was attacked by the commission with a complaint against International Paper Company issued in November, 1956, the day after it acquired the assets of the Long Bell Lumber company in exchange for the stock. Long Bell had held stock in a leading paper company on the west coast—Longview Fibre Company. On June 25, 1957, International consented to an order by the commission. International must divest itself of all stock interest in the Longview Fibre Company, and not acquire any stock in competing companies for 10 years. In addition, for 10 years it must sell 40 per cent of the paper and paperboard production of its west coast mill to nonintegrated, independent wholesalers, converters, and other purchasers located in the western states.[96]

The Automatic Canteen Company has also consented to an order by the commission in a case arising out of its acquisition of the Rowe Corporation. Both firms were operators of vending machines. Rowe had been a leading manufacturer of vending machines as well. The order issued July 3, 1958, allowed the Automatic Canteen Company to keep the acquired manufacturing

---

[96] *In the Matter of International Paper Co.* (F.T.C. Docket No. 6676, Nov. 6, 1956), and *CCH Trade Regulation Reporter,* Par. 26,560.

plants, but forced the divestiture of several vending machine subsidiaries formerly operated by Rowe.[97] Thus the commission agreed to allow the vertical acquisition but not the horizontal.

In several other cases, preliminary orders have been issued by hearing examiners. In July, 1958, an initial order dismissing a complaint against Scott Paper Company was issued by a hearing examiner on the grounds that Scott was not dominant in its field. Two years earlier the commission had issued a complaint charging that the acquisitions of three firms in the pulp and paper industry had individually and collectively violated Section 7 of the Clayton Act. Scott's share of the sanitary paper market in the United States had risen from 30 per cent to 38 per cent between 1950 and 1955, whereas its nearest competitor's share in 1955 was only 11 per cent.[98]

The acquisition by Brillo Manufacturing Company of a competitor—the Williams Company—led to a Federal Trade Commission complaint in 1956. In his initial opinion, the Hearing Examiner Robert L. Piper interpreted the standard of illegality of Section 7 to prohibit Brillo's acquisition of Williams with no other showing of probable market affect than that its share of the industrial steel wool market had been increased from 29 to 47 per cent. On May 23, 1958, the commission remanded the case to the examiner, saying:

> . . . informed determination as to actual or probable competitive effects can only be based on an analysis of all facts of record pertaining to the relevant market. In addition to the facts concerning market shares, likewise important is such evidence as was received herein pertaining to the general competitive situation, number of competitors and degree of concentration prevailing in the industry. . . .
>
> The test . . . is whether their products are shown by the facts to have such peculiar characteristics and uses as to constitute them sufficiently distinct from others to make them a "line of commerce" within the meaning of the Act.[99]

---

[97] *In the Matter of Automatic Canteen Co., Consent Order to Cease and Desist* (F.T.C. Docket No. 6820, July 3, 1958).

[98] *In the Matter of Scott Paper Co., Initial Order Dismissing Complaint* (F.T.C. Docket No. 6559, July 14, 1958).

[99] *In the Matter of Brillo Manufacturing Company* (F.T.C. Docket No. 6557). *CCH Trade Regulation Reporter,* Par. 27,243.

After further hearings, in December, 1958, the examiner dismissed the complaint. Piper concluded that even though Brillo is the largest producer of industrial steel wool, it is not dominant in the market because it has not, among other things, depressed prices unduly or exercised price leadership. He concluded that entry is relatively easy—two new firms had entered that market in recent years. Although Brillo and S.O.S. shared about equally over 96 per cent of the household steel wool market, Piper found that the Williams acquisition added less than 1 per cent to Brillo's share and that it was not dominant in that market either.[100]

At the end of 1958, about a dozen and a half other complaints were in the course of hearings before Federal Trade Commission hearing examiners. No commission decision had yet been reviewed by the courts.

Justice Department Complaints—For more than four years after the amendment of Section 7 of the Clayton Act, the Justice Department brought no actions. In February, 1955, the antitrust division brought a civil action against Schenley Industries, Inc. It sought a preliminary injunction enjoining the company from voting the 70 per cent of the common stock of Park and Tilford Distillers Corporation, which Schenley had acquired in December, 1954, and the divestment of the stock. The complaint indicated that Schenley was one of the four largest firms in the United States whisky market prior to the acquisition, and that Park and Tilford was about one-fifth as large in terms of sales, capacity to produce, whisky in storage, and similar measures. The Justice Department followed closely the policy of the Federal Trade Commission in similar cases in justifying the complaint. The complaint charged:

> The effect of the acquisition of these shares of Park and Tilford by Schenley may be substantially to lessen competition, or to tend to create a monopoly in violation of Section 7 of the Clayton Act in the following ways, among others: (a) actual and potential competition between Schenley and Park and Tilford in the production and sale of whisky will be eliminated; (b) actual and potential competition generally in the produc-

[100] *Wall Street Journal,* XXXIX (Dec. 11, 1958), Midwest Edition, p. 4.

tion and sale of whisky may be lessened; (c) Park and Tilford may be permanently eliminated as an independent competitive factor in the whisky industry; (d) the acquisition of Park and Tilford by Schenley may enhance Schenley's competitive advantage in the production and sale of whisky to the detriment of actual and potential competition; (e) Park and Tilford may be permanently eliminated as an independent outlet for the sale of cooperage by manufacturers other than Schenley; (f) independent distributors may be denied access to whisky produced and sold by Park and Tilford; (g) industry-wide concentration of the production and sale of whisky will be increased.[101]

On April 3, 1957, Schenley consented to a decree preventing it for ten years from acquiring other whisky distilling or distributing firms without Department of Justice or court approval.[102]

The second action brought by the Justice Department under the Celler-Kefauver Act was a complaint brought against General Shoe Corporation in March, 1955.[103] Since its organization in 1925, General had been engaged in the manufacture, distribution, and sale of men's, women's, and children's shoes, and by 1955 had become one of the five leading manufacturers of shoes in the United States. The complaint made no allegation about the *relative share* of the total sales of shoes in any market attributable to General. The complaint charged that General in December, 1954, acquired the assets of Delman, Inc., as a part of a series of eighteen acquisitions after 1950 of firms engaged in the shoe manufacturing or distribution business. It alleged that the *cumulative* effect of the entire series of acquisitions "may be substantially to lessen competition or to tend to create a monopoly." The complaint then listed seven ways, as in the Schenley case, in which the illegal effect may occur. The government asked that the court adjudge General to have violated Section 7 of the Clayton Act, that General be required to divest itself of stock and assets sufficient to dissipate the effects of the unlawful acquisitions, and that the defendant be "perpetually enjoined from

---

[101] *United States* v. *Schenley Industries, Inc., Complaint* (D.C., D. Del., Civil No. 1686, Feb. 14, 1955), pp. 5–6.

[102] *CCH Trade Cases,* 1957, Par. 68,664.

[103] *United States* v. *General Shoe Corporation, Complaint* (D.C., M.D. Tenn., Civil No. 2001, March 29, 1955).

acquiring the stock or assets of any corporation engaged in the manufacture, distribution or sale of shoes." [104]

In February, 1956, General Shoe Company accepted a consent decree.[105] Under the terms of the decree, General was enjoined from acquiring any shoe manufacturer, wholesaler, or retailer until October 1, 1956. After that, for a period of five years, General was enjoined from making any such acquisition without the approval of the Department of Justice or the affirmative showing to the satisfaction of the court that such an acquisition would not substantially lessen competition or tend to create a monopoly, unless the acquired firm is in danger of imminent bankruptcy and has made efforts to sell to at least three other buyers, or unless the acquired firm is a replacement for an affiliated outlet that has been lost. In addition, for the five-year period General must purchase sufficient shoes manufactured by other firms to constitute 20 per cent of the sales of its affiliated outlets, and must license its patents at a reasonable royalty to small shoe manufacturers on a nondiscriminatory basis. General was ordered to divest itself of all stock in shoe manufacturing and distributing firms other than those in which it has a controlling interest—that is, its subsidiaries.

In these cases the Justice Department did not succeed in preventing or dissolving the mergers, but it appears to have stopped the cumulative growth of the acquiring firms by a series of acquisitions of small firms. At least, in any additional acquisitions during the next few years, the burden of proof is on the acquiring firm to show that the illegal effect will not occur.

In April, 1955, the Justice Department brought a civil action against Hilton Hotels Corporation charging that the acquisition of the stock and assets of the Hotels Statler Company had violated Section 7 of the Clayton Act.[106] The complaint alleged that prior to the acquisition the Hilton chain was the largest in the nation, and did a large part of the convention business of those

[104] *Ibid.*, pp. 5–6.

[105] *United States* v. *General Shoe Corporation, Final Judgment* (D.C., M.D. Tenn., Civil No. 2001, Feb. 17, 1956).

[106] *United States* v. *Hilton Hotels Corporation, Complaint* (D.C., D. of Col., Civil No. 1889–55, April 27, 1955).

cities possessing Hilton hotels. In terms of the number of hotel rooms under its control, Statler had been the second largest hotel chain. The complaint charged that the acquisition had eliminated competition between the firms—particularly in New York, Washington, St. Louis, and Los Angeles—in the hotel business generally and in the servicing of conventions. It also alleged that: actual and potential competition in those lines of commerce may be substantially lessened; Hilton's competitive advantage may be enhanced to the detriment of competition; Statler has been eliminated as a competitive factor; and concentration has been increased.

In February, 1956, a consent decree was entered under which the Hilton interests agreed to dispose of the Jefferson Hotel in St. Louis, the Mayflower Hotel in Washington, and either the Roosevelt or the New Yorker Hotel in New York. In addition, the court enjoined Hilton from acquiring any hotel before January 1, 1961, if the acquisition would result in the Hilton chain controlling more than one of a group of the chief hotels (listed in the order) in Washington, St. Louis, or Los Angeles (including Beverly Hills), or more than four in New York. As in the General Shoe and Schenley cases, the decree provides that such an acquisition can be allowed if it is approved by the Department of Justice, or if the defendant proves to the satisfaction of the court that the acquisition will not substantially lessen competition or tend to create a monopoly.[107]

In September, 1955, the Justice Department filed a complaint against Minute Maid Corporation and on the same day entered a consent decree.[108] In November of the previous year, Minute Maid had acquired all the assets of the Snow Crop Division of Clinton Foods. Prior to the acquisition, Minute Maid was the largest producer of frozen citrus juice concentrates in the United States, with 20 per cent of the total industry capacity and 15 per cent of total national sales in 1954. Snow Crop's capacity represented 15 per cent of the total industry capacity and its sales in

[107] *United States* v. *Hilton Hotels Corporation, Final Judgment* (D.C., N.D. Ill., E. Div., Civil No. 55 C 1658, Feb. 6, 1956).

[108] *United States* v. *Minute Maid Corporation, Complaint and Final Judgment* (D.C., S.D. Fla., Civil No. 6429 M, Sept. 7, 1955).

1954 amounted to 10 per cent of the total sales of frozen citrus juice concentrates. This complaint followed the usual pattern in alleging that the effect of the acquisition had been to eliminate competition between the acquiring and the acquired firms, that its effect may be to substantially lessen potential and actual competition in the line of commerce generally, that it enhanced the acquiring firm's competitive advantage to the possible detriment of competition, eliminated the acquired firm as a competitor in the purchase of citrus fruit, and increased industry-wide concentration, tending to create a monopoly.

The consent decree provided that Minute Maid is perpetually enjoined from operating certain frozen concentrate facilities at Davenport, Florida, which it had previously operated under contract with Ridge Citrus Concentrates, Inc. Minute Maid was ordered to dispose of the plants acquired from Snow Crop in Dunedin and Frostproof, Florida. Minute Maid was allowed to retain the properties obtained from Snow Crop at Auburndale, Florida. In addition, the court enjoined Minute Maid from acquiring for a period of five years any other frozen citrus juice concentrate plants without first applying to the court and showing that such acquisitions would not tend to create a monopoly or substantially lessen competition.

In November, 1955, another shoe manufacturer was charged with violating Section 7.[109] Brown Shoe Company, the nation's third largest seller of shoes in 1954, had announced plans to acquire G. R. Kinney Company, the ninth largest seller of shoes. Since 1950 Brown had acquired ten other firms engaged in the manufacture, distribution, or sale of shoes. The complaint alleged that the proposed merger would eliminate competition between Brown and Kinney; it would have the effect of substantially lessening competition in the production, distribution, and sale of shoes; it might enhance Brown's competitive advantage; it might foreclose competing manufacturers from selling to Kinney's retail outlets; the effect may be to deprive independent retailers of a

[109] *United States* v. *Brown Shoe Company, Inc., Complaint* (D.C., E.D. Mo., Civil No. 10527, Nov. 28, 1955).

fair opportunity to compete with Brown's retail outlets; and industry-wide concentration of control of retail outlets may be increased. The Justice Department asked that a temporary restraining order be issued and that Brown Shoe Company be perpetually enjoined from acquiring the stock or assets of Kinney or any other corporation in the shoe industry.

The court granted the temporary restraining order pending a hearing to determine whether a preliminary injunction should be issued. In March, 1956, the court issued a memorandum denying an injunction to prevent the merger, but granting a temporary injunction to insure that the properties of the acquired company would not be commingled with those of the acquiring company until the trial of the case has been completed.[110] In his memorandum, Judge Hulen said that, if the evidence presented at that point in the case were the only basis of a final decision, then the judgment would be for the defendants. For that reason he was unwilling to enjoin the merger.

Judge Hulen said that the court was called upon to settle the issue, as a matter of law, on the basis merely of figures showing Brown's sales and production increases if the merger took place. The government, in its briefs, alleged that the acquisition would add 360 stores to Brown's retail chain, increasing its sales at retail from about twenty-eight million dollars to about fifty-nine million. Brown's manufacturing capacity would be increased from about one hundred one million dollars to about one hundred nine million. Of the additional 360 stores to be acquired from Kinney, 118 are located in cities in which Brown has retail stores already. The government cited a number of cases under Section 3 of the Clayton Act to justify its contention that the evidence was sufficient to make a *prima facie* case. Judge Hulen rejected the argument that the Section 3 rulings were applicable to a Section 7 case, quoting the circuit court decision in the Transamerica case.

The government filed affidavits reciting figures on the manufacturing and sales of shoes. The defendants filed affidavits deny-

[110] *United States* v. *Brown Shoe Company, Inc., Memorandum* (D.C., E.D. Mo., Civil No. 10527 [2], March 14, 1956).

ing that the two firms competed in the same markets because of the difference in prices charged for their products. Judge Hulen said:

> The affidavits filed by the plaintiff are made by an economist in the Department of Justice who claims no experience in any branch of the shoe industry. The affidavits of defendants are by officers of the defendant corporations, each reciting many years of experience in the shoe industry. Comparing the record of plaintiff and defendants as shown by affidavits, we are not prepared to give equal probative value to an affidavit made by a stranger to the shoe industry, and based wholly on figures obtained from public and private sources, and affidavits made by officers of the defendant companies who have had years of experience in the shoe industry.[111]

Judge Hulen then quoted the International Shoe Company decision, in which the Supreme Court said that competition is a matter of observation rather than logic. In a speech to the American Bar Association a few weeks later, Assistant Attorney General Stanley N. Barnes said that these remarks of Judge Hulen may complicate market proof for prosecutors and practitioners.[112]

In February, 1958, the Justice Department charged Lucky Lager Brewing Company with violating Section 7 by its acquisition of Fisher Brewing Company. The case was terminated October 6, 1958, with a consent decree requiring Lucky Lager to sell its interest in Fisher within nine months. Lucky Lager could continue to own and operate the Fisher plant, if it could not be sold. However, Lucky Lager was enjoined from selling over 39 per cent of the beer sold in Utah. Following the pattern of the other consent decrees, the court enjoined Lucky Lager, for five years, from acquiring any brewery in the United States without court approval.[113]

In November, 1958, as this was going to press, victories were announced for the Justice Department in two contested Section 7 cases in the district courts. The Maryland-Virginia Milk Producers Association's acquisition of the Embassy Dairy was held to be in violation of the statute, although the acquisition of another

[111] *Ibid.*, pp. 10–11.

[112] Stanley N. Barnes, "Quantitative Substantiality," An Address Prepared for Delivery before the American Bar Association (Washington: April 6, 1956).

[113] *CCH Trade Regulation Reporter*, Par. 45,058.

dairy in financial straits was allowed. Another district court granted the government's request for an injunction prohibiting the merger of Bethlehem Steel Corporation and Youngstown Sheet and Tube Company.[114] Several other Justice Department cases are pending in the district courts.

Some Problems in the Administration of Section 7

The large number of corporate mergers taking place each year, and the scope of the investigations necessary to decide even whether a complaint should be brought, have given rise to several administrative problems. The 1950 legislation did not provide for notification of the intention of a firm to make an acquisition, so it is up to the administrative agencies to find out about them from the press and to request information. In addition, the Federal Trade Commission has no authority to take action until an acquisition has been consummated. Several bills were introduced in the 84th Congress to amend again Section 7 of the Clayton Act to remedy these problems.[115]

On March 15, 1956, the House Judiciary Committee favorably reported H.R. 9424,[116] and it was passed by the House of Representatives on April 16, 1956. On July 27, 1956, the Senate Judiciary Committee reported the bill with some changes,[117] but Congress adjourned without Senate action. The House version of this bill would require that acquisitions involving all but very small corporations must not be consummated until ninety days after notifying both the Attorney General and the appropriate administrative commission or board. Along with notification, the acquiring firm would have to furnish information on the nature and size of

---

[114] *Business Week* (Nov. 29, 1958), pp. 25 and 38.

[115] 84th Cong., 2d sess., H.R. 6748, H.R. 7229, H.R. 8332, H.R. 8690, H.R. 9424, S. 3424, S. 3341.

[116] *Amending the Clayton Act, As Amended, By Requiring Prior Notification of Certain Corporate Mergers*, U.S. House Committee on the Judiciary, 84th Cong., 2d sess., H. Rept. 1889 (Washington: 1956).

[117] *Corporate Mergers and Price Discrimination*, U.S. Senate Committee on the Judiciary, 84th Cong., 2d sess., S. Rept. 2817 (Washington: 1956).

the businesses involved and, upon request, such additional information as may be required by the enforcement agencies. Such legislation would improve the effectiveness of the antimerger law, and with exemptions for the bulk of the small acquisitions of assets that normally have little competitive effect, would not seem to place an unnecessary burden on business firms.

Legislation requiring prior notification, however, has one inherent danger. Even if Congress specifies that failure of the enforcement agencies to act within a specified time would not make an acquisition legal, the courts would probably be reluctant to support dissolution of a merger that the commission and the Justice Department had made no attempt to stop after notification. If prior-notification legislation is enacted, in the future it will become even more important to make adequate appropriations to enable the commission and the antitrust division to consider fully each acquisition before it takes place. Professor Jesse W. Markham has pointed out that in recent years the total budget of the Federal Trade Commission was about the same as that of the Smithsonian institution, or the advertising budget of the sixth largest tobacco producer! [118] The effectiveness of Section 7 will be primarily as a deterrent of decisions to merge, but this depends upon a high probability of a complaint being brought if an illegal merger is effected.

The recent bills introduced in Congress have also proposed some sort of amendment to empower the Federal Trade Commission to seek an injunction to forestall a merger. Such legislation would appear to be definitely desirable, since it is obviously difficult to unscramble corporate assets once they have been mingled. H.R. 9424 would have also empowered the commission to seek a court order of the type granted the Justice Department in the Brown Shoe Company case to prevent the destruction of the acquired company as a separate entity, even though the acquisition had taken place before a complaint was brought. These changes would greatly increase the effectiveness of the commis-

[118] *A Study of the Antitrust Laws,* Hearings pursuant to S. Res. 61, U.S. Subcommittee on Antitrust and Monopoly of the Senate Committee on the Judiciary, 84th Cong., 1st sess. (Washington, 1955), part 1, p. 438.

sion in administering the law, but again it would become necessary to provide the commission with sufficient funds to enable it to expedite its investigations.

Conclusions

The original Section 7 of the Clayton Act, as interpreted before its amendment, served merely to prevent the continued use of the intercorporate stockholding device as the form of organization of a combination of previously independent corporations. The acquisition of stock control in a competitor was not discouraged by law, since assets could be transferred should a complaint be issued by the Federal Trade Commission. The law, therefore, served to encourage the complete fusion of the merging corporations. It may have achieved one of its original purposes of preventing the secret acquisition by one corporation of the control of a competitor.

Prior to its amendment, however, the interpretation of Section 7 did not make even a stock acquisition illegal unless it resulted in a reasonable probability of a substantial lessening of competition between the corporations involved. As the statute was interpreted, it was necessary for the commission to prove that: (1) a substantial proportion of each corporation's business was done in direct competition with the other, and (2) the elimination of the competition between the corporations would injuriously affect the public to the extent necessary to constitute an unreasonable restraint of trade.[119]

Acquisitions of assets and statutory mergers of corporations were not affected by Section 7 of the Clayton Act. Mergers and asset acquisitions were subject to control only by the Sherman Act. There have been only a few cases in which a corporate merger alone has been the subject of court action. In several Sherman Act cases decided just before 1950, the opinions of the Supreme Court made it quite clear that a corporate acquisition or merger is not illegal *per se*. It might violate Section 1 of the

[119] See chaps. 3–6.

Sherman Act if there is *specific intent* to restrain trade. It might violate Section 2 of the Sherman Act if there is *specific intent* to monopolize. In the absence of specific intent, the question of the legality of a merger under the Sherman Act rested on the reasonableness of the result. If the effect of an acquisition were to restrain trade unreasonably, then the court would infer intent.

The rule of reason has always been a highly flexible criterion. As applied to corporate acquisitions, its meaning in recent years was sharply defined in the Supreme Court's opinion in the Columbia Steel case.[120] The market in which the firms compete must first be delimited. In determining whether the merger unreasonably restrains trade in the relevant market, dollar volume of sales is not of compelling significance. Instead the court looks to the *percentage* of business controlled after the merger and the strength of the remaining competition, and other market characteristics. The court has given no set of percentage figures, but said that the relevant percentage of the market varies from case to case.

The Celler-Kefauver Act changed Section 7 of the Clayton Act so as to cover all types of mergers and acquisitions made by firms subject to the jurisdiction of the Federal Trade Commission. Thus, for industrial corporations engaged in interstate commerce, the amended Clayton Act has replaced the Sherman Act as the relevant statute for the control of mergers. The implications of the new statute must be found by comparing the standard of illegality provided in it with that of the Sherman Act, as well as the original Section 7 of the Clayton Act.

The amendment changed Section 7 to prohibit the acquisition by one corporation of the stock or, for corporations other than common carriers and banks, assets of one or more corporations engaged in commerce, if the effect may be substantially to lessen competition in any line of commerce in any section of the country or to tend to create a monopoly in any line of commerce in any section of the country. The statements of Congressional intent in the House and Senate Judiciary Committee reports, as well as

[120] 334 U.S. 446, 527–529.

the record of recent cases before the Federal Trade Commission and the district courts, indicate that the administration of the new law will be based on a policy of consideration of the probable effect of an acquisition on competition in the relevant markets. Although in many of the complaints issued since 1950, the commission and the Justice Department have alleged elimination of the competition between the acquiring and the acquired firms, neither agency has required that most of the sales of each firm must have been of the same products to the same customers, as the commission did prior to 1950. In this respect the change in the Clayton Act made by Congressional action in 1950 and by Supreme Court reinterpretation in 1957 has made possible an economically more meaningful standard of illegality.

Under the new statute, in ascertaining whether the acquisition violates the law, it is not necessary to find the equivalent of an unreasonable restraint of trade. Nor is it necessary to prove that the acquisition was made with the *intent* of lessening competition. On the other hand, acquisitions have not been placed in the category of *per se* violations, which would undoubtedly have resulted in the prohibition of many acquisitions that would increase competition. The new law seems to require the same sort of examination of market effects as the Sherman Act, but less proof of adverse effect on competition than that statute.

If the Supreme Court interprets the amended Section 7 in this manner, then the 1950 amendment will have resulted in several salutary changes in the law. First, as compared with the original Clayton Act, the new law will be an improvement in that consideration will no longer be centered on the frequently economically meaningless concept of competition between two firms, which dominated the administration of the original statute. Second, for most corporations, mergers of all types, rather than those merely involving stock acquisitions, will be subject to the Clayton Act and the varied means of administration which it provides. Third, as compared with the Sherman Act, the new law of mergers will be an improvement in that decisions will be based on the *effect* of acquisitions rather than on the *intent* of the parties involved. In addition, the "incipiency doctrine" of the original authors of the Clayton Act has finally been put into operation in the determination of the legality of mergers. The law on close-knit combinations has been brought into much closer correspondence with the law on loose forms of agreement.

Although the Supreme Court has not yet interpreted the Celler-Kefauver Act, the administration of the law has already shown that it can be used to stop the growth of monopoly in its incipiency. The consent decrees obtained by the Justice Department in some of its cases have succeeded in several industries in stalling a pattern of development of increased concentration of control of productive facilities under a few firms. In these few cases, for a period of five or ten years, the burden of proof has been shifted to the corporations making acquisitions.

A judgment of the economic implications of the legislation must await the case-by-case development of this new antitrust law policy. There is nothing in the record of administration of the law so far to indicate that unfavorable economic consequences necessarily must result. The legality of each merger must be considered separately within the context of its effect on the degree of competition in the relevant markets. The time and financial resources necessary to handle such a case will inevitably mean prosecution of selected cases so as to indirectly influence business decisions. The full force of this influence will not be felt until the statute has received Supreme Court interpretation. The stated aim of the proponents of the legislation to halt the rising tide of mergers will not be realized, of course.

The change in the law will not affect the legality of mergers accomplished prior to its passage, but the subsequent reinterpretation of the old law in the du Pont–General Motors decision has made it possible to apply a more meaningful standard to stock acquisitions made between 1914 and 1950 in cases in which the intercorporate stockholding continued until after the 1950 amendment. It may have the effect of halting the movement toward an oligopolistic market structure in many industries—for example, the flour-base mix industry, the shoe industry, and the frozen citrus juice industry. This result could prove to be of major importance over a period of years as new products are introduced in a dynamic economy. A continuous enforcement of the new law may in time produce an over-all market structure much more conducive to workable competition than now exists after sixty years of an antitrust policy that encouraged fusion of independent firms.

Possibly, however, the application of the new law might produce unfavorable economic consequences. For example, the commission and the courts could become overzealous in prohibiting mergers that would increase the economic power of small firms operating in markets dominated by one or more large firms, which would not be subject to dissolution, since the Sherman Act criteria of illegality require a greater degree of monopoly power than the criterion to which the merging firms would be subject. Also, the administration of the new law might hinder the changes in market structure which are necessarily incident to technological changes that make possible economies of scale and economic growth. This does not appear to be a great danger, however, since the new standard will not be applicable in judging the legality of the result of growth of a firm by means other than merger. If technological changes make economies of scale possible, they could generally be realized by internal expansion rather than by merger.

The law on mergers, although definitely changed by the 1950 amendment, represents a general statement of policy which is now subject to implementation by an administrative commission as well as by the district courts. The Federal Trade Commission gives every indication of a willingness to decide each case on its merits, with careful consideration of the economic implications of its actions. It is faced, however, with the very difficult problem of ascertaining empirically the probable effect of a merger on the degree of competition in a market. The problem is made more difficult by the reluctance of the courts to give weight to economic evidence. Judge Hulen's statements on this question in the Brown Shoe Company case disclose that the amendment of the statute has not succeeded in completely overcoming the ill effects of the International Shoe Company case a quarter-century earlier. The Federal Trade Commission, however, in both the Pillsbury case and the Crown-Zellerbach case, has indicated that it will give strong support to the effort to focus attention upon the many complex market factors that must be considered if economically meaningful criteria are to be developed in the implementation of the new antimerger statute.

9. Corporate Mergers and Antitrust Policy

Section 7 of the Clayton Act, as it existed between 1914 and 1950, was but a small part of the federal antitrust law. The original Section 7 placed some restriction on one particular corporate practice—intercorporate stockholding. The 1950 amendment created a statutory provision designed to cope with the broader problem of fusion of industrial corporations. Rather than being merely a "plugging of the loophole" in the Clayton Act, the new law is a major substantive change in the federal antitrust law policy. The original Section 7, as interpreted before 1957, prohibited one corporation from acquiring *stock* in another corporation, if the acquisition might have the effect of substantially lessening competition *between* the acquiring and the acquired corporation. As amended, Section 7 of the Clayton Act prohibits industrial corporations from acquiring either the stock or *assets* of another corporation, if there is a reasonable probability that the effect will be substantially to lessen competition *in a market.* Thus, the amendment not only replaces the original Section 7 of the Clayton Act, but also has the effect of replacing the Sherman Act, as the basic statutory statement of Congressional policy on all types of mergers of industrial corporations. Therefore, the new

Clayton Act may become an effective instrument with which to deal with the fundamental problem in monopoly and combination to which the use of the corporate form of organization of industrial firms has given rise.

The Antitrust Problem Presented by Corporate Mergers

The use of the corporate form of business organization has for many years presented some difficult problems in antitrust policy. Basically, the act of incorporation itself constitutes a form of centralization of control of productive assets, and the corporate device facilitates further centralization by means of intercorporate stockholding and outright merger of existing corporations. It has long been recognized that market control that would be unlawful if achieved by agreement among otherwise independent control groups, can be achieved lawfully by the elimination of the element of agreement through the use of the corporate form to completely unify control of a group of productive assets. The elimination of agreement may eliminate the illegality even though the degree of market control remains the same.

Freedom to centralize control of productive assets through the use of the corporate form has not been unlimited, however, since the Northern Securities case in 1904.[1] The legal limitation on such centralization was vaguely defined by the Supreme Court's enunciation of the rule of reason in 1911.[2] The illegality of cartel-type agreements among firms in the United States has undoubtedly encouraged the growth of large corporations—in many instances growth up to a point close to the limitation placed on such growth by the application of the rule of reason in the interpretation of the Sherman Act.

In examining this question of public policy presented by the corporation, it is useful to distinguish four types of centralization

[1] 193 U.S. 197. See chap. 1.

[2] *United States* v. *Standard Oil Co.*, 221 U.S. 1, and *United States* v. *American Tobacco Co.*, 221 U.S. 106. See chap. 1.

of control of productive assets: (1) loose agreements among otherwise separate business firms by which centralized decisions are made with respect to certain specific variables, (2) intercorporate stock acquisitions that centralize decision-making in varying degrees, (3) mergers of separate corporations to form a larger corporation and thus centralize decision-making to whatever degree desired, and (4) growth of a particular business firm by internal expansion and the displacement of other firms in the market. Centralization of the first type has long been considered unlawful *per se*. Under the Sherman Act as interpreted in the 1911 cases, the other three types were not distinguished and the rule of reason was applied to all three, except in cases of specific intent to monopolize or restrain trade. In 1914, Congress attempted to place intercorporate stockholding in a separate category with a criterion of illegality intermediate between *per se* illegality and the rule of reason. The Supreme Court, however, applied the rule of reason until the 1957 du Pont case.[3] The 1950 amendment of Section 7 placed intercorporate stockholding and mergers together in a separate category intermediate between agreements that are illegal *per se* and growth by displacement, which is unlawful only if it actually results in unreasonable restraint of trade or monopoly.

The new Section 7 is characterized by the same "convenient vagueness" that has made the Sherman Act such a flexible instrument of national policy. The new law is a very general statement of the policy that some mergers permitted by the Sherman Act are to be prohibited. Congress wisely avoided specifically answering the basic question: Which mergers are to be permitted and which are to be prohibited? The commission, board, or court that initially decides the legality of a particular merger has much discretion in implementing and giving specific content to the general statement of policy. Since so much discretion is allowed the initial enforcement agencies, it is particularly important for economists to consider some of the economic questions inherent in the

[3] *United States* v. *E. I. du Pont de Nemours and Co., et al.*, 353 U.S. 568. See chap. 8.

problem of establishing legal criteria for evaluating mergers and intercorporate stock ownership.

From the viewpoint of the economist, the basic issues in merger policy differ from the more general questions relating to "big business" in two ways: (1) the law itself is different, and (2) mergers have unique economic effects.

The legal standards provided by the Sherman Act, as interpreted, for the evaluation of a large firm that has grown by the creation of new plant capacity and the displacement of other firms, requires proof of either a *specific intent* to monopolize or restrain trade, or the *actual* achievement of market control sufficient to be deemed unreasonable in terms of injury to the public. The legal standards provided by Section 7 of the Clayton Act for the evaluation of mergers and intercorporate stockholding require proof only of a *reasonable probability* of a *tendency toward* or a *substantial degree* of the market control that constitutes illegality under the Sherman Act. Thus, the problem of economic analysis in Section 7 cases is not only that of providing insight into the relationship between particular market structures and the existence or absence of public injury, but also that of providing some basis for ascertaining the *probability* that a particular merger or stock acquisition will have the effect of bringing about a market structure or pattern of behavior which is not quite, but in the direction of, the sort of situation that is unlawful under the Sherman Act.

If economists had achieved substantial agreement on the Sherman Act problem, the economic questions raised by the Clayton Act would still be formidable, since the basic economic issues inherent in the new merger policy differ from the more general questions of "big business" in a second way as well. Even if the same legal standard were to be applied to all types of growth to positions of market power, there would remain the necessity of ascertaining what unique effects mergers and intercorporate stockholding have which distinguish them from centralization of control brought about by internal expansion and displacement of other firms in the market. Some views of economists on these questions need to be considered.

Centralization of Control and Antitrust Objectives

The antitrust laws are justified by the acceptance of the principle of competitive markets as the central organizing feature of our economic system.[4] The desirability of maintaining competitive markets is generally accepted by most segments of our society on the grounds that it best serves the interests of individuals, in their capacity as both producers and consumers. The maximum decentralization of authority to make decisions directing economic activity, however, would require an economy of small single proprietorships. The granting of charters to corporations to engage in general business activities was a move in the direction of centralization of authority in the decision-making process. The evolution of the corporate device as the primary means of organizing industrial activity in the United States made possible larger firms that could take advantage of new technological developments, which made possible greater production of economic goods. At the turn of the century, however, the use of the corporate form for larger firms was extended far beyond the necessities of technology for the purpose of gaining monopoly power. The antitrust policy of the federal government during the last half-century has been concerned with counteracting the trend toward centralization inherent in the liberal corporate charters granted by some states. The chief issues in discussions of antitrust policy in the pre–First World War period and in the past decade have been focused on the problem of reconciling the desire to achieve technical efficiency and economic progress with the desire to avoid so high a degree of centralization as to threaten individual freedom in the economic sphere. Herein seems to lie the basis of much of the disagreement among economists on antitrust policy.

Some economists hold that, if the market economy is to be

[4] See Clare E. Griffin, *An Economic Approach to Antitrust Problems*, National Economic Problems Series No. 441 (New York: American Enterprise Association, Inc., [1951]), p. xi.

preserved, more vigorous antitrust enforcement is necessary to prevent too much departure from a pattern of many small firms. Others fear that too much interference with the growth of large corporations will have adverse effects on technological innovation.

Corwin D. Edwards has listed several structural characteristics necessary for markets to be sufficiently competitive. Although firms need not be so numerous that no firm has individual influence, there must be enough alternative traders that buyers or sellers may readily turn to others, and no firm must be so powerful that he can coerce his rivals. Edwards makes the important, but frequently overlooked, point that effective competition requires that no trader be so large that his rivals do not have the productive capacity to take over a substantial proportion of his business. Each firm must be responsive to incentives of profit and loss *in a particular market,* if it is to be effectively competitive. Decisions must be made without agreement among rival traders. Freedom of entry should be restricted only by the fact that other traders are already established in a market. Access of buyers and sellers to each other must not be impaired by obstacles deliberately introduced. Preferential status must not exist for any traders "on the basis of law, politics, or commercial alliances." [5] Edwards concedes that efficiency must be considered in determining policy with respect to big business, and that advantages of size should be preserved, if possible. He says, however, that ". . . if at any point choice must be made between effective competition and any of these advantages, the decision should follow a careful weighing of the pros and cons." [6]

Some economists have criticized the emphasis placed on the structure of markets in antitrust discussions. Clare E. Griffin, for example, says that the acceptance of the model of many small firms as the one and only meaning of competition has led to two undesirable reactions. On the one hand, the view has arisen that the greatest progress in our economy has been made during the

[5] Corwin D. Edwards, *Maintaining Competition; Requisites of a Governmental Policy* (New York: McGraw-Hill, 1949), pp. 9–10.

[6] *Ibid.,* p. 108.

period in which competition in this sense was declining. This, he says, has led to the abandonment of the principle of competition on the part of some persons. On the other hand, the acceptance of the model of many small firms has led many persons to advocate bringing it about.[7] A. D. H. Kaplan points out that even though a firm has control of all the supply of a particular product, it may not be able to "sit back and enjoy high margins" because of the potential innovation of new products in a dynamic economy. His study of big business serves to emphasize the limitations of the concept of an industry and various measures of concentration in industries.[8]

It is clear that the professional economist qua economist cannot provide specific answers to specific questions about the effects on the general welfare of alternative decisions in the implementation of the antitrust policy. On the more general questions concerning the goals to be achieved, there is general agreement. If the free enterprise system is not to drift into a native American form of centralization of control of economic activity, the antitrust laws must be preserved to limit the centralization of control of productive facilities. Disagreement arises over whether the evolution of the structure of control in the past three-quarters of a century has resulted in too much centralization, and whether the Sherman Act should be used to dissolve existing large corporations.

Mergers as a Means of Centralization—Economists seem to be more generally agreed on the desirability of limiting further centralization of control by corporate mergers and intercorporate stockholding than on the desirability of changing existing market structures by dissolution. The primary reason for allowing large aggregations of capital under unified control is to achieve the

[7] Griffin, *op. cit.*, pp. 18–19. This distinction between the competitive model as an "ideal" for purposes of analysis and as an "ideal" in the sense of a policy goal was clearly recognized by John B. Clark. See chap. 1. After the refinement of the model of perfect competition in connection with the development of monopolistic and imperfect competition theory, the attention of economists was redirected to the older approach by the famous article by John M. Clark: "Toward a Concept of Workable Competition," *The American Economic Review* (June, 1940), pp. 241–256.

[8] *Big Enterprise in a Competitive System* (Washington: Brookings Institute, 1954), p. 59.

economies of scale possible only with centralization. The creation of a large firm simply by the centralization of decision-making within the corporate framework without the integration of the productive processes is much more likely to be viewed as a device for achieving market power than as a means of more efficiently organizing production.

Kaplan points out, however, that a merger may be an economical way of achieving integration. He says:

> It may avoid wasteful duplication of existing facilities; it may speed the pooling of services, physical resources, and talents; it may fit into a more economical plan of management with centralized services, less cross-hauling, and better spread of overhead.[9]

He goes on to say that a merger should not be condemned merely because it has the initial effect of eliminating a competitor. The result of a merger can be weighed, he says, "only after seeing whether entry remains essentially open, whether the merger actually increases or diminishes the number of consumer alternatives. . . ."[10] The law, however, empowers the Federal Trade Commission or the Justice Department to proceed against a merger if its effect *may be* substantially to lessen competition. Certainly, more difficulty is encountered in dissolving a corporation than in preventing its growth by merger. It is necessary for the enforcement agencies to anticipate the effect of a merger and to take action against those *likely* to result in a substantial lessening of competition.

Stocking and Watkins consider the primary requirement of effective competition to be the maintenance of the largest practical number of producers consistent with economies of scale in production and distribution. Writing before the amendment of the Clayton Act, they said:

> Even though suitable standards are lacking by which to determine precisely how many firms the most economical scale of production requires, it is evident that it would be possible, without sacrifice of efficiency, to have far more producers in many industries than at present. Two steps would be necessary to increase the number: first, a broader interpretation and

[9] *Ibid.*, p. 213.
[10] *Ibid.*, p. 215.

more vigorous enforcement of antitrust laws; second, a modification of the Clayton Act with a view to preventing the merger of competing businesses.[11]

Stocking and Watkins point out that the antitrust laws have been far more effective in preventing market control brought about by collusive agreements than in preventing the creation of large firms for the purpose of market control. This double standard, however, is not necessarily inconsistent with their own criteria of public policy. They would like to see the antitrust laws interpreted in such a way as to require the largest number of firms consistent with technical efficiency. The reason for wanting many firms is to make collusion, tacit or overt, more difficult. They admit that it is impossible to draw the lines sharply. In the case of collusive agreements, the courts can easily justify condemnation because there are clearly no economies of large scale and such agreements are obviously designed to achieve market control. In the case of a large firm, created years ago by merger, there is a presumption of economies of scale—or at least no diseconomies—and the possibility that market control was neither intended nor achieved. Therefore, the courts are reluctant to break up successful going-concerns even if they have been convicted of monopolizing. If it were possible to precisely measure the effect of centralization of decision-making power both on competition and on economies of scale, the double standard would not be warranted, and probably would not exist.

Over the past half-century the courts have applied this double standard in enforcing the Sherman Act by formulating some *per se* offenses deemed unlawful, and by applying the "rule of reason" in other types of cases. On the one hand, the courts have declared to be illegal agreements that centralize decision-making power over a few specific business decisions. On the other hand, they have been reluctant to dissolve the centers of decision-making power created by the large corporations that have grown both by internal expansion and by merger and have demonstrated by their survival some evidence of technical efficiency. There is,

[11] George W. Stocking and Myron W. Watkins, *Monopoly and Free Enterprise* (New York: Twentieth Century Fund, 1951), p. 506.

however, a third category: firms that have not yet demonstrated their technical efficiency by survival, but have recently arranged for centralized decision-making authority by way of merger. In this third category, there is good reason for applying a standard somewhere in between the two aspects of the traditional double standard. The desirability of such an intermediate standard seems to be generally accepted by economists who are students of antitrust problems. Congress has provided for such a standard by the amendment of the Clayton Act. Economics should be able to contribute to the formulation of criteria with which the Congressional policy can be implemented.

Economically Meaningful Criteria for Mergers

It is the function of the Federal Trade Commission and the Justice Department to prevent or dissolve those mergers that are likely to hinder the achievement of the goals of the antitrust policy. In the long run, the most important effect of the work of these agencies will be in establishing a new legal framework, within which corporation managers will decide whether to make acquisitions. As in the administration of the Sherman Act, the policy will be effectively implemented by affecting corporate decisions rather than by court orders directly. The development, on a case by case basis, of this new legal framework should discourage mergers that would have the effect of unnecessarily further concentrating economic power and creating control of markets. At the same time, the freedom of private business firms to rearrange the control of industrial capital should not be unnecessarily infringed.

The Federal Trade Commission has set up a procedure for reviewing acquisitions and deciding which ones warrant action. Unlike the over-simplified methods used in administering the original Section 7, the commission's new procedure utilizes a staff of economists to systematically analyze the competitive effects of important mergers. The complexity of this task is indicated in a recent article by the chief of the Division of Economic Evidence of the Bureau of Industrial Economics of the Commission.[12]

The new Section 7 of the Clayton Act embodies the general policy that a merger is illegal if there is a reasonable probability that its effect will be either substantially to lessen competition or to tend to create a monopoly in any line of commerce in any section of the country. This new standard suffers from neither the disadvantage of focusing on the competition between the firms involved nor the disadvantage of looking to the *intent* of the persons responsible for the merger. It directs the enforcing agency to develop criteria around the question of the *probable effect* of the merger on competition in a market for some product.

For purposes of simplification in inquiring into the market effects of mergers, it is convenient to classify them into three types: (1) horizontal mergers that unite two or more firms formerly selling the same product in the same market, (2) vertical mergers between firms that formerly bought and sold from each other, and (3) conglomerate mergers between firms that formerly bought and sold products neither horizontally nor vertically related to each other. Of course mergers may involve firms whose operations are so varied that they overlap these simplified categories.

In considering the economic effects of horizontal mergers, several factors must be examined. "Products" and "markets" are not easily defined, nor is a firm's participation in a particular market. A firm may affect the degree of competition in a market for a product merely by having means that would facilitate its active entry into the market. A merger involving such a firm may have as much effect as one involving only firms actively in the market. Differentiation of products and the existence of transportation costs also create difficulties in defining the relevant market. Economists have frequently found it useful to work within the conceptual framework of an industry consisting of one or more firms selling (or buying) a particular product in a particular market.

[12] Irston R. Barnes, "Economic Issues in the Regulation of Acquisitions and Mergers," *Ohio State Law Journal,* 14 (1953), 279–306.

Many variants of the basic model have been introduced by specifying the characteristics of the industry with respect to such things as the degree of differentiation of product among the firms, the number of firms, the degree of freedom of entry, and the reactions of each firm to the actions of the other firms.[13]

The usefulness of such a model in considering the effect on competition of the fusion of two of the firms is greatly limited. Even on the purely formal level, the analysis yields no conclusive answer to the question of the effect of a merger on the degree of competition in the industry. The inherent difficulty is that it is possible conceptually merely to rank—not measure cardinally—the degree of competition under the assumption of (1) many firms, wherein no firm can raise price without losing most of or all its sales, (2) few firms, and (3) one firm. Therefore, the change in the degree of competition which occurs when the number of firms is reduced by one cannot be measured even ordinally. It cannot be deduced that the degree of competition varies in one-to-one correspondence with the reduction in the number of firms. Consider the situation of "many" firms selling the same product in the same market. If all these firms were united by merger into a single firm, competition would be eliminated and a single-firm monopoly would be created. But even in this extreme instance, the degree of market control obtained would be negligible if the product has been defined so narrowly or the ease of entry is so great that the market demand curve is highly elastic. In considering the market share of firms involved in a merger, it is necessary to carefully consider the relevant definition of the product.

If the product is defined broadly enough and if entry is not easy, then the creation of a single firm out of many small firms would clearly lessen competition. If, however, prior to a merger of two firms there were "several" firms in the industry, then the effect on competition is not clear. A merger of the two largest firms in the group would seem to increase the probability of the mo-

[13] The literature of recent years contains innumerable illustrations of this type of analysis, but usually the economists using such models have considered the question of the effect of mergers only incidentally, if at all. See William Fellner, *Competition Among the Few: Oligopoly and Similar Market Structures* (New York: Alfred A. Knopf, 1949), and the references cited there.

nopoly equilibrium adjustment resulting, since it would not only eliminate an important decision-making unit, but would also increase the size of the largest firm relative to the industry. The merger of several small firms in such an industry, though, might increase the probability of an oligopoly adjustment closer to that of perfect competition, particularly if it had the effect of increasing the number of firms of substantial size in the group, and prevented the failure and disappearance of the smaller firms.[14] In such cases, the goals of antitrust policy might better be served if the Sherman Act could be used to dissolve the large dominant firms.

The effects on competition of mergers among firms that formerly bought and sold from each other are more difficult to evaluate. Such mergers constitute one means of vertically integrating. Certainly, the antitrust laws should not be used to prevent changes in productive processes. Few consumer goods are produced by a simple transformation of resources directly into finished goods. The problem of deciding how much of the productive process will be undertaken in a particular plant or by a particular firm is a prerogative of management which cannot be taken away without defeating the aims of antitrust policy. As technological change takes place, changes are made both in products and in methods of producing them. The decisions on what part of the process to undertake within the firm and what part to leave to other firms—that is, whether to integrate vertically either backward or forward—must be continually reëvaluated. If the antitrust laws were to prevent all vertical integration, such changes would be prevented and the public interest would not be served. An extension of a firm's operations to either earlier or later stages of the productive process may serve to reduce the over-all cost of production of a final good by making possible more efficient productive methods. Vertical integration may also increase competition by increasing the number of firms engaging

[14] It was for this reason that the Federal Trade Commission took no action against the recent mergers of the small firms in the automobile industry. See *Report on Corporate Mergers and Acquisitions*, Federal Trade Commission (Washington: 1955), p. 135.

in the various stages of production. The desirable results of vertical integration may not result, however, if integration is achieved by merger.

Vertical integration by internal expansion—by the building of new plants, facilities, and organization—may not always conform with the goals of antitrust policy. Such growth of firms removes certain transfers of intermediate goods from the direct influence of the market mechanism. A firm will buy raw materials instead of manufactured products or use its products to make more-finished products instead of selling them. Such integration will remove the firm from the market as a buyer of the manufactured products it now produces itself, or remove it as a seller of intermediate products it will now use. It will, however, enter the market as a purchaser of raw materials and as a seller of finished products. If all manufacturing firms were completely vertically integrated from the raw material to the retail sales stages, then many of the markets in the economy would disappear completely.

When one firm integrates vertically either by merger or otherwise, the remaining firms may lose a customer or a source of supply. This may provide incentive for those firms also to integrate. The effect may be to increase competition in the markets not eliminated by increasing the number of firms. But if integration is accomplished by acquisition of suppliers or customers, the effect is to remove firms as well as markets. The net result of a large number of such acquisitions might be to substantially reduce the number of markets as well as the number of independent firms operating in the markets that remain.

If a firm integrates vertically, but does not maintain its capacity at each stage of production at just the level that will supply all of its own needs and no more, then it will have to trade with firms with which it is in competition. This sort of disproportionate vertical integration is likely to have the greatest effect on competition. It enables a firm to use the price squeeze on other firms. It makes it possible for a firm to transfer its market control from one market to another. Whenever a vertical integration by merger takes place, the enforcement agency must consider the possibility that the acquiring firm is extending monopoly power that it has in one market by virtue of patents, control of a scarce resource, or other means. If the monopoly power could be attacked under the Sherman Act in all such instances, it would be unnecessary to prevent vertical acquisitions to prevent its extension to other markets. Since it is not always possible to do so, however, the Clayton Act should be used to prevent such extensions of legal market control by acquisition of control of the plant facilities of previously independent firms.

A firm already integrated vertically also may substantially lessen competition in the markets at various levels by acquiring either distribution outlets or sources of raw materials and thus making entry into intermediate markets difficult. Therefore, acquisitions that have the effect of disproportionately integrating a large firm should be carefully scrutinized.

Vertical integration resulting in more economical production should be encouraged. However, integration really motivated by the aim of increased efficiency usually can be achieved better by construction of new plant capacity than by acquisition of existing plants. If the social advantages of uniting under the control of a single firm various stages of the productive process are really available, then the integrating firm should be able to hold its own in the market with the existing firms without the artificial aid received by removing from the market existing firms with which it otherwise would have to compete.

The economic effects of conglomerate mergers involving firms that previously bought and sold goods neither horizontally nor vertically related are the most difficult to evaluate. Many of the mergers of the last few years are acquisitions by multiproduct firms of small firms that sell entirely different products. The merging firms may or may not be functionally related in their productive processes. If existing firms were growing larger by building new plants with which to produce different products and enter new markets, the effect would be to increase the number of firms in each market and to increase competition. But extension of operations into new lines by acquiring existing firms concentrates productive capacity into the control of fewer firms in the aggregate. The merger movement at the turn of the century transformed the ownership structure of industry in the United States by creating a pattern of a few large corporations in most industries. It has been fully recognized in recent years that many large firms now engage in operations that overlap several industries. If the current merger movement continues unabated, we shall probably see the development of a quite different pattern of organization and control of American industry. A few very large firms may achieve control of a very large portion of industrial production with each firm operating in many different industries. Many small firms might continue to exist as suppliers to the few giants or as distributors of their products, but such firms might be merely satellites of the giants, with little real independence.

The most difficult problems of merger policy arise out of the degrees of concentration of control already achieved. In the administration of the law a particular merger must be evaluated within the context of existing market structures. The antitrust enforcement agencies are able directly to effect a reorganization of market structures only by seeking remedies for particular unlawful situations.

In many industrial markets, one or two firms are so outstandingly important that it is not too difficult to decide to restrict the absorption of smaller firms by the largest ones. In instances involving the lesser orders of bigness, the arguments of technical and marketing efficiency are often very persuasive. A large amount of leeway for mergers of small firms seems to be unavoidable if the existing giant firms are not to be dissolved.

There is a great need for further development of economic theory along lines that will enable it to provide discerning insight into the probable effect of corporate mergers and acquisitions.

APPENDIX

Text of Section 11 of the Original Clayton Act

Sec. 11. That authority to enforce compliance with sections two, three, seven, and eight of this Act by the persons respectively subject thereto is hereby vested: in the Interstate Commerce Commission where applicable to common carriers, in the Federal Reserve Board where applicable to banks, banking associations, and trust companies, and in the Federal Trade Commission where applicable to all other character of commerce, to be exercised as follows:

Whenever the commission or board vested with jurisdiction thereof shall have reason to believe that any person is violating or has violated any of the provisions of sections two, three, seven, and eight of this Act, it shall issue and serve upon such person a complaint stating its charges in that respect, and containing a notice of a hearing upon a day and at a place therein fixed at least thirty days after the service of said complaint. The person so complained of shall have the right to appear at the place and time so fixed and show cause why an order should not be entered by the commission or board requiring such person to cease and desist from the violation of the law so charged in said complaint. Any person may make application, and upon good cause shown may be allowed by the commission or board, to intervene and appear in said proceeding by counsel or in person. The testimony in any such proceeding shall be reduced to writing and filed in the office of the commission or board. If upon such hearing the commission or board, as the case may be, shall be of the opinion that any of the provisions of said sections have been or are being violated, it shall make a report in writing in which it shall state its findings as to the facts, and shall issue and cause to be served on such person an order requiring such person to cease and desist from such violations, and divest itself of the stock held or rid itself of the directors chosen contrary to the provisions of sections seven and eight of this Act, if any there be, in the manner and within the time fixed by said order. Until a transcript of the record in such hearing shall have been filed in a circuit court of appeals of the United States, as hereinafter provided, the commission or board may at any time, upon such notice and in such manner as it shall deem proper, modify or set aside, in whole or in part, any report or any order made or issued by it under this section.

If such person fails or neglects to obey such order of the commission or board while the same is in effect, the commission or board may apply to the circuit court of appeals of the United States, within any circuit where the violation complained of was or is being committed or where such person resides or carries on business, for the enforcement of its order, and shall certify and file with its application a transcript of the entire record in the proceeding, including all the testimony taken and the report and order of the commission or board. Upon such filing of the application or transcript the court shall cause notice thereof to be served upon such person and thereupon shall have jurisdiction of the proceeding and of the question determined therein, and shall have power to make and enter upon the pleadings, testimony, and proceedings set forth in such transcript a decree affirming, modifying, or setting aside the order of the commission or board. The findings of the commission or board as to the facts, if supported by testimony, shall be conclusive. If either party shall apply to the court for leave to adduce additional evidence, and show to the satisfaction of the court that such additional evidence is material and that there were reasonable grounds for the failure to adduce such evidence in the proceeding before the commission or board, the court may order such additional evidence to be taken before the commission or board and to be adduced upon the hearings in such manner and upon such terms and conditions as to the court may seem proper. The commission or board may modify its findings as to the facts, or make new findings, by reason of the additional evidence so taken, and it shall file such modified or new findings, which, if supported by testimony, shall be conclusive, and its recommendation, if any, for the modification or setting aside of its original order, with the return of such additional evidence. The judgment and decree of the court shall be final, except that the same shall be subject to review by the Supreme Court upon certiorari as provided in section two hundred and forty of the Judicial Code.

Any party required by such order of the commission or board to cease and desist from a violation charged may obtain a review of such order in said circuit court of appeals by filing in the court a written petition praying that the order of the commission or board be set aside. A copy of such petition shall be forthwith served upon the commission or board, and thereupon the commission or board forthwith shall certify and file in the court a transcript of the record as hereinbefore provided. Upon the filing of the transcript the court shall have the same jurisdiction to affirm, set aside, or modify the order of the commission or board as in the case of an application by the commission or board for the enforcement of its order, and the findings of the commission or board as to the facts, if supported by testimony, shall in like manner be conclusive.

The jurisdiction of the circuit court of appeals of the United States to enforce, set aside, or modify orders of the commission or board shall be exclusive.

Such proceedings in the circuit court of appeals shall be given precedence over other cases pending therein, and shall be in every way expedited. No order of the commission or board or the judgment of the court to enforce the same shall in any wise relieve or absolve any person from any liability under the antitrust Acts.

Complaints, orders, and other processes of the commission or board under this section may be served by anyone duly authorized by the commission or board, either (a) by delivering a copy thereof to the person to be served, or to a member of the partnership to be served, or to the president, secretary, or other executive officer or a director of the corporation to be served; or (b) by leaving a copy thereof at the principal office or place of business of such person; or (c) by registering and mailing a copy thereof addressed to such person at his principal office or place of business. The verified return by the person so serving said complaint, order, or other process setting forth the manner of said service shall be proof of the same, and the return post-office receipt for said complaint, order, or other process registered and mailed as aforesaid shall be proof of the service of the same.

Bibliography

BOOKS

Butters, John Keith, John Lintner, and William L. Cary. *Effects of Taxation: Corporate Mergers.* Boston: Harvard Graduate School of Business Administration, 1951. 364 pp.

Chamberlin, Edward H., ed. *Monopoly and Competition and Their Regulation.* Papers and proceedings of a conference held by the International Economic Association, 1951. New York: St. Martin's Press, 1954. 549 pp.

Chicago Conference on Trusts: Speeches, Debates, Resolutions, Lists of Delegates, Committees, etc. Held September 13–16, 1899. Chicago: the Civic Federation of Chicago, 1900. 626 pp.

Clark, John Bates. *The Problem of Monopoly. A Study of a Grave Danger and of the Natural Mode of Averting It.* New York: Columbia University Press, 1904. 128 pp.

Clark, John Bates, and John Maurice Clark. *The Control of Trusts.* Rewritten and enlarged. New York: Macmillan, [1912]. 202 pp.

Dewing, Arthur S. *Corporate Promotions and Reorganizations.* Cambridge: Harvard University Press, 1914. 615 pp.

———. *Financial Policy of Corporations.* 4th ed. New York: Ronald, 1941. 2 vols.

Dirlam, Joel B., and Alfred E. Kahn. *Fair Competition: The Law and Economics of Antitrust Policy.* Ithaca: Cornell University Press, 1954. 307 pp.

Edwards, Corwin D. *Maintaining Competition; Requisites of a Governmental Policy.* New York: McGraw-Hill, 1949. 337 pp.

Fellner, William. *Competition Among the Few: Oligopoly and Similar Market Structures.* New York: Knopf, 1949. 328 pp.

Galbraith, John Kenneth. *American Capitalism; The Concept of Countervailing Power.* Boston: Houghton Mifflin, 1952. 217 pp.

Griffin, Clare E. *An Economic Approach to Antitrust Problems.* National Economic Problem Series No. 441. New York: American Enterprise Association, Inc., [1951]. 93 pp.

Haney, Lewis. *Business Organization and Combination.* Rev. ed. New York: Macmillan, 1914. 523 pp.

Henderson, Gerard C. *The Federal Trade Commission; A Study in Administrative Law and Procedure.* New Haven: Yale University Press, 1924. 382 pp.

Holt, W. Stull. *The Federal Trade Commission, Its History, Activities and Organization.* Institute for Government Research, Service Monographs of the United States Government, No. 7. New York: Appleton, 1922. 80 pp.

Kaplan, A. D. H. *Big Enterprise in a Competitive System.* Washington: The Brookings Institute, 1954. 269 pp.

Meade, Edward S. *Trust Finance.* New York: Appleton, 1903. 387 pp.

National Bureau of Economic Research. *Business Concentration and Price Policy: A Conference of the Universities-National Bureau Committee for Economic Research.* Princeton University Press, 1955. 514 pp.

Pegrum, Dudley F. *Regulation of Industry.* Chicago: Irwin, 1949. 497 pp.

Republican Party. *Official Report of the Proceedings of the Fifteenth Republican National Convention.* New York: Tenny, 1912. 460 pp.

Ripley, W. Z., ed. *Trusts, Pools and Corporations.* Rev. ed. Boston: Ginn, 1916.

Schumpeter, Joseph A. *Capitalism, Socialism, and Democracy.* 3d ed. New York: Harper, 1950. 431 pp.

Seager, H. R., and C. A. Gulick, Jr. *Trust and Corporation Problems.* New York: Harper, [1929]. 719 pp.

Stevens, William S., ed. *Industrial Combinations and Trusts.* New York: Macmillan, 1922. 593 pp.

Stocking, George W., and Myron W. Watkins. *Monopoly and Free Enterprise.* New York: The Twentieth Century Fund, 1951. 596 pp.

Thorelli, Hans B. *The Federal Antitrust Policy, Origination of an American Tradition.* Baltimore: The Johns Hopkins Press, 1955. 658 pp.

Thornton, W. W. *A Treatise on Combinations in Restraint of Trade.* Cincinnati: Anderson, 1928. 1751 pp.

Weston, J. Fred. *The Role of Mergers in the Growth of Large Firms.* Berkeley and Los Angeles: University of California Press, 1953. 159 pp.

Wyman, Bruce. *Control of the Market; a Legal Solution of the Trust Problem.* New York: Moffat, Yard, 1911. 282 pp.

PERIODICAL PUBLICATIONS

American Academy of Political and Social Science. "Industrial Competition and Combination," *The Annals,* XLII (July, 1912), 1–341.

Barnes, Irston R. "Economic Issues in the Regulation of Acquisitions and Mergers," *Ohio State Law Journal,* 14 (1953), 297–306.

Barnes, Stanley N. "Quantitative Substantiality." An address prepared for delivery before the American Bar Association. (Washington: April 6, 1956). 20 pp. Mimeographed.

Clark, John M. "Toward a Concept of Workable Competition," *American Economic Review,* XXX (June, 1940), 241–256.

"Clayton Act Proceeding: Transamerica Corporation," *Federal Reserve Bulletin,* 38 (April, 1952), 368–398.

Conant, Luther, Jr. "Industrial Consolidations in the United States," *Publications of the American Statistical Association,* VII (March, 1901), 207–226.

Homan, Paul T. "Notes on the Anti-trust Law Policy," *Quarterly Journal of Economics,* LIV (November, 1939), 73–102.

———. "Trusts," *Encyclopedia of the Social Sciences,* XV (Macmillan, 1931), 111–14.

"Section 7 of the Clayton Act: A Legislative History," *Columbia Law Review,* 52 (June, 1952), 766–781.

Stigler, George J. "Monopoly and Oligopoly by Merger," *American Economic Review,* XL (May, 1950), 23–34.

Whitney, Edward B. "Governmental Interference with Industrial Combinations," *Publications of the American Economic Association,* 3d Series, VI (May, 1905), 1–19.

Young, Allyn A. "The Sherman Act and the New Anti-trust Legislation," *Journal of Political Economy,* 23 (March, April, and May, 1915), 201–220, 305–326, and 417–436.

UNITED STATES GOVERNMENT PUBLICATIONS

Bureau of Corporations. *Trust Laws and Unfair Competition.* Washington: 1916. 832 pp.

Congress. House. Antitrust Subcommittee of the Committee on the Judiciary. *Interim Report on Corporate and Bank Mergers.* 84th Cong., 1st sess., pursuant to H. Res. 22. Washington: 1955. 188 pp.

———.———. Committee of Conference. *Antitrust Legislation.* 63d Cong., 2d sess., H. Rept. 1168 to accompany H.R. 15657. Washington: 1914. 18 pp. Serial no. 6560.

———.———. Committee on Interstate and Foreign Commerce. *Interstate Trade Commission.* 63d Cong., 2d sess., H. Rept. 533 to accompany H.R. 15613. Washington: 1914. 39 pp. Serial no. 6559.

———.———. Committee on the Judiciary. *Amending an Act Approved October 15, 1914.* 81st Cong., 1st sess., H. Rept. 1191 to accompany H.R. 2734. Washington: 1949. 15 pp. Serial no. 11300.

———.———.———. *Amending Sections 7 and 11 of the Clayton Act.* 79th Cong., 2d sess., H. Rept. 1480 to accompany H.R. 4810. Washington: 1946. 8 pp. Serial no. 11022.

———.———.———. *Amending Sections 7 and 11 of the Clayton Act.* 79th Cong., 2d sess., H. Rept. 1820 to accompany H.R. 5535. Washington: 1946. 8 pp. Serial no. 11023.

———.———.———. *Amending Sections 7 and 11 of the Clayton Act.* 80th Cong., 1st sess., H. Rept. 596 to accompany H.R. 3736. Washington: 1947. 16 pp. Serial no. 11120.

———.———.———. *Amending the Clayton Act, as Amended, By Requiring Prior Notification of Certain Corporate Mergers.* 84th Cong., 2d sess., H. Rept. 1889 to accompany H.R. 9424. Washington: 1956. 8 pp.

———.———. *Federal Trade Commission Report on the Agricultural Implement and Machinery Industry.* 75th Cong., 3d sess., H. Doc. 702. Washington: 1938. 1176 pp. Serial no. 10261.

———.———. *Report of the Industrial Commission—Trusts and Combinations.* 57th Cong., 1st sess., H. Doc. 182. Washington: [1902]. 1013 pp. Serial no. 4343.

———.———. Subcommittee No. 2 of the Committee on the Judiciary. *Amending Sections 7 and 11 of the Clayton Act.* Hearings, 80th Cong., 1st sess., on H.R. 515. Washington: 1945. 551 pp.

———.———. Subcommittee No. 3 of the Committee on the Judiciary. *Amending Sections 7 and 11 of the Clayton Act.* Hearings, 81st Cong., 1st sess., on H.R. 988, H.R. 1240, H.R. 2006, H.R. 2734. Washington: 1949. 148 pp.

———.———. Subcommittee of the Committee on Banking and Currency. *Money Trust Investigation.* 62d Cong., 2d sess., Exhibits and Report pursuant to H. Res. Nos. 429 and 504. Washington: 1912 and 1913. 3 vols.

———.———. Subcommittee of the Committee on the Judiciary. *To Amend Sections 7 and 11 of the Clayton Act.* Hearings, 79th Cong., 1st sess., on H.R. 2357. Washington: 1945. 373 pp.

———.———. *Trusts and Monopolies.* Address of the President of the United States before the Joint Session of Congress, Tuesday, January 20, 1914. 63d Cong., 2d sess., H. Doc. 625. Washington: 1914. 8 pp. Serial no. 6754.

———. Senate. *Chain Stores; Final Report on the Chain-Store Investigation, Federal Trade Commission.* 74th Cong., 1st sess., S. Doc. 4. Washington: 1935. 110 pp. Serial no. 9896.

———.———. Committee on Interstate Commerce. *Federal Trade Com-*

mission. 63d Cong., 2d sess., S. Rept. 597 to accompany H.R. 15613. Washington: 1914. 42 pp. Serial no. 6553.

———.———. Committee on the Judiciary. *Amending an Act . . . Approved October 15, 1914, (38 Stat. 730). . . .* 81st Cong., 2d sess., S. Rept. 1775 to accompany H.R. 2734. Washington: 1950. 10 pp. Serial no. 11368.

———.———.———. *Corporate Mergers and Price Discrimination.* 84th Cong., 2d sess., S. Rept. 2817 to accompany H.R. 9424. Washington: 1956. 25 pp.

———.———.———. *Unlawful Restraints and Monopolies.* 63d Cong., 2d sess., S. Rept. 698 to accompany H.R. 15657. Washington: 1914. 83 pp. Serial no. 6553.

———.———. *Federal Antitrust Bill, Comparative Print.* 63d Cong., 2d sess., S. Doc. 584. Washington: 1914. 27 pp. Serial no. 6592.

———.———. *Principal Farm Products, Agricultural Income Inquiry; Report of the Federal Trade Commission.* 75th Cong., 1st sess., S. Doc. 54. Washington: 1937. 40 pp. Serial no. 10104.

———.———. Subcommittee on Antitrust and Monopoly of the Committee on the Judiciary. *A Study of the Antitrust Laws.* Hearings, Part 1, 84th Cong., 1st sess., pursuant to S. Res. 61. Washington: 1955. 479 pp.

———.———. Subcommittee of the Committee on the Judiciary. *Corporate Mergers and Acquisitions.* Hearings, 81st Cong., 1st and 2d sess., on H.R. 2734. Washington: 1950. 419 pp.

———. Temporary National Economic Committee. *A Preliminary Report.* 76th Cong., 1st sess., S. Doc. 95. Washington: 1939. 39 pp. Serial no. 10316.

———.———. *Federal Trade Commission Report on Monopolistic Practices in Industries.* Hearings, Part 5-A, 76th Cong., 1st sess., pursuant to Public Res. 113. Washington: 1939. [112 pp.]

———.———. *Final Report and Recommendations.* 77th Cong., 1st sess., S. Doc. 35. Washington: 1941. 783 pp. Serial no. 10564.

Congressional Record. 62d Cong., 2d sess., vol. 48 (December 4, 1911–August 26, 1912).

———. 63d Cong., 2d sess., vol. 51 (May 22, 1914–October 8, 1914).

———. 81st Cong., 1st sess., vol. 95 (August 15, 1949).

———. 81st Cong., 2d sess., vol. 96 (December 13, 1950–January 2, 1951).

Department of Commerce. *Annual Reports of the Department of Commerce.* Washington: 1913–1914.

Department of Commerce and Labor. *Annual Reports of the Department of Commerce and Labor.* Washington: 1906–1912.

Department of Justice. *Report of the Attorney General's National Committee to Study the Antitrust Laws.* Washington: 1955. 393 pp.

Federal Trade Commission. *Annual Reports of the Federal Trade Commission.* Washington: 1915–1958.

———. *Appeal Brief.* In the Matter of Pillsbury Mills, Inc., Docket No. 6000. (Washington: 1953). 70 pp. Mimeographed.

———. *Reply to Respondent's Opposing Brief.* In the Matter of Pillsbury Mills, Inc., Docket No. 6000. (Washington: 1953). 29 pp. Mimeographed.

———. *Report and Comment of the Federal Trade Commission on H.R. 2357.* By W. T. Kelley. [Washington: 1945]. 34 pp. Mimeographed.

———. *Report of the Federal Trade Commission on the Merger Movement, a Summary Report.* Washington: 1948. 134 pp.

———. *Report on Corporate Mergers and Acquisitions.* Washington: 1955. 210 pp.

———. *Respondent's Brief in Support of Motion to Hearing Examiner to Dismiss Complaint.* In the Matter of Pillsbury Mills, Inc., Docket No. 6000. (Washington: 1953). 67 pp. Mimeographed.

UNPUBLISHED MATERIALS

United States Federal Trade Commission. "Digest of Formal Complaints Issued by the Federal Trade Commission under Sections 7 and 8 of the Clayton Act," *Federal Trade Commission Exhibit No. 168 Included within Temporary National Economic Committee Exhibit No. 305.* National Archives, Washington: n.d. Typewritten.

———. "Digest of Informal Investigations Made by the Federal Trade Commission under Section 7 of the Clayton Act," *Federal Trade Commission Exhibit No. 192 Included within Temporary National Economic Committee Exhibit No. 305.* National Archives, Washington: n.d. Typewritten.

———. *Drafted Material, for Consideration by the Temporary National Economic Committee for its Final Report, as to Corporate Mergers and Section Seven of the Clayton Act.* Box 259, National Archives, Washington: 1941. 16 pp. Typewritten.

———. "Photostatic Copies of Papers from File No. 17–11–2886, General Carpet Corporation," *Federal Trade Commission Exhibit No. 191 Included within Temporary National Economic Committee Exhibit No. 305.* National Archives, Washington.

LAWS, STATUTES, AND COURT AND COMMISSION REPORTS

Commerce Clearing House Trade Regulation Reports.

Federal Reporter.

Federal Reporter, Second Series.

Federal Rules Decisions.

Federal Supplement.
Federal Trade Commission Decisions.
Georgia Reports.
Illinois Reports.
Interstate Commerce Commission Reports.
Michigan Reports.
New Jersey Equity Reports.
North Eastern Reporter.
Ohio State Reports.
United States Code (1952 ed.).
United States Code Annotated (1951 ed.).
United States Statutes at Large.
United States Supreme Court Reports.

Table of Cases

Index

www.ingramcontent.com/pod-product-compliance
Ingram Content Group UK Ltd.
Pitfield, Milton Keynes, MK11 3LW, UK
UKHW040234290926
15471UKWH00002B/184

9 780520 345706